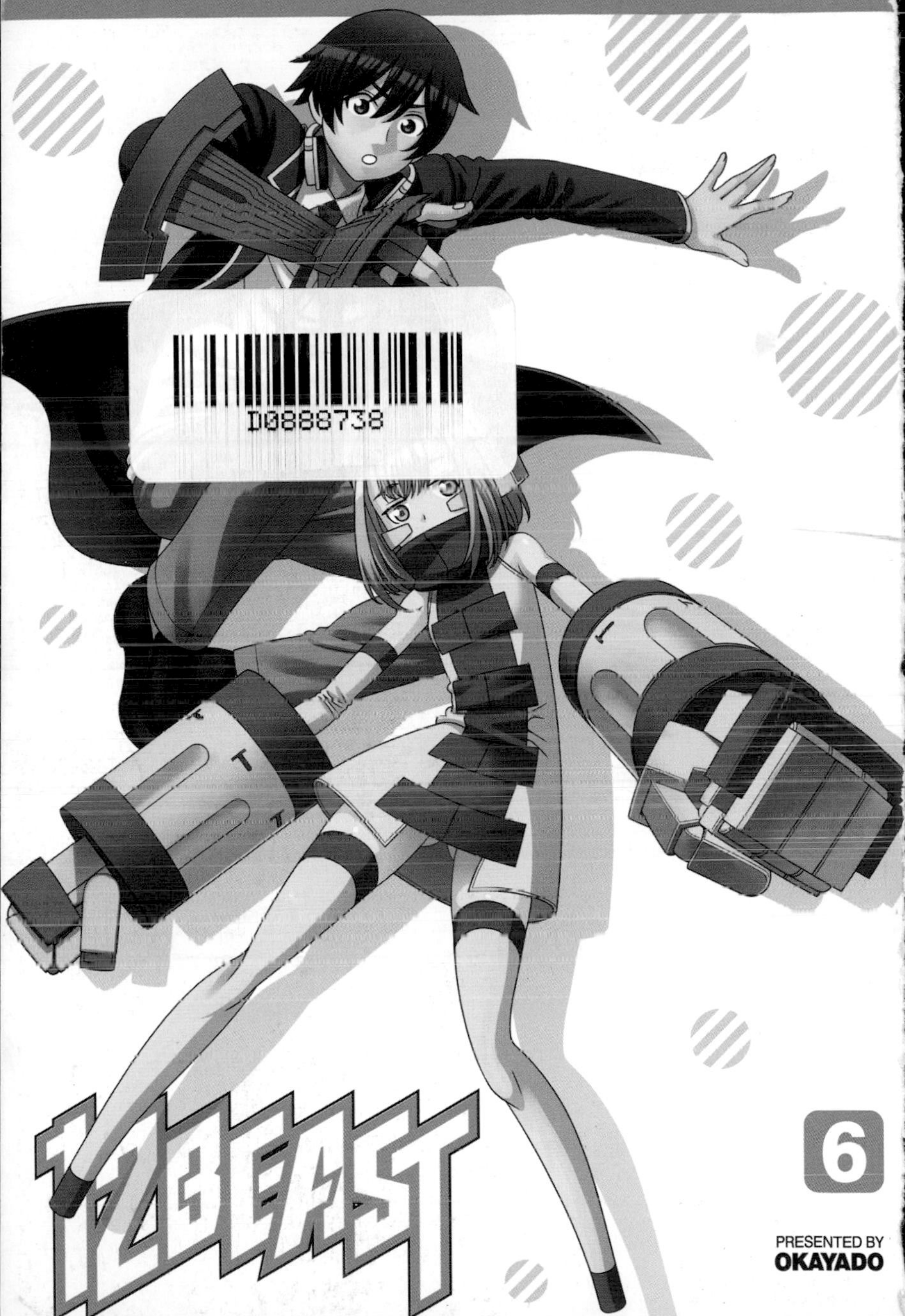

12 BEAST

6

PRESENTED BY
OKAYADO

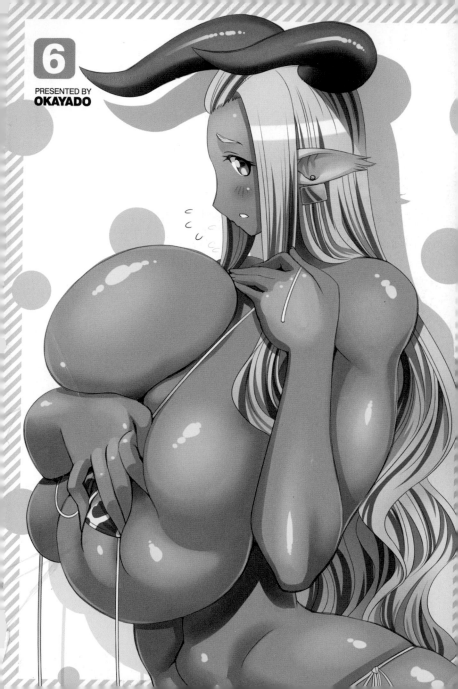

6

PRESENTED BY
OKAYADO

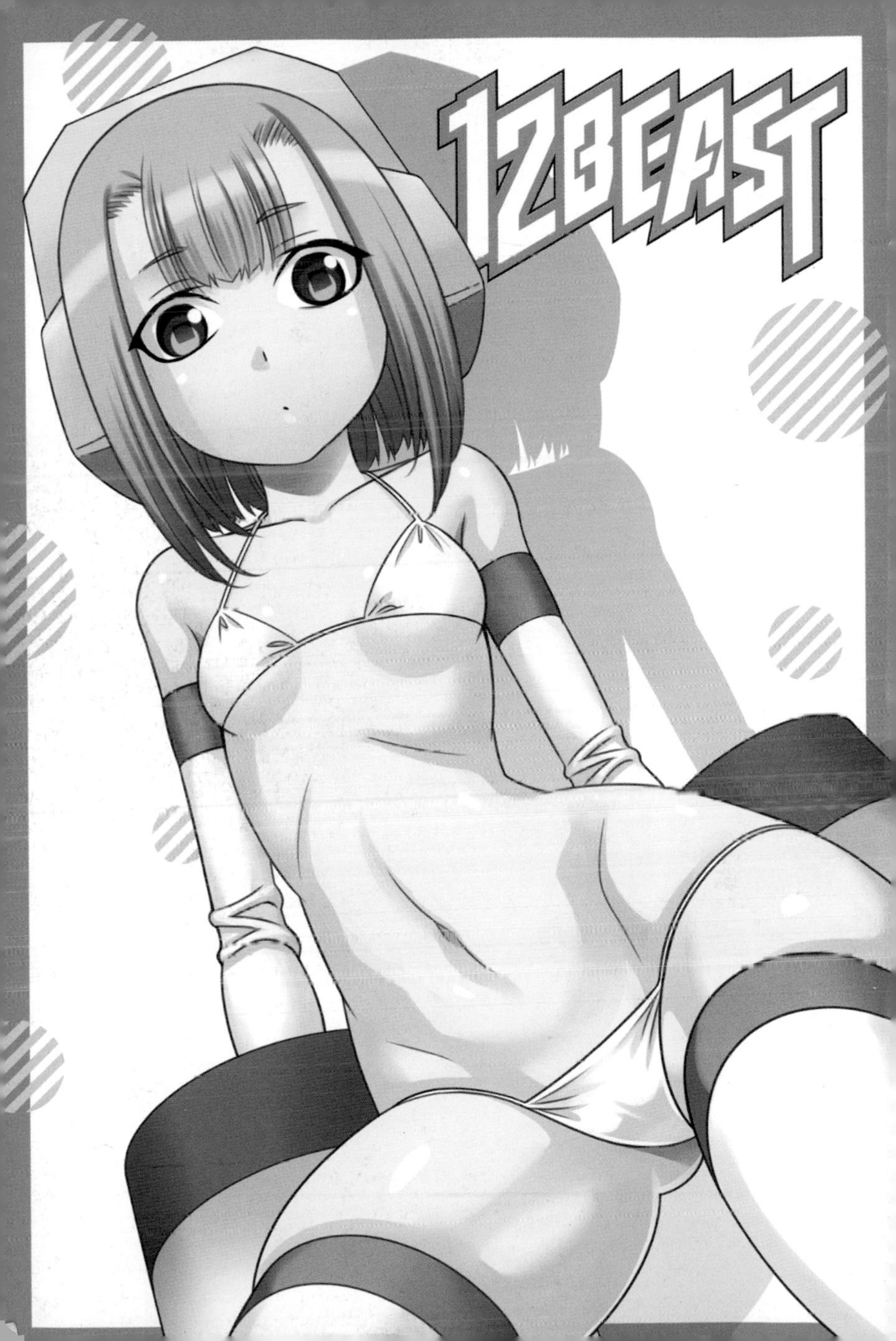
12BEAST

12 BEAST

PRESENTED BY **OKAYADO**

6

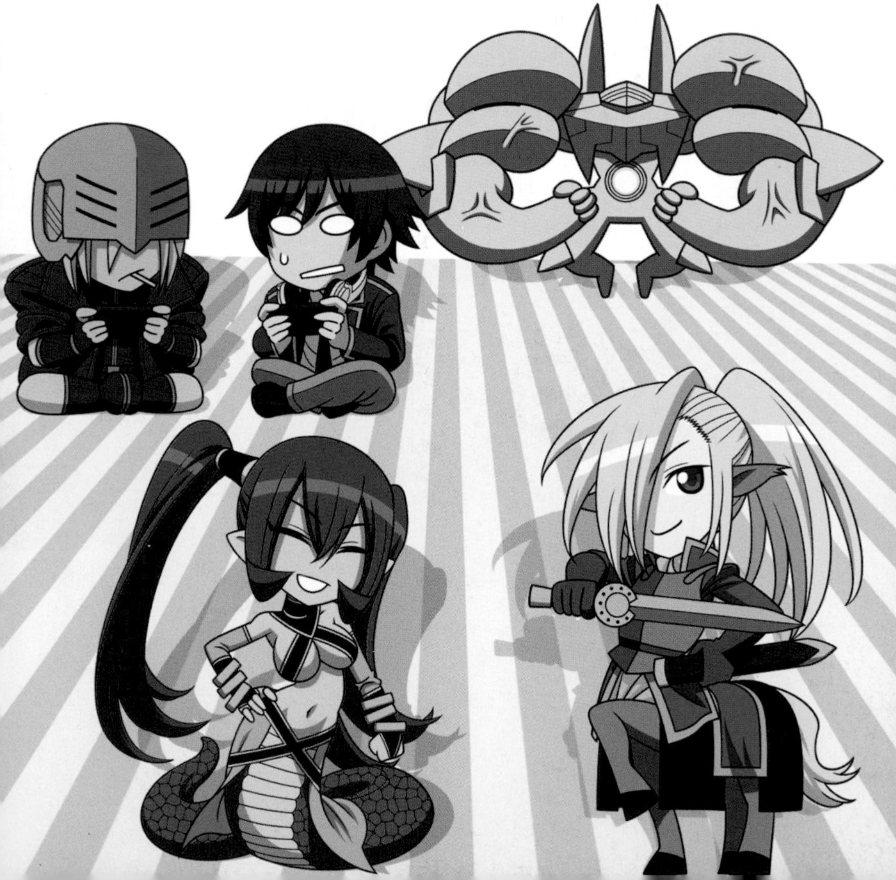

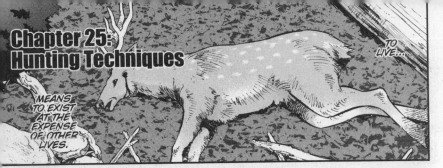

Chapter 25: Hunting Techniques
TO LIVE...
MEANS TO EXIST AT THE EXPENSE OF OTHER LIVES.
THOSE LIVES BECOME PART OF OUR BODIES...
AND WE EXPRESS OUR GRATITUDE TOWARDS THEM.
BUT TODAY, LIFE IS PACKAGED, SHRINK WRAPPED, AND SOLD.
Native Japanese Sirloin Tip Roast
783
JUST ANOTHER COMMODITY TO BE CONSUMED.
I BECAME A HUNTER...
SO THAT I COULD TRULY FEEL ALIVE.

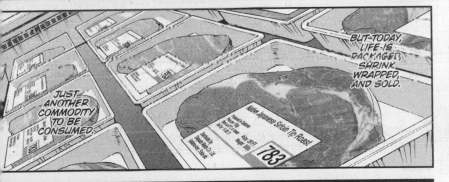

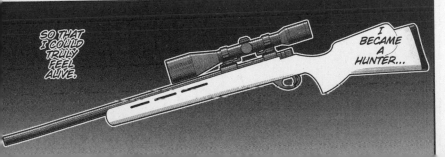

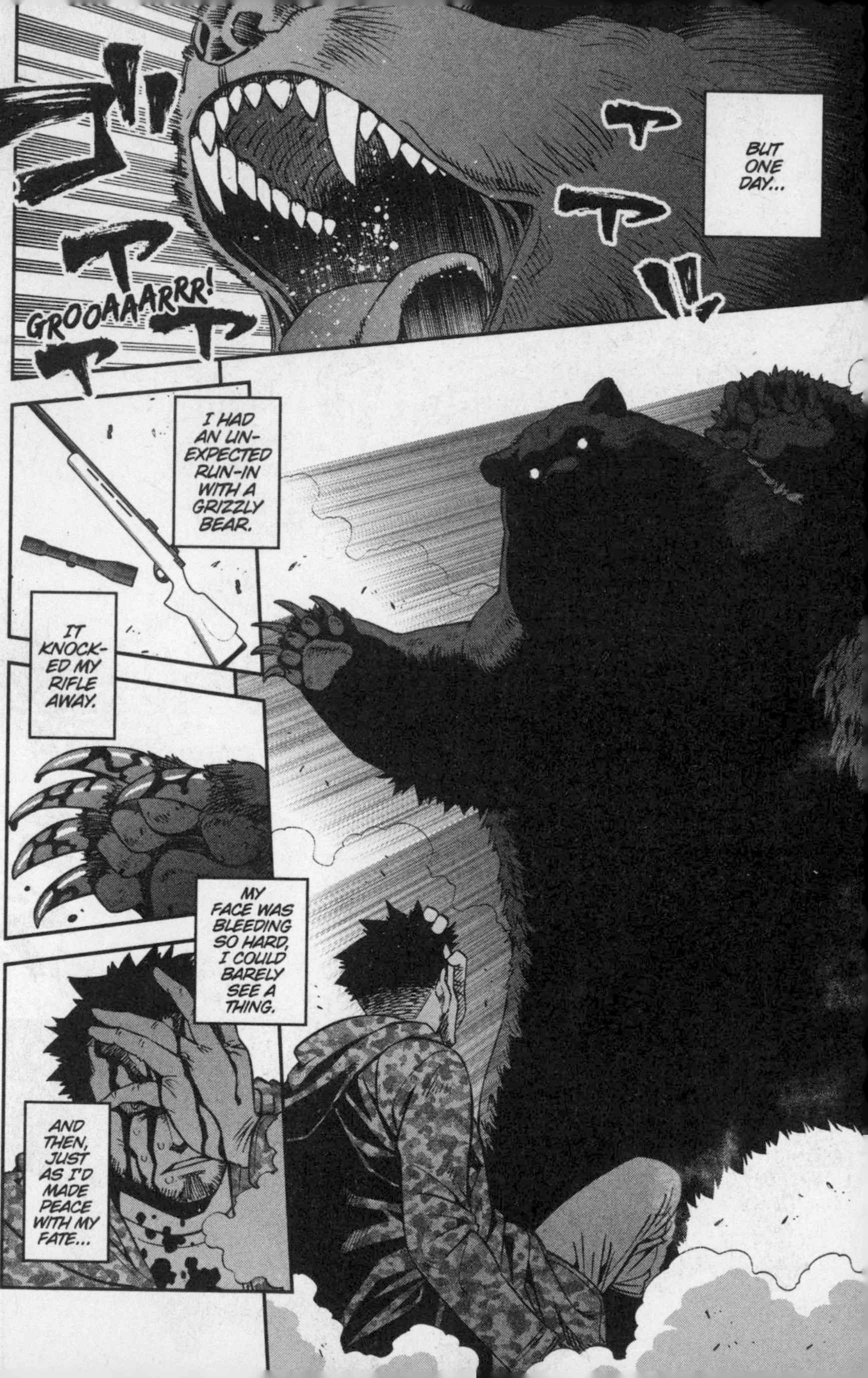
BUT ONE DAY...
GROOAAARRR!
I HAD AN UN-EXPECTED RUN-IN WITH A GRIZZLY BEAR.
IT KNOCK-ED MY RIFLE AWAY.
MY FACE WAS BLEEDING SO HARD, I COULD BARELY SEE A THING.
AND THEN, JUST AS I'D MADE PEACE WITH MY FATE...

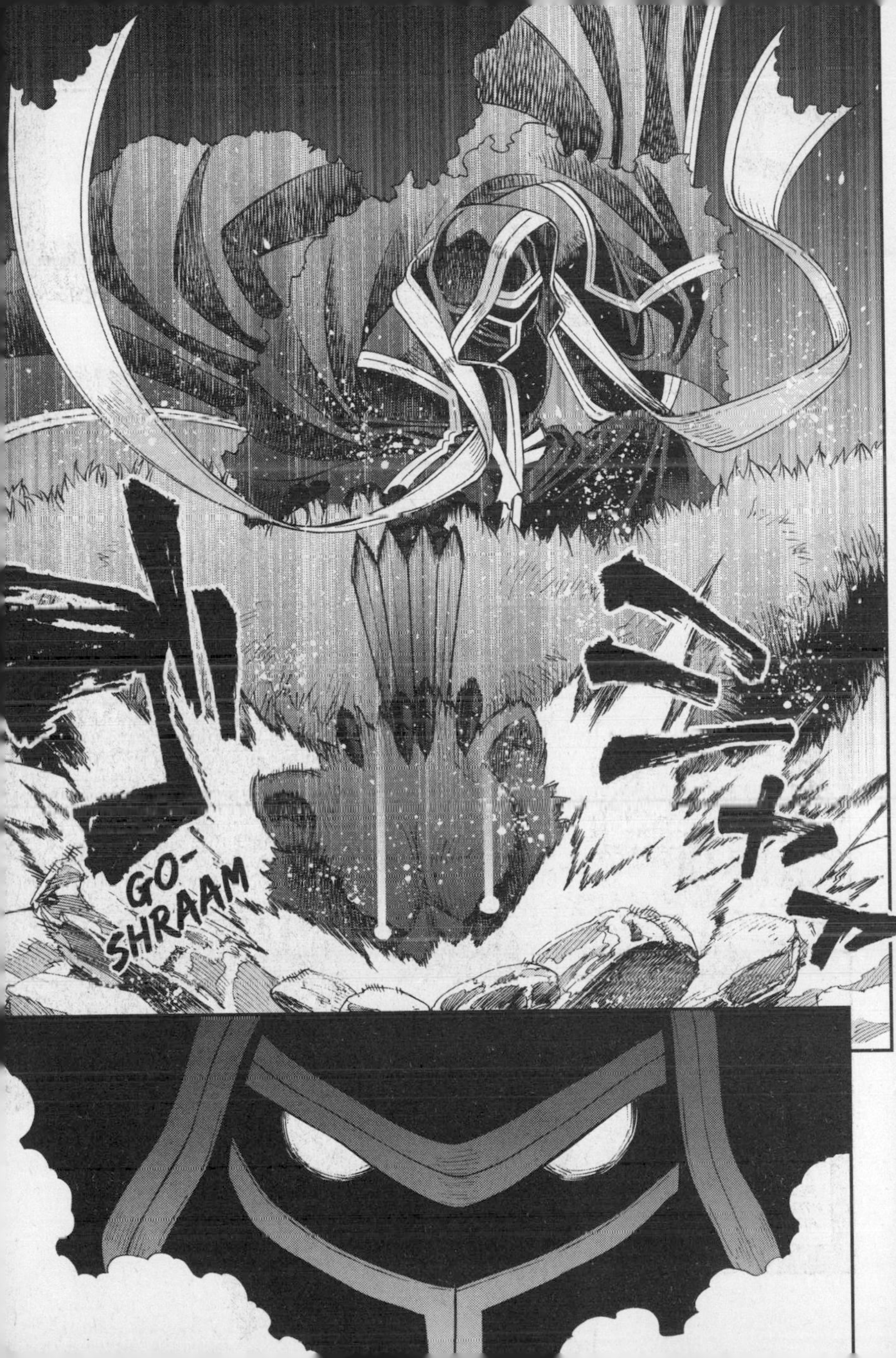
GO-SHRAAM

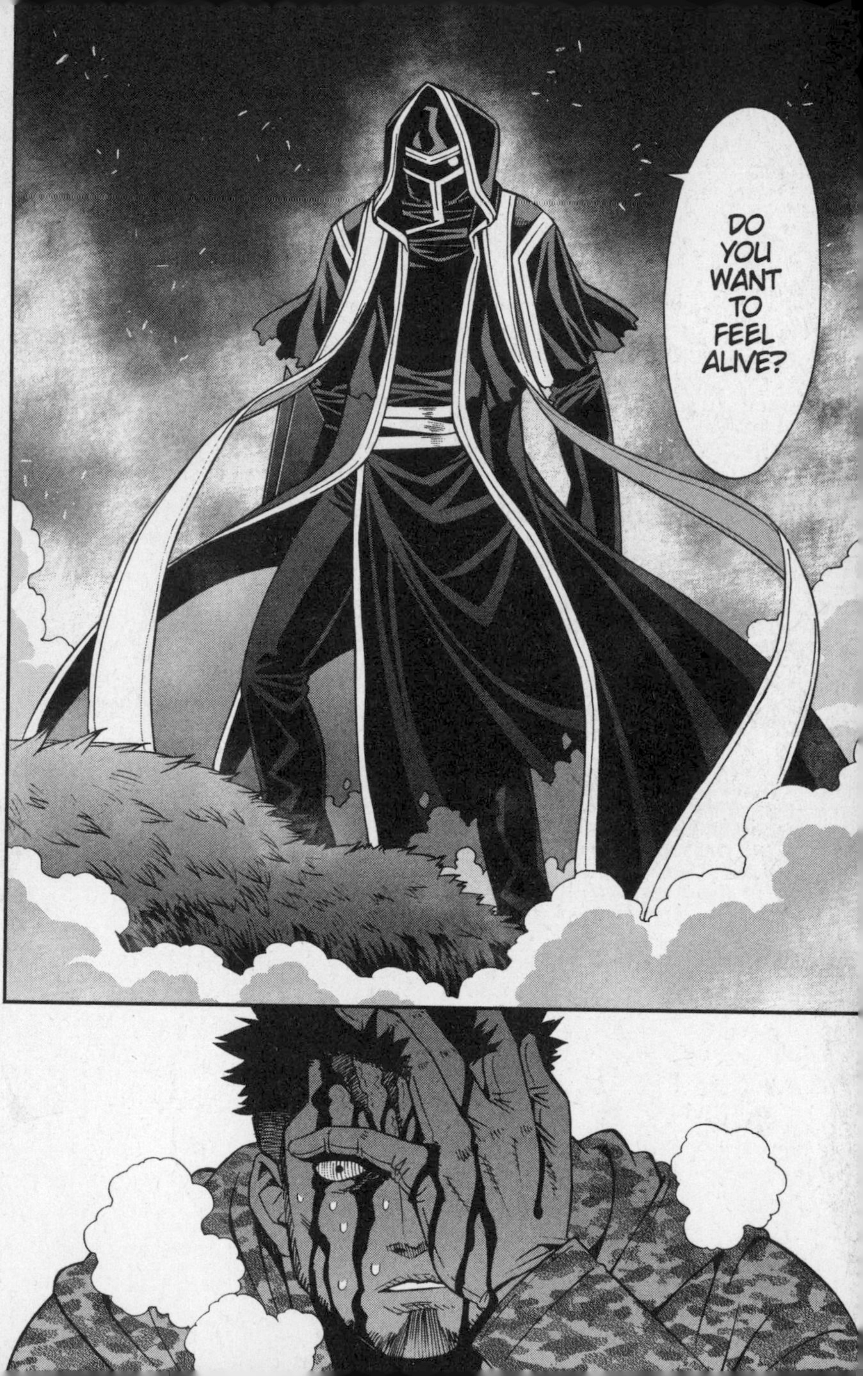
DO YOU WANT TO FEEL ALIVE?

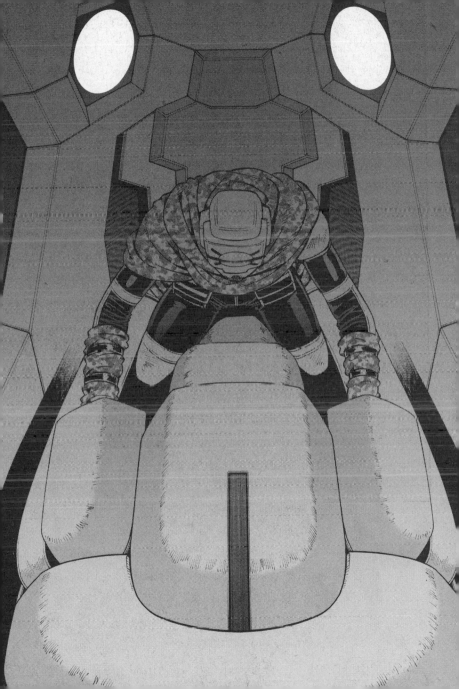

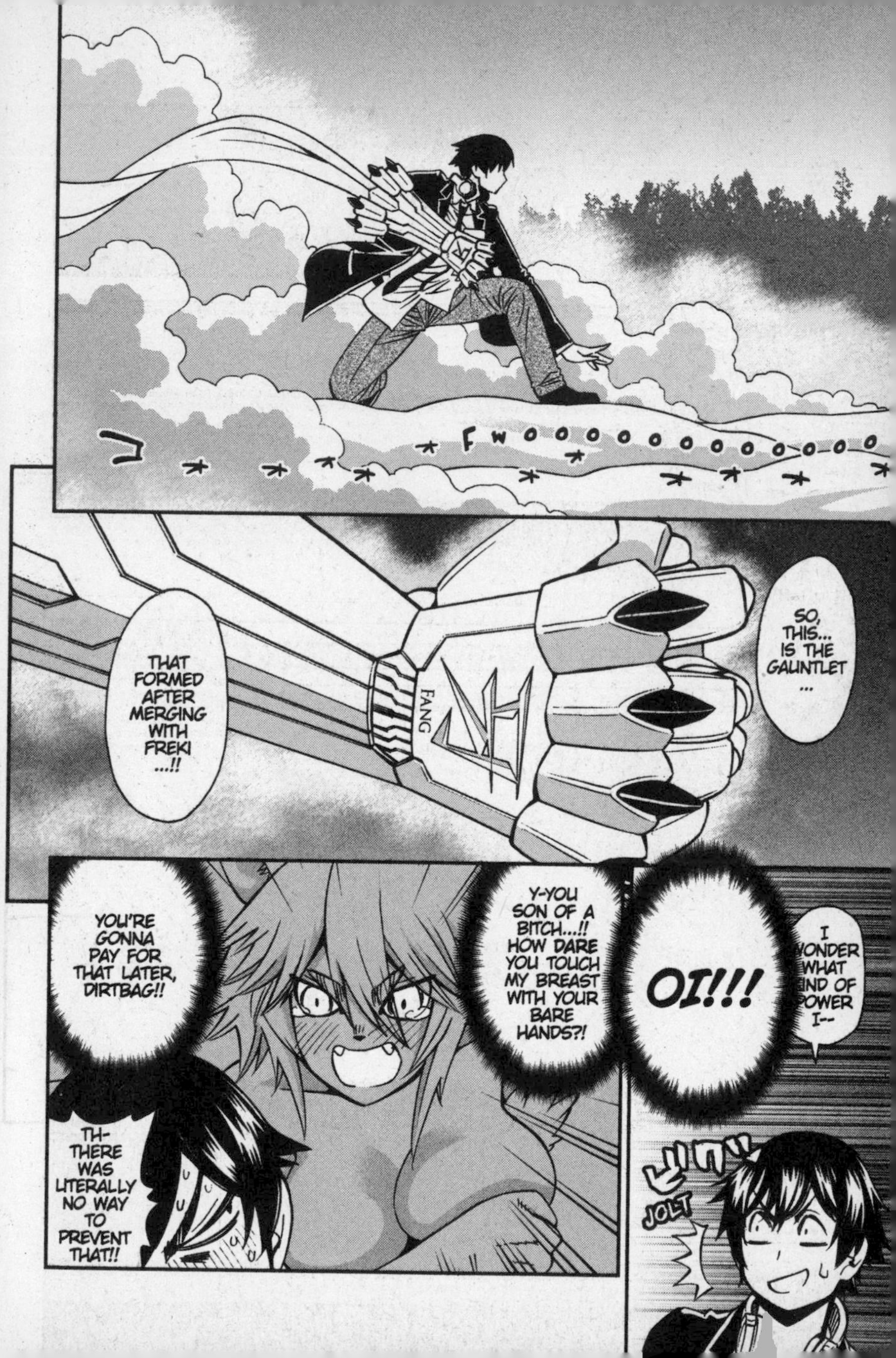
FWOOOOOOOOOOOO
SO, THIS... IS THE GAUNTLET ...
THAT FORMED AFTER MERGING WITH FREKI ...!!
FANG
I WONDER WHAT KIND OF POWER I--
OI!!!
JOLT
Y-YOU SON OF A BITCH...!! HOW DARE YOU TOUCH MY BREAST WITH YOUR BARE HANDS?!
YOU'RE GONNA PAY FOR THAT LATER, DIRTBAG!!
TH-THERE WAS LITERALLY NO WAY TO PREVENT THAT!!

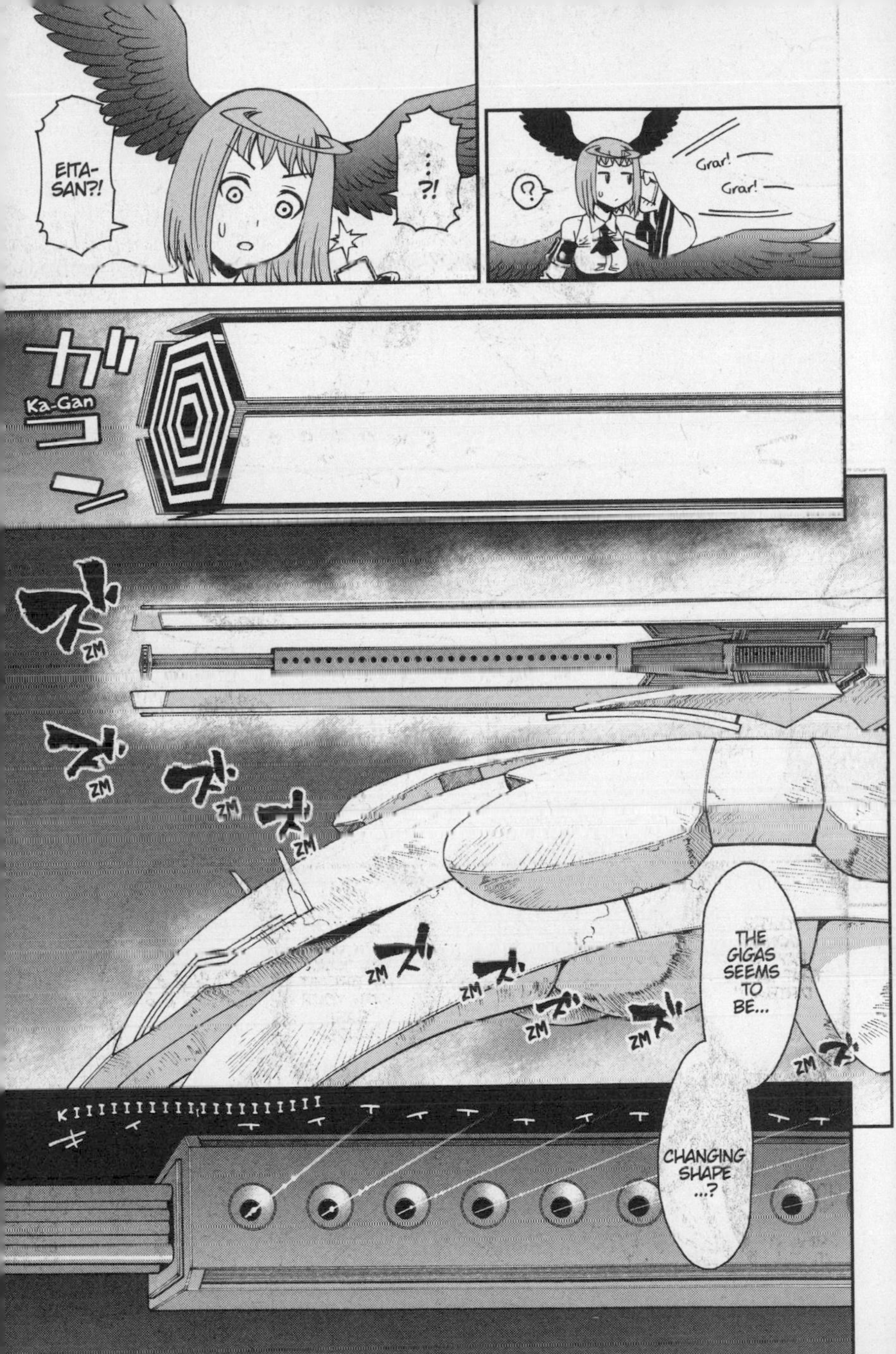

Grar!
Grar!
?
...?!
EITA-SAN?!
Ka-Gan
ZM
ZM
ZM
ZM
ZM
ZM
ZM
ZM
ZM
THE GIGAS SEEMS TO BE...
KIIIIIIIIIIIIIIIIIIIII
CHANGING SHAPE ...?

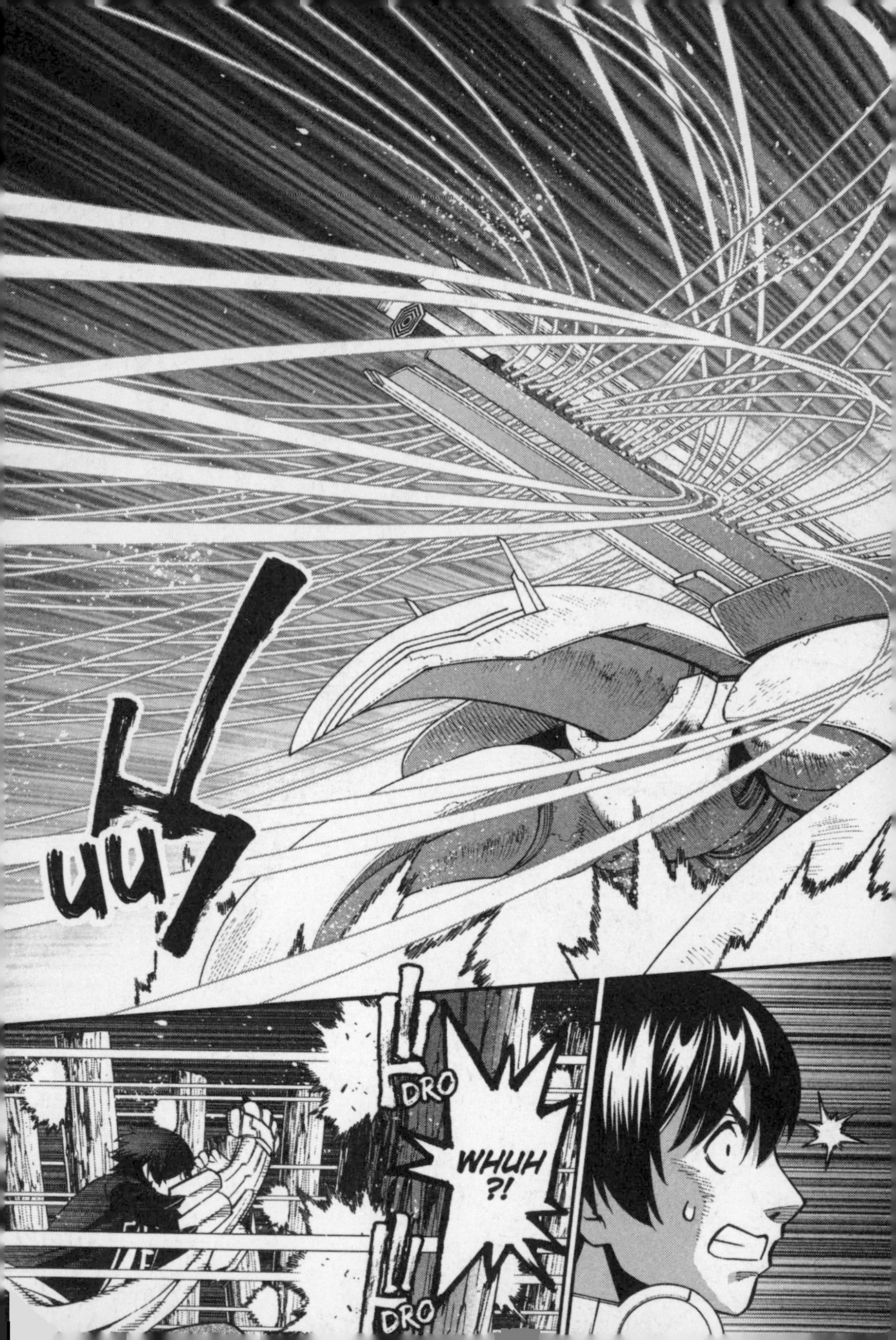

WHUH ?!
DRO
DRO

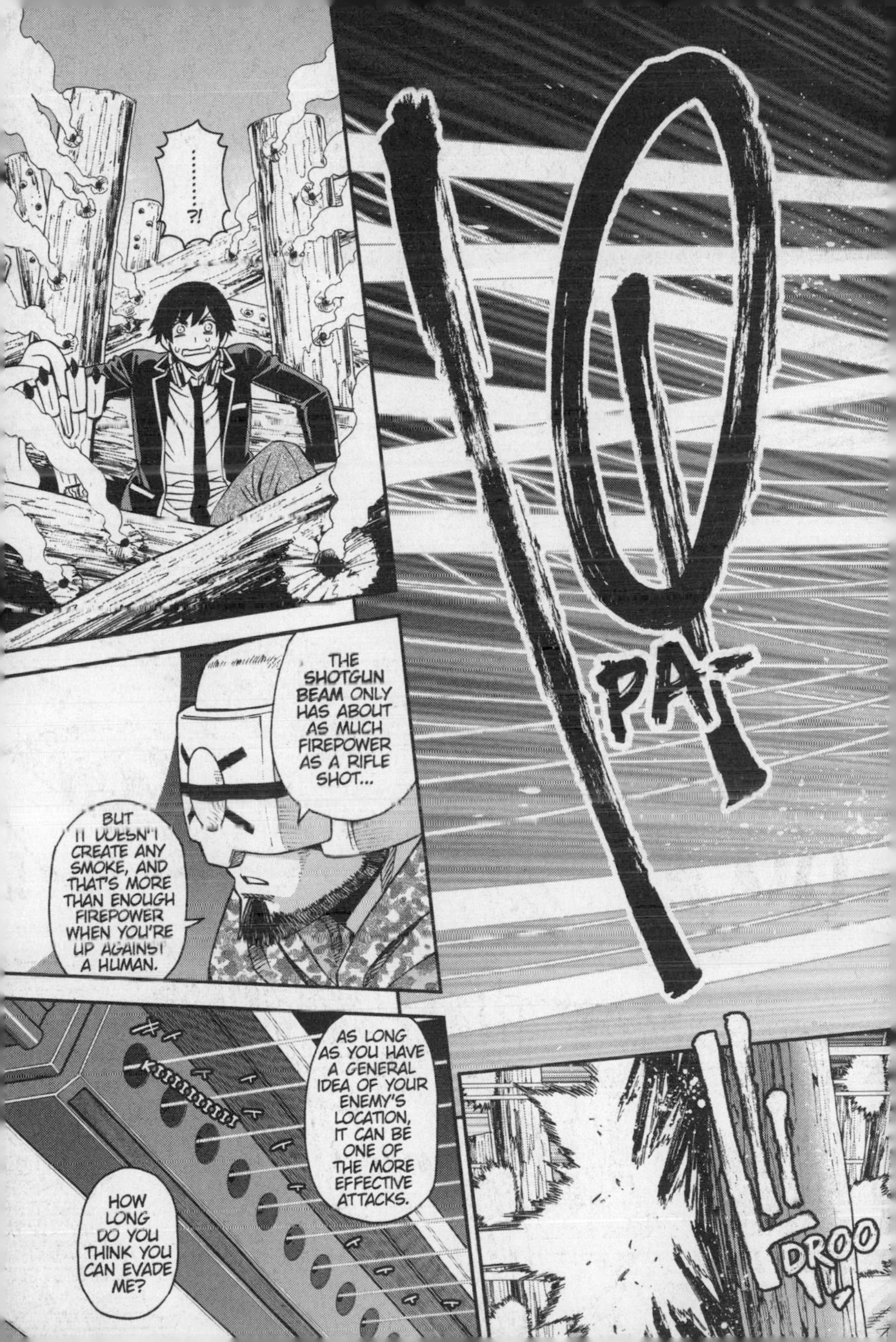
PA
......?!
THE SHOTGUN BEAM ONLY HAS ABOUT AS MUCH FIREPOWER AS A RIFLE SHOT...
BUT IT DOESN'T CREATE ANY SMOKE, AND THAT'S MORE THAN ENOUGH FIREPOWER WHEN YOU'RE UP AGAINST A HUMAN.
DROO
KIIIIIIIII
AS LONG AS YOU HAVE A GENERAL IDEA OF YOUR ENEMY'S LOCATION, IT CAN BE ONE OF THE MORE EFFECTIVE ATTACKS.
HOW LONG DO YOU THINK YOU CAN EVADE ME?

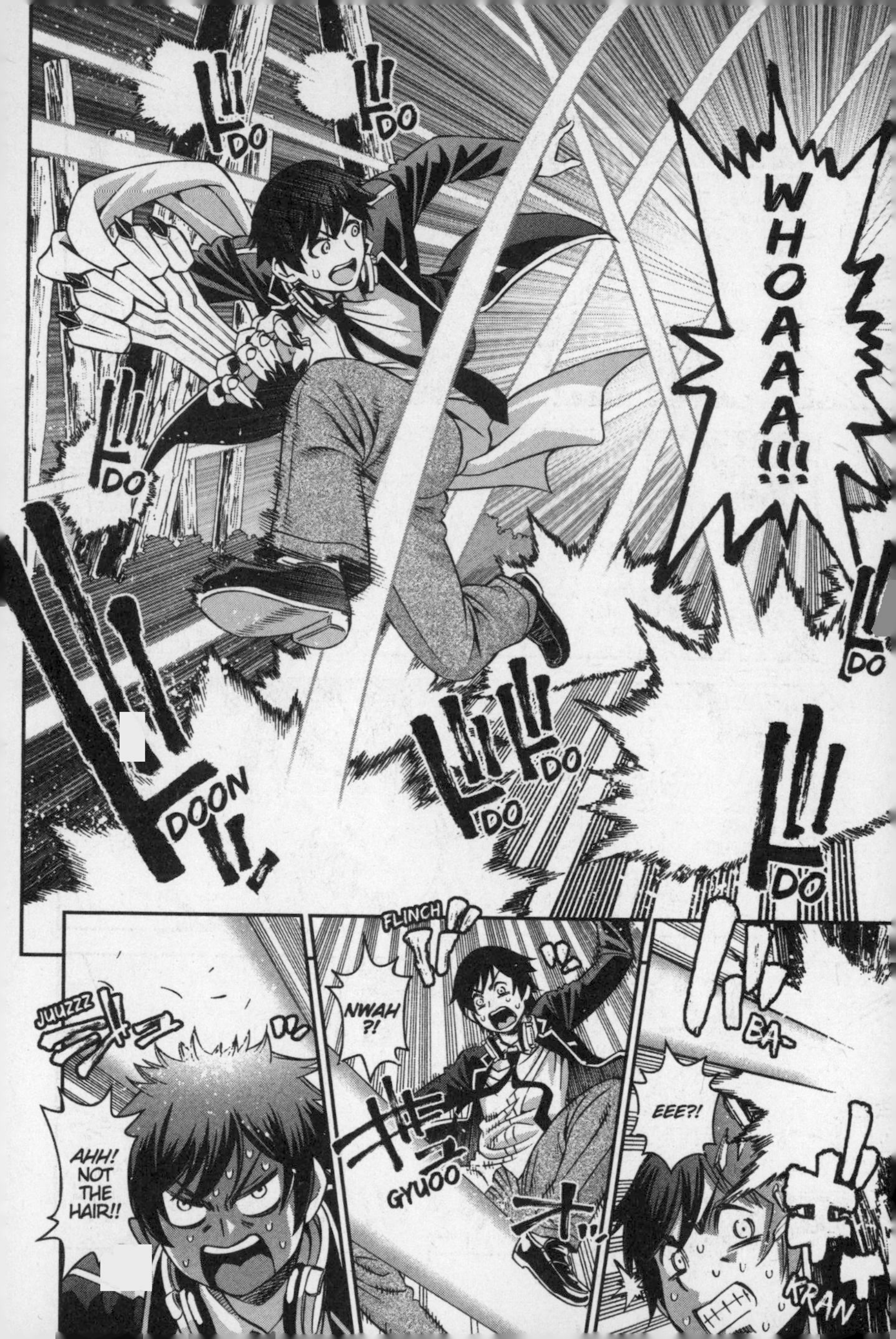
WHOAAA!!!
DO
DO
DO
DO
DO
DO
DO
DOON
BA-
EEE?!
KRAN
FLINCH
NWAH?!
GYUOO
JUUZZZ
AHH! NOT THE HAIR!!

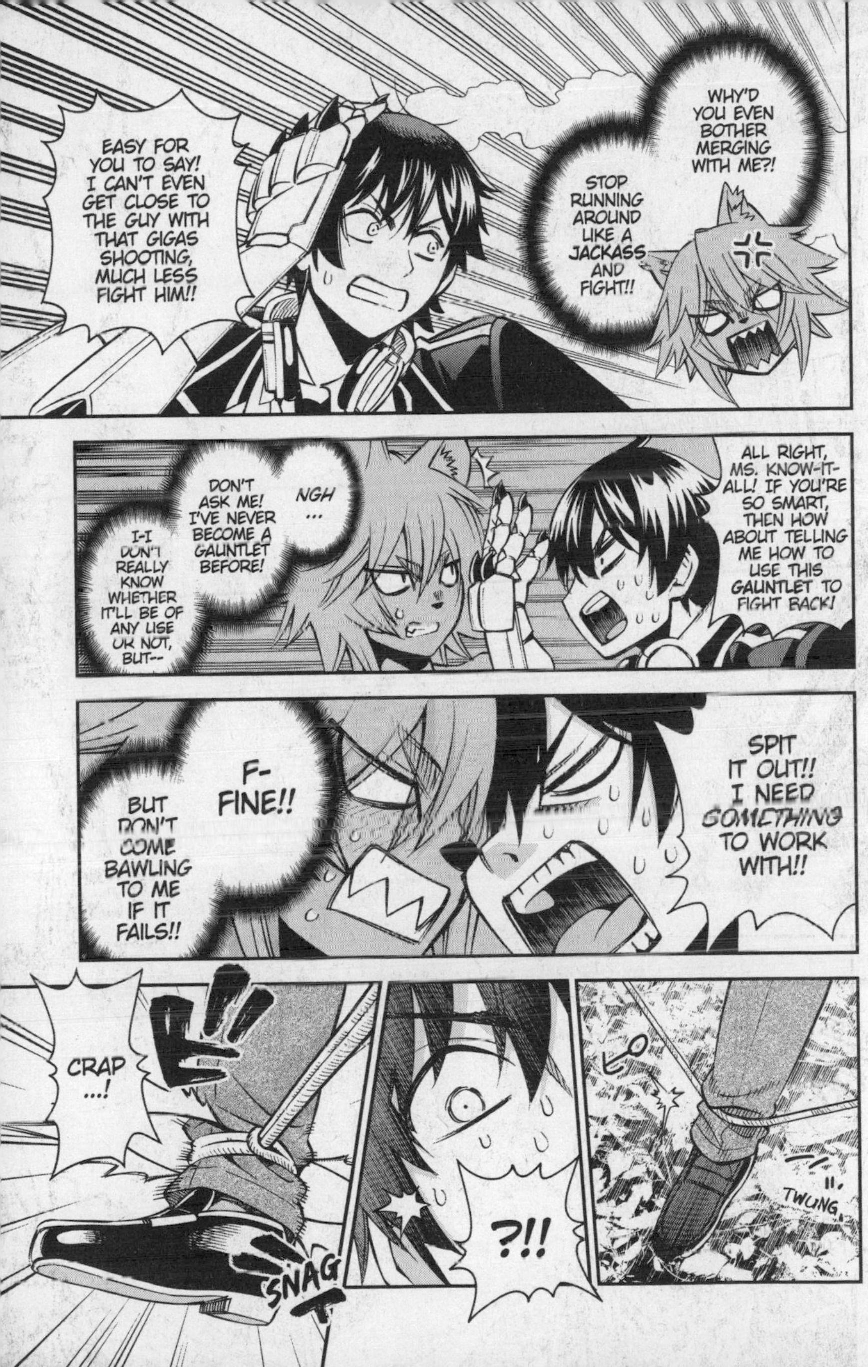

WHY'D YOU EVEN BOTHER MERGING WITH ME?!
STOP RUNNING AROUND LIKE A JACKASS AND FIGHT!!
EASY FOR YOU TO SAY! I CAN'T EVEN GET CLOSE TO THE GUY WITH THAT GIGAS SHOOTING, MUCH LESS FIGHT HIM!!
ALL RIGHT, MS. KNOW-IT-ALL! IF YOU'RE SO SMART, THEN HOW ABOUT TELLING ME HOW TO USE THIS GAUNTLET TO FIGHT BACK!
NGH ...
DON'T ASK ME! I'VE NEVER BECOME A GAUNTLET BEFORE!
I-I DON'T REALLY KNOW WHETHER IT'LL BE OF ANY USE OR NOT, BUT--
SPIT IT OUT!! I NEED SOMETHING TO WORK WITH!!
F-FINE!!
BUT DON'T COME BAWLING TO ME IF IT FAILS!!
TWUNG
?!!
CRAP ...!
SNAG

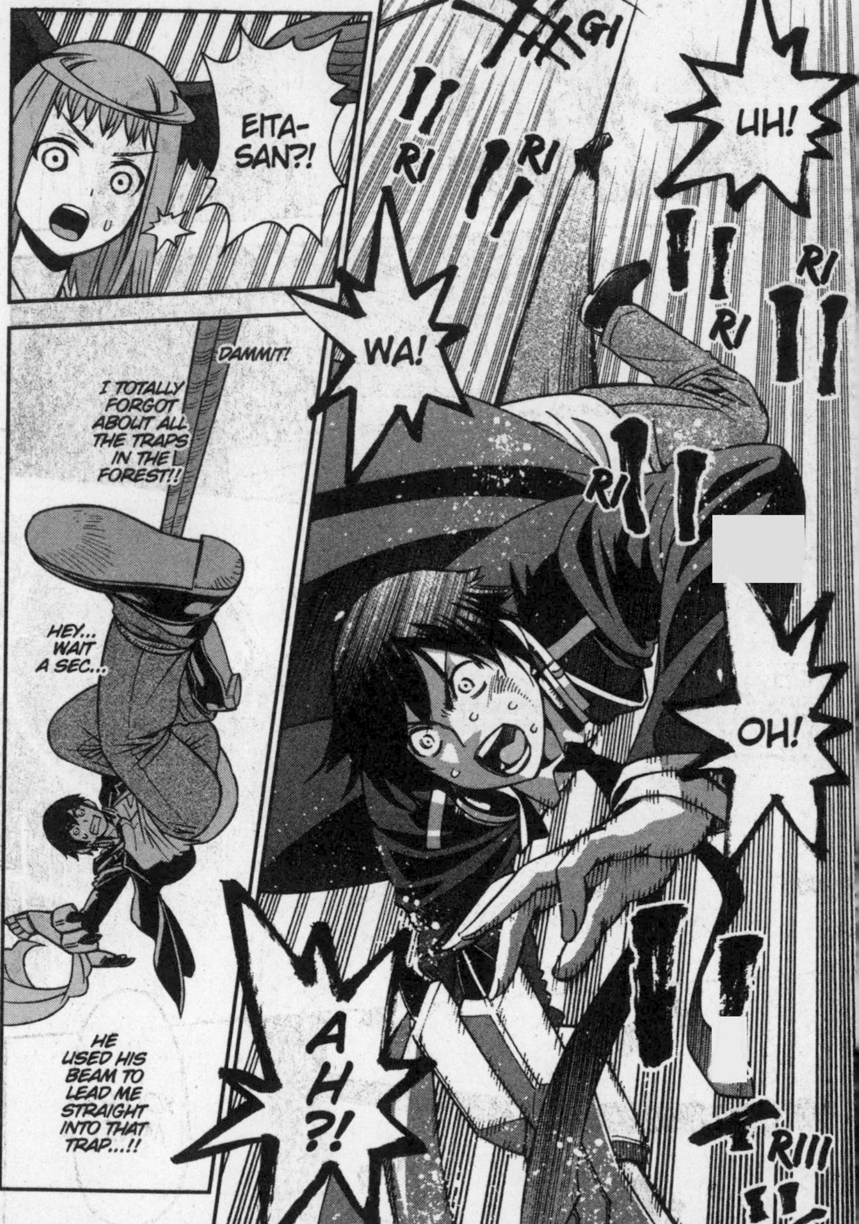
UH!
GI
RI
RI
RI
RI
WA!
RI
OH!
RIII
AH?!
EITA-SAN?!
DAMMIT!
I TOTALLY FORGOT ABOUT ALL THE TRAPS IN THE FOREST!!
HEY... WAIT A SEC...
HE USED HIS BEAM TO LEAD ME STRAIGHT INTO THAT TRAP...!!

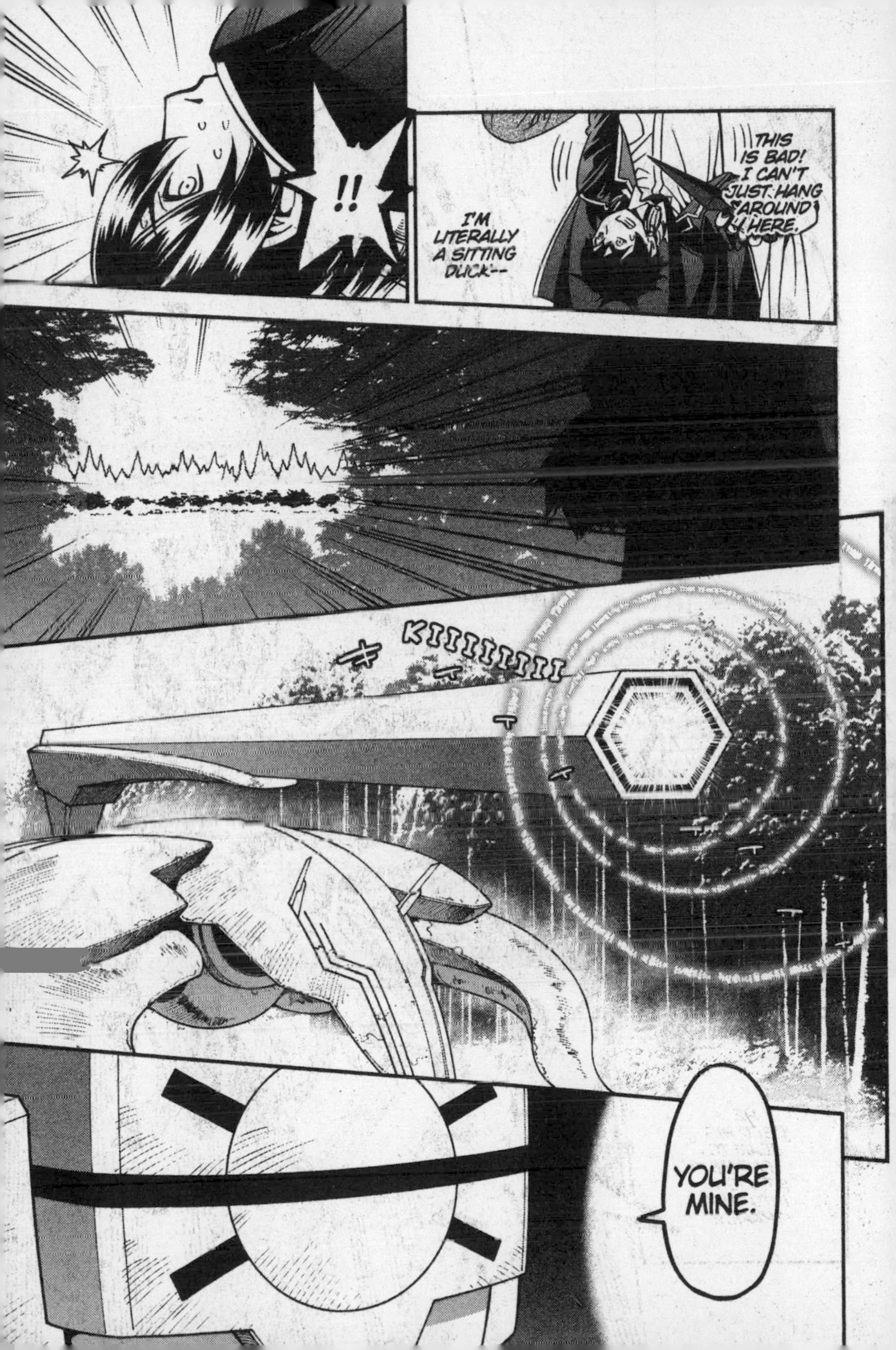
THIS IS BAD! I CAN'T JUST HANG AROUND HERE.
I'M LITERALLY A SITTING DUCK--
!!
KIIIIIIII
YOU'RE MINE.

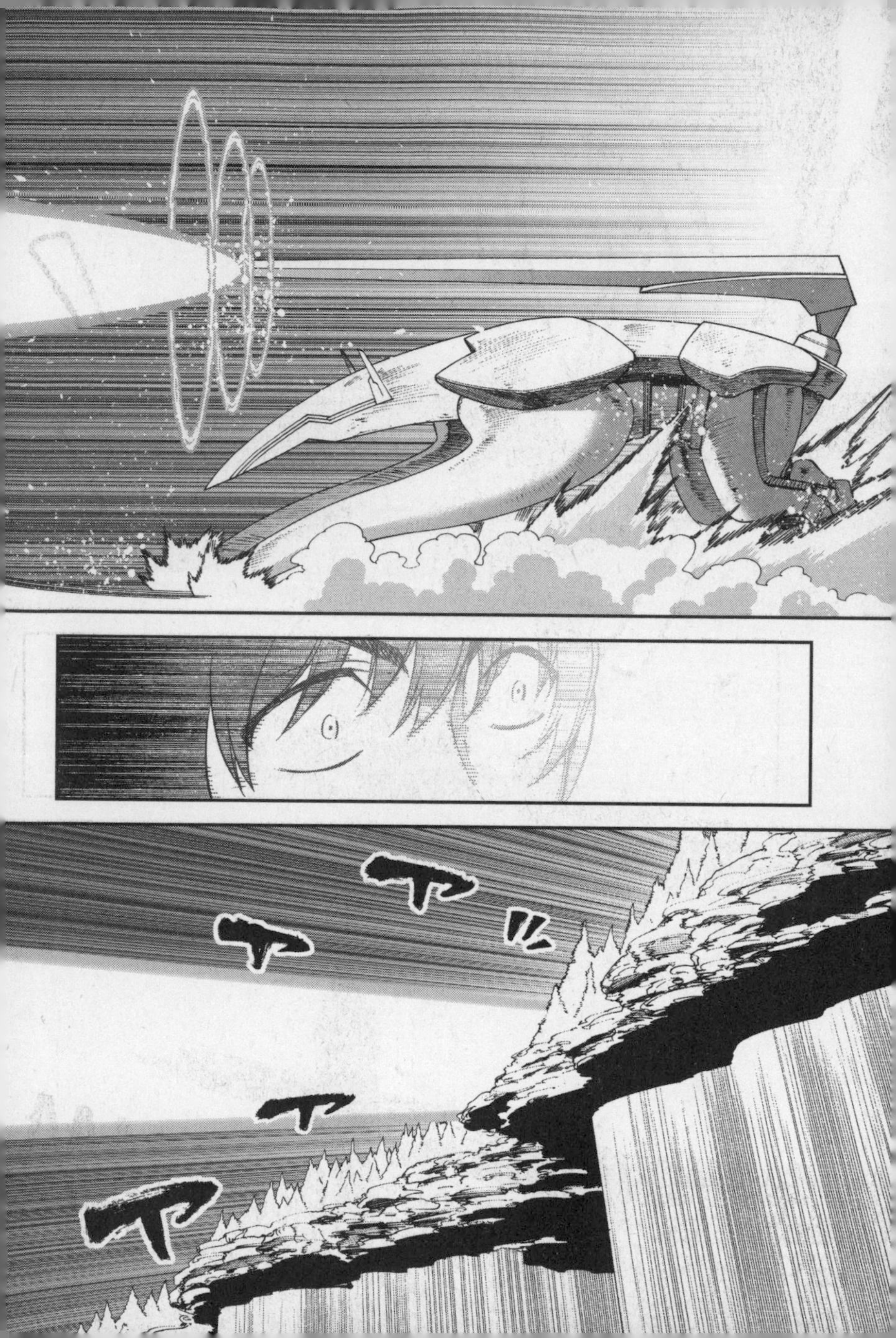
アァァァッ

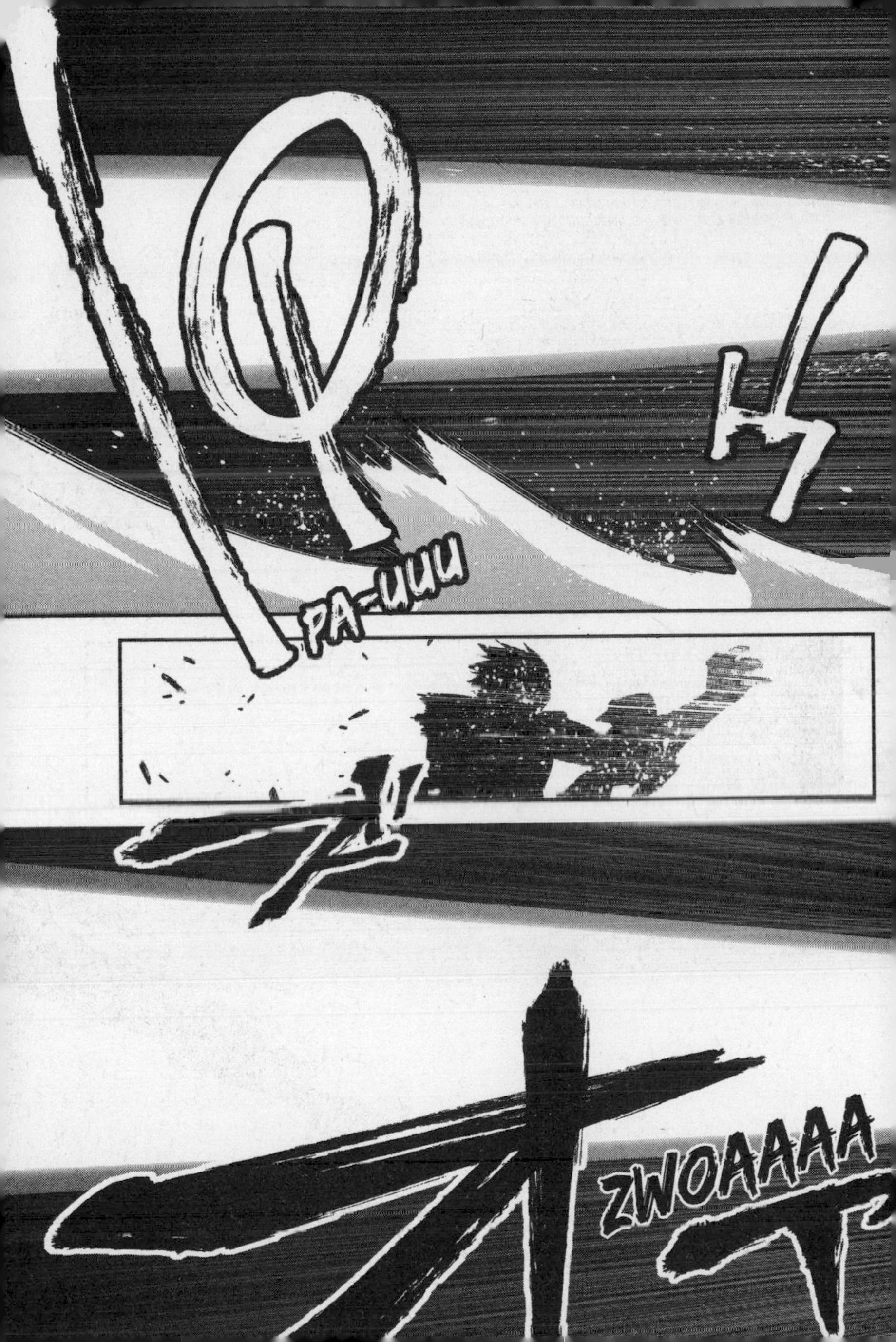
PA-UUU
ZWOAAAA

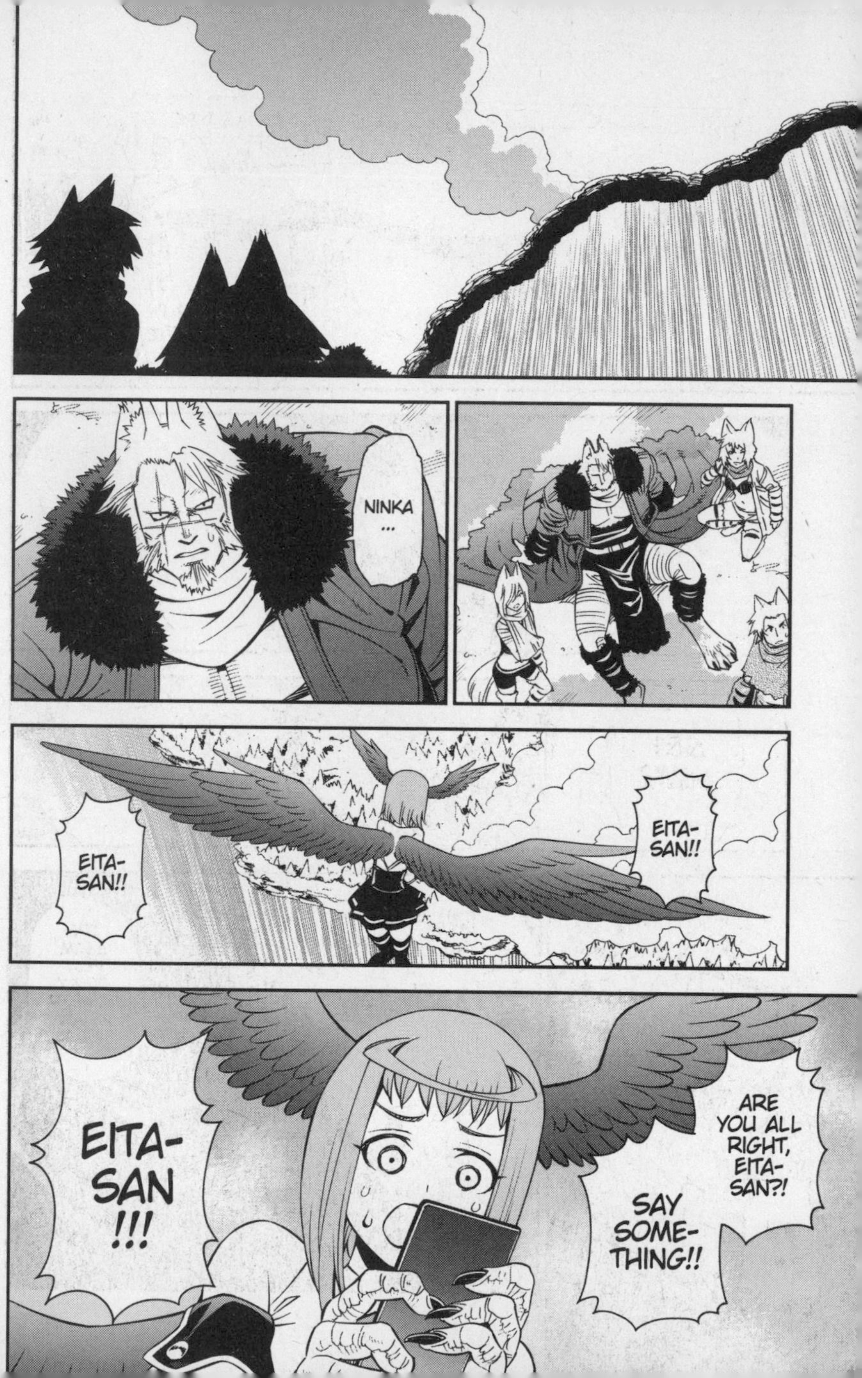
NINKA ...
EITA-SAN!!
EITA-SAN!!
ARE YOU ALL RIGHT, EITA-SAN?!
SAY SOME-THING!!
EITA-SAN!!!

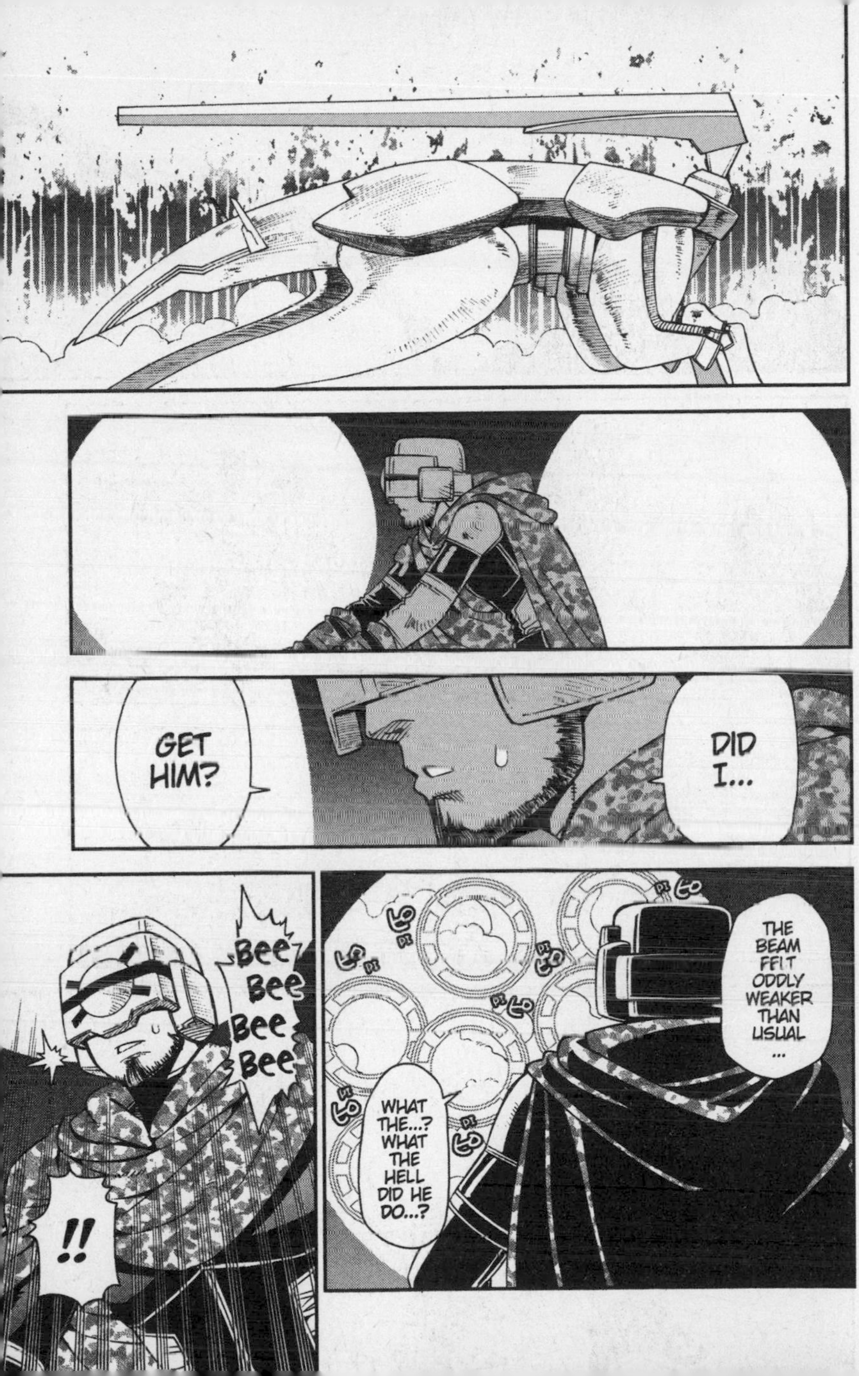
DID I...
GET HIM?
THE BEAM FELT ODDLY WEAKER THAN USUAL ...
WHAT THE...? WHAT THE HELL DID HE DO...?
Bee Bee Bee Bee
!!

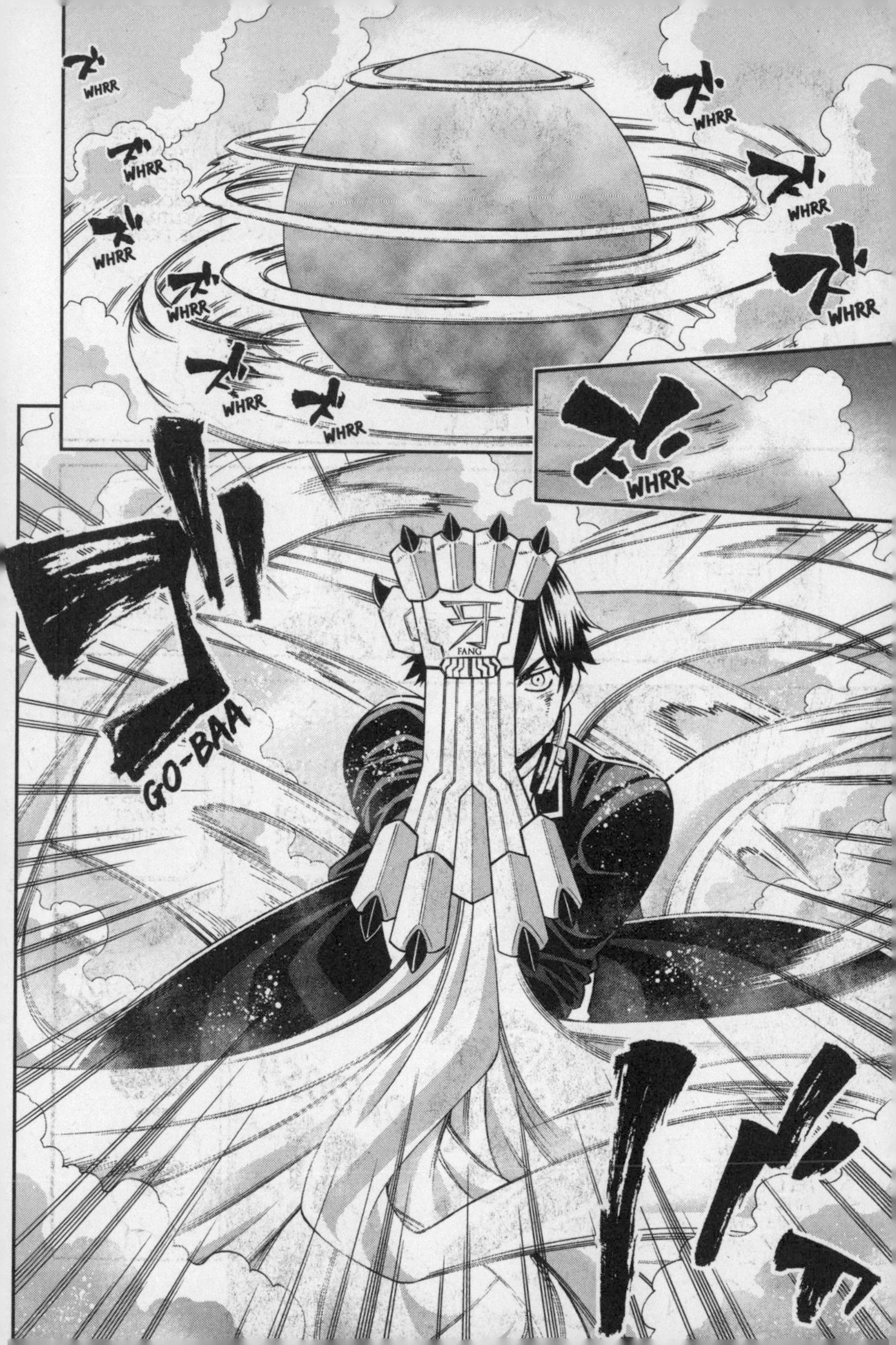
WHRR
WHRR
WHRR
WHRR
WHRR
WHRR
WHRR
WHRR
WHRR
WHRR
FANG
GO-BAA

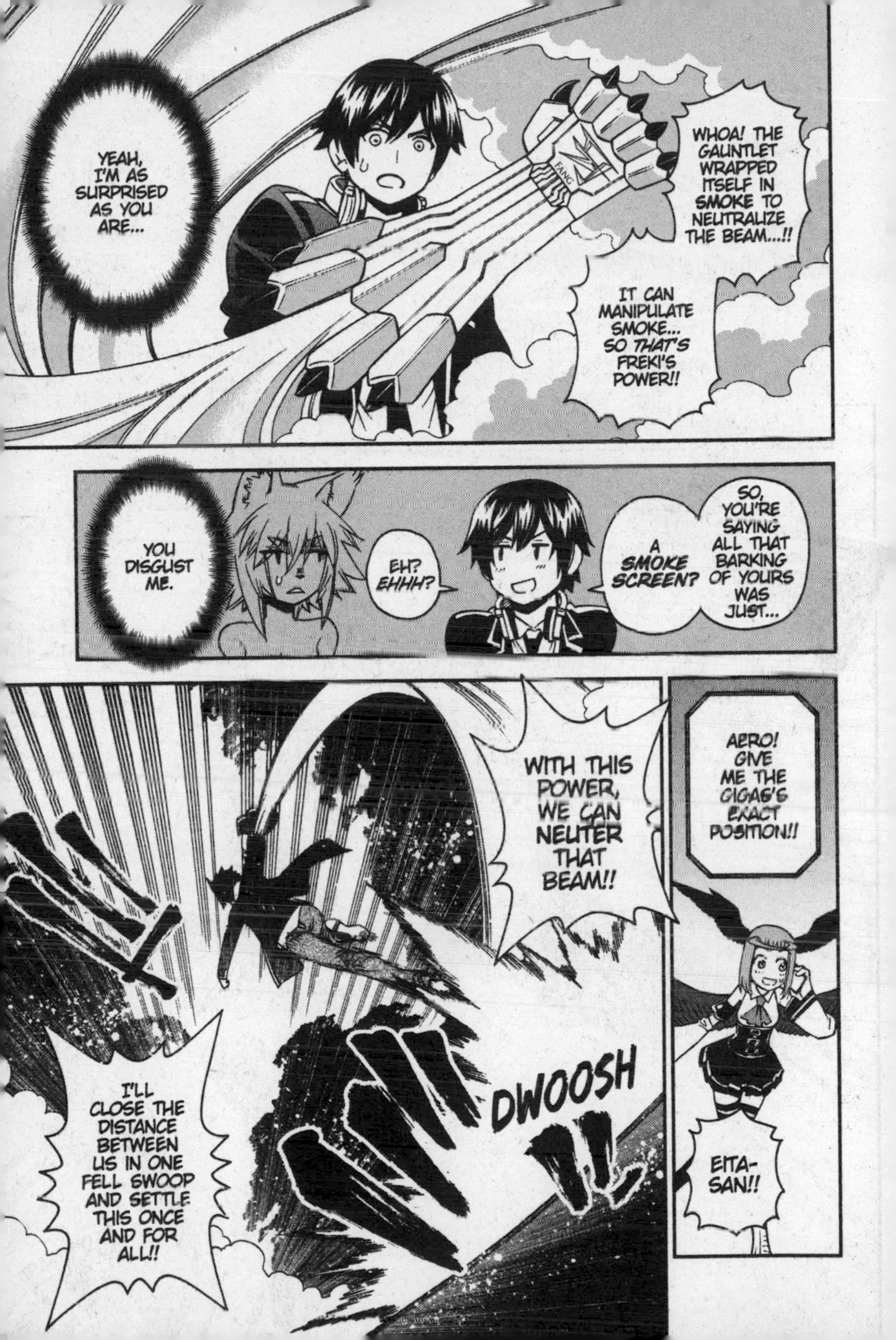
WHOA! THE GAUNTLET WRAPPED ITSELF IN SMOKE TO NEUTRALIZE THE BEAM...!!
IT CAN MANIPULATE SMOKE... SO *THAT'S* FREKI'S POWER!!
YEAH, I'M AS SURPRISED AS YOU ARE...
SO, YOU'RE SAYING ALL THAT BARKING OF YOURS WAS JUST...
A *SMOKE SCREEN?*
EH? *EHHH?*
YOU DISGUST ME.
AERO! GIVE ME THE GIGAS'S EXACT POSITION!!
EITA-SAN!!
WITH THIS POWER, WE CAN NEUTER THAT BEAM!!
DWOOSH
I'LL CLOSE THE DISTANCE BETWEEN US IN ONE FELL SWOOP AND SETTLE THIS ONCE AND FOR ALL!!

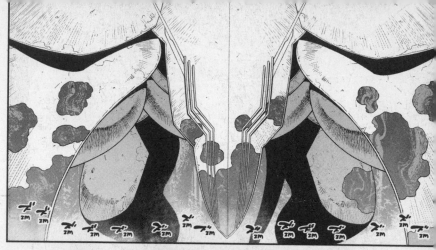

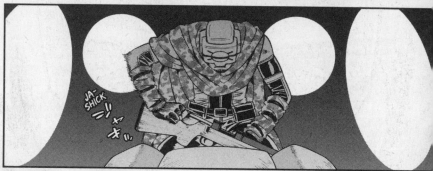

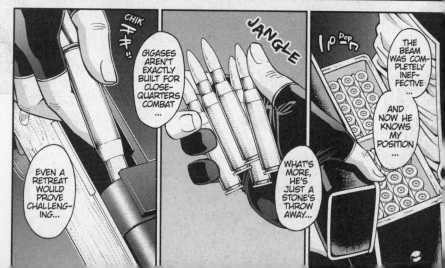

ZM ZM ZM ZM ZM ZM ZM ZM ZM ZM ZM ZM ZM ZM ZM ZM
JA-SHICK
POP
THE BEAM WAS COMPLETELY INEFFECTIVE...
AND NOW HE KNOWS MY POSITION...
JANGLE
GIGASES AREN'T EXACTLY BUILT FOR CLOSE-QUARTERS COMBAT...
WHAT'S MORE, HE'S JUST A STONE'S THROW AWAY...
CHIK
EVEN A RETREAT WOULD PROVE CHALLENGING...

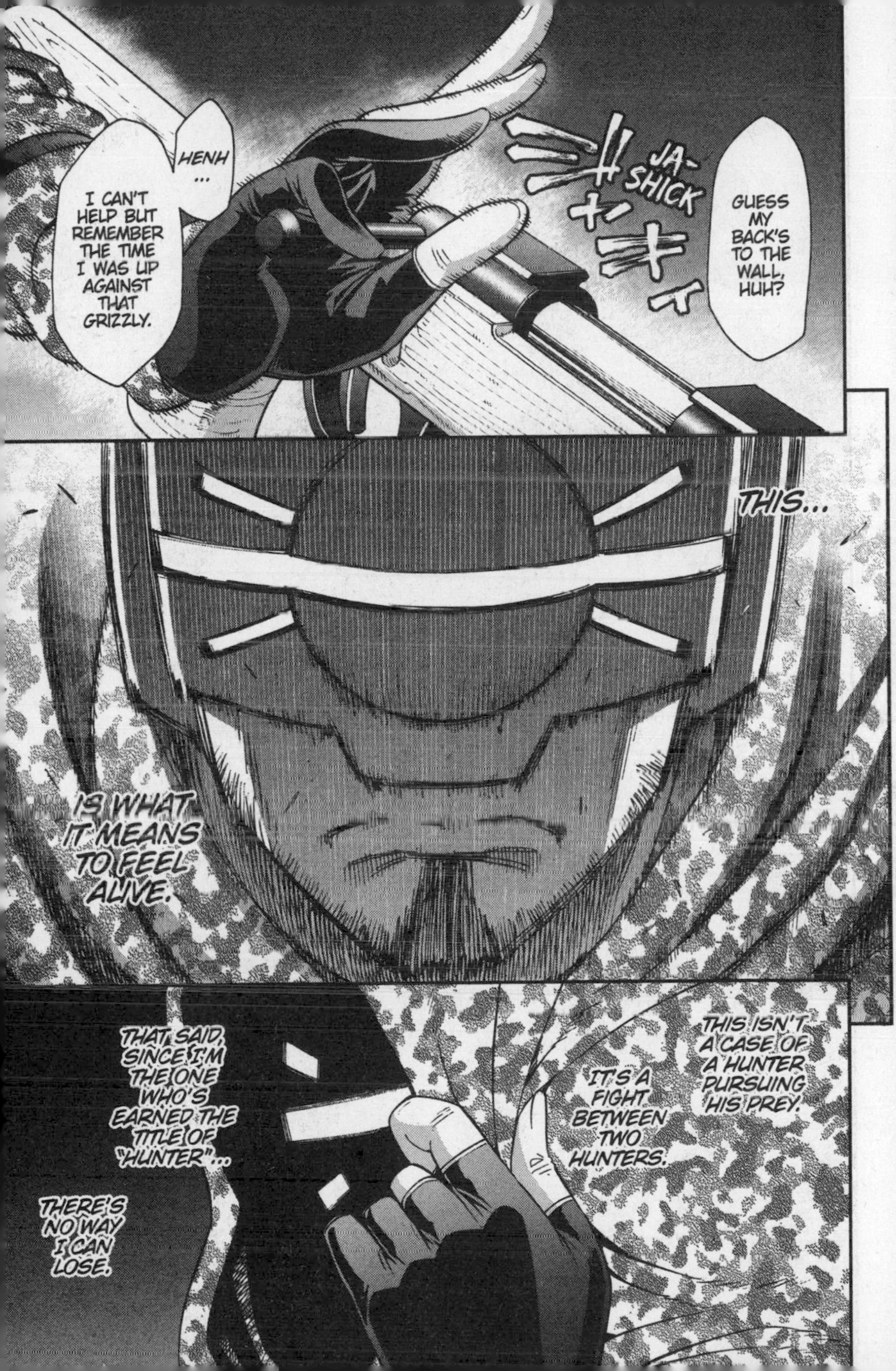
GUESS MY BACK'S TO THE WALL, HUH?
JA-SHICK
HENH...
I CAN'T HELP BUT REMEMBER THE TIME I WAS UP AGAINST THAT GRIZZLY.
THIS...
IS WHAT IT MEANS TO FEEL ALIVE.
THIS ISN'T A CASE OF A HUNTER PURSUING HIS PREY.
IT'S A FIGHT BETWEEN TWO HUNTERS.
THAT SAID, SINCE I'M THE ONE WHO'S EARNED THE TITLE OF "HUNTER"...
THERE'S NO WAY I CAN LOSE.

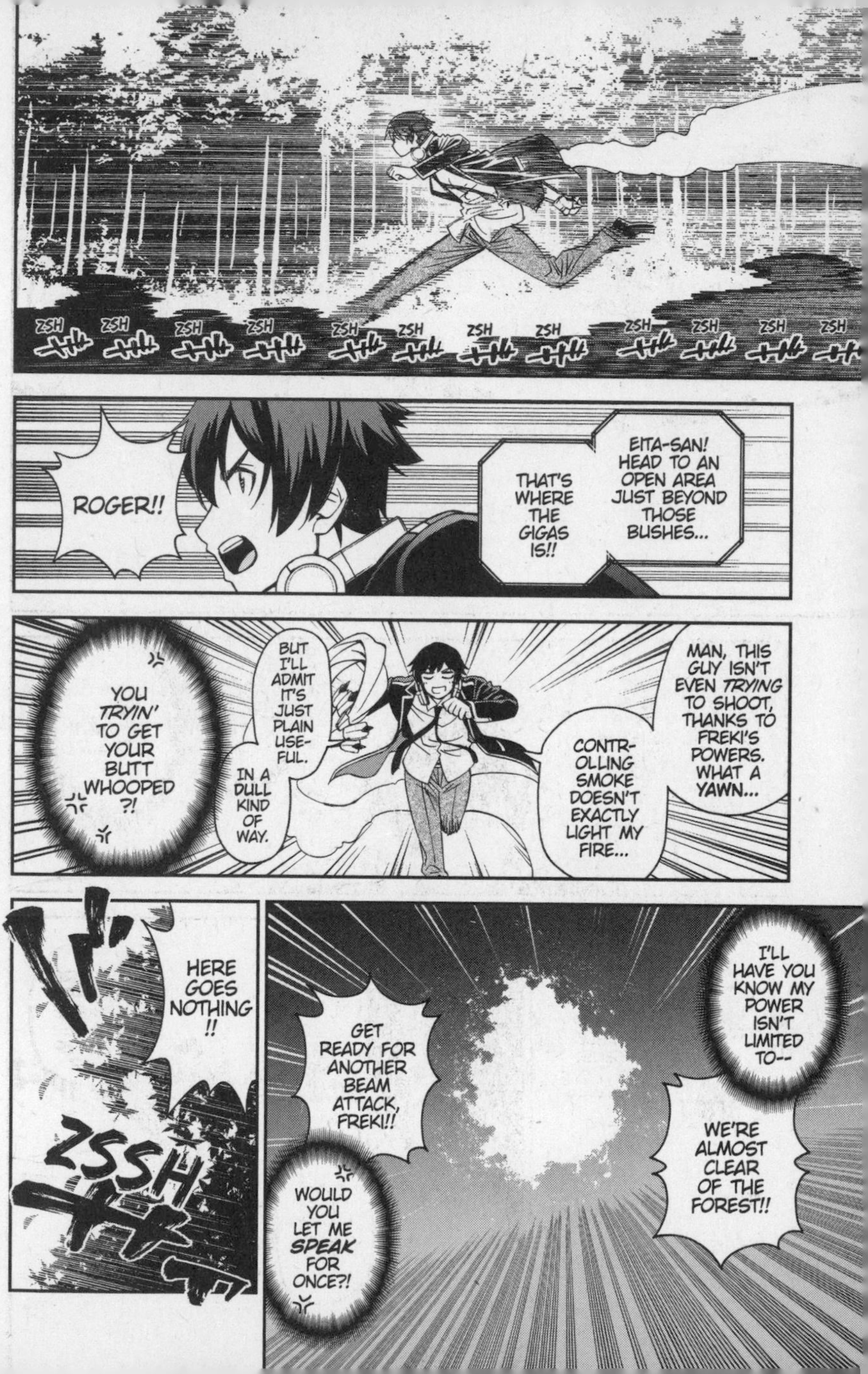
ZSH ZSH ZSH ZSH ZSH ZSH ZSH ZSH ZSH ZSH ZSH ZSH
EITA-SAN! HEAD TO AN OPEN AREA JUST BEYOND THOSE BUSHES...
THAT'S WHERE THE GIGAS IS!!
ROGER!!
MAN, THIS GUY ISN'T EVEN *TRYING* TO SHOOT, THANKS TO FREKI'S POWERS. WHAT A YAWN...
CONTROLLING SMOKE DOESN'T EXACTLY LIGHT MY FIRE...
BUT I'LL ADMIT IT'S JUST PLAIN USEFUL.
IN A DULL KIND OF WAY.
YOU *TRYIN'* TO GET YOUR BUTT WHOOPED?!
I'LL HAVE YOU KNOW MY POWER ISN'T LIMITED TO--
WE'RE ALMOST CLEAR OF THE FOREST!!
GET READY FOR ANOTHER BEAM ATTACK, FREKI!!
WOULD YOU LET ME ***SPEAK*** FOR ONCE?!
HERE GOES NOTHING!!
ZSSH

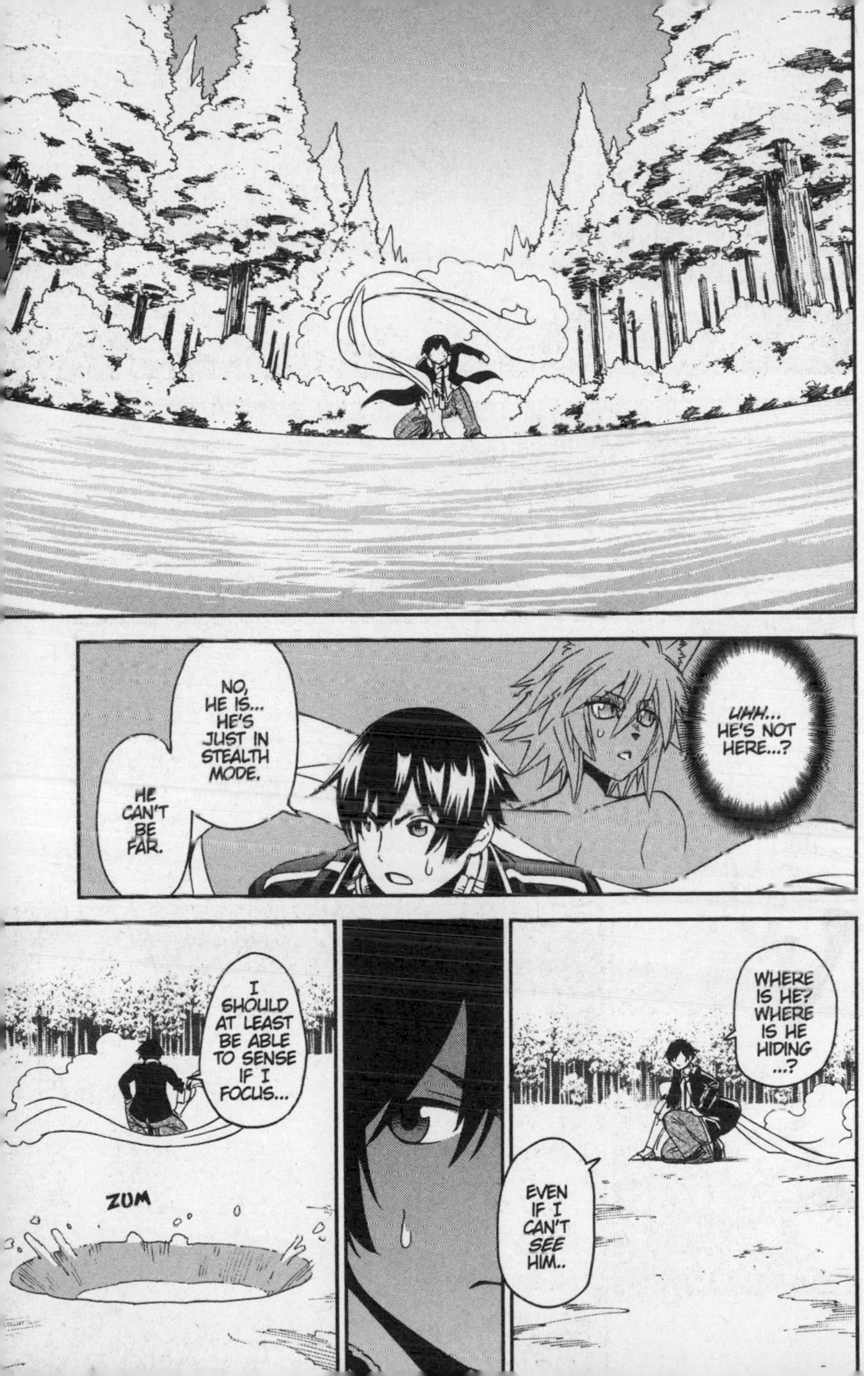
UHH... HE'S NOT HERE...?
NO, HE IS... HE'S JUST IN STEALTH MODE.
HE CAN'T BE FAR.
WHERE IS HE? WHERE IS HE HIDING ...?
EVEN IF I CAN'T SEE HIM..
I SHOULD AT LEAST BE ABLE TO SENSE IF I FOCUS...
ZUM

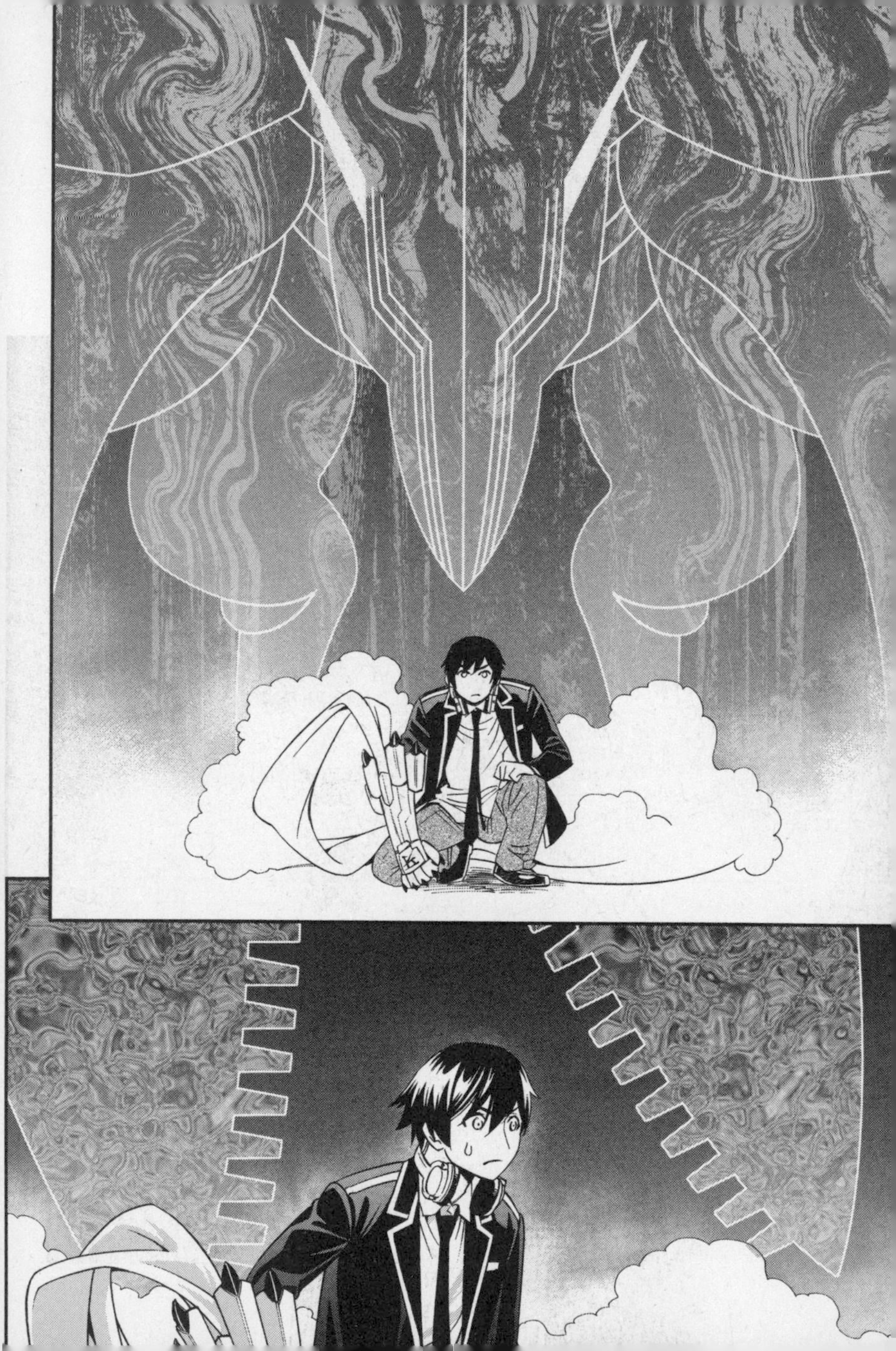

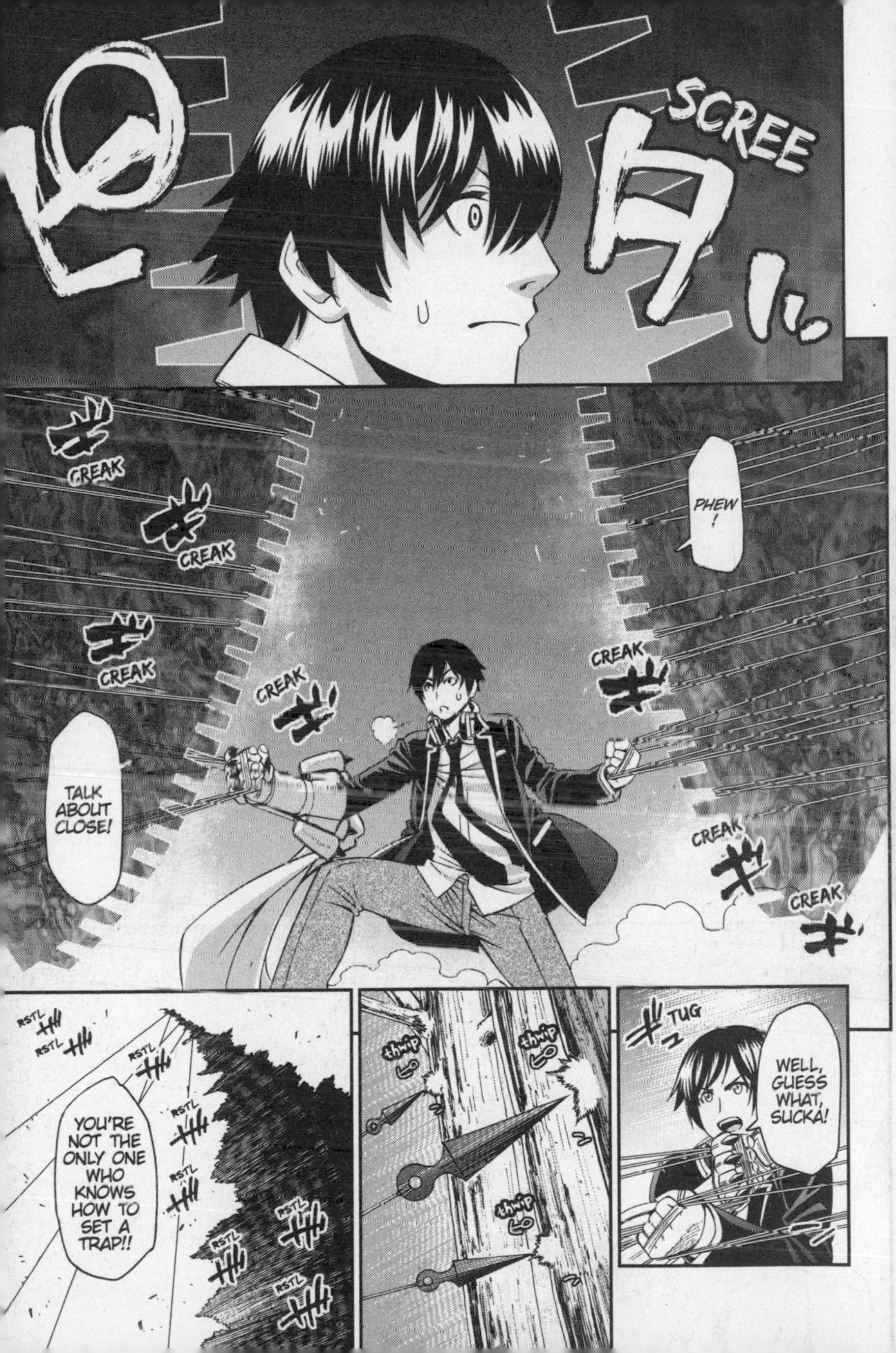
SCREE
PHEW!
CREAK
CREAK
CREAK
CREAK
CREAK
CREAK
CREAK
TALK ABOUT CLOSE!
TUG
WELL, GUESS WHAT, SUCKA!
thwip
thwip
thwip
RSTL
RSTL
RSTL
RSTL
RSTL
RSTL
RSTL
RSTL
YOU'RE NOT THE ONLY ONE WHO KNOWS HOW TO SET A TRAP!!

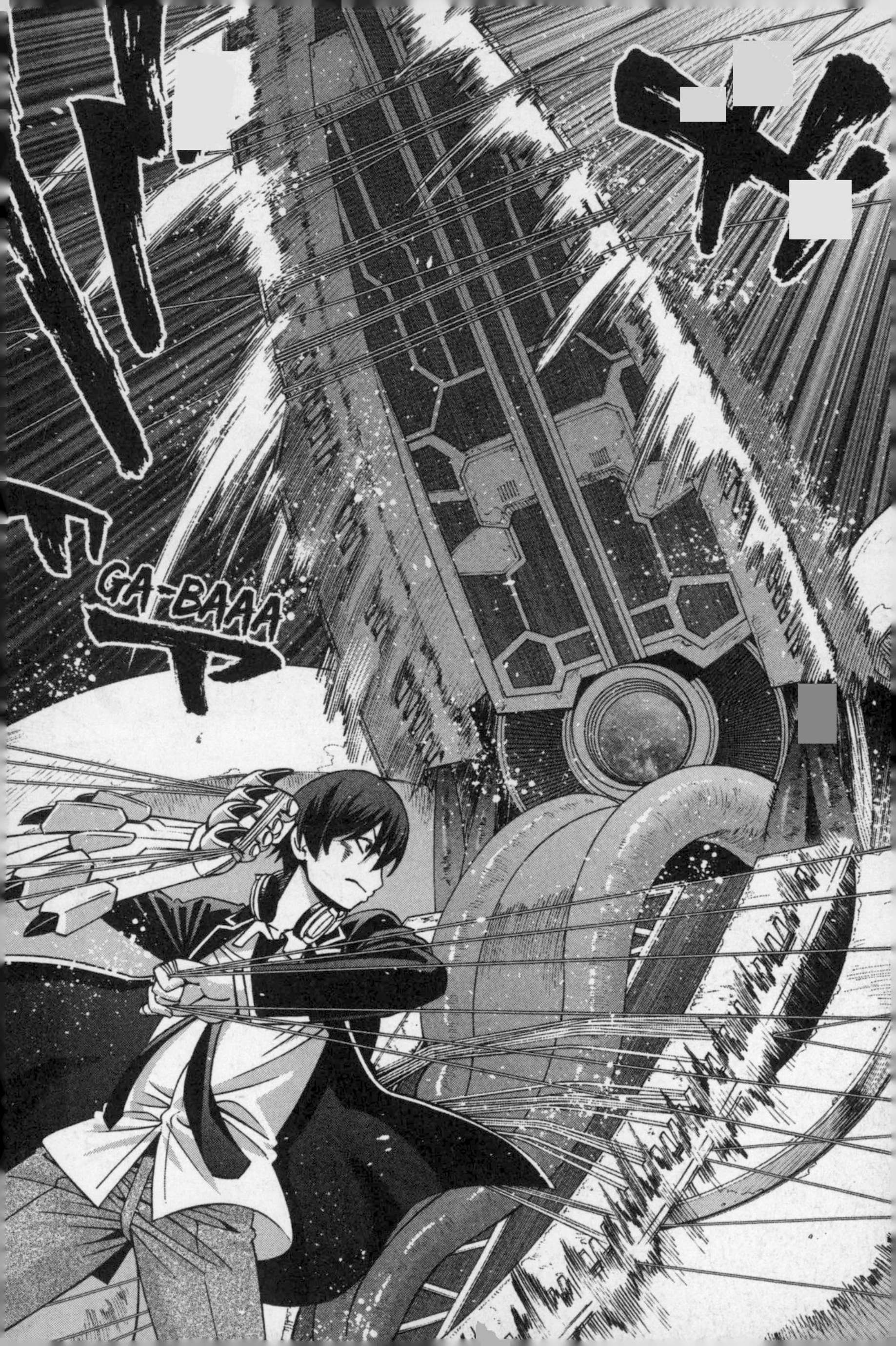
GA-BAAA

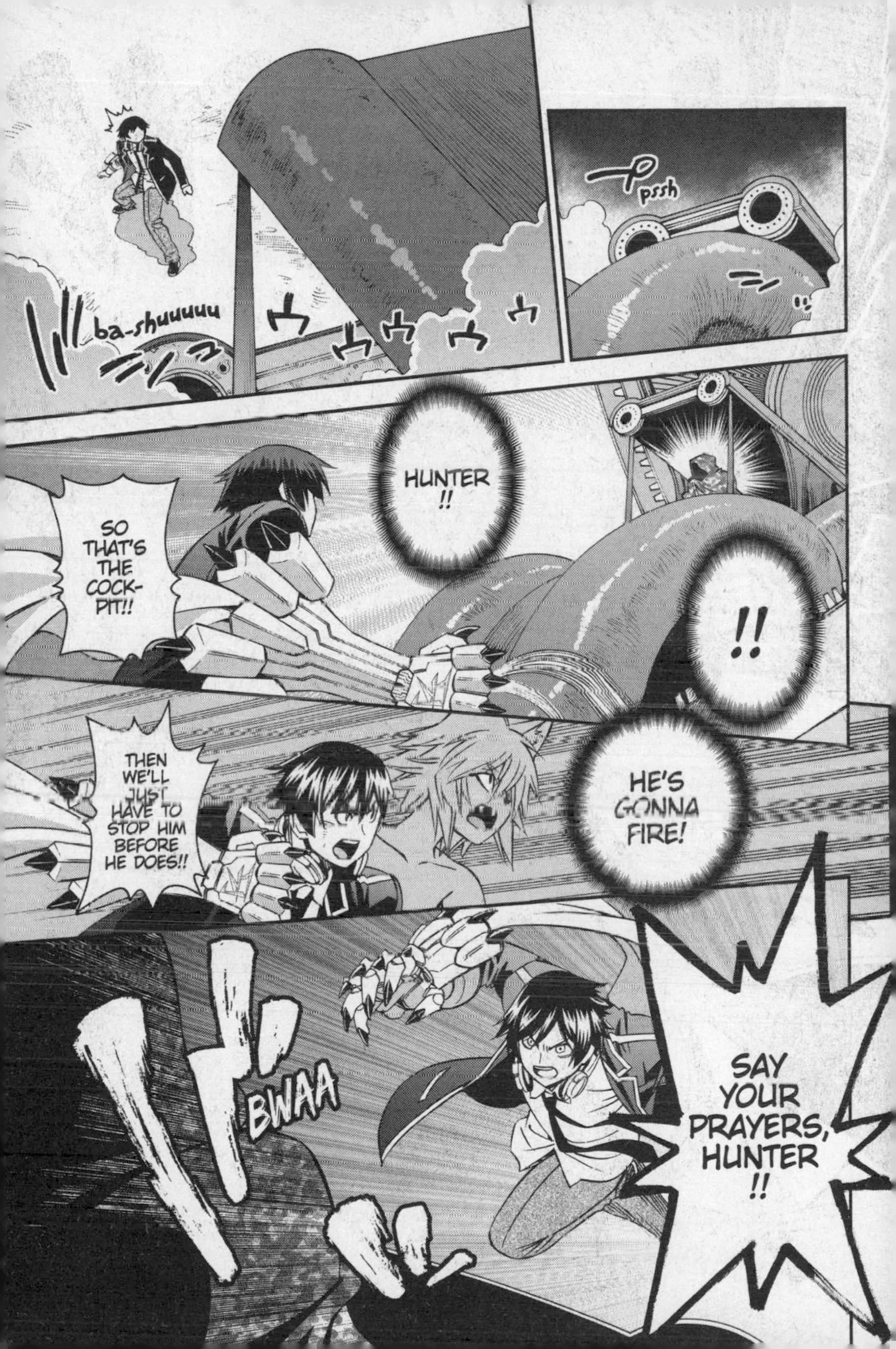
pssh
ba-shuuuu
HUNTER!!
SO THAT'S THE COCK-PIT!!
!!
HE'S GONNA FIRE!
THEN WE'LL JUST HAVE TO STOP HIM BEFORE HE DOES!!
SAY YOUR PRAYERS, HUNTER!!
BWAA

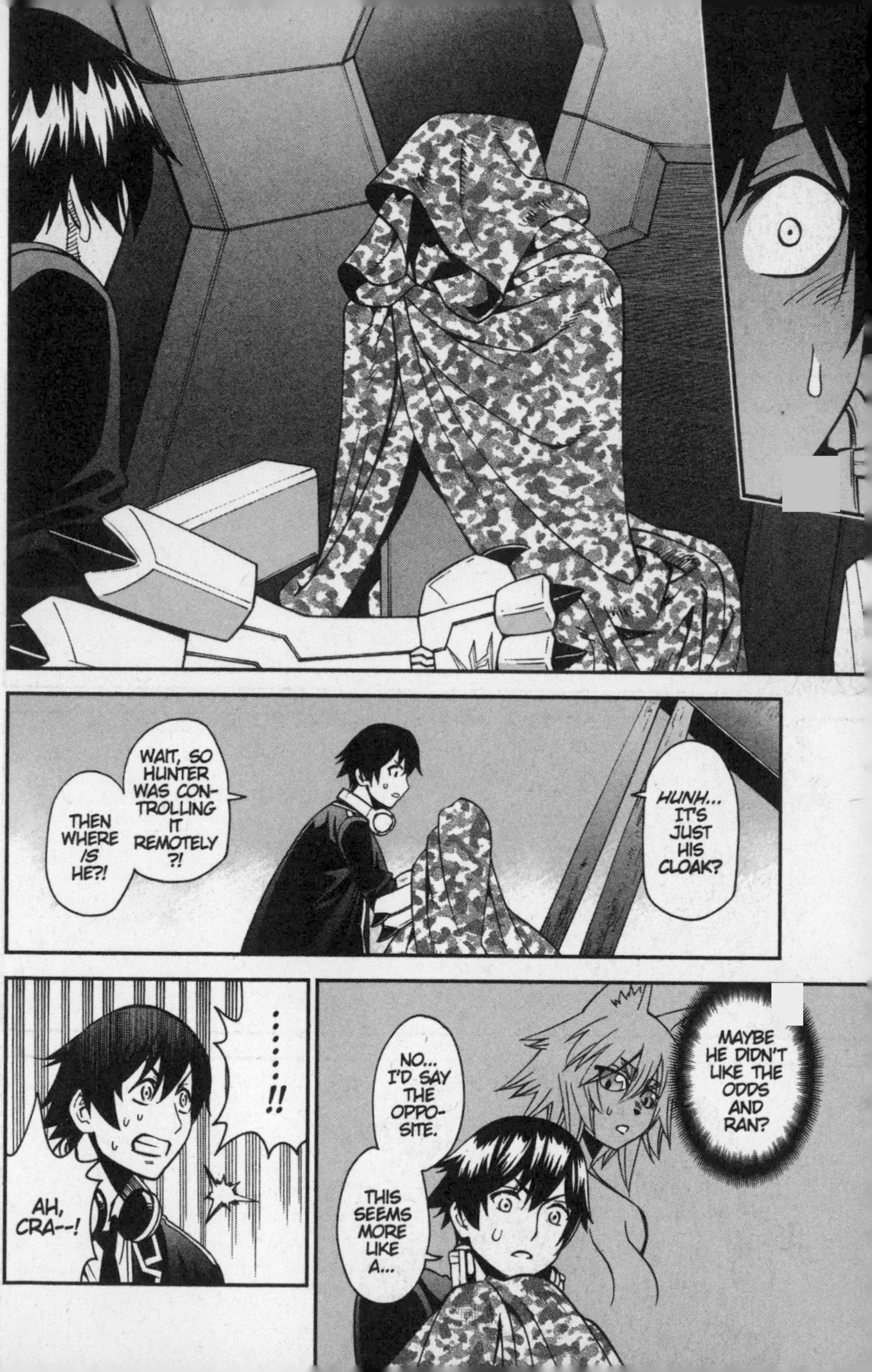
HUNH... IT'S JUST HIS CLOAK?
WAIT, SO HUNTER WAS CONTROLLING IT REMOTELY?!
THEN WHERE IS HE?!
MAYBE HE DIDN'T LIKE THE ODDS AND RAN?
NO... I'D SAY THE OPPOSITE.
THIS SEEMS MORE LIKE A...
......!!
AH, CRA--!

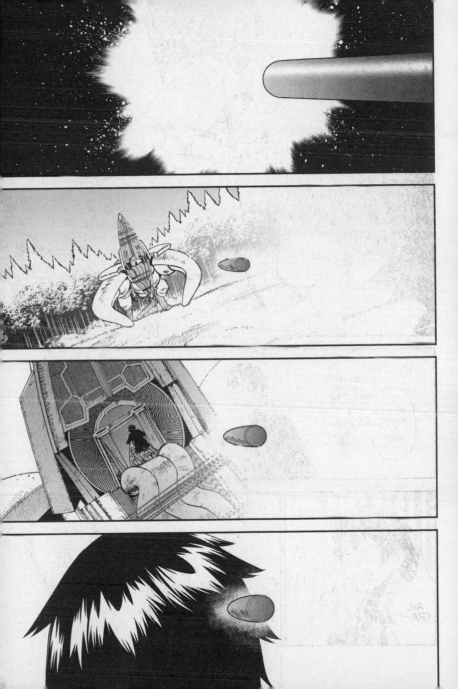

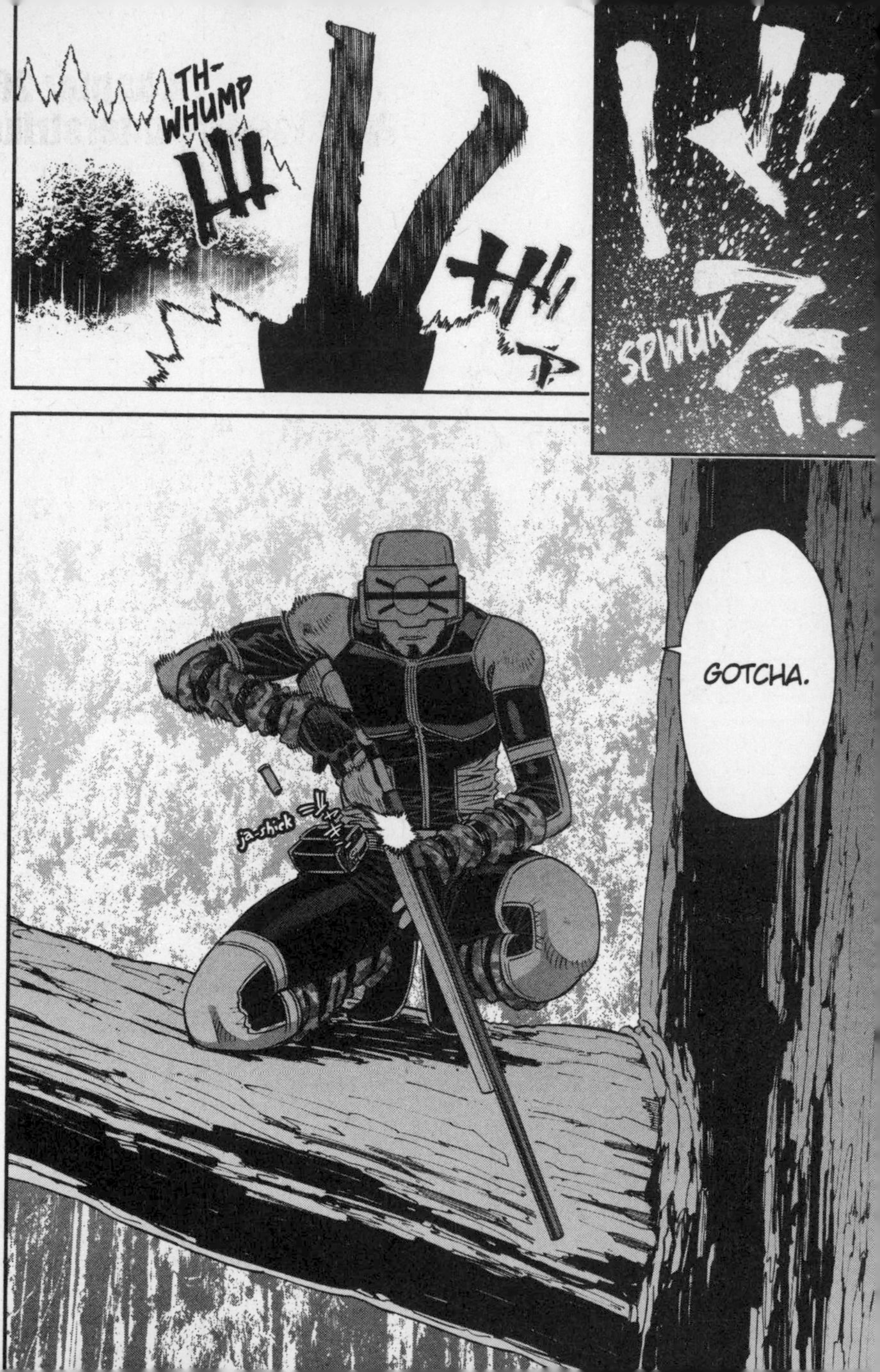
SPWUK
TH-WHUMP
ja-shick
GOTCHA.

Chapter 26: Wolf-fang Counterstrike

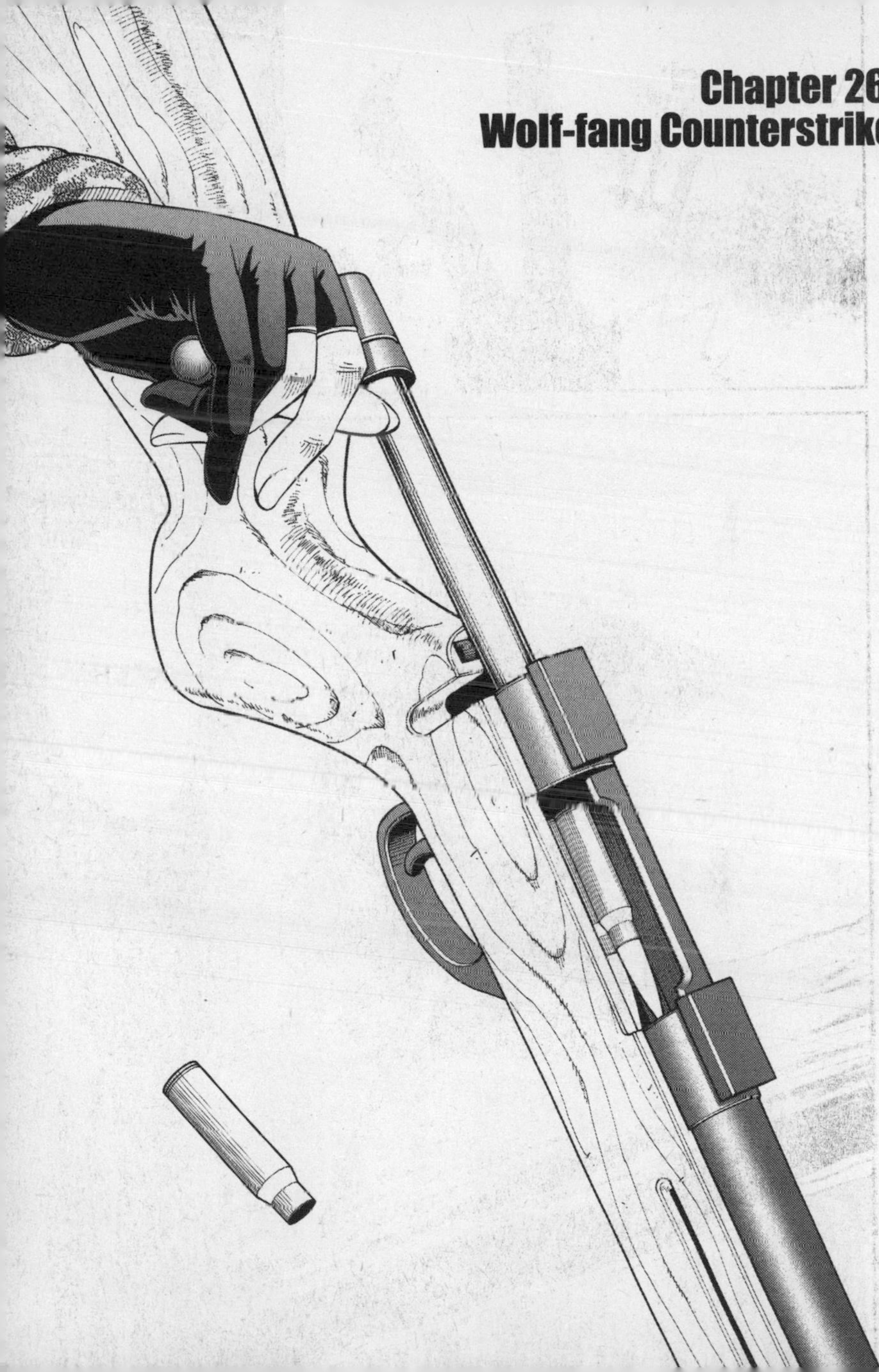

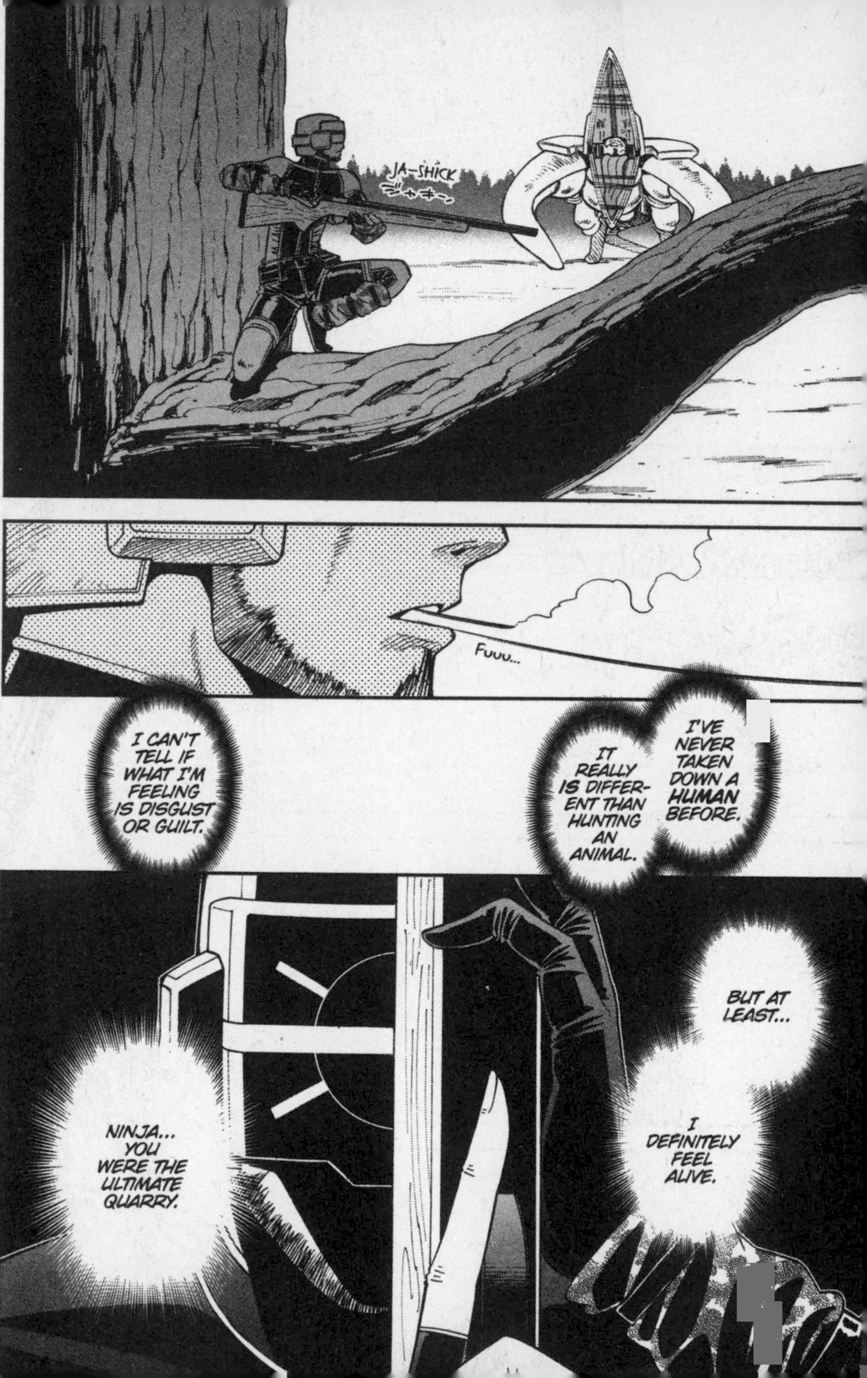
JA-SHICK
Fuuu...
I'VE NEVER TAKEN DOWN A HUMAN BEFORE.
IT REALLY IS DIFFER-ENT THAN HUNTING AN ANIMAL.
I CAN'T TELL IF WHAT I'M FEELING IS DISGUST OR GUILT.
BUT AT LEAST...
I DEFINITELY FEEL ALIVE.
NINJA... YOU WERE THE ULTIMATE QUARRY.

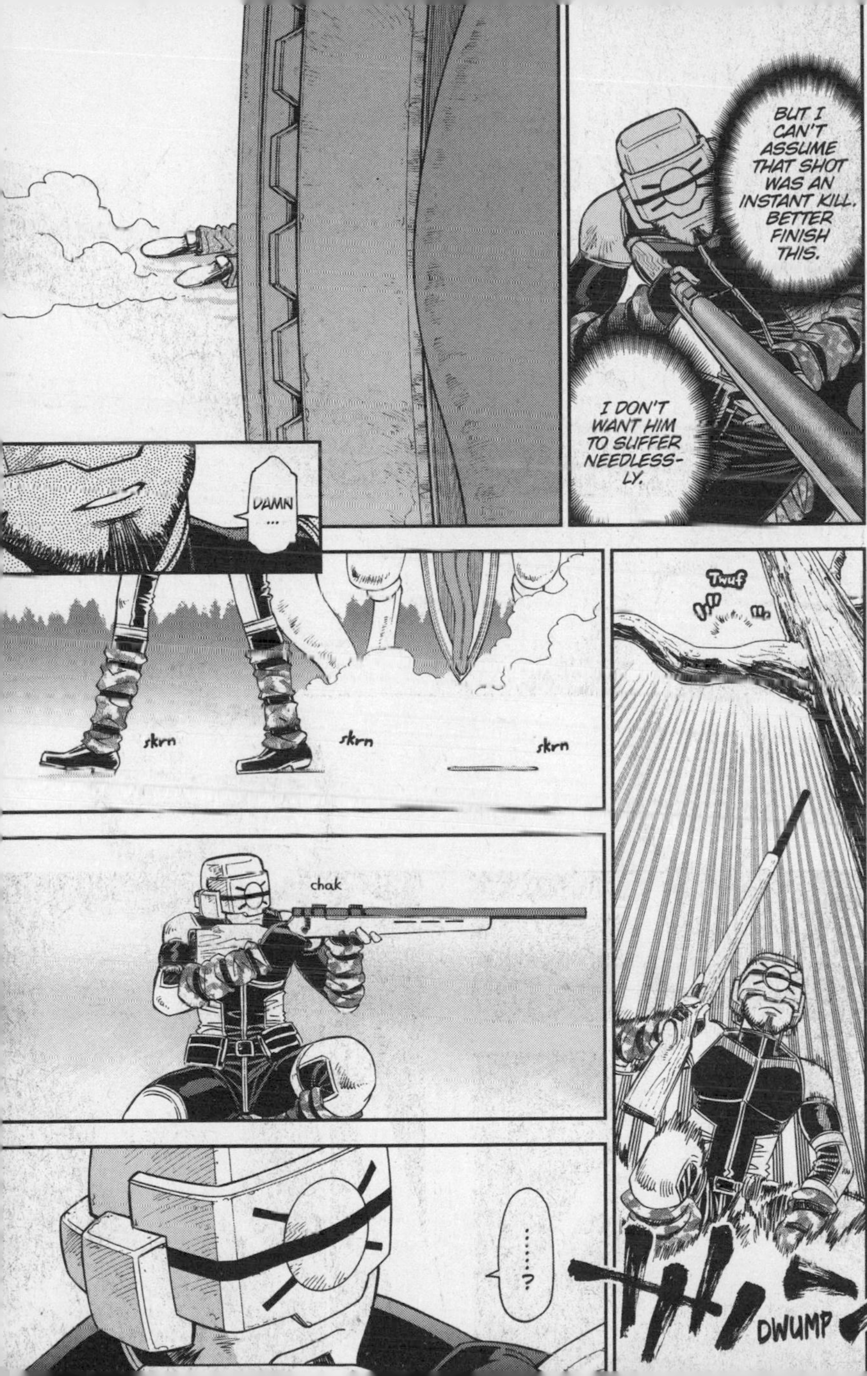
BUT I CAN'T ASSUME THAT SHOT WAS AN INSTANT KILL. BETTER FINISH THIS.
I DON'T WANT HIM TO SUFFER NEEDLESS-LY.
DAMN ...
Twuf
DWUMP
skrn
skrn
skrn
chak
......?

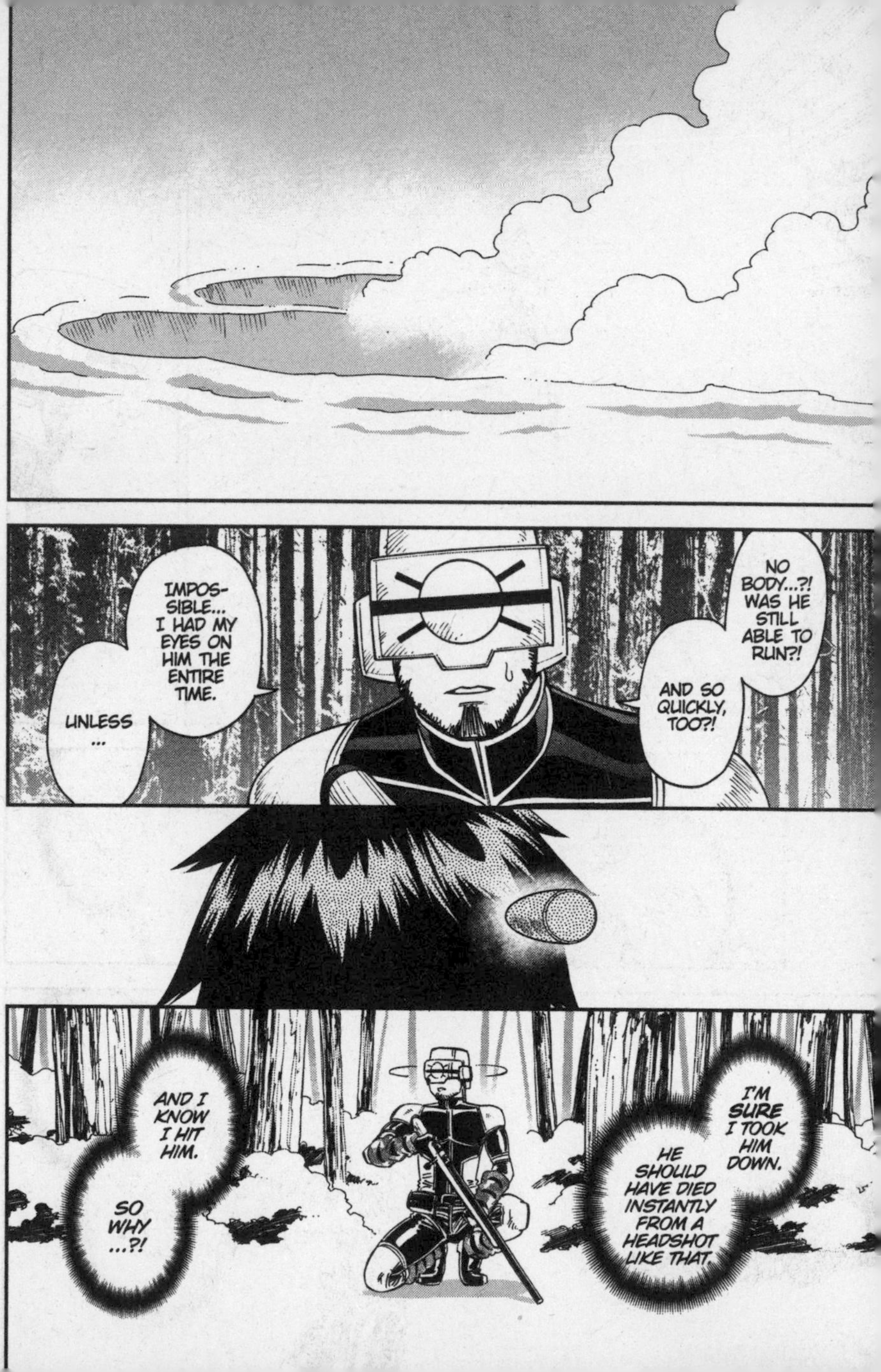
NO BODY...?! WAS HE STILL ABLE TO RUN?!
AND SO QUICKLY, TOO?!
IMPOSSIBLE... I HAD MY EYES ON HIM THE ENTIRE TIME.
UNLESS ...
I'M SURE I TOOK HIM DOWN.
HE SHOULD HAVE DIED INSTANTLY FROM A HEADSHOT LIKE THAT.
AND I KNOW I HIT HIM.
SO WHY ...?!

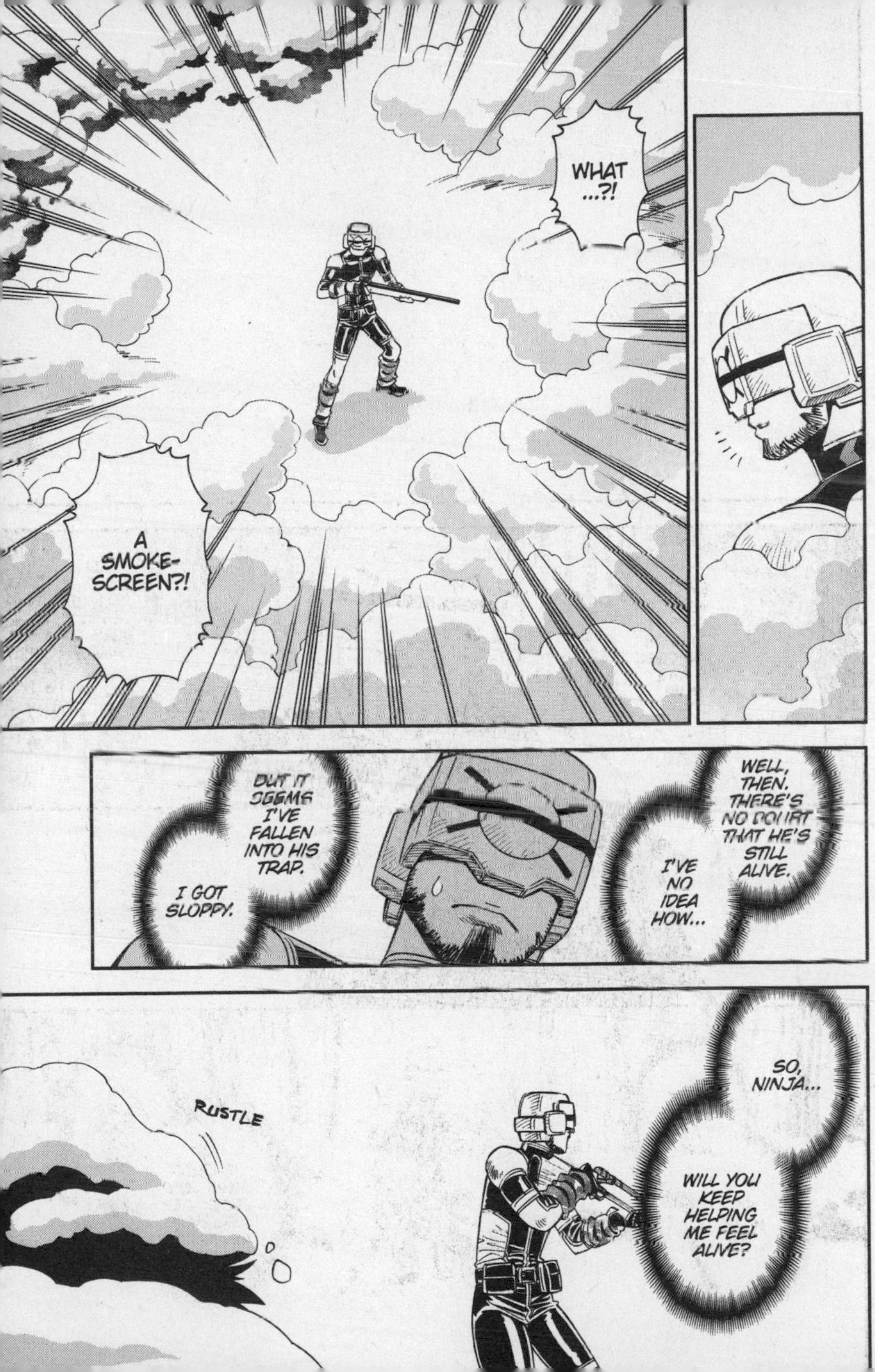
WHAT ...?!
A SMOKE-SCREEN?!
WELL, THEN. THERE'S NO DOUBT THAT HE'S STILL ALIVE.
I'VE NO IDEA HOW...
BUT IT SEEMS I'VE FALLEN INTO HIS TRAP.
I GOT SLOPPY.
SO, NINJA...
WILL YOU KEEP HELPING ME FEEL ALIVE?
RUSTLE

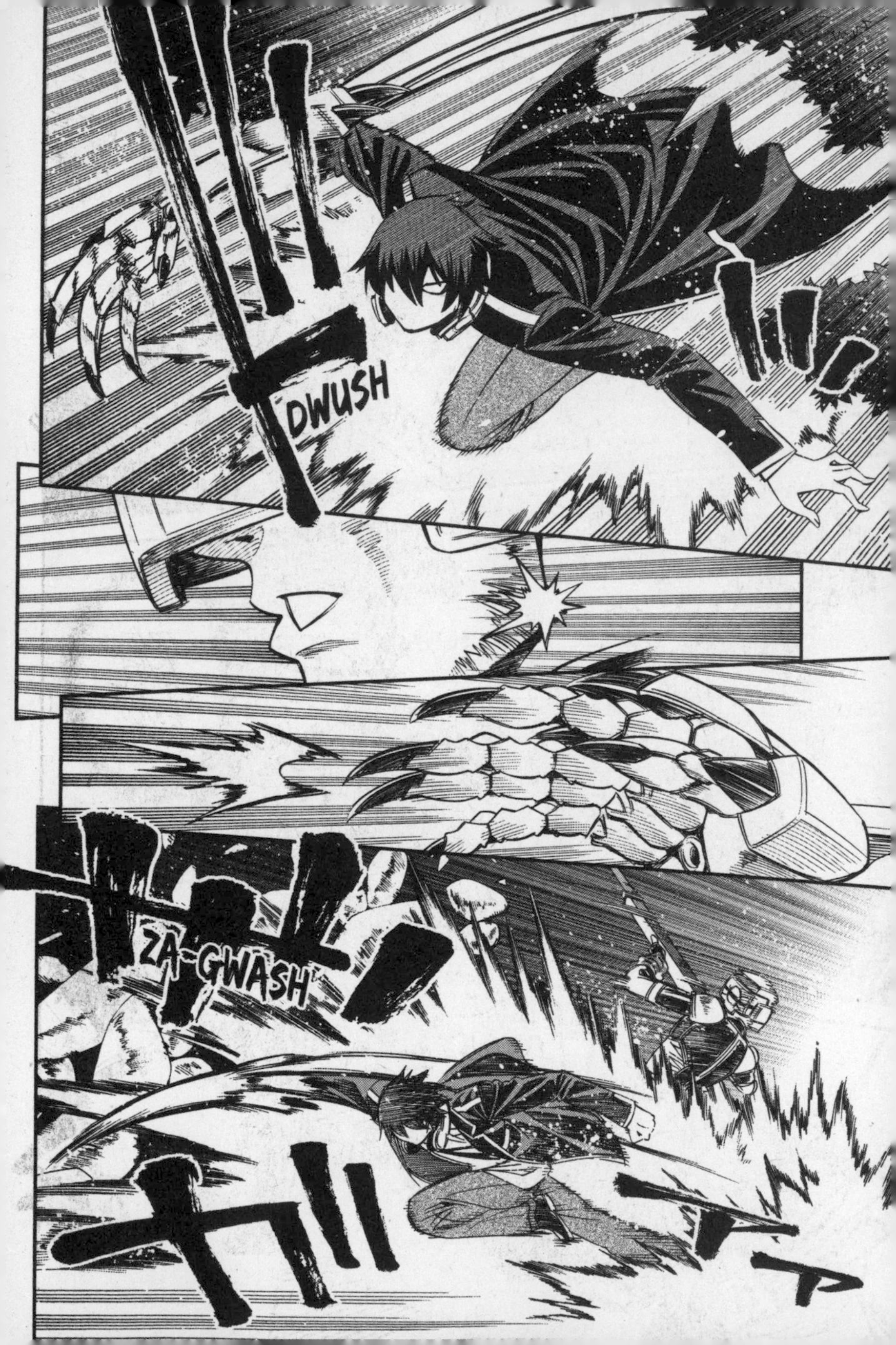
DWUSH
ZA-GWASH

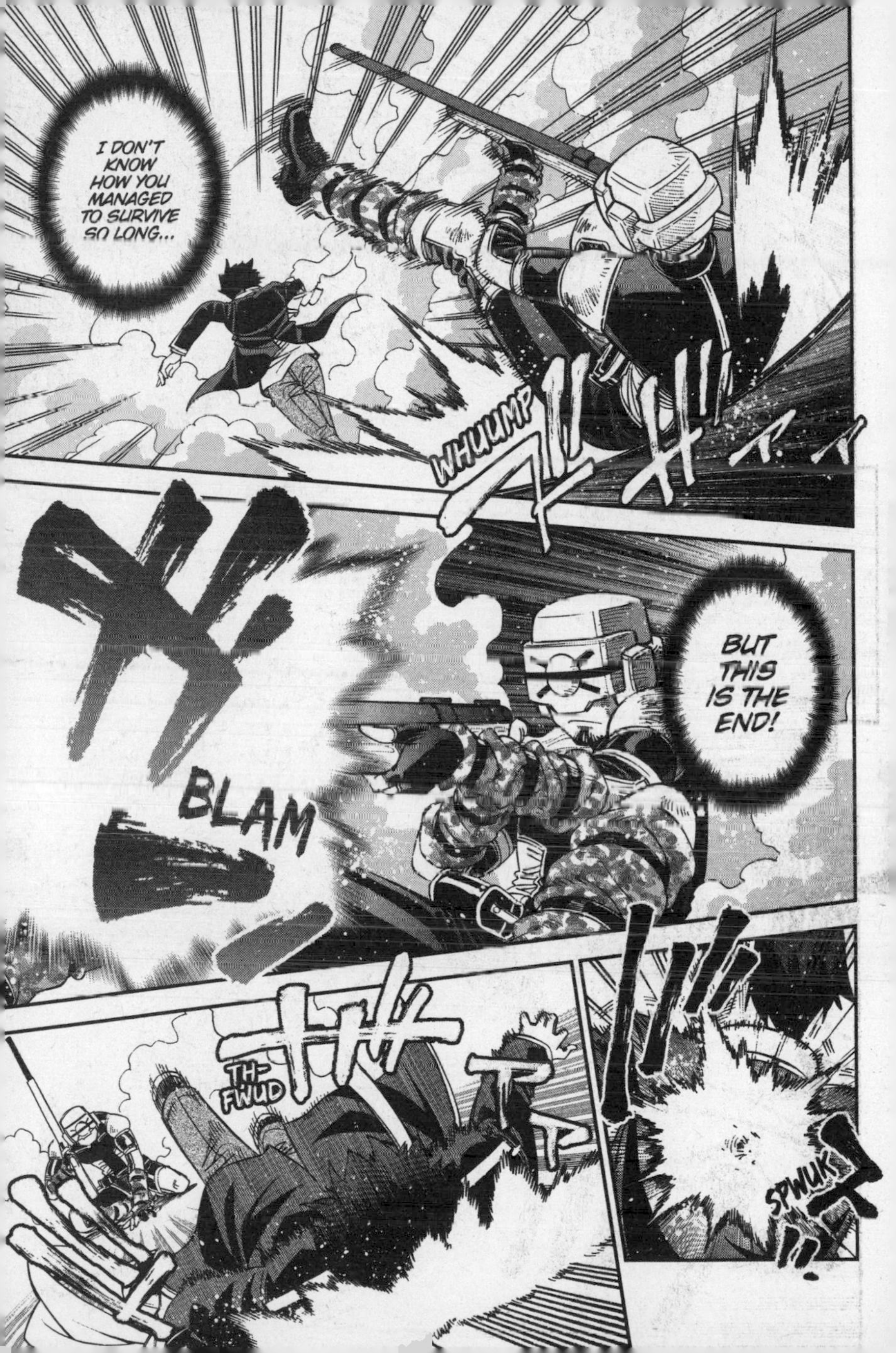
I DON'T KNOW HOW YOU MANAGED TO SURVIVE SO LONG...
WHUUMP
BUT THIS IS THE END!
BLAM
SPWUK
TH-FWUD

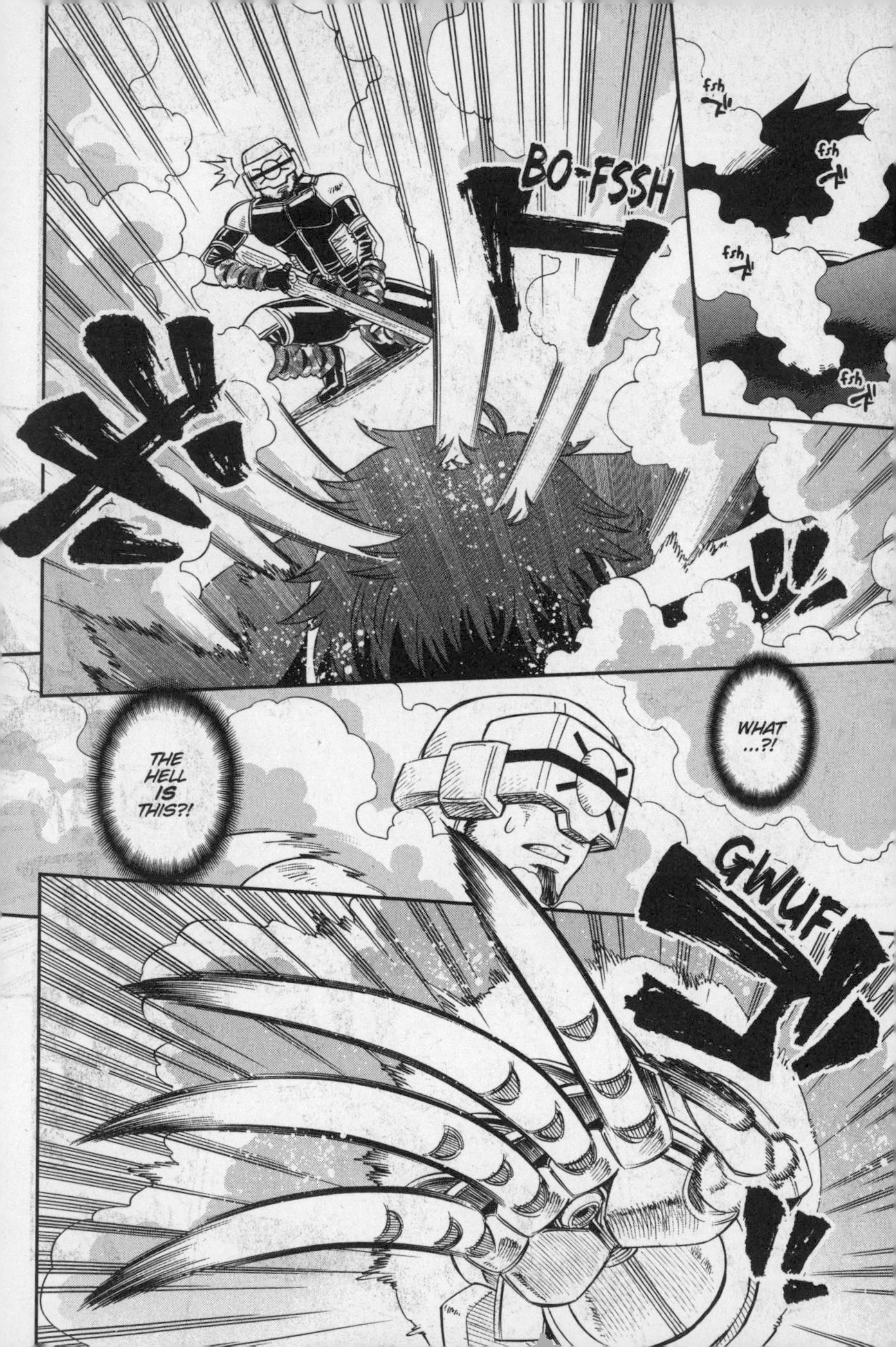
fsh
fsh
fsh
fsh
BO-FSSH
WHAT ...?!
THE HELL IS THIS?!
GWUF

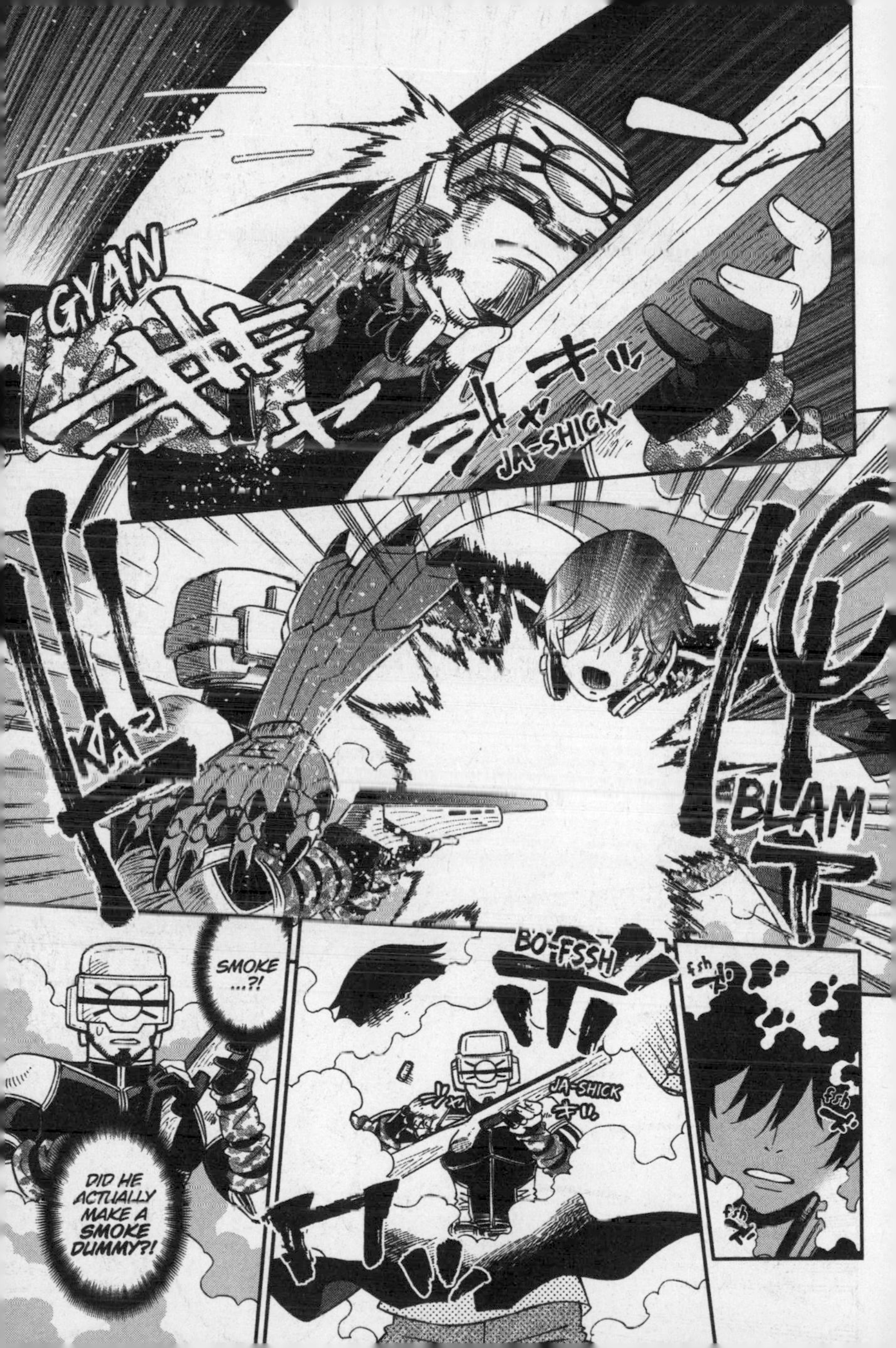
JA-SHICK
GYAN
BLAM
KA
fsh
fsh
fsh
BO-FSSH
JA-SHICK
SMOKE ...?!
DID HE ACTUALLY MAKE A SMOKE DUMMY?!

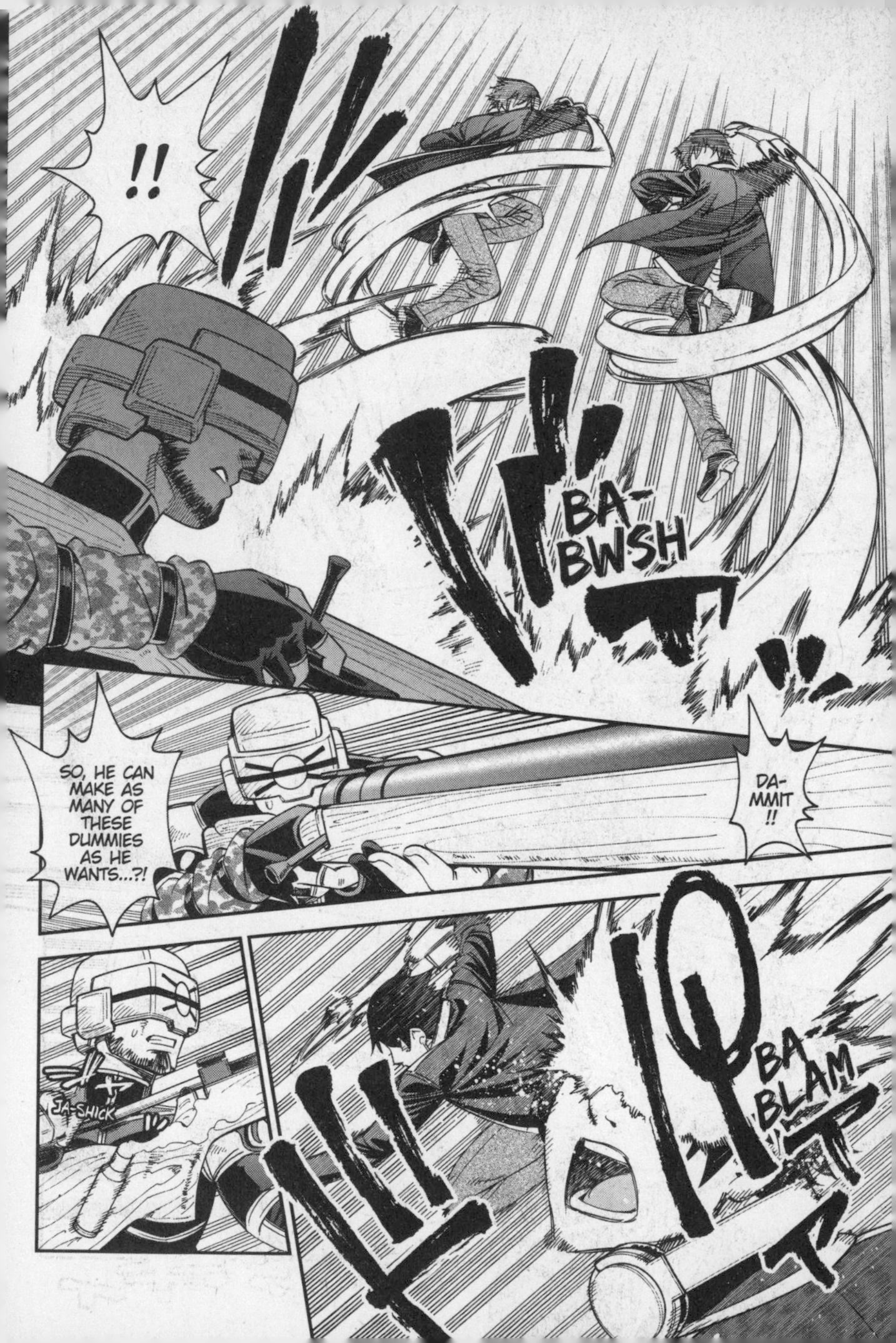
!!
BA-BWSH
DA-MMIT !!
SO, HE CAN MAKE AS MANY OF THESE DUMMIES AS HE WANTS...?!
BA-BLAM
JA-SHICK

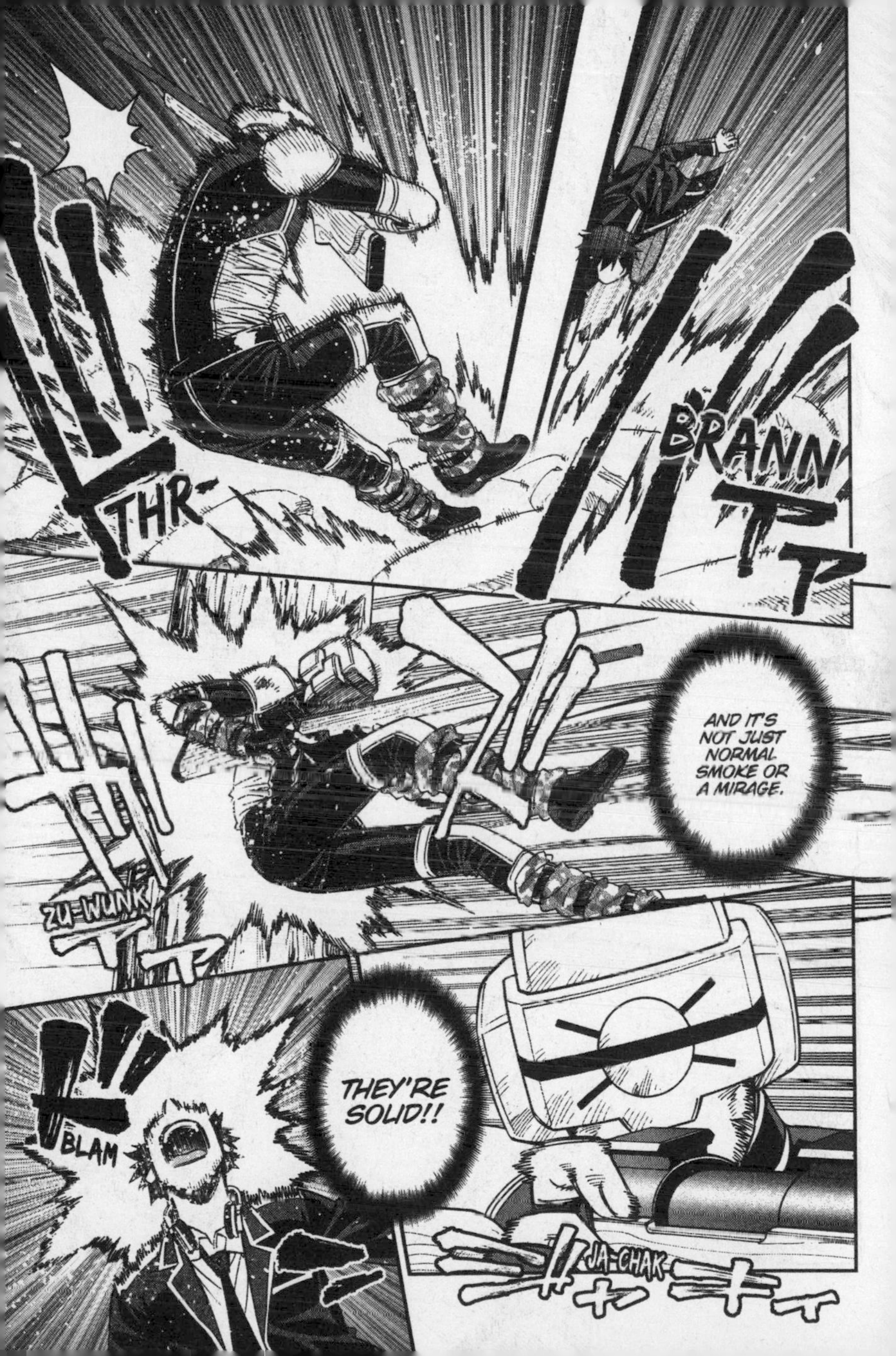
BRANN
THR-
AND IT'S NOT JUST NORMAL SMOKE OR A MIRAGE.
ZU-WUNK
JA-CHAK
THEY'RE SOLID!!
BLAM

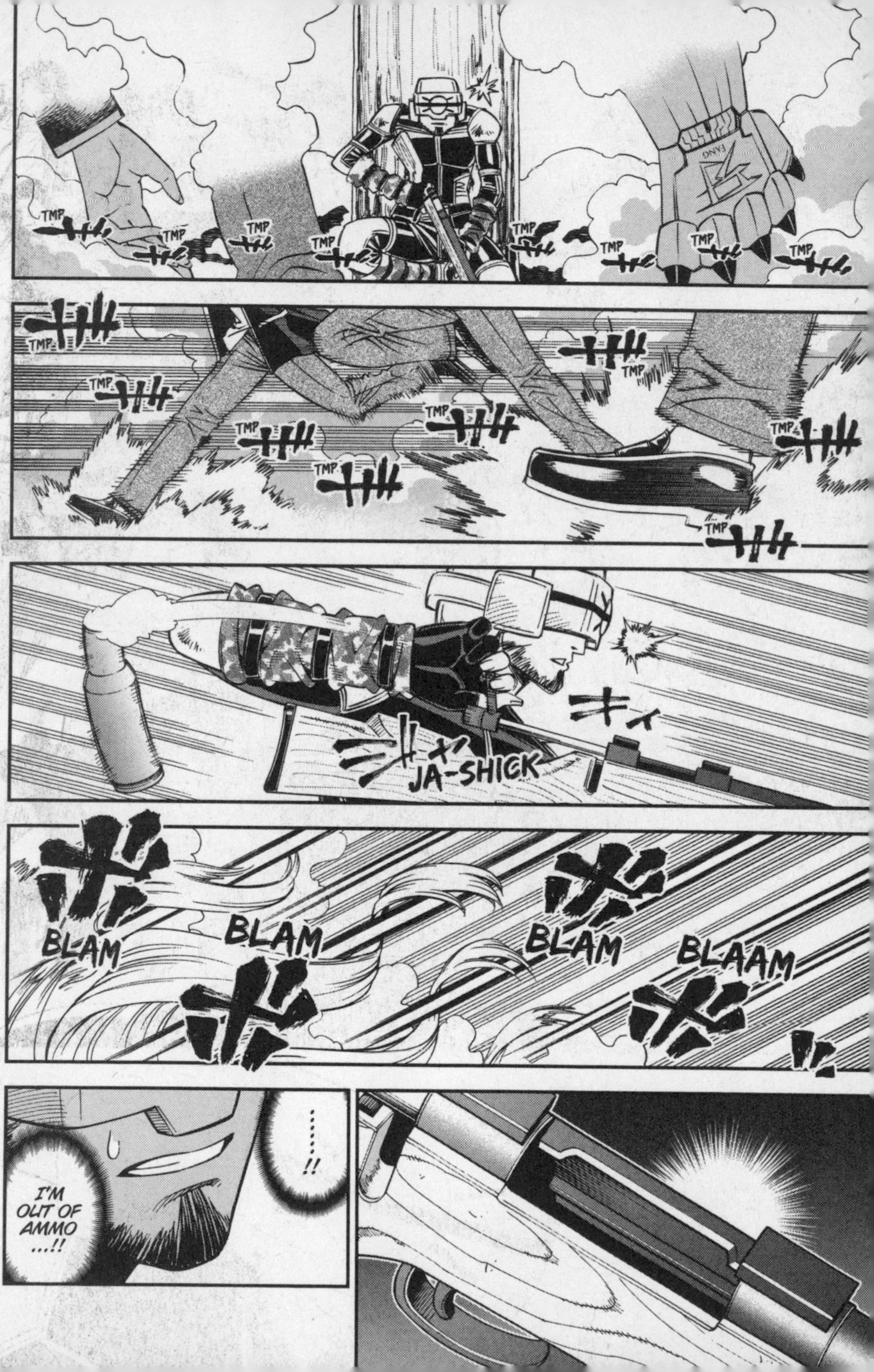
TMP
TMP
TMP
TMP
TMP
TMP
TMP
TMP
TMP
TMP
TMP
TMP
TMP
TMP
TMP
JA-SHICK
BLAAM
BLAM
BLAM
BLAM
......!!
I'M OUT OF AMMO ...!!

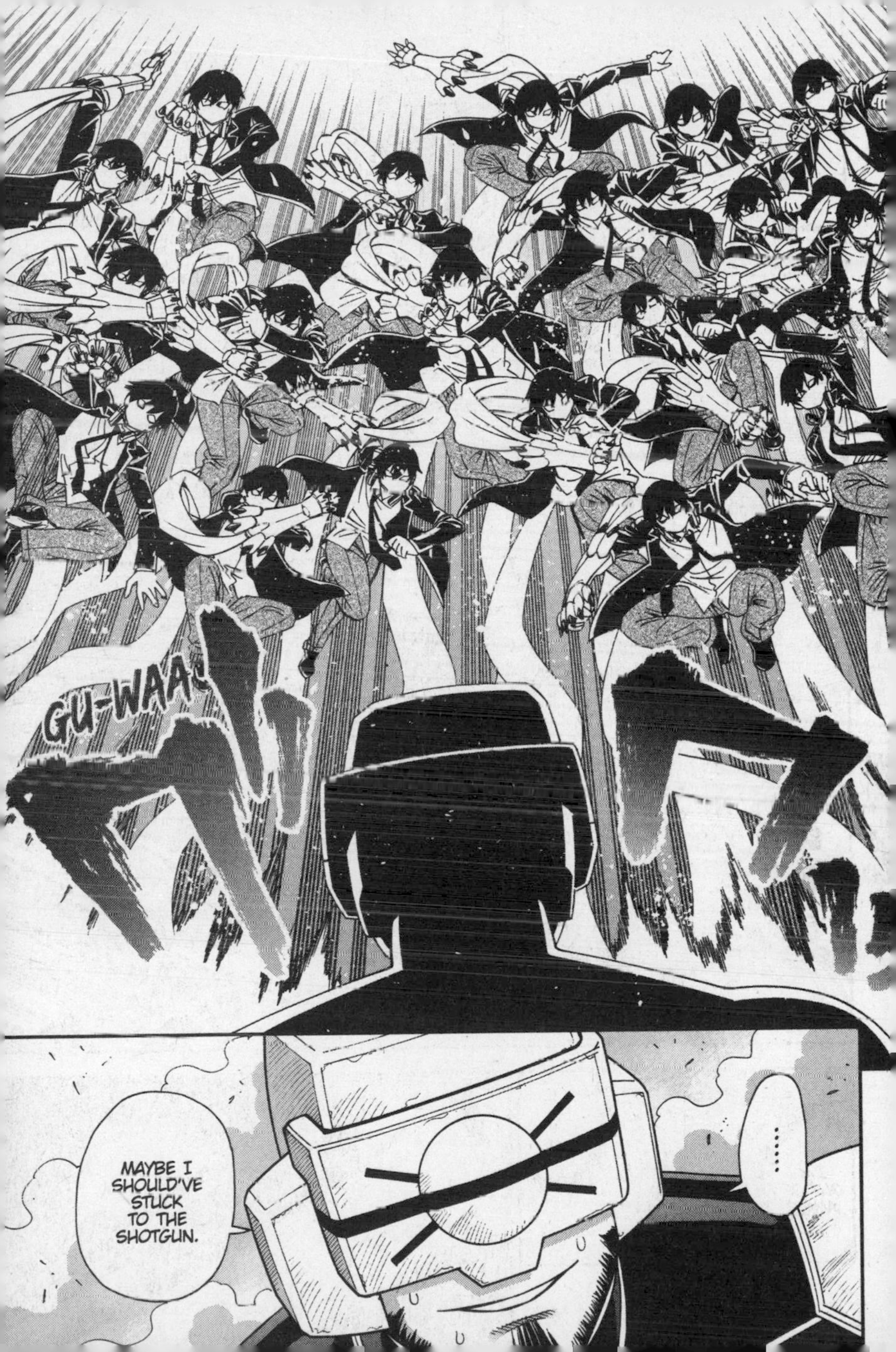
GU-WAA
......
MAYBE I SHOULD'VE STUCK TO THE SHOTGUN.

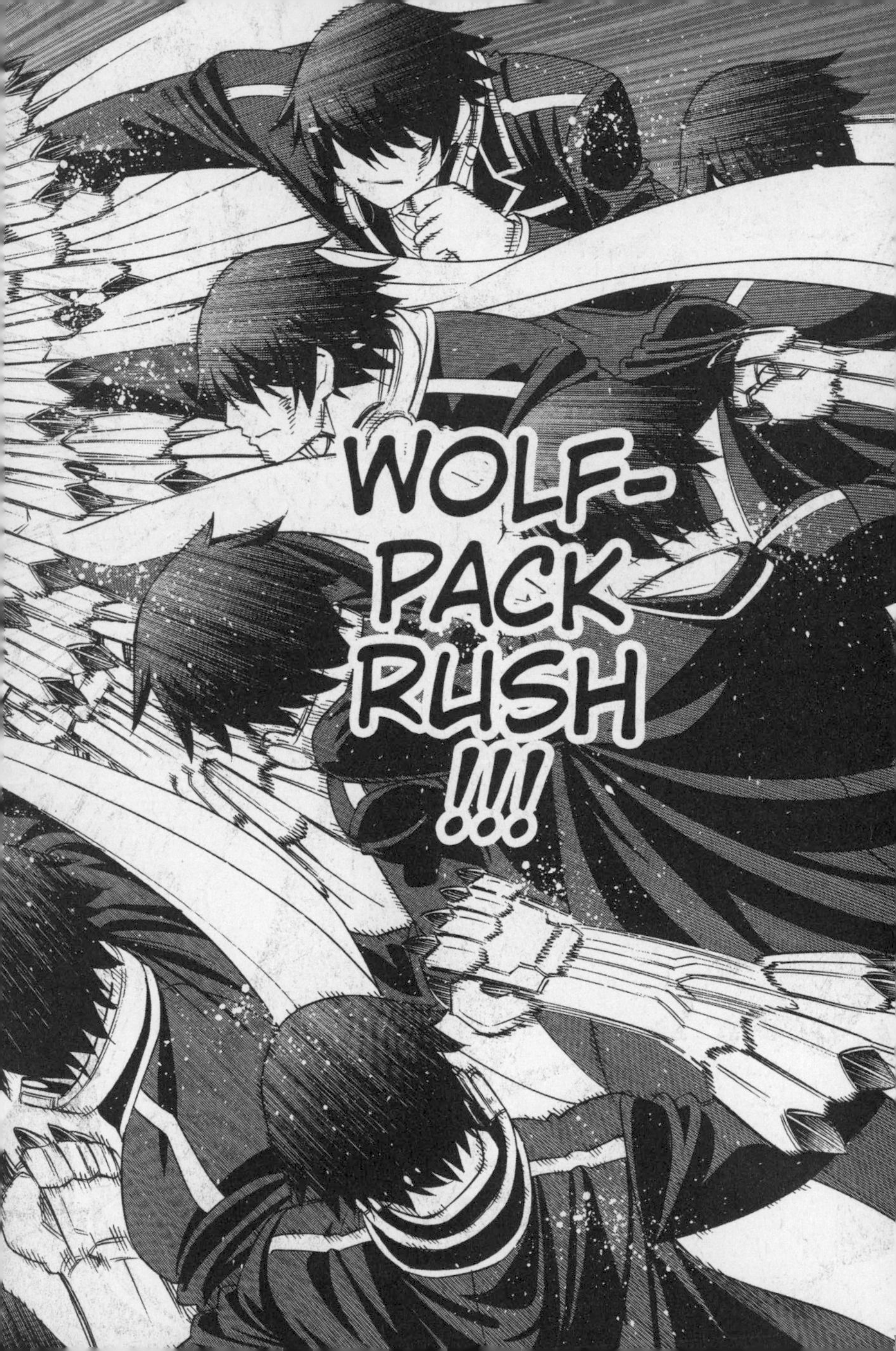
WOLF-PACK RUSH!!!!

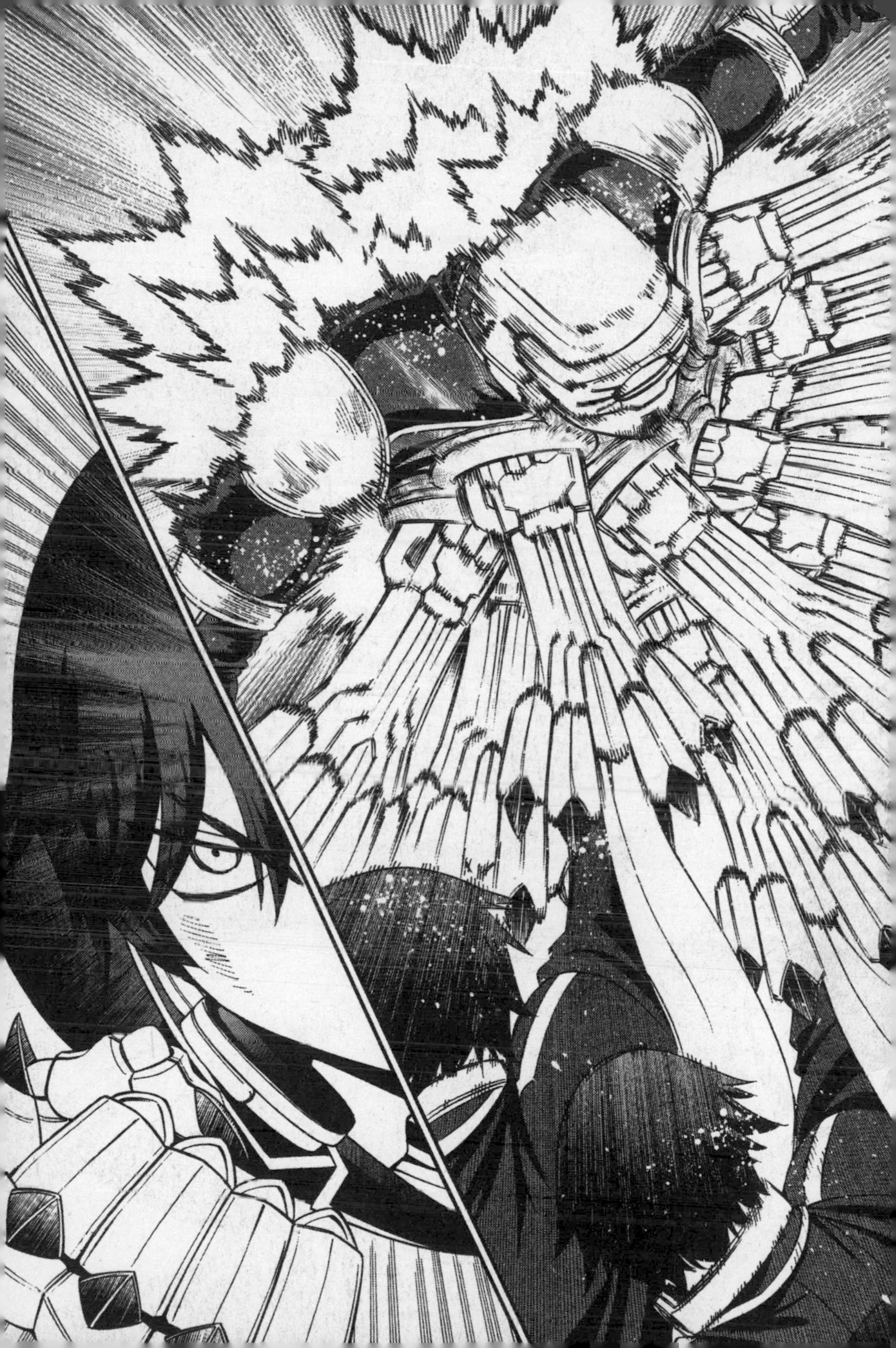

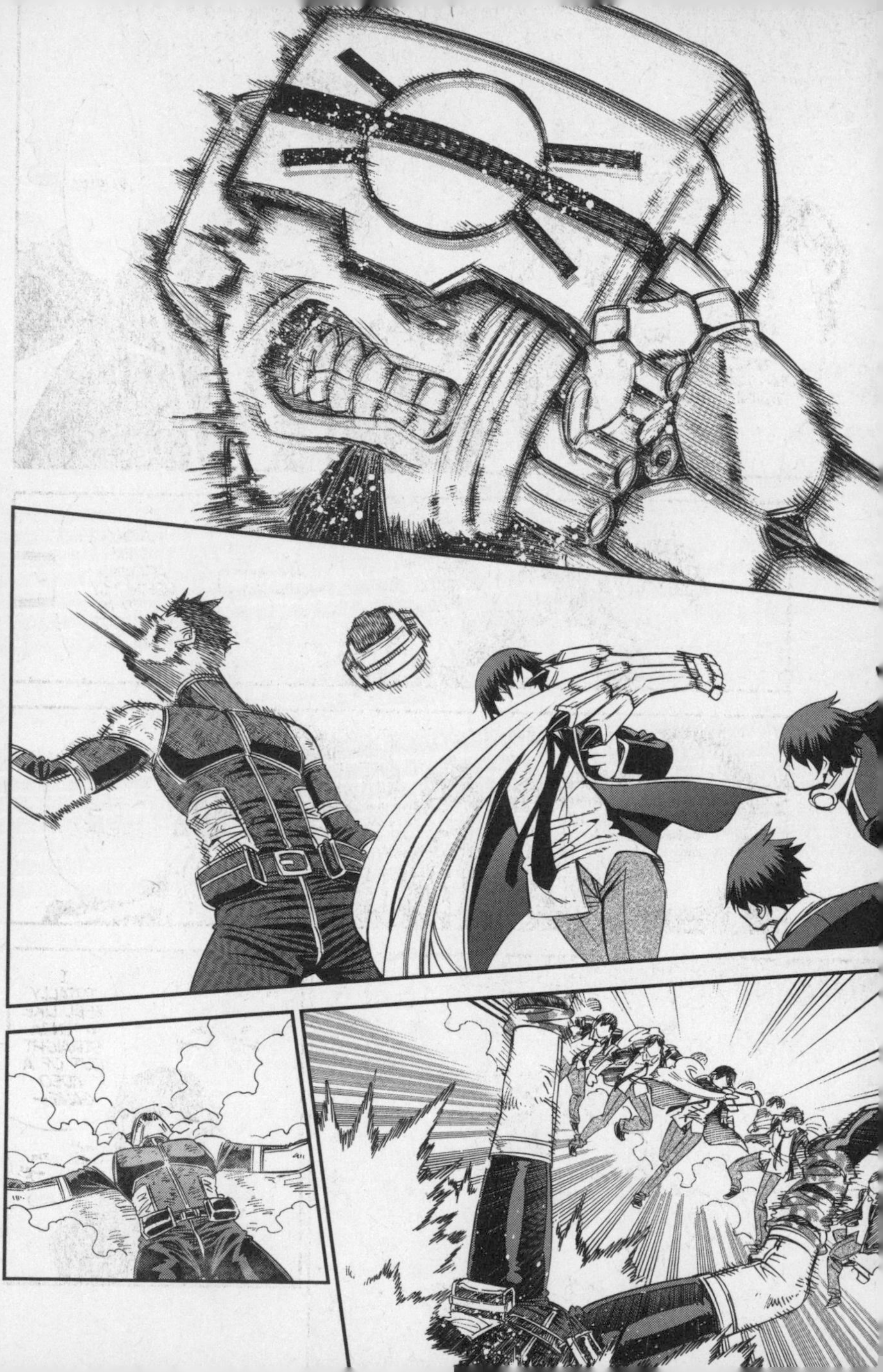

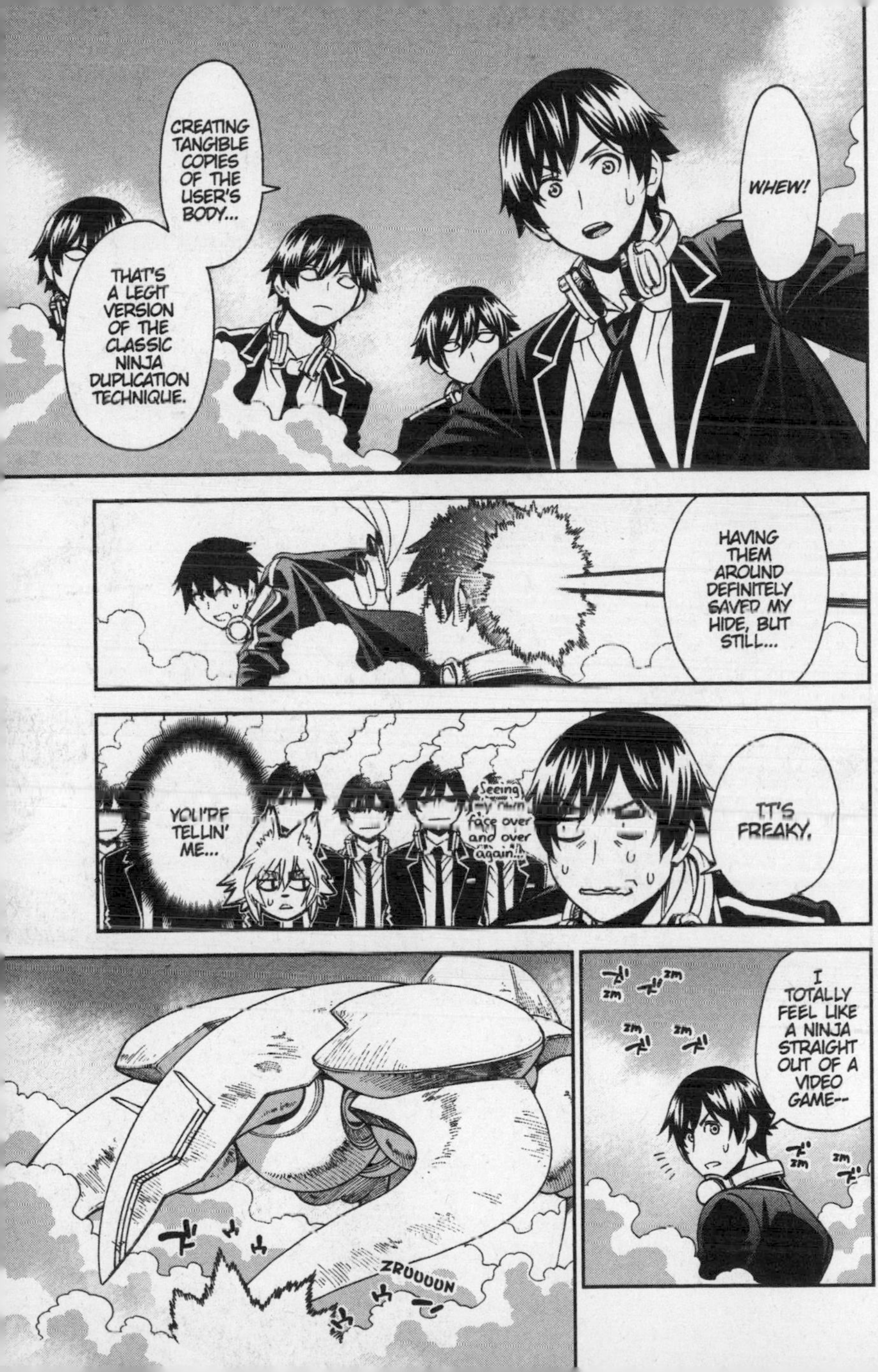
WHEW!
CREATING TANGIBLE COPIES OF THE USER'S BODY...
THAT'S A LEGIT VERSION OF THE CLASSIC NINJA DUPLICATION TECHNIQUE.
HAVING THEM AROUND DEFINITELY SAVED MY HIDE, BUT STILL...
IT'S FREAKY.
Seeing my own face over and over again...
YOU'RE TELLIN' ME...
I TOTALLY FEEL LIKE A NINJA STRAIGHT OUT OF A VIDEO GAME--
zm zm zm zm zm zm
ZRUUUUN

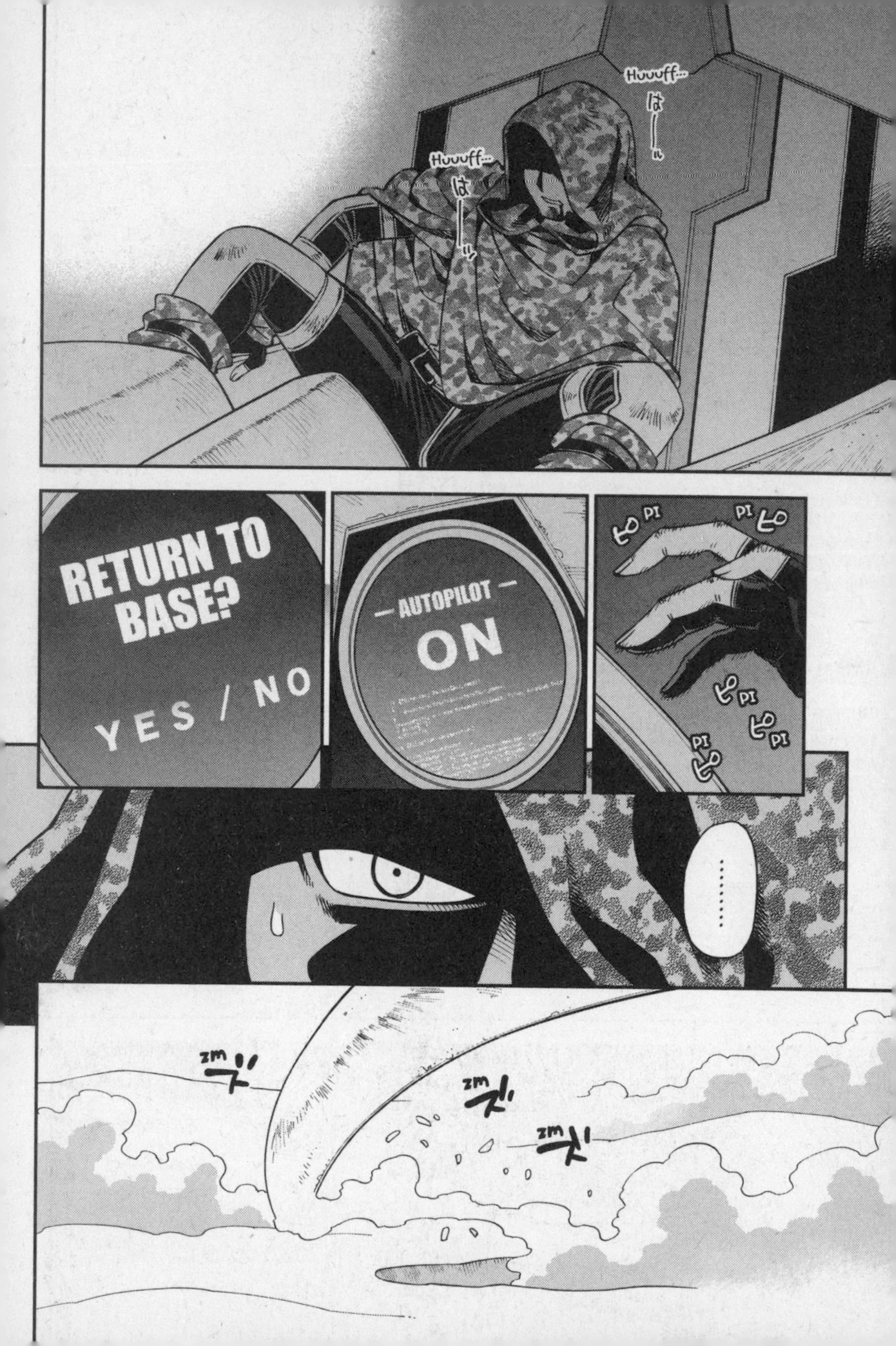
Huuuff...
はーー…
Huuuff...
はーー…
RETURN TO BASE?
YES / NO
AUTOPILOT
ON
PI ピ
ピ PI
ピ PI
ピ PI
PI ピ
……
zm ズ
zm ズ
zm ズ

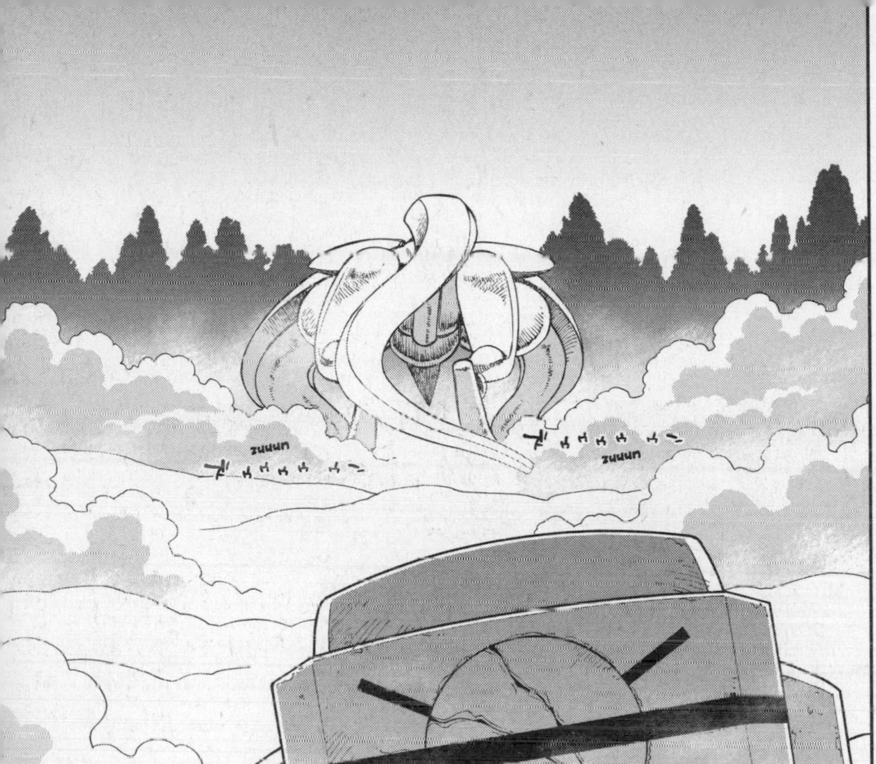
zuuun
zuuun
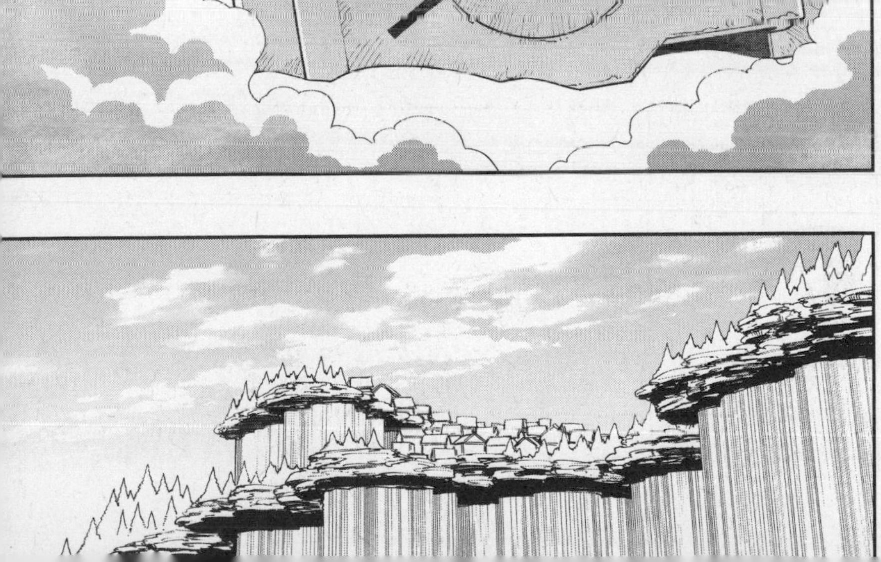

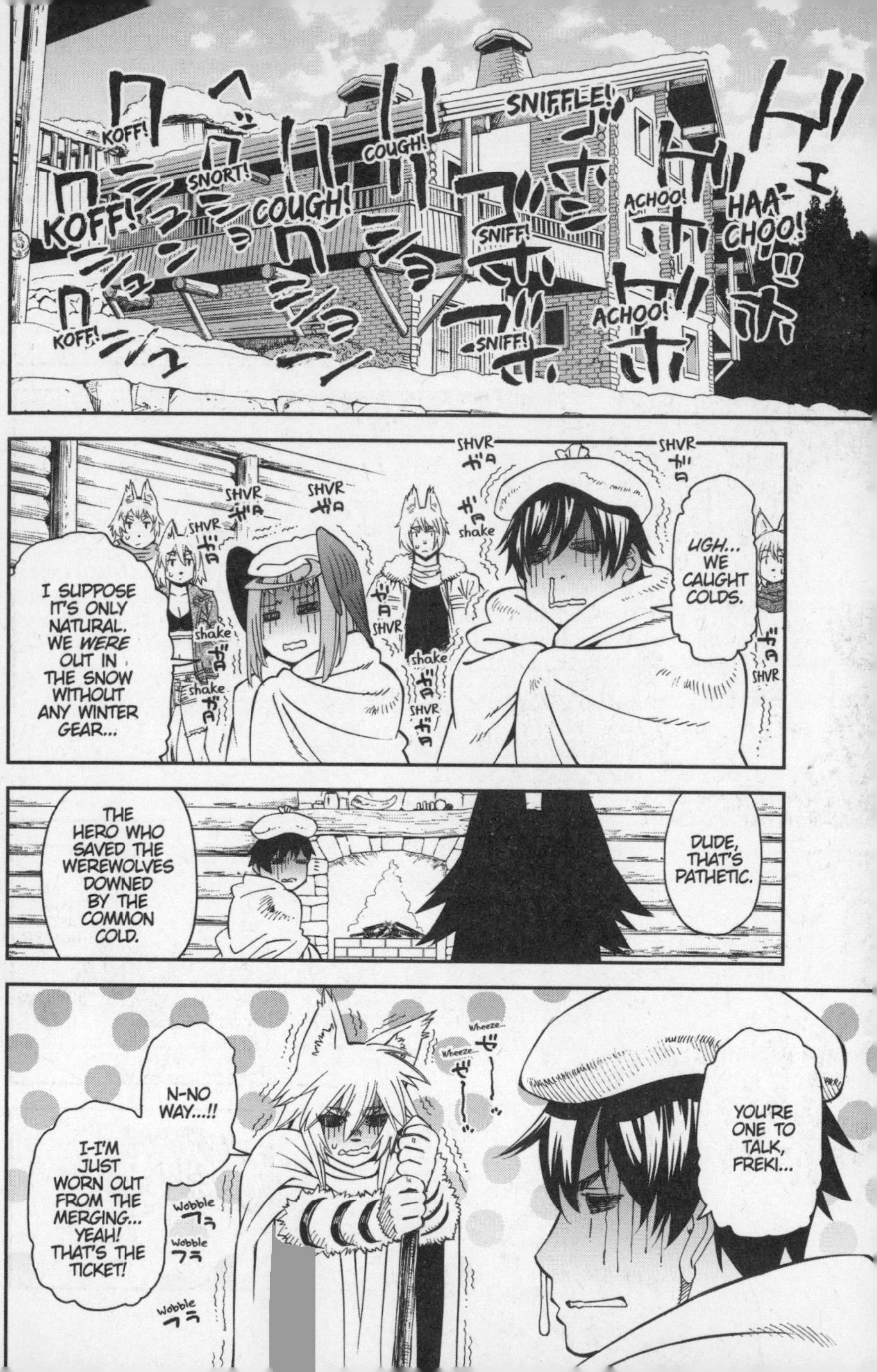
HAA-CHOO!!
ACHOO!
ACHOO!
SNIFFLE!
SNIFF!
SNIFF!
COUGH!
COUGH!
SNORT!
KOFF!
KOFF!
KOFF!
SHVR
UGH... WE CAUGHT COLDS.
SHVR
SHVR
shake
SHVR
shake
SHVR
SHVR
SHVR
shake
shake
I SUPPOSE IT'S ONLY NATURAL. WE WERE OUT IN THE SNOW WITHOUT ANY WINTER GEAR...
DUDE, THAT'S PATHETIC.
THE HERO WHO SAVED THE WEREWOLVES DOWNED BY THE COMMON COLD.
YOU'RE ONE TO TALK, FREKI...
Wheeze...
Wheeze...
N-NO WAY...!!
I-I'M JUST WORN OUT FROM THE MERGING... YEAH! THAT'S THE TICKET!
Wobble
Wobble
Wobble

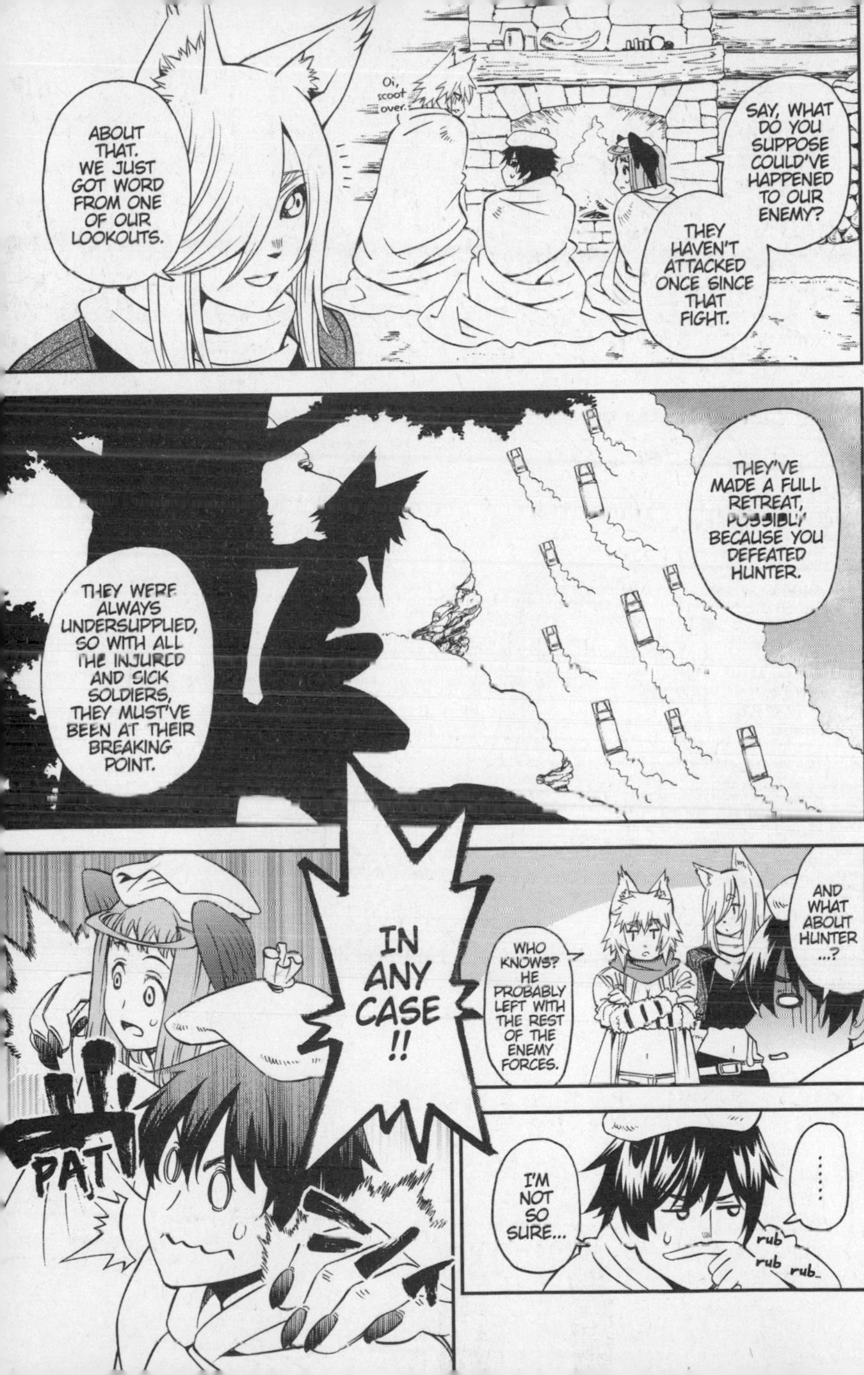
SAY, WHAT DO YOU SUPPOSE COULD'VE HAPPENED TO OUR ENEMY?
THEY HAVEN'T ATTACKED ONCE SINCE THAT FIGHT.
Oi, scoot over.
ABOUT THAT. WE JUST GOT WORD FROM ONE OF OUR LOOKOUTS.
THEY'VE MADE A FULL RETREAT, POSSIBLY BECAUSE YOU DEFEATED HUNTER.
THEY WERE ALWAYS UNDERSUPPLIED, SO WITH ALL THE INJURED AND SICK SOLDIERS, THEY MUST'VE BEEN AT THEIR BREAKING POINT.
AND WHAT ABOUT HUNTER ...?
WHO KNOWS? HE PROBABLY LEFT WITH THE REST OF THE ENEMY FORCES.
......
rub rub rub..
I'M NOT SO SURE...
IN ANY CASE !!
PAT

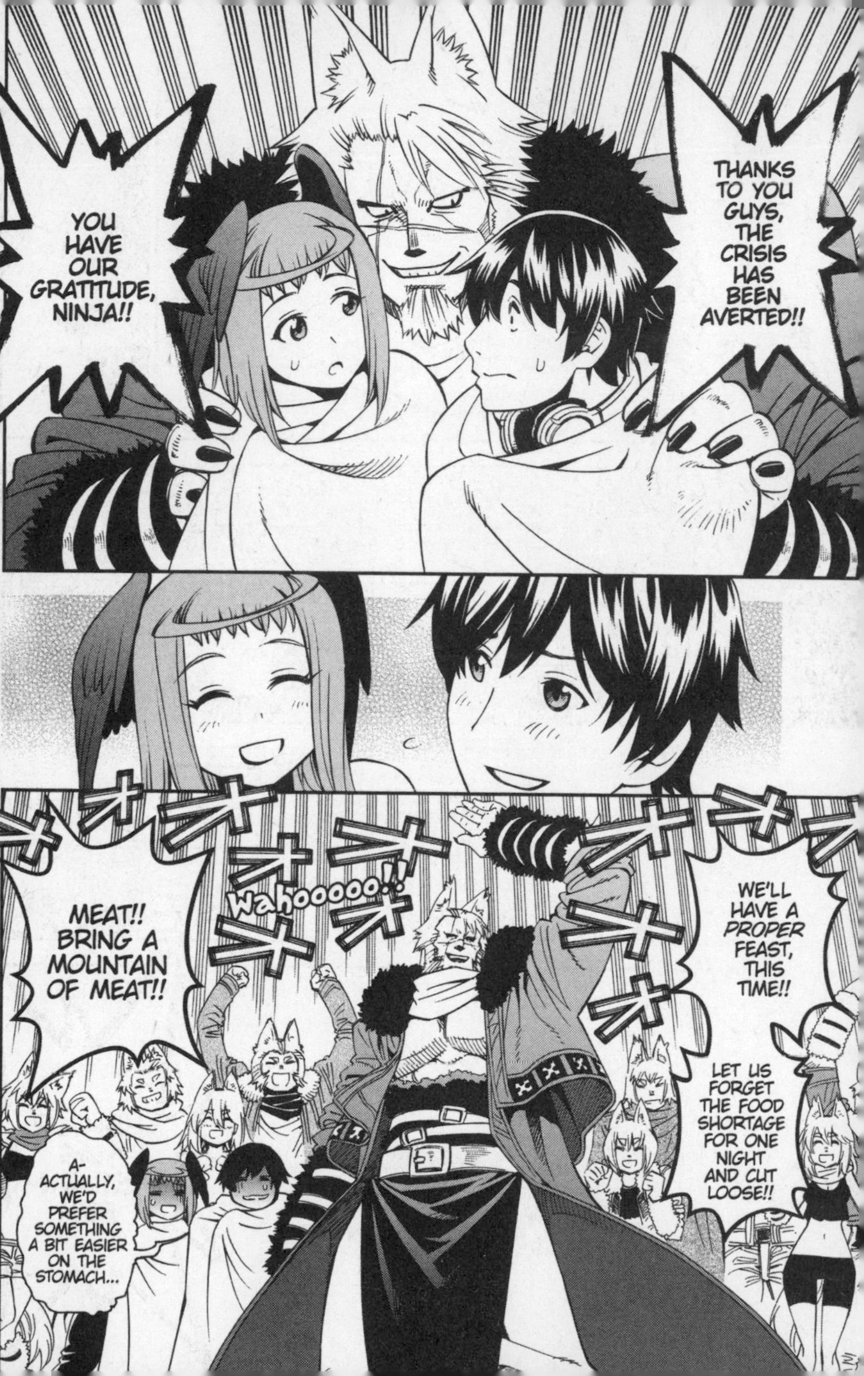
THANKS TO YOU GUYS, THE CRISIS HAS BEEN AVERTED!!
YOU HAVE OUR GRATITUDE, NINJA!!
Wahoooooo!!
WE'LL HAVE A *PROPER* FEAST, THIS TIME!!
MEAT!! BRING A MOUNTAIN OF MEAT!!
LET US FORGET THE FOOD SHORTAGE FOR ONE NIGHT AND CUT LOOSE!!
A- ACTUALLY, WE'D PREFER SOMETHING A BIT EASIER ON THE STOMACH...

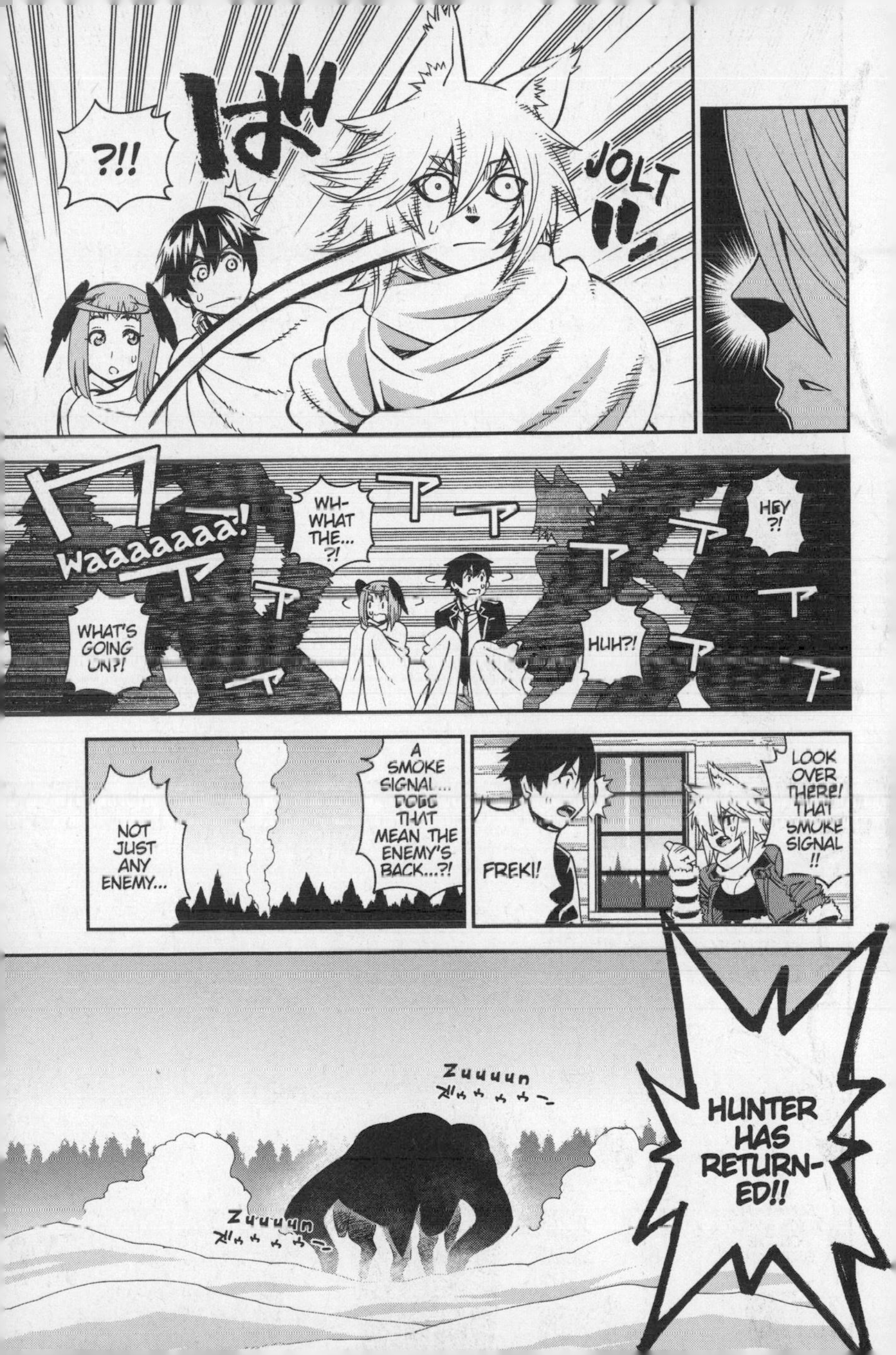
JOLT!!
?!!
HEY?!
HUH?!
WH-WHAT THE...?!
Waaaaaaa!
WHAT'S GOING ON?!
LOOK OVER THERE! THAT SMOKE SIGNAL!!
FREKI!
A SMOKE SIGNAL... DOES THAT MEAN THE ENEMY'S BACK...?!
NOT JUST ANY ENEMY...
HUNTER HAS RETURN-ED!!
Zuuuun
Zuuuuun

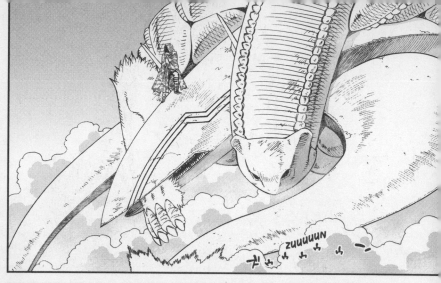

zuuuuun

THWUNK

shaa

WHA
...

WHAT'S HAPPEN-ING?

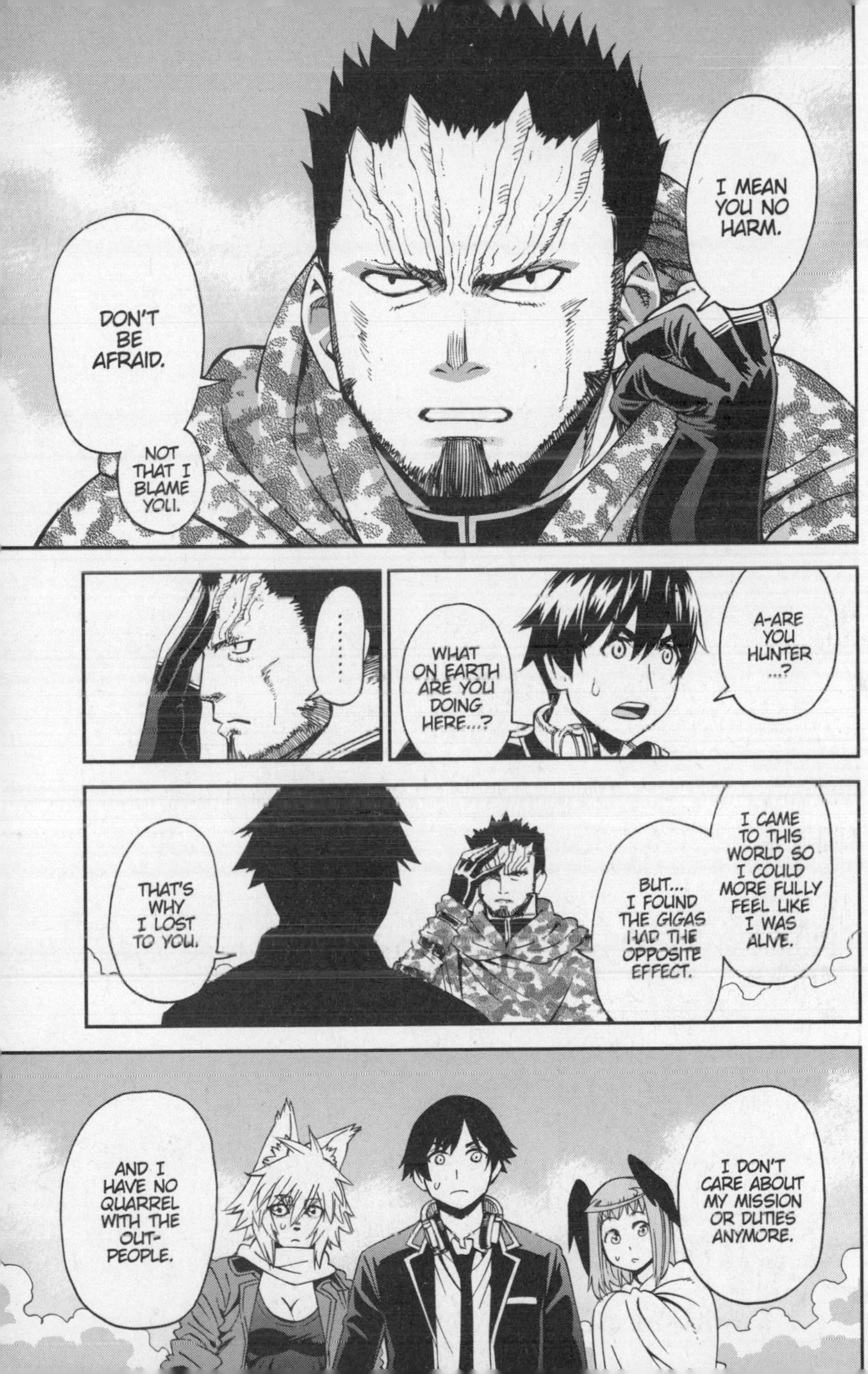
I MEAN YOU NO HARM.
DON'T BE AFRAID.
NOT THAT I BLAME YOU.
A-ARE YOU HUNTER ...?
WHAT ON EARTH ARE YOU DOING HERE...?
......
I CAME TO THIS WORLD SO I COULD MORE FULLY FEEL LIKE I WAS ALIVE.
BUT... I FOUND THE GIGAS HAD THE OPPOSITE EFFECT.
THAT'S WHY I LOST TO YOU.
I DON'T CARE ABOUT MY MISSION OR DUTIES ANYMORE.
AND I HAVE NO QUARREL WITH THE OUT-PEOPLE.

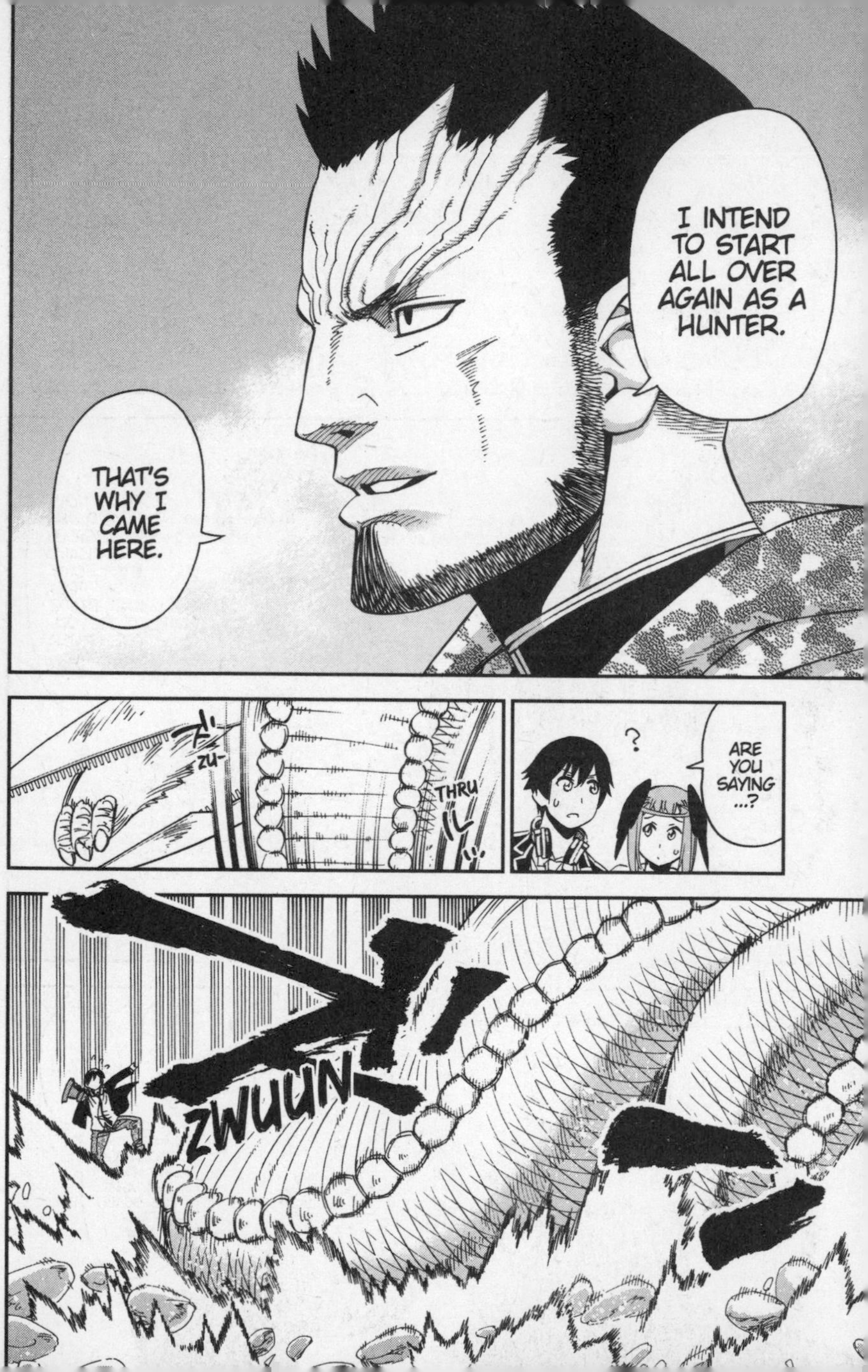
I INTEND TO START ALL OVER AGAIN AS A HUNTER.
THAT'S WHY I CAME HERE.
?
ARE YOU SAYING ...?
ZU-
THRU
ZWUUN

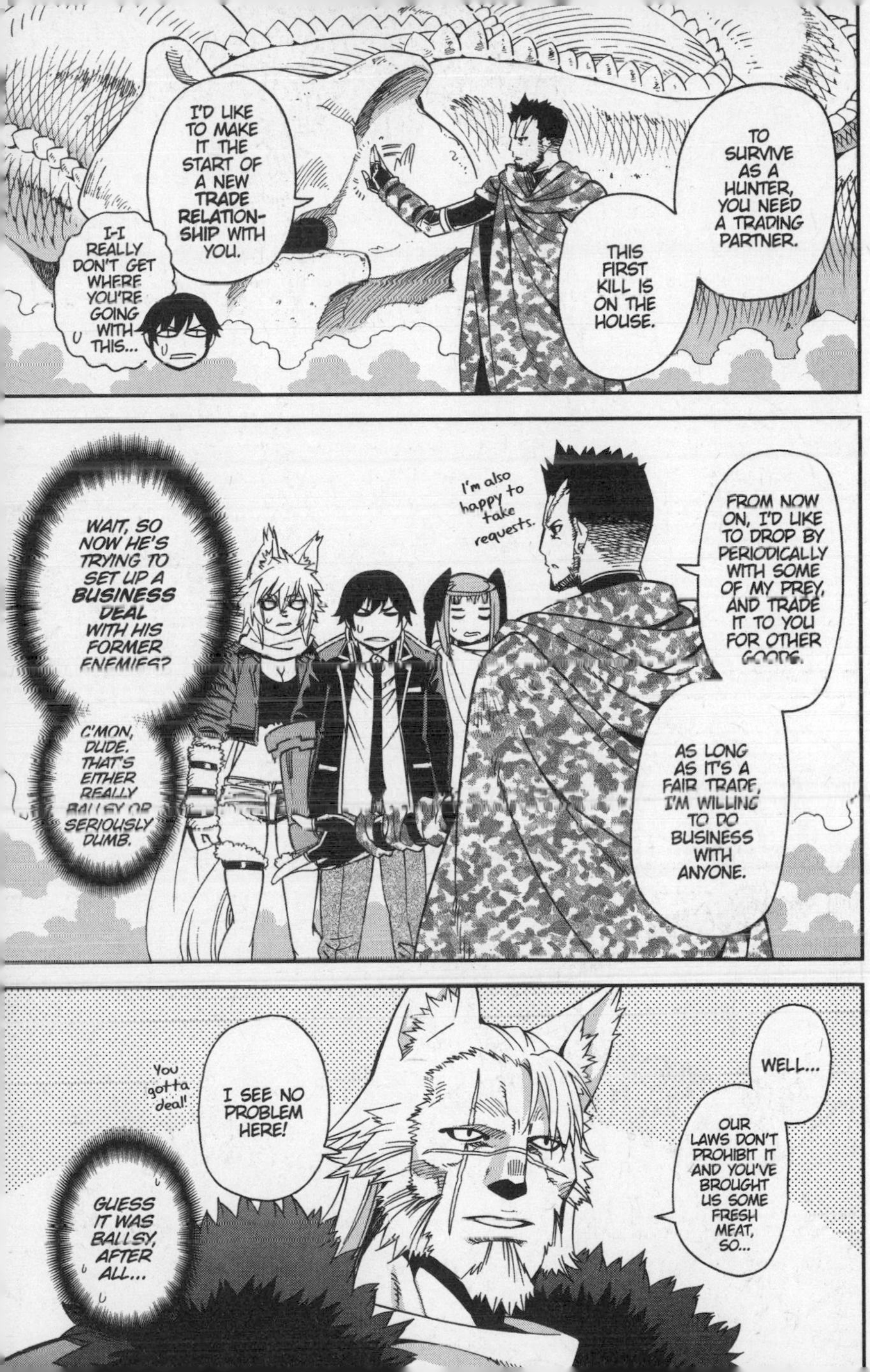
TO SURVIVE AS A HUNTER, YOU NEED A TRADING PARTNER.
THIS FIRST KILL IS ON THE HOUSE.
I'D LIKE TO MAKE IT THE START OF A NEW TRADE RELATIONSHIP WITH YOU.
I-I REALLY DON'T GET WHERE YOU'RE GOING WITH THIS...
FROM NOW ON, I'D LIKE TO DROP BY PERIODICALLY WITH SOME OF MY PREY, AND TRADE IT TO YOU FOR OTHER GOODS.
I'm also happy to take requests.
AS LONG AS IT'S A FAIR TRADE, I'M WILLING TO DO BUSINESS WITH ANYONE.
WAIT, SO NOW HE'S TRYING TO SET UP A **BUSINESS DEAL** WITH HIS FORMER ENEMIES?
C'MON, DUDE. THAT'S EITHER REALLY BALLSY OR SERIOUSLY DUMB.
WELL...
OUR LAWS DON'T PROHIBIT IT AND YOU'VE BROUGHT US SOME FRESH MEAT, SO...
I SEE NO PROBLEM HERE!
You gotta deal!
GUESS IT WAS BALLSY, AFTER ALL...

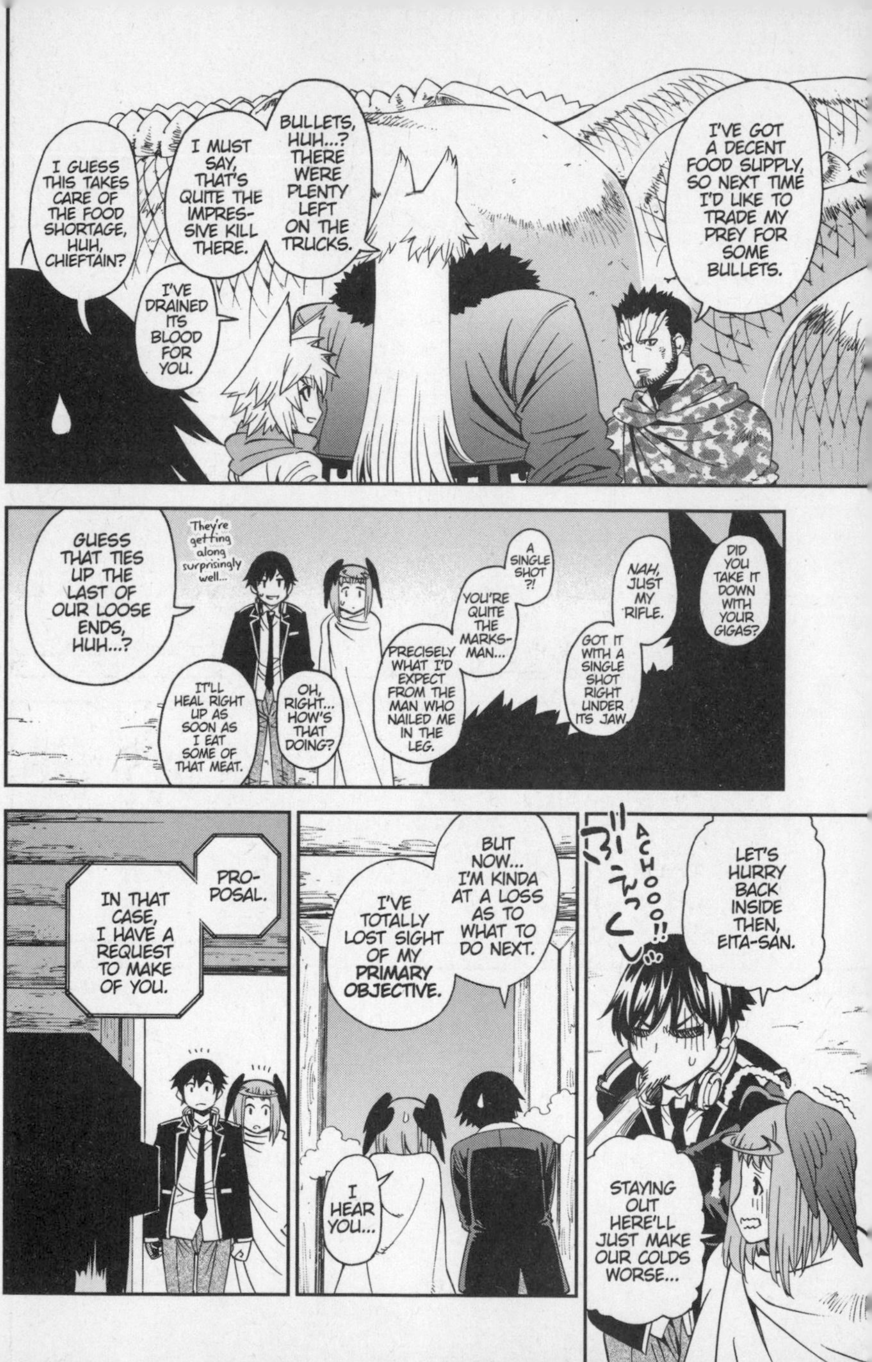
I'VE GOT A DECENT FOOD SUPPLY, SO NEXT TIME I'D LIKE TO TRADE MY PREY FOR SOME BULLETS.
BULLETS, HUH...? THERE WERE PLENTY LEFT ON THE TRUCKS.
I MUST SAY, THAT'S QUITE THE IMPRES-SIVE KILL THERE.
I'VE DRAINED ITS BLOOD FOR YOU.
I GUESS THIS TAKES CARE OF THE FOOD SHORTAGE, HUH, CHIEFTAIN?
DID YOU TAKE IT DOWN WITH YOUR GIGAS?
NAH, JUST MY RIFLE.
GOT IT WITH A SINGLE SHOT RIGHT UNDER ITS JAW.
A SINGLE SHOT?!
YOU'RE QUITE THE MARKS-MAN...
PRECISELY WHAT I'D EXPECT FROM THE MAN WHO NAILED ME IN THE LEG.
OH, RIGHT... HOW'S THAT DOING?
IT'LL HEAL RIGHT UP AS SOON AS I EAT SOME OF THAT MEAT.
They're getting along surprisingly well...
GUESS THAT TIES UP THE LAST OF OUR LOOSE ENDS, HUH...?
ACHOOOO!!
LET'S HURRY BACK INSIDE THEN, EITA-SAN.
STAYING OUT HERE'LL JUST MAKE OUR COLDS WORSE...
BUT NOW... I'M KINDA AT A LOSS AS TO WHAT TO DO NEXT.
I'VE TOTALLY LOST SIGHT OF MY PRIMARY OBJECTIVE.
I HEAR YOU...
PRO-POSAL.
IN THAT CASE, I HAVE A REQUEST TO MAKE OF YOU.

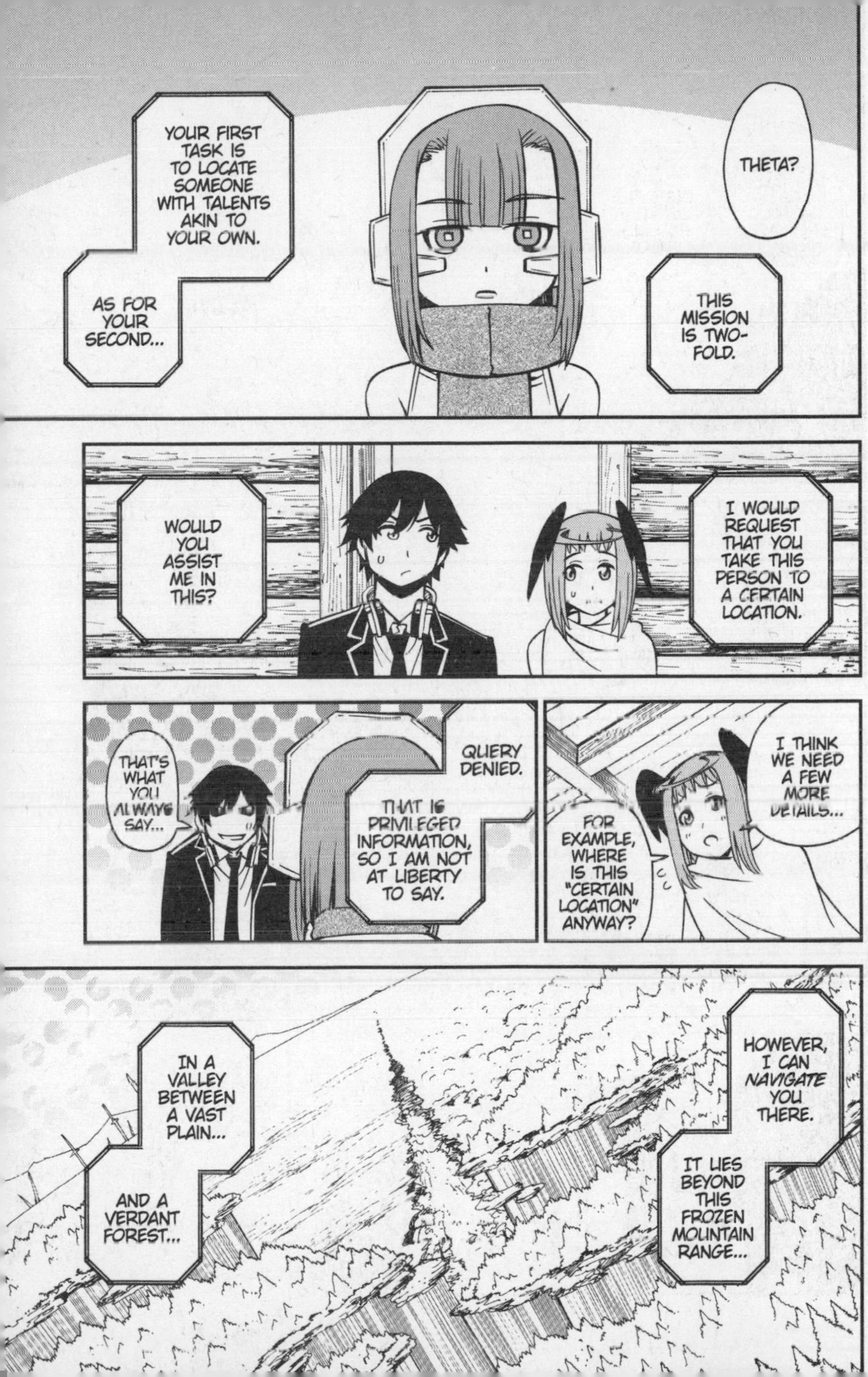
THETA?
THIS MISSION IS TWO-FOLD.
YOUR FIRST TASK IS TO LOCATE SOMEONE WITH TALENTS AKIN TO YOUR OWN.
AS FOR YOUR SECOND...
I WOULD REQUEST THAT YOU TAKE THIS PERSON TO A CERTAIN LOCATION.
WOULD YOU ASSIST ME IN THIS?
I THINK WE NEED A FEW MORE DETAILS...
FOR EXAMPLE, WHERE IS THIS "CERTAIN LOCATION" ANYWAY?
QUERY DENIED.
THAT IS PRIVILEGED INFORMATION, SO I AM NOT AT LIBERTY TO SAY.
THAT'S WHAT YOU ALWAYS SAY...
HOWEVER, I CAN *NAVIGATE* YOU THERE.
IT LIES BEYOND THIS FROZEN MOUNTAIN RANGE...
IN A VALLEY BETWEEN A VAST PLAIN...
AND A VERDANT FOREST...

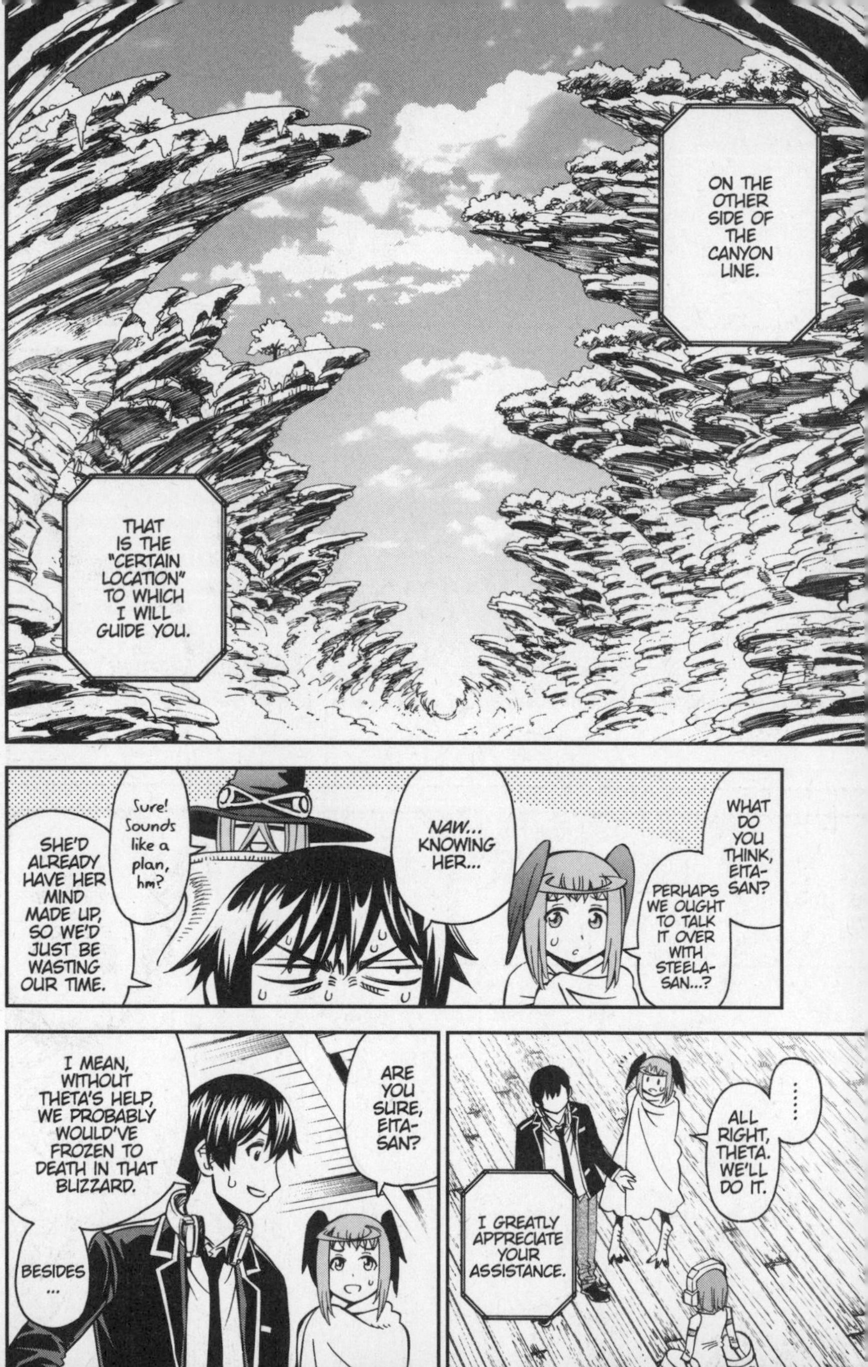
ON THE OTHER SIDE OF THE CANYON LINE.
THAT IS THE "CERTAIN LOCATION" TO WHICH I WILL GUIDE YOU.
WHAT DO YOU THINK, EITA-SAN?
PERHAPS WE OUGHT TO TALK IT OVER WITH STEELA-SAN...?
NAW... KNOWING HER...
Sure! Sounds like a plan, hm?
SHE'D ALREADY HAVE HER MIND MADE UP, SO WE'D JUST BE WASTING OUR TIME.
......
ALL RIGHT, THETA. WE'LL DO IT.
I GREATLY APPRECIATE YOUR ASSISTANCE.
ARE YOU SURE, EITA-SAN?
I MEAN, WITHOUT THETA'S HELP, WE PROBABLY WOULD'VE FROZEN TO DEATH IN THAT BLIZZARD.
BESIDES...

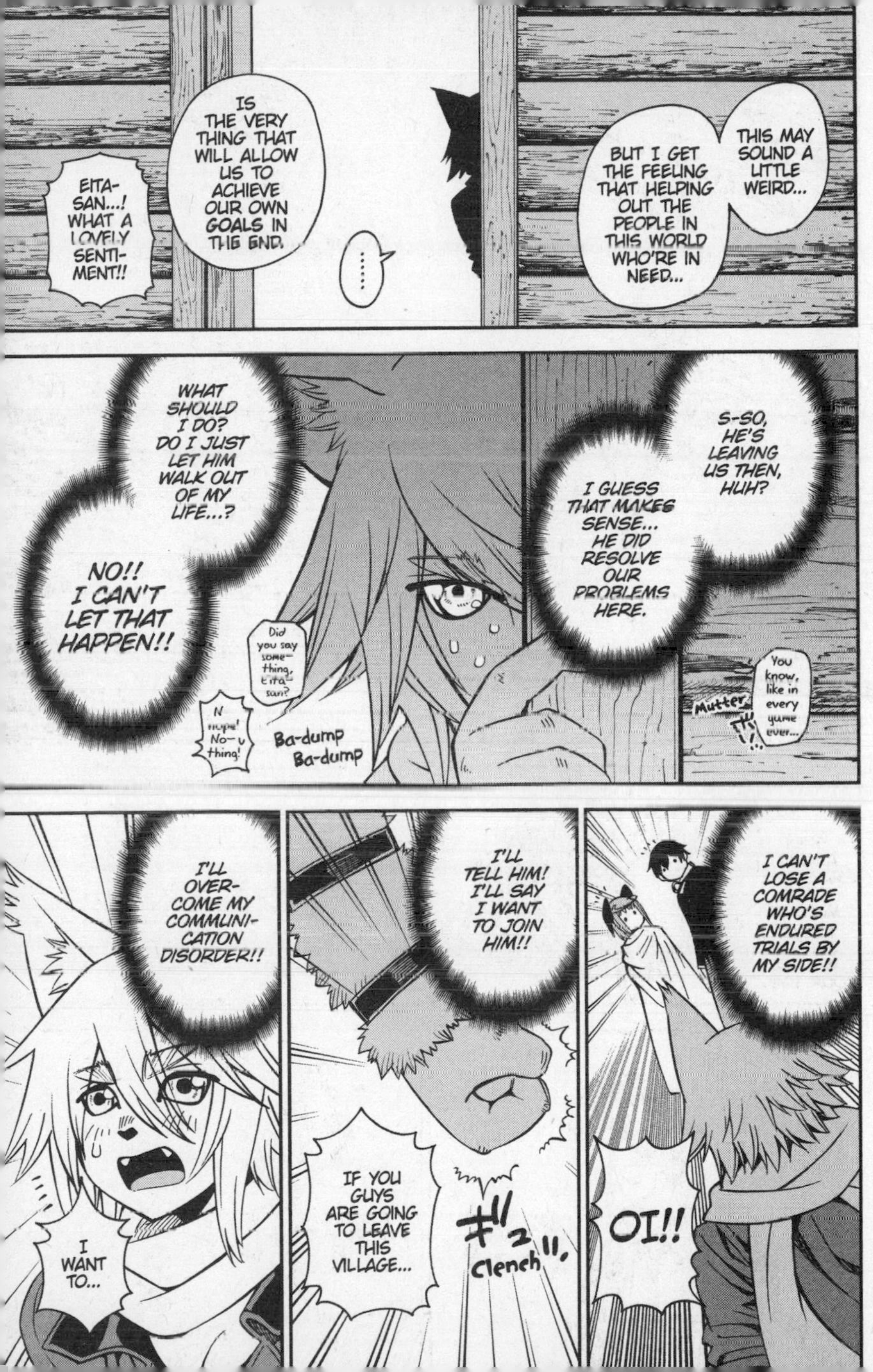
THIS MAY SOUND A LITTLE WEIRD...
BUT I GET THE FEELING THAT HELPING OUT THE PEOPLE IN THIS WORLD WHO'RE IN NEED...
IS THE VERY THING THAT WILL ALLOW US TO ACHIEVE OUR OWN GOALS IN THE END.
......
EITA-SAN...! WHAT A LOVELY SENTIMENT!!
S-SO, HE'S LEAVING US THEN, HUH?
I GUESS THAT MAKES SENSE... HE DID RESOLVE OUR PROBLEMS HERE.
You know, like in every game ever...
Mutter
WHAT SHOULD I DO? DO I JUST LET HIM WALK OUT OF MY LIFE...?
NO!! I CAN'T LET THAT HAPPEN!!
Did you say something, Eita-san?
N-nope! No-thing!
Ba-dump Ba-dump
I CAN'T LOSE A COMRADE WHO'S ENDURED TRIALS BY MY SIDE!!
OI!!
I'LL TELL HIM! I'LL SAY I WANT TO JOIN HIM!!
Clench
IF YOU GUYS ARE GOING TO LEAVE THIS VILLAGE...
I'LL OVERCOME MY COMMUNICATION DISORDER!!
I WANT TO...

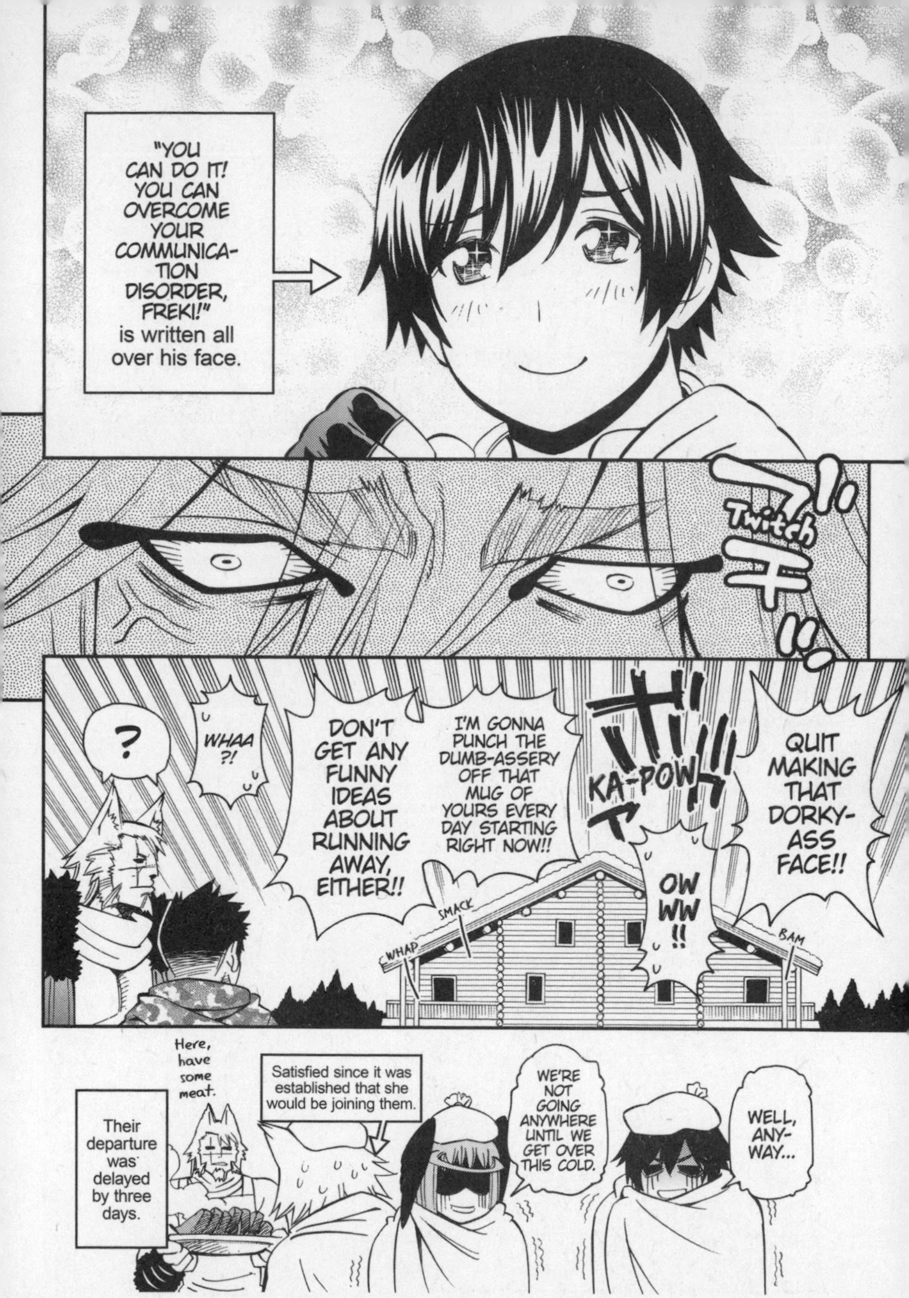
"YOU CAN DO IT! YOU CAN OVERCOME YOUR COMMUNICATION DISORDER, FREKI!" is written all over his face.
Twitch
QUIT MAKING THAT DORKY-ASS FACE!!
KA-POW
OW WW!!
BAM
I'M GONNA PUNCH THE DUMB-ASSERY OFF THAT MUG OF YOURS EVERY DAY STARTING RIGHT NOW!!
SMACK
WHAP
DON'T GET ANY FUNNY IDEAS ABOUT RUNNING AWAY, EITHER!!
WHAA?!
?
WELL, ANYWAY...
WE'RE NOT GOING ANYWHERE UNTIL WE GET OVER THIS COLD.
Satisfied since it was established that she would be joining them.
Here, have some meat.
Their departure was delayed by three days.

Life with Hunter

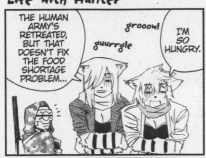

I'M SO HUNGRY.
groooowl
guurrgle
THE HUMAN ARMY'S RETREATED, BUT THAT DOESN'T FIX THE FOOD SHORTAGE PROBLEM...
ALL RIGHT. GET RID OF THESE GUTS FOR ME, WOULD YA?
MAN, THERE'S ALWAYS A TON OF THIS OFFAL CRAP AFTER A HUNT...
offal
FWUFF

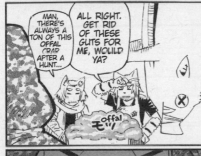

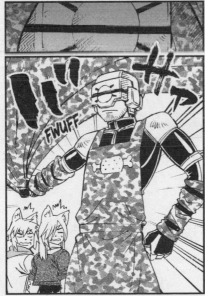

offal モツ
offal モツ
offal モツ
offal モツ
offal モツ
offal モツ
offal モツ
offal モツ
offal モツ
offal モツ
offal モツ
完成!
Hot and ready!
INGREDIENTS
Boar offal: A ton.
Vegetables: As many of any one veggie as you can find.
Soy sauce: Lots.
Alcohol: A generous pour.
Mirin: A good amount.
Chicken broth: Plenty.
Sugar: On the heavy side.
Chili pepper: A sizeable portion.
Garlic: As much as you like.
Ginger: To taste.
Hunter-style Boar Offal Stew
猟師風猪モツ鍋
うめーっ!!
Mmmmm!!
Seconds, please!
Me too!
Thus, the food shortage crisis was resolved.
brbl
brbl
brbl
brbl

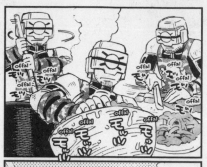

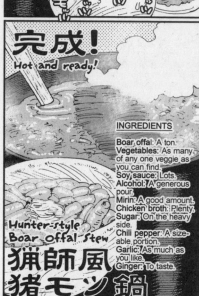

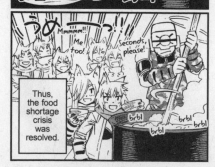

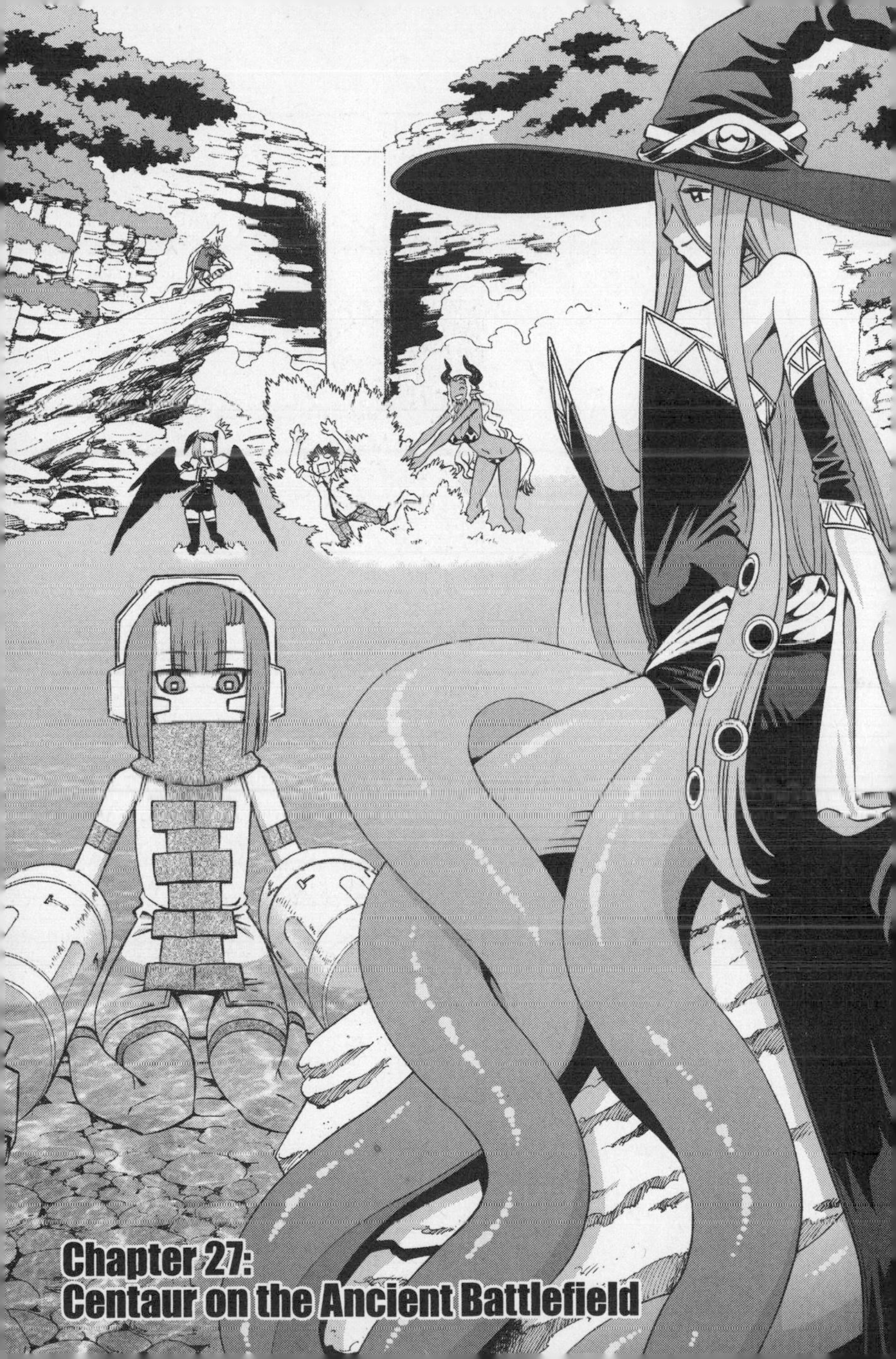

Chapter 27: Centaur on the Ancient Battlefield

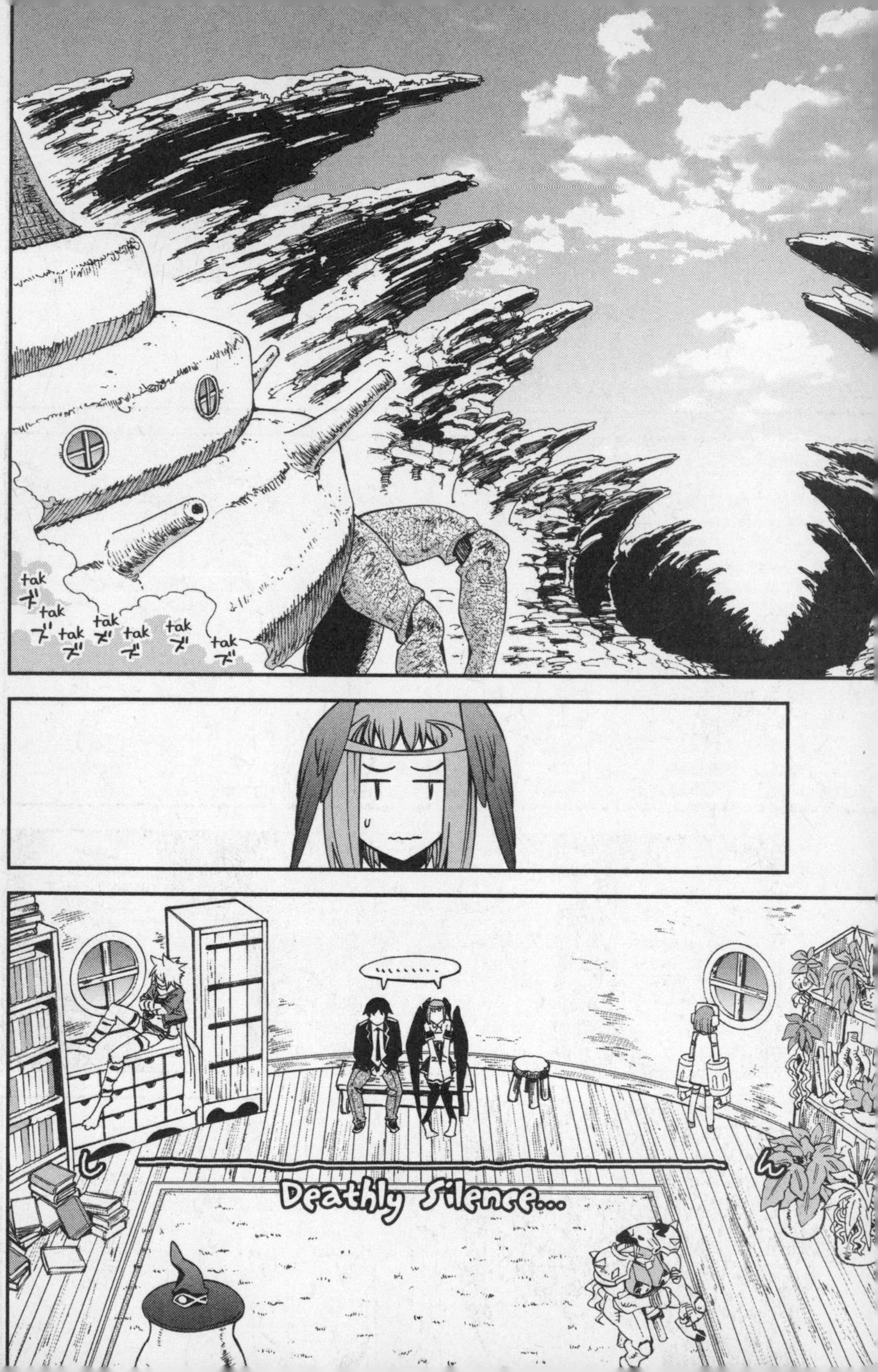
tak ズ tak ズ tak ズ tak ズ tak ズ tak ズ tak ズ
....
しん
Deathly Silence...

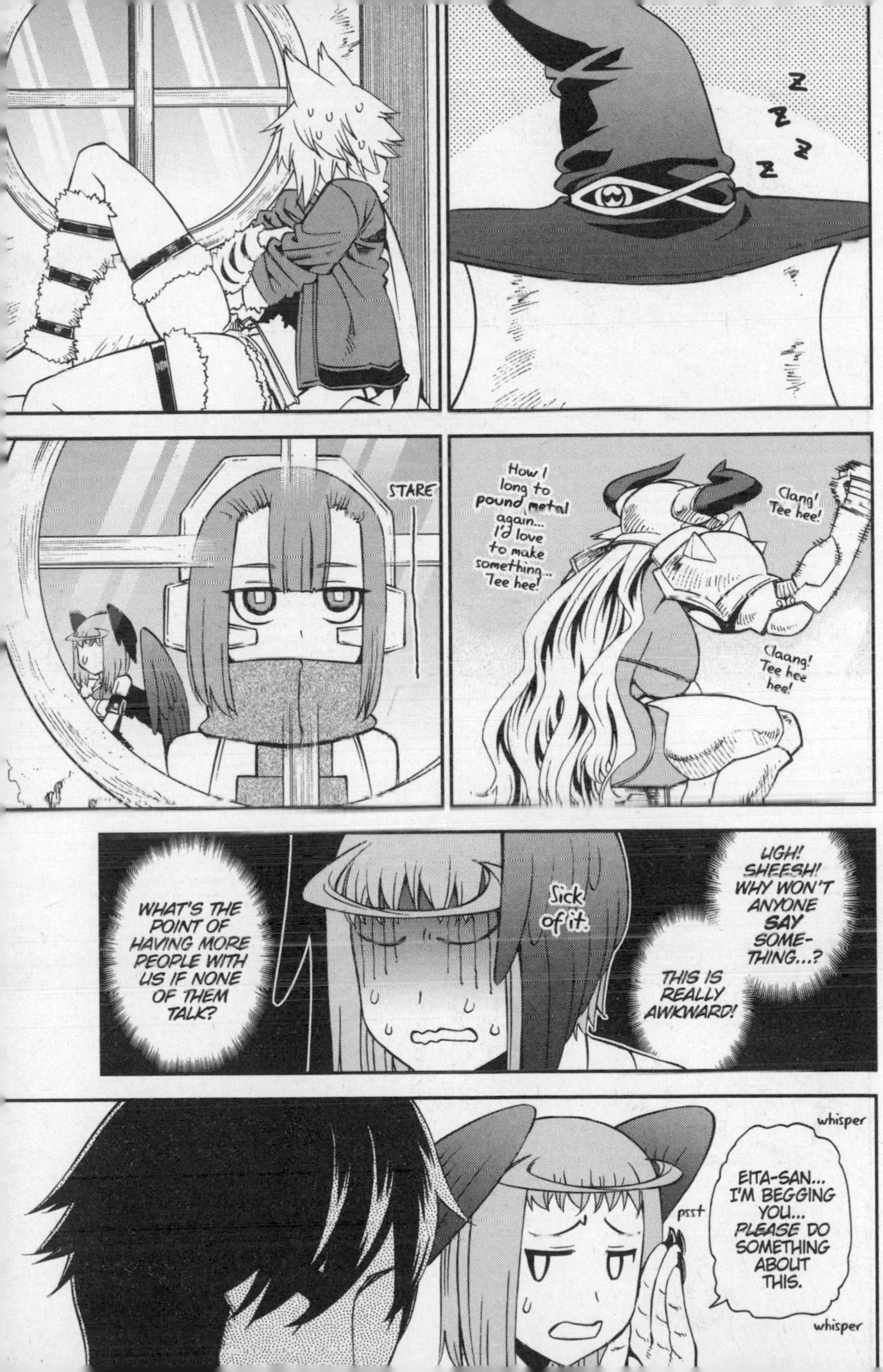
Z
Z
Z
Z
Clang! Tee hee!
How I long to pound metal again... I'd love to make something... Tee hee!
Claang! Tee hee hee!
STARE
UGH! SHEESH! WHY WON'T ANYONE SAY SOMETHING...?
THIS IS REALLY AWKWARD!
Sick of it.
WHAT'S THE POINT OF HAVING MORE PEOPLE WITH US IF NONE OF THEM TALK?
whisper
EITA-SAN... I'M BEGGING YOU... PLEASE DO SOMETHING ABOUT THIS.
psst
whisper

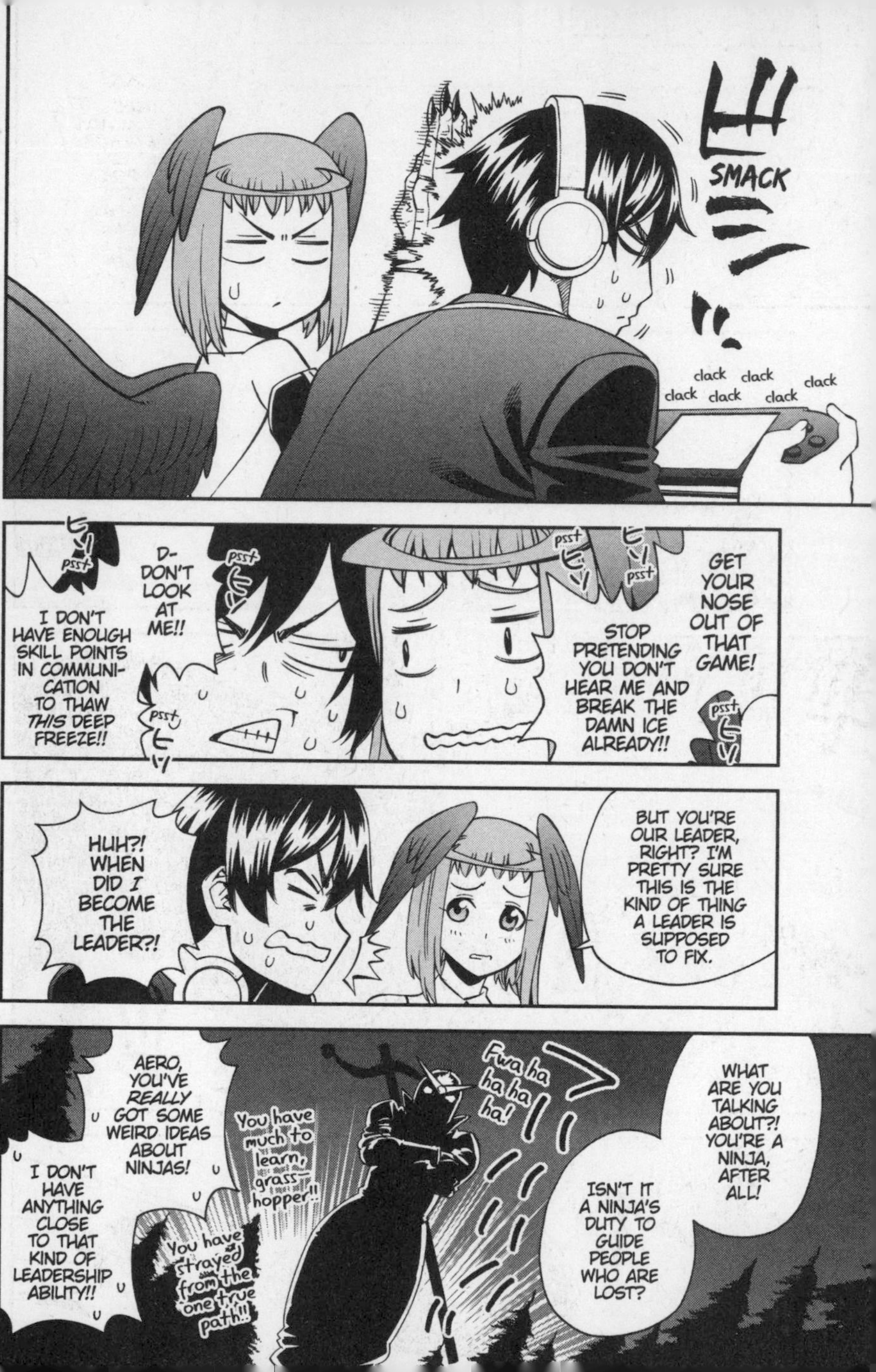
SMACK
clack clack clack clack clack clack
GET YOUR NOSE OUT OF THAT GAME!
STOP PRETENDING YOU DON'T HEAR ME AND BREAK THE DAMN ICE ALREADY!!
psst psst psst
D-DON'T LOOK AT ME!!
psst psst psst
I DON'T HAVE ENOUGH SKILL POINTS IN COMMUNICATION TO THAW *THIS* DEEP FREEZE!!
BUT YOU'RE OUR LEADER, RIGHT? I'M PRETTY SURE THIS IS THE KIND OF THING A LEADER IS SUPPOSED TO FIX.
HUH?! WHEN DID *I* BECOME THE LEADER?!
WHAT ARE YOU TALKING ABOUT?! YOU'RE A NINJA, AFTER ALL!
ISN'T IT A NINJA'S DUTY TO GUIDE PEOPLE WHO ARE LOST?
Fwa ha ha ha ha!
You have much to learn, grasshopper!!
You have strayed from the one true path!!
AERO, YOU'VE *REALLY* GOT SOME WEIRD IDEAS ABOUT NINJAS!
I DON'T HAVE ANYTHING CLOSE TO THAT KIND OF LEADERSHIP ABILITY!!

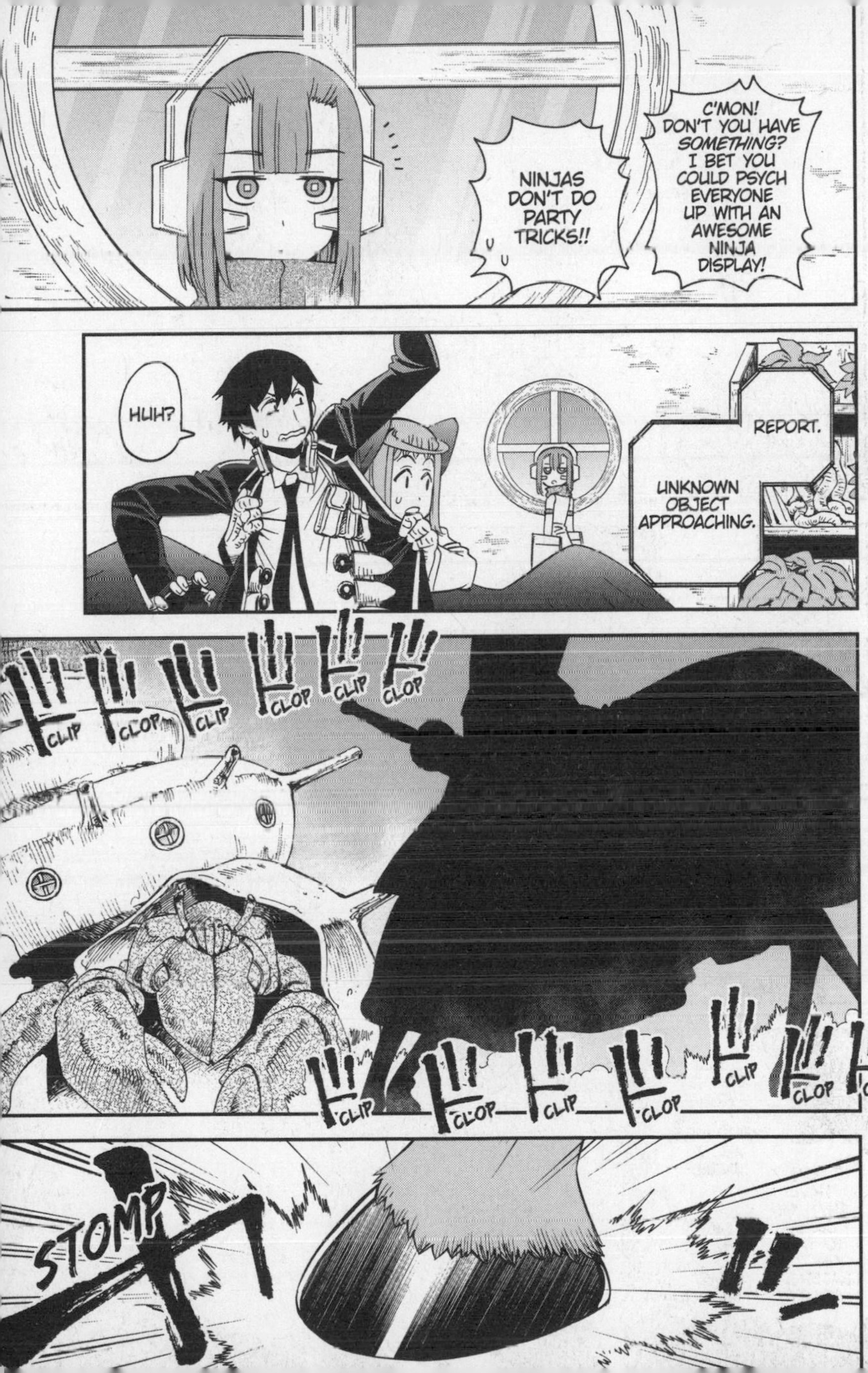
C'MON! DON'T YOU HAVE *SOMETHING?* I BET YOU COULD PSYCH EVERYONE UP WITH AN AWESOME NINJA DISPLAY!
NINJAS DON'T DO PARTY TRICKS!!
REPORT.
UNKNOWN OBJECT APPROACHING.
HUH?
CLIP CLOP CLIP CLOP CLIP CLOP
CLIP CLOP CLIP CLOP CLIP CLOP CLIP
STOMP

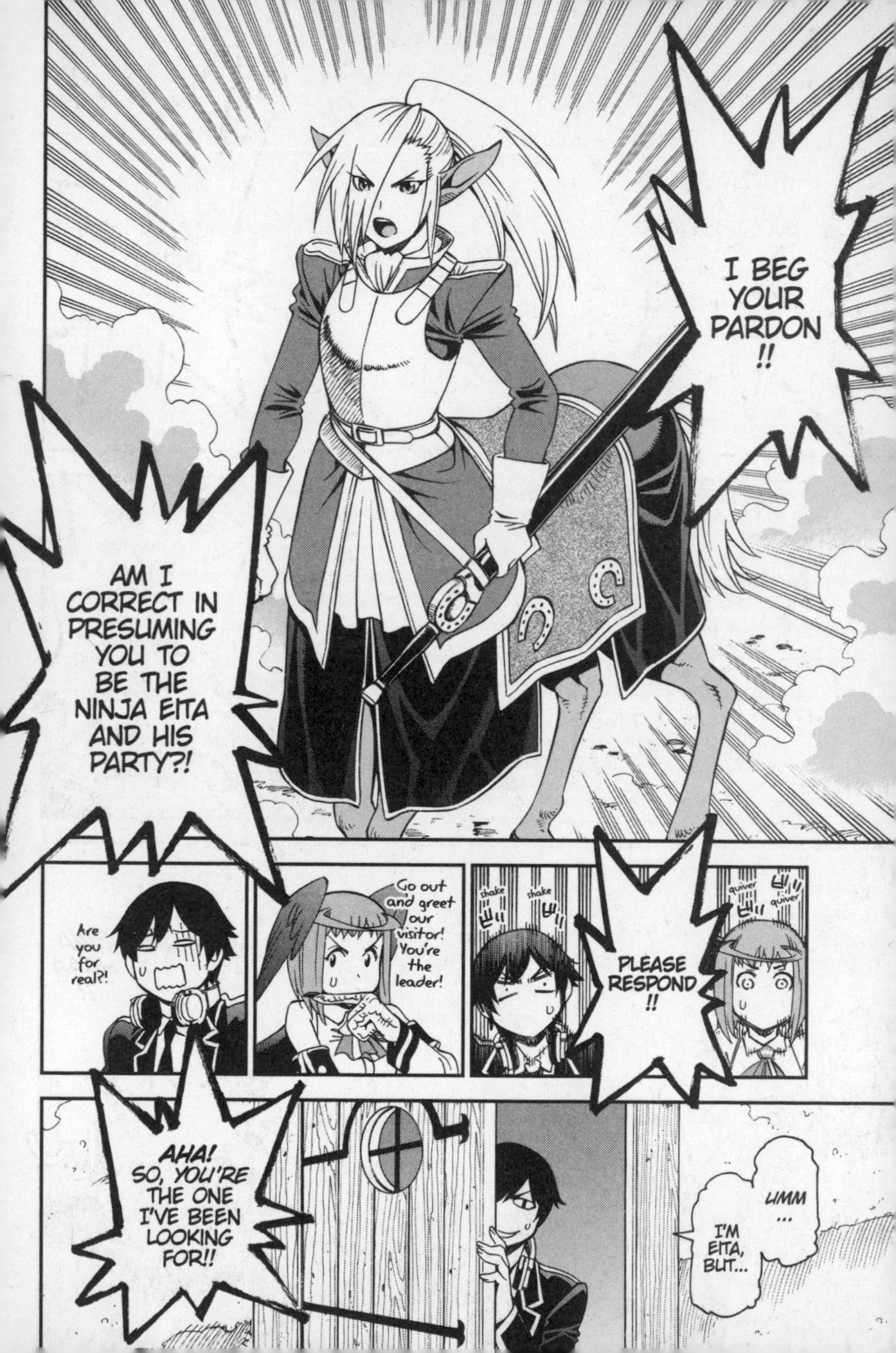
I BEG YOUR PARDON!!
AM I CORRECT IN PRESUMING YOU TO BE THE NINJA EITA AND HIS PARTY?!
quiver
quiver
PLEASE RESPOND!!
shake
shake
Go out and greet our visitor! You're the leader!
Are you for real?!
UMM...
I'M EITA, BUT...
AHA! SO, YOU'RE THE ONE I'VE BEEN LOOKING FOR!!

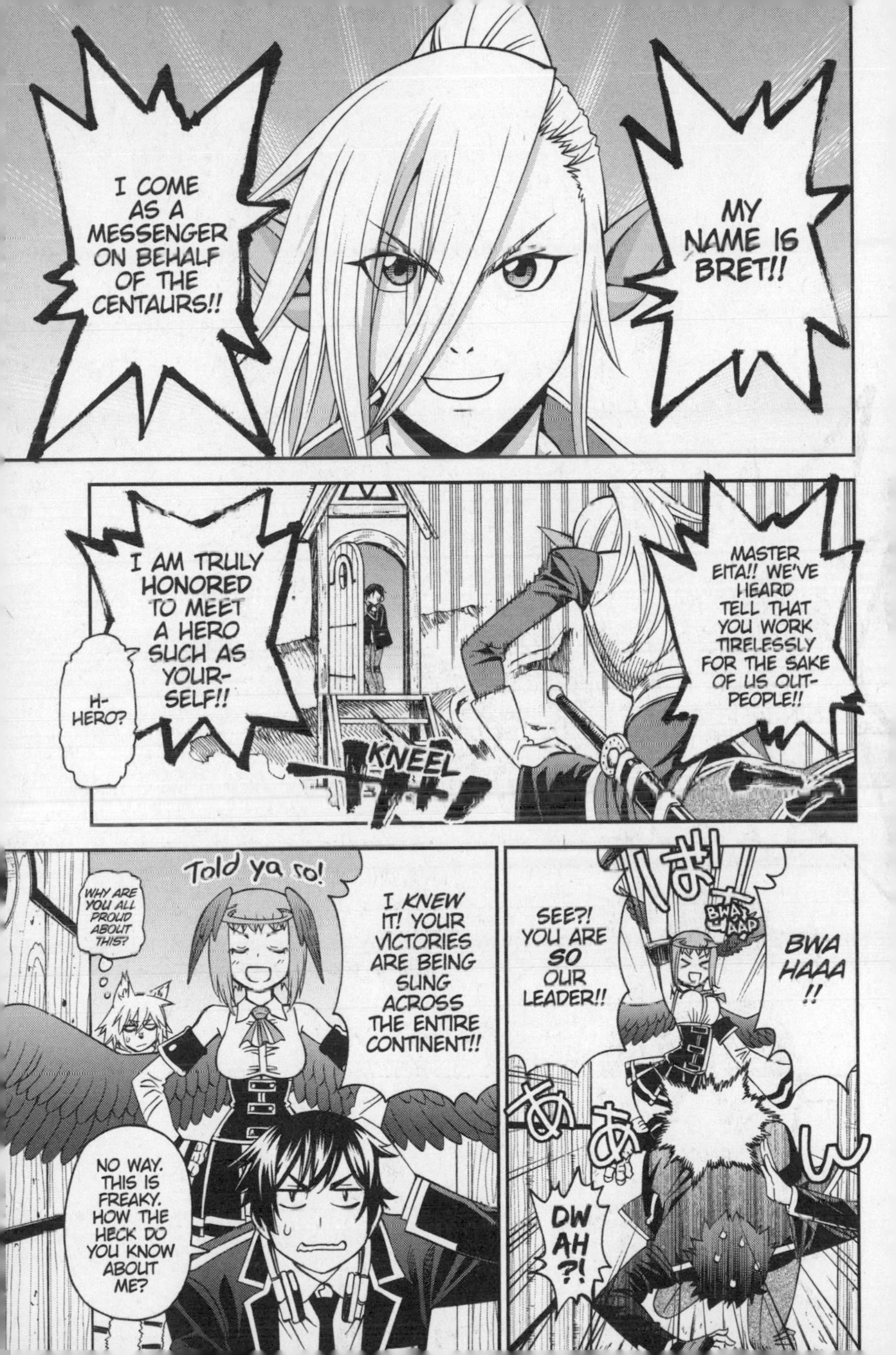
MY NAME IS BRET!!
I COME AS A MESSENGER ON BEHALF OF THE CENTAURS!!
MASTER EITA!! WE'VE HEARD TELL THAT YOU WORK TIRELESSLY FOR THE SAKE OF US OUT-PEOPLE!!
KNEEL
I AM TRULY HONORED TO MEET A HERO SUCH AS YOURSELF!!
H-HERO?
BWA HAAA!!
SEE?! YOU ARE SO OUR LEADER!!
DWAH?!
Told ya so!
I KNEW IT! YOUR VICTORIES ARE BEING SUNG ACROSS THE ENTIRE CONTINENT!!
WHY ARE YOU ALL PROUD ABOUT THIS?
NO WAY. THIS IS FREAKY. HOW THE HECK DO YOU KNOW ABOUT ME?

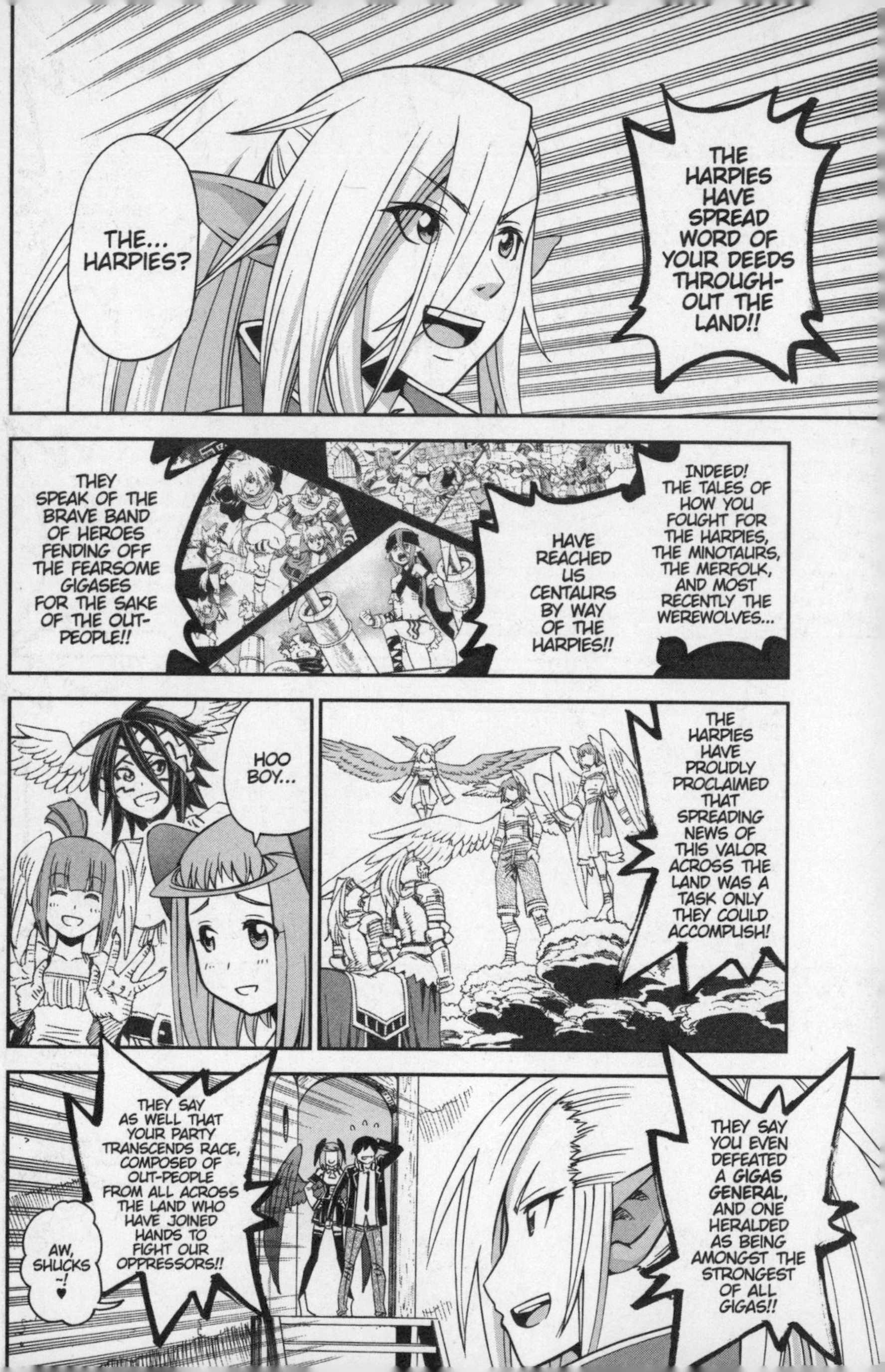
THE HARPIES HAVE SPREAD WORD OF YOUR DEEDS THROUGH-OUT THE LAND!!
THE... HARPIES?
INDEED! THE TALES OF HOW YOU FOUGHT FOR THE HARPIES, THE MINOTAURS, THE MERFOLK, AND MOST RECENTLY THE WEREWOLVES...
HAVE REACHED US CENTAURS BY WAY OF THE HARPIES!!
THEY SPEAK OF THE BRAVE BAND OF HEROES FENDING OFF THE FEARSOME GIGASES FOR THE SAKE OF THE OUT-PEOPLE!!
THE HARPIES HAVE PROUDLY PROCLAIMED THAT SPREADING NEWS OF THIS VALOR ACROSS THE LAND WAS A TASK ONLY THEY COULD ACCOMPLISH!
HOO BOY...
THEY SAY YOU EVEN DEFEATED A GIGAS GENERAL, AND ONE HERALDED AS BEING AMONGST THE STRONGEST OF ALL GIGAS!!
THEY SAY AS WELL THAT YOUR PARTY TRANSCENDS RACE, COMPOSED OF OUT-PEOPLE FROM ALL ACROSS THE LAND WHO HAVE JOINED HANDS TO FIGHT OUR OPPRESSORS!!
AW, SHUCKS ~! ♥

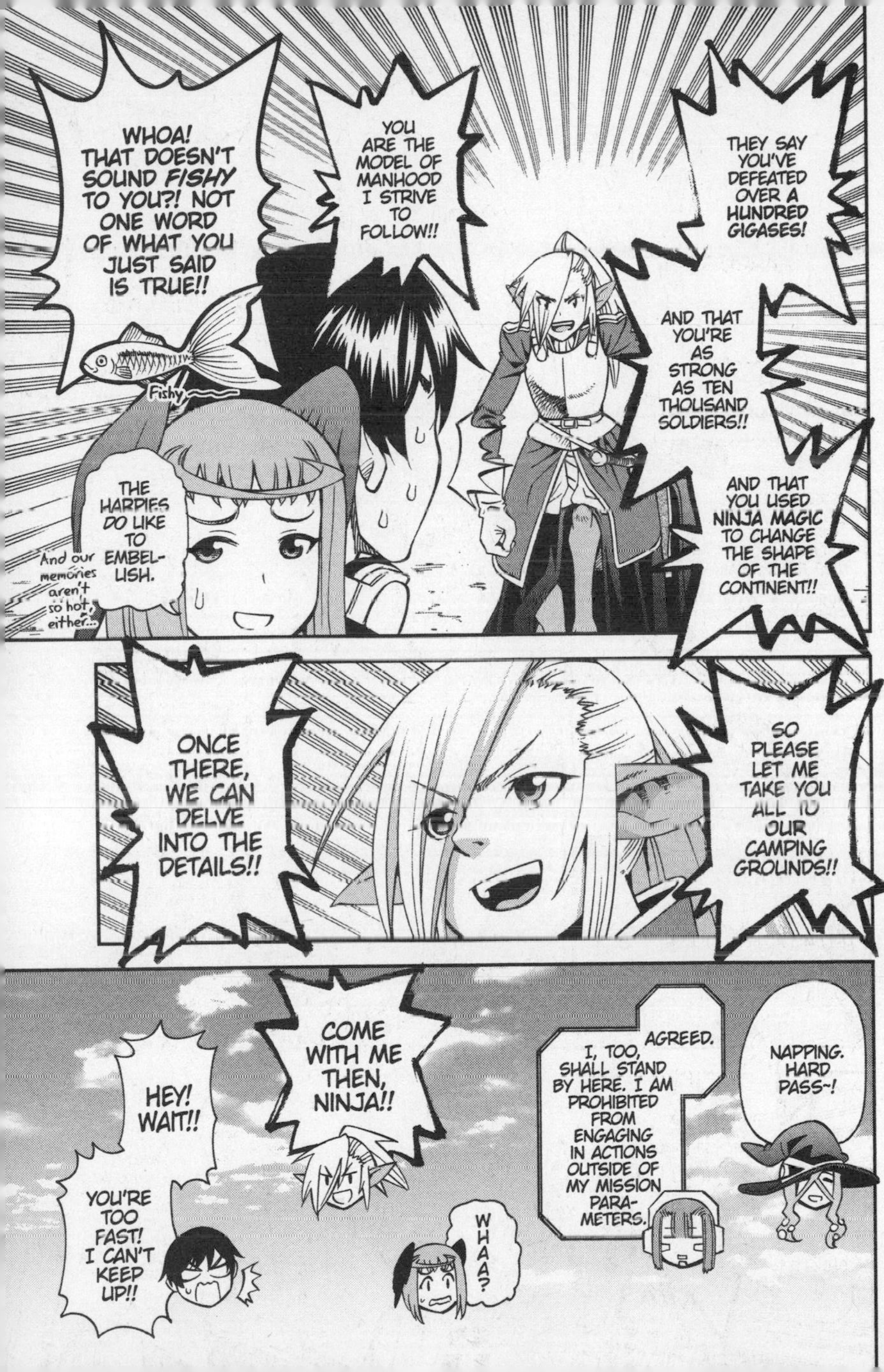
THEY SAY YOU'VE DEFEATED OVER A HUNDRED GIGASES!
AND THAT YOU'RE AS STRONG AS TEN THOUSAND SOLDIERS!!
AND THAT YOU USED NINJA MAGIC TO CHANGE THE SHAPE OF THE CONTINENT!!
YOU ARE THE MODEL OF MANHOOD I STRIVE TO FOLLOW!!
WHOA! THAT DOESN'T SOUND *FISHY* TO YOU?! NOT ONE WORD OF WHAT YOU JUST SAID IS TRUE!!
Fishy~
THE HARPIES *DO* LIKE TO EMBELLISH.
And our memories aren't so hot, either...
SO PLEASE LET ME TAKE YOU ALL TO OUR CAMPING GROUNDS!!
ONCE THERE, WE CAN DELVE INTO THE DETAILS!!
NAPPING. HARD PASS~!
AGREED. I, TOO, SHALL STAND BY HERE. I AM PROHIBITED FROM ENGAGING IN ACTIONS OUTSIDE OF MY MISSION PARAMETERS.
WHAA?
COME WITH ME THEN, NINJA!!
HEY! WAIT!!
YOU'RE TOO FAST! I CAN'T KEEP UP!!

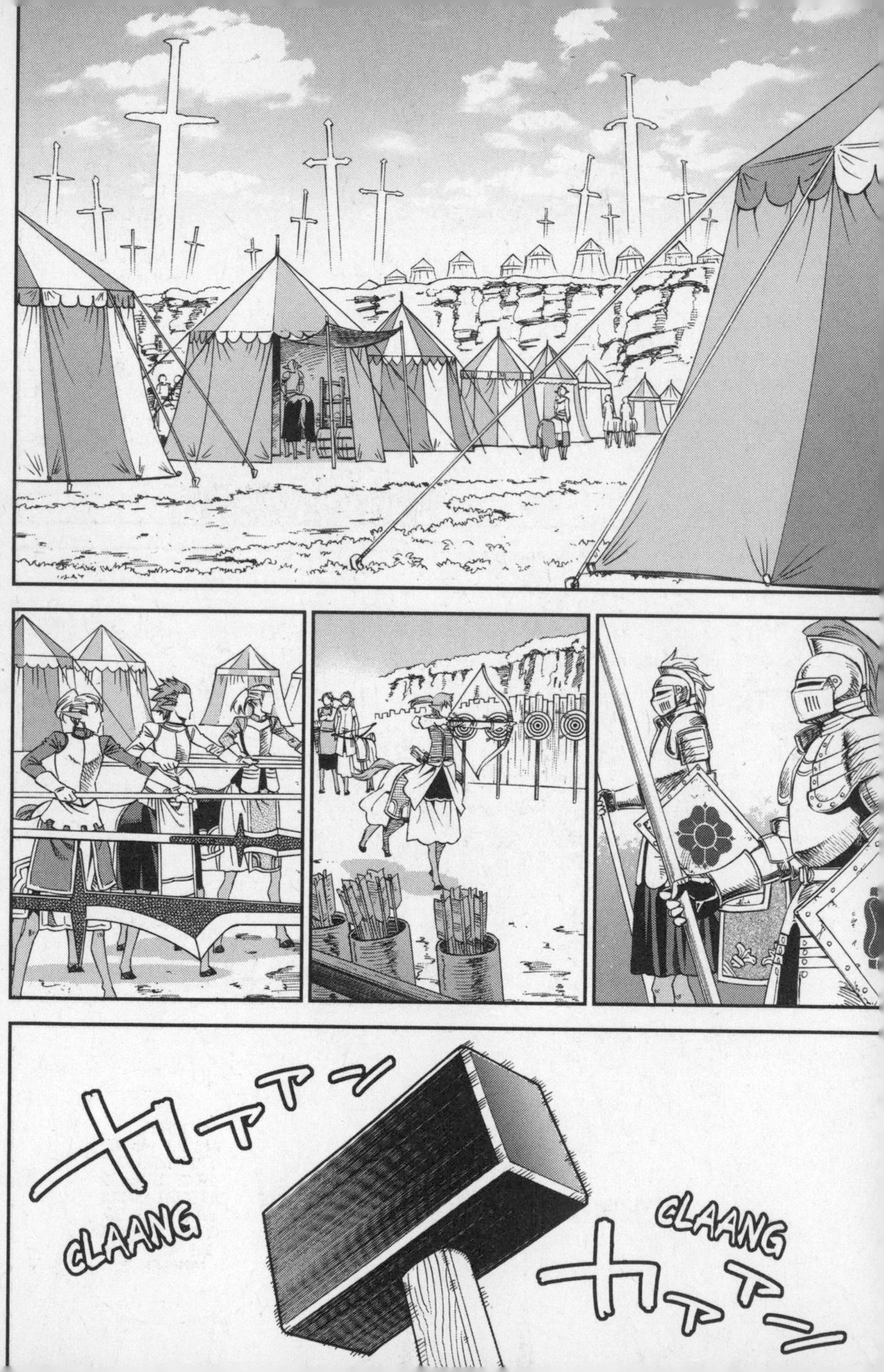
CLAANG
CLAANG

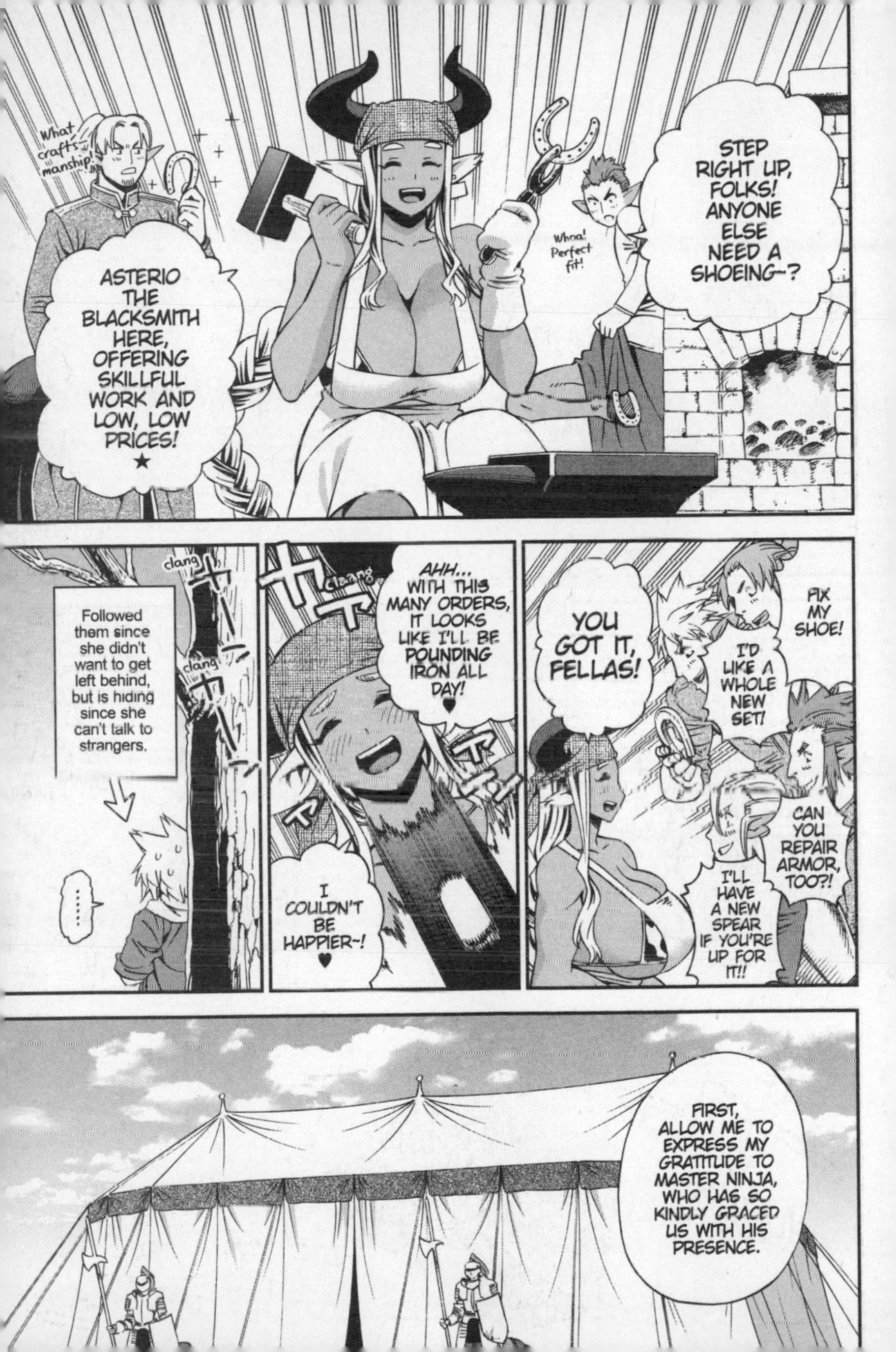
STEP RIGHT UP, FOLKS! ANYONE ELSE NEED A SHOEING~?
Whoa! Perfect fit!
What craftsmanship!
ASTERIO THE BLACKSMITH HERE, OFFERING SKILLFUL WORK AND LOW, LOW PRICES! ★
FIX MY SHOE!
I'D LIKE A WHOLE NEW SET!
YOU GOT IT, FELLAS!
CAN YOU REPAIR ARMOR, TOO?!
I'LL HAVE A NEW SPEAR IF YOU'RE UP FOR IT!!
clang
AHH... WITH THIS MANY ORDERS, IT LOOKS LIKE I'LL BE POUNDING IRON ALL DAY! ♥
I COULDN'T BE HAPPIER~! ♥
clang
clang
Followed them since she didn't want to get left behind, but is hiding since she can't talk to strangers.
......
FIRST, ALLOW ME TO EXPRESS MY GRATITUDE TO MASTER NINJA, WHO HAS SO KINDLY GRACED US WITH HIS PRESENCE.

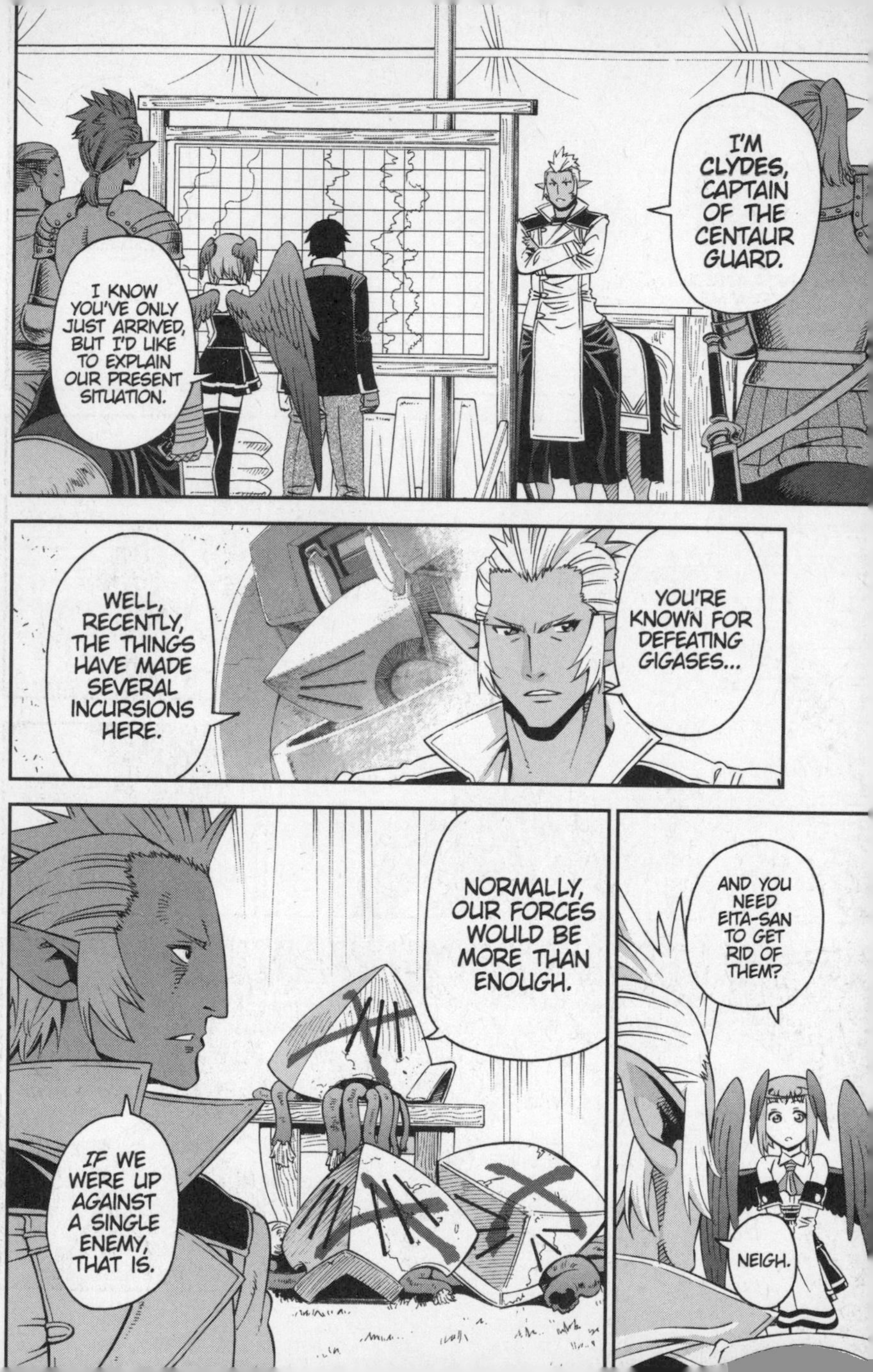
I'M CLYDES, CAPTAIN OF THE CENTAUR GUARD.
I KNOW YOU'VE ONLY JUST ARRIVED, BUT I'D LIKE TO EXPLAIN OUR PRESENT SITUATION.
YOU'RE KNOWN FOR DEFEATING GIGASES...
WELL, RECENTLY, THE THINGS HAVE MADE SEVERAL INCURSIONS HERE.
AND YOU NEED EITA-SAN TO GET RID OF THEM?
NEIGH.
NORMALLY, OUR FORCES WOULD BE MORE THAN ENOUGH.
IF WE WERE UP AGAINST A SINGLE ENEMY, THAT IS.

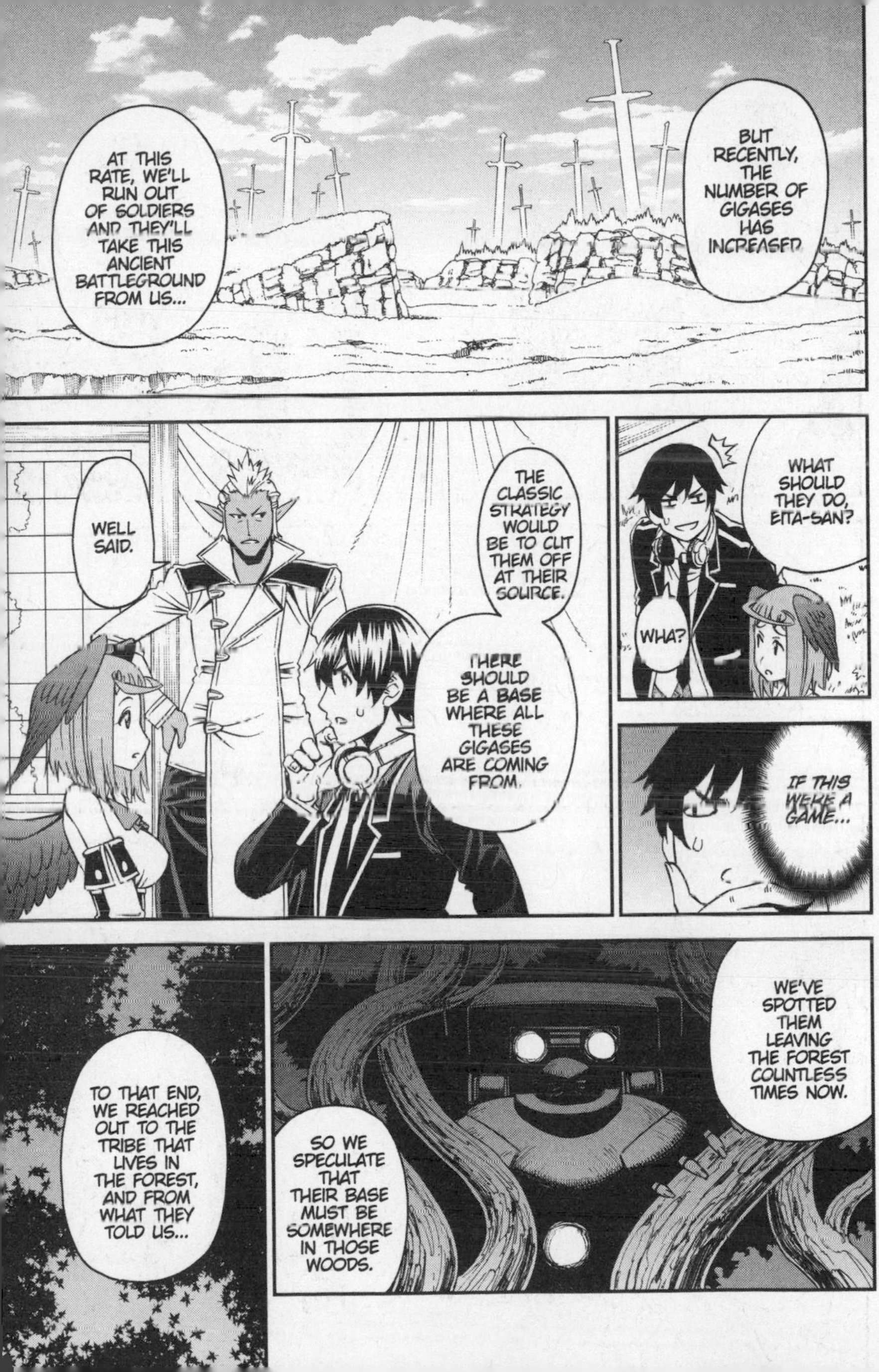
BUT RECENTLY, THE NUMBER OF GIGASES HAS INCREASED
AT THIS RATE, WE'LL RUN OUT OF SOLDIERS AND THEY'LL TAKE THIS ANCIENT BATTLEGROUND FROM US...
WHAT SHOULD THEY DO, EITA-SAN?
WHA?
IF THIS WERE A GAME...
THE CLASSIC STRATEGY WOULD BE TO CUT THEM OFF AT THEIR SOURCE.
THERE SHOULD BE A BASE WHERE ALL THESE GIGASES ARE COMING FROM.
WELL SAID.
WE'VE SPOTTED THEM LEAVING THE FOREST COUNTLESS TIMES NOW.
SO WE SPECULATE THAT THEIR BASE MUST BE SOMEWHERE IN THOSE WOODS.
TO THAT END, WE REACHED OUT TO THE TRIBE THAT LIVES IN THE FOREST, AND FROM WHAT THEY TOLD US...

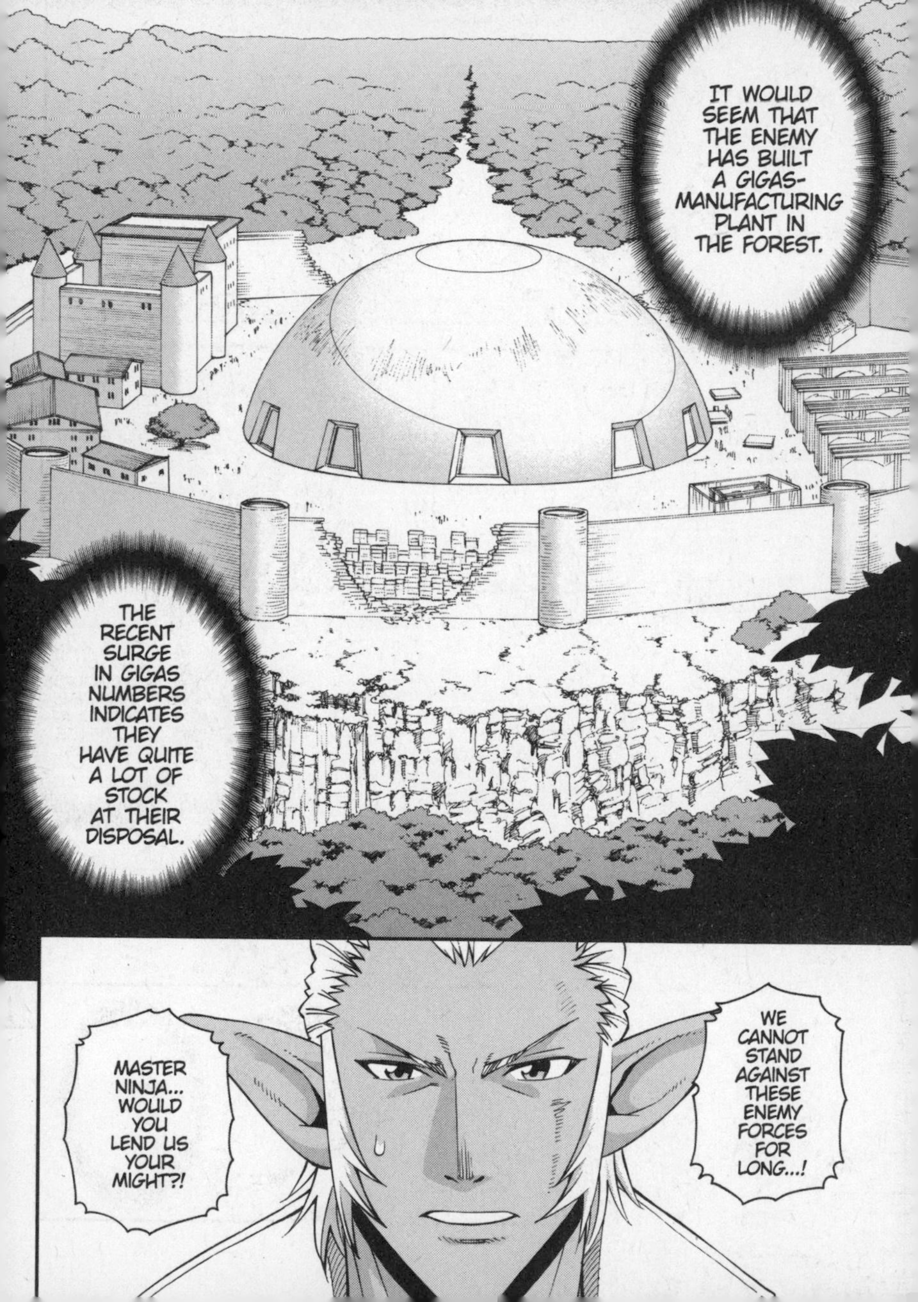
IT WOULD SEEM THAT THE ENEMY HAS BUILT A GIGAS-MANUFACTURING PLANT IN THE FOREST.
THE RECENT SURGE IN GIGAS NUMBERS INDICATES THEY HAVE QUITE A LOT OF STOCK AT THEIR DISPOSAL.
WE CANNOT STAND AGAINST THESE ENEMY FORCES FOR LONG...!
MASTER NINJA... WOULD YOU LEND US YOUR MIGHT?!

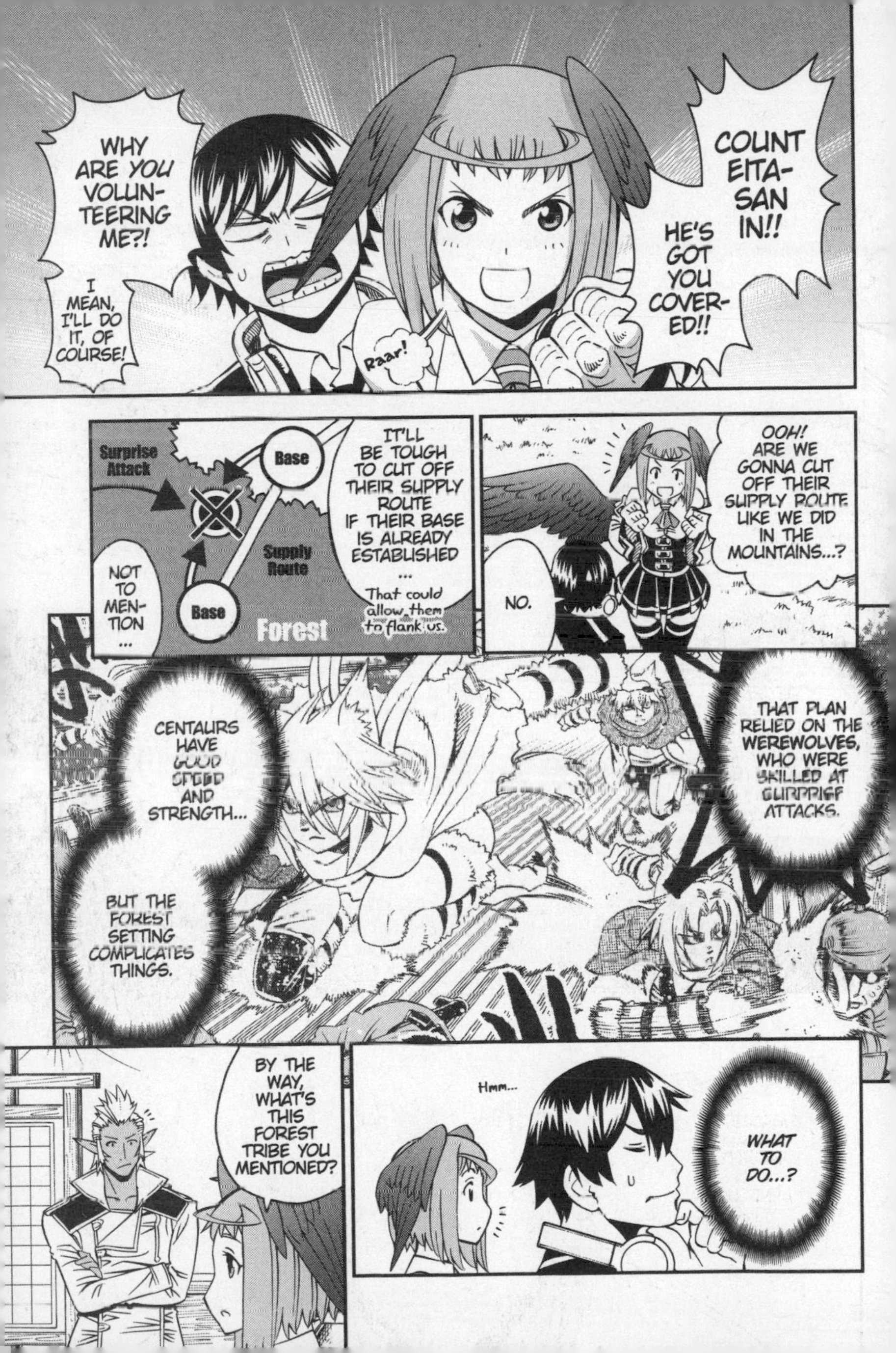
COUNT EITA-SAN IN!!
HE'S GOT YOU COVERED-ED!!
WHY ARE YOU VOLUNTEERING ME?!
I MEAN, I'LL DO IT, OF COURSE!
Raar!
OOH! ARE WE GONNA CUT OFF THEIR SUPPLY ROUTE LIKE WE DID IN THE MOUNTAINS...?
NO.
IT'LL BE TOUGH TO CUT OFF THEIR SUPPLY ROUTE IF THEIR BASE IS ALREADY ESTABLISHED...
That could allow them to flank us.
Surprise Attack
Base
Supply Route
Base
Forest
NOT TO MENTION...
THAT PLAN RELIED ON THE WEREWOLVES, WHO WERE SKILLED AT SURPRISE ATTACKS.
CENTAURS HAVE GOOD SPEED AND STRENGTH...
BUT THE FOREST SETTING COMPLICATES THINGS.
Hmm...
WHAT TO DO...?
BY THE WAY, WHAT'S THIS FOREST TRIBE YOU MENTIONED?

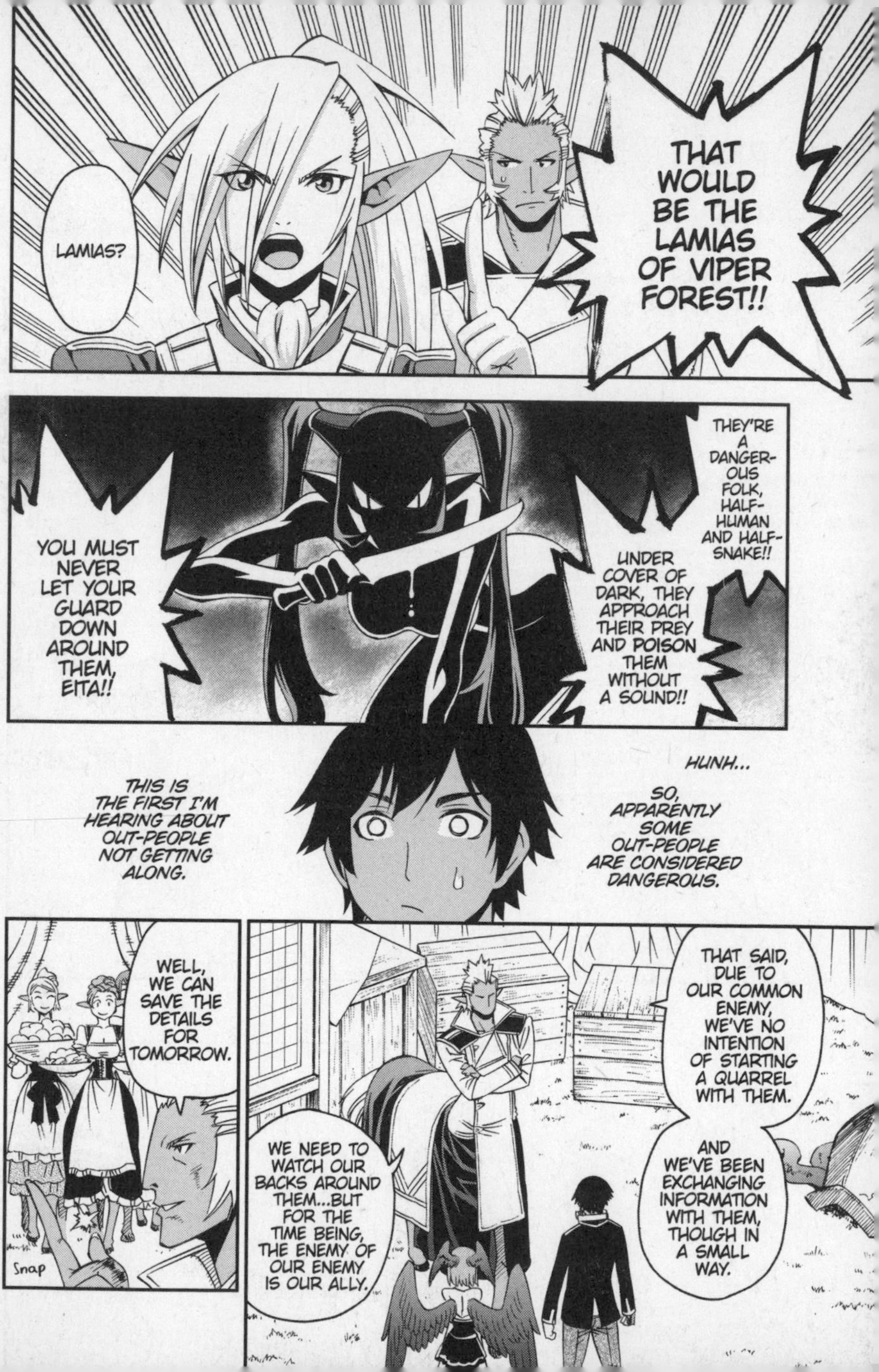

THAT WOULD BE THE LAMIAS OF VIPER FOREST!!
LAMIAS?
THEY'RE A DANGER-OUS FOLK, HALF-HUMAN AND HALF-SNAKE!!
UNDER COVER OF DARK, THEY APPROACH THEIR PREY AND POISON THEM WITHOUT A SOUND!!
YOU MUST NEVER LET YOUR GUARD DOWN AROUND THEM, EITA!!
HUNH...
SO, APPARENTLY SOME OUT-PEOPLE ARE CONSIDERED DANGEROUS.
THIS IS THE FIRST I'M HEARING ABOUT OUT-PEOPLE NOT GETTING ALONG.
THAT SAID, DUE TO OUR COMMON ENEMY, WE'VE NO INTENTION OF STARTING A QUARREL WITH THEM.
AND WE'VE BEEN EXCHANGING INFORMATION WITH THEM, THOUGH IN A SMALL WAY.
WE NEED TO WATCH OUR BACKS AROUND THEM...BUT FOR THE TIME BEING, THE ENEMY OF OUR ENEMY IS OUR ALLY.
WELL, WE CAN SAVE THE DETAILS FOR TOMORROW.
Snap

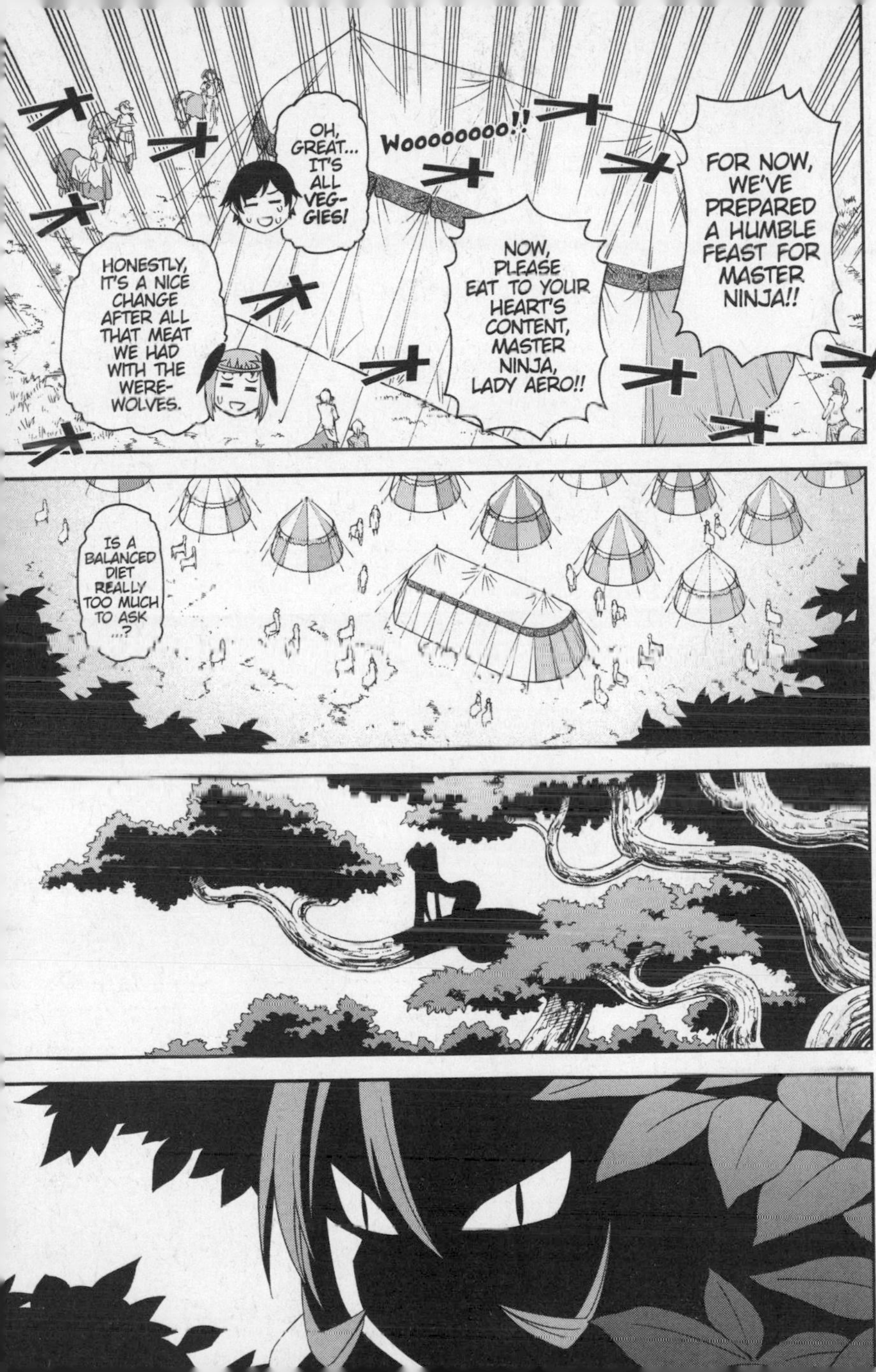
FOR NOW, WE'VE PREPARED A HUMBLE FEAST FOR MASTER NINJA!!
Wooooooooo!!
NOW, PLEASE EAT TO YOUR HEART'S CONTENT, MASTER NINJA, LADY AERO!!
OH, GREAT... IT'S ALL VEG-GIES!
HONESTLY, IT'S A NICE CHANGE AFTER ALL THAT MEAT WE HAD WITH THE WERE-WOLVES.
IS A BALANCED DIET REALLY TOO MUCH TO ASK ...?

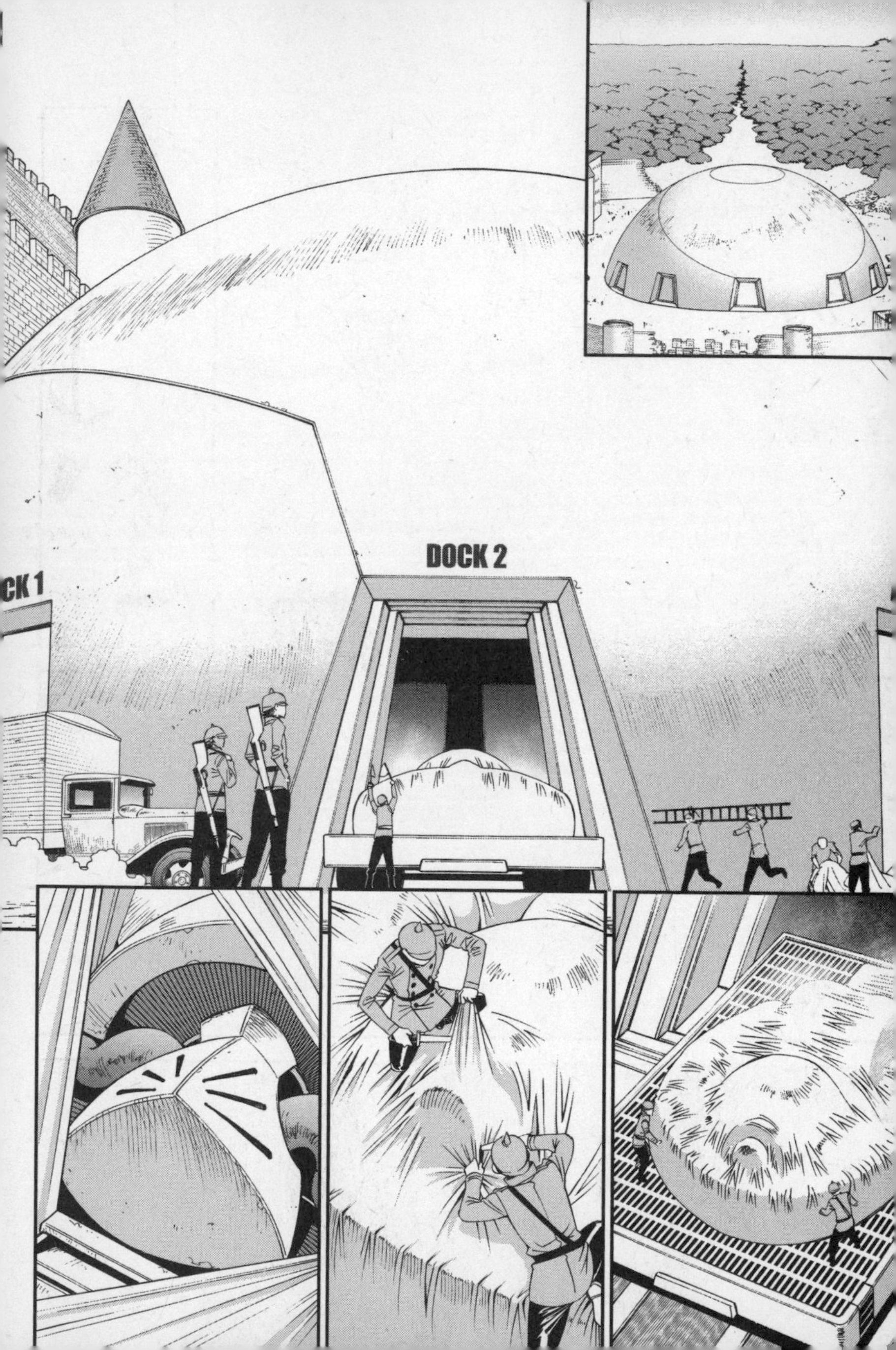
DOCK 2
CK 1

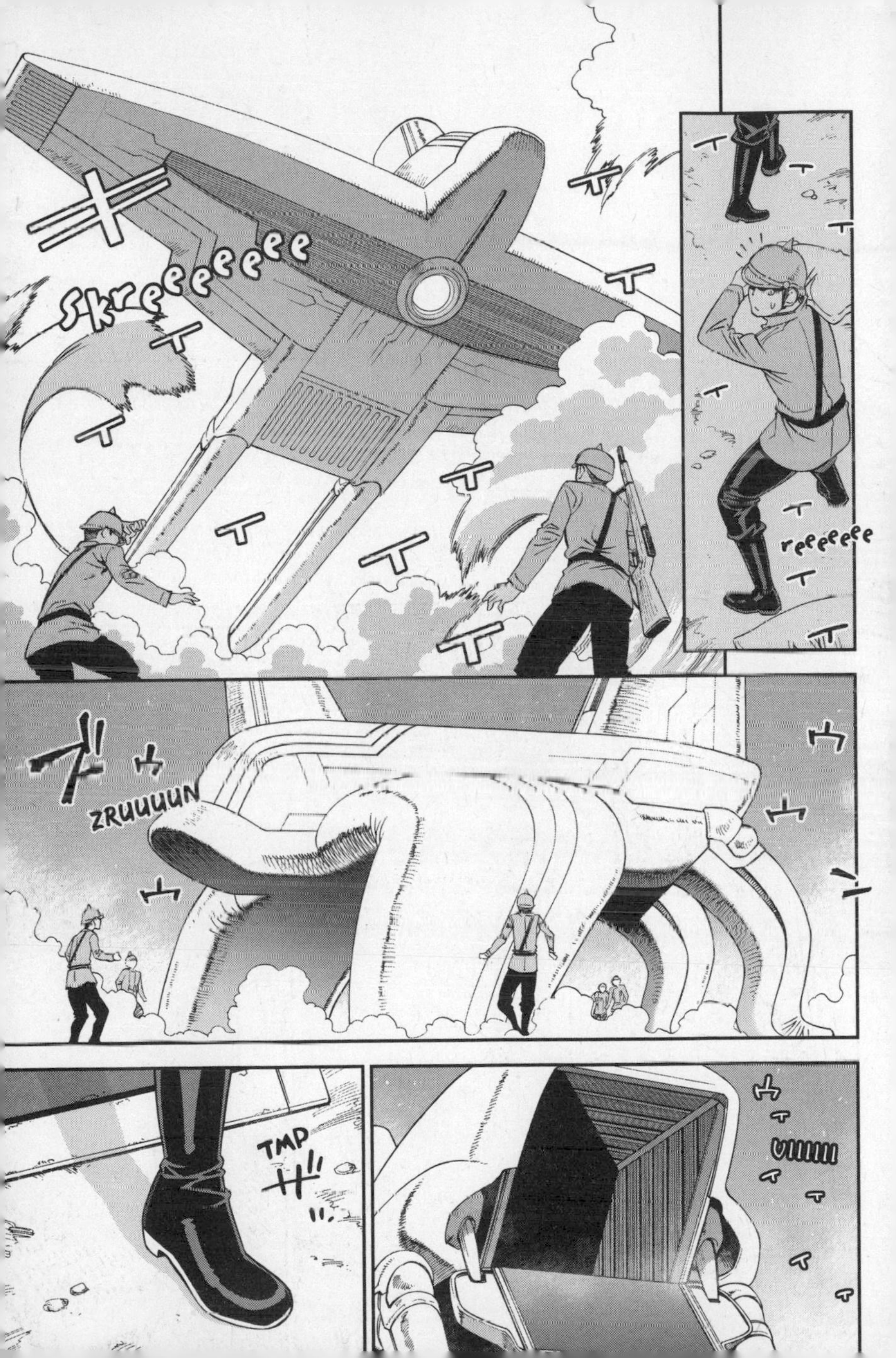
reeeeeee
Skreeeeeeee
ZRUUUUN
UIIIII
TMP

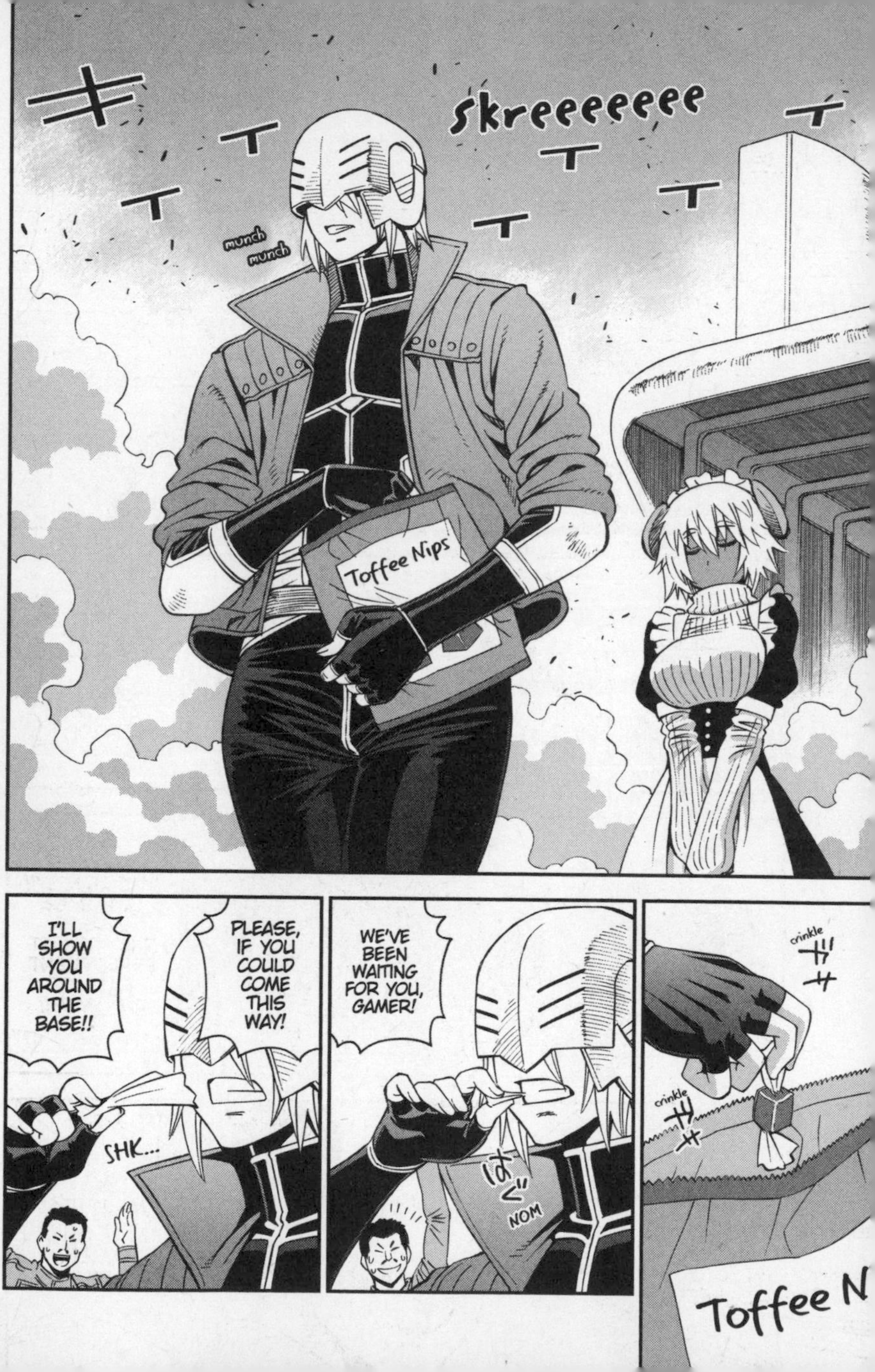

Skreeeeeee
munch munch
Toffee Nips
crinkle
crinkle
Toffee N
WE'VE BEEN WAITING FOR YOU, GAMER!
はぐ
NOM
PLEASE, IF YOU COULD COME THIS WAY!
I'LL SHOW YOU AROUND THE BASE!!
SHK...

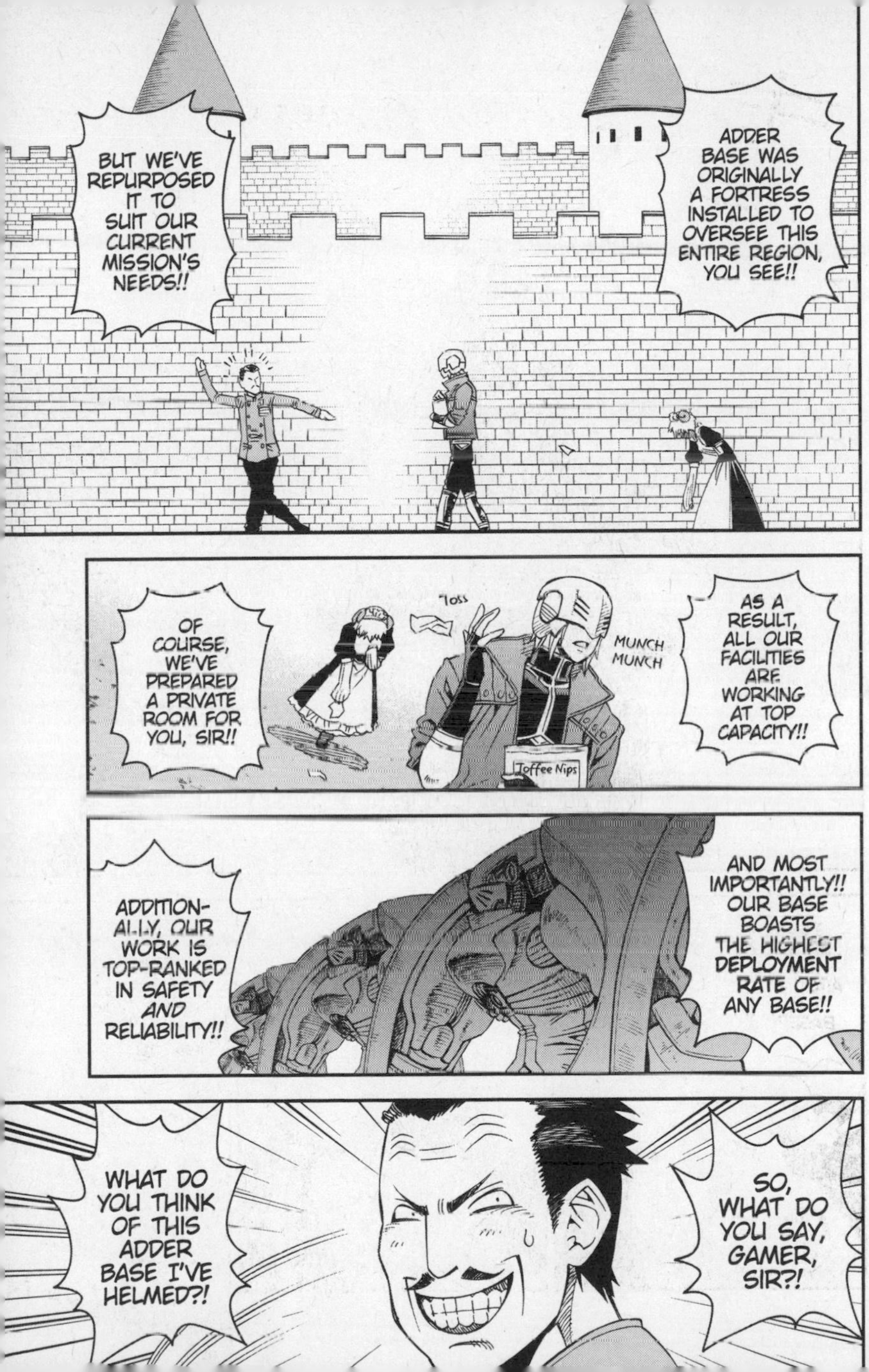
ADDER BASE WAS ORIGINALLY A FORTRESS INSTALLED TO OVERSEE THIS ENTIRE REGION, YOU SEE!!
BUT WE'VE REPURPOSED IT TO SUIT OUR CURRENT MISSION'S NEEDS!!
AS A RESULT, ALL OUR FACILITIES ARE WORKING AT TOP CAPACITY!!
MUNCH MUNCH
TOSS
Toffee Nips
OF COURSE, WE'VE PREPARED A PRIVATE ROOM FOR YOU, SIR!!
AND MOST IMPORTANTLY!! OUR BASE BOASTS THE HIGHEST DEPLOYMENT RATE OF ANY BASE!!
ADDITION-ALLY, OUR WORK IS TOP-RANKED IN SAFETY AND RELIABILITY!!
SO, WHAT DO YOU SAY, GAMER, SIR?!
WHAT DO YOU THINK OF THIS ADDER BASE I'VE HELMED?!

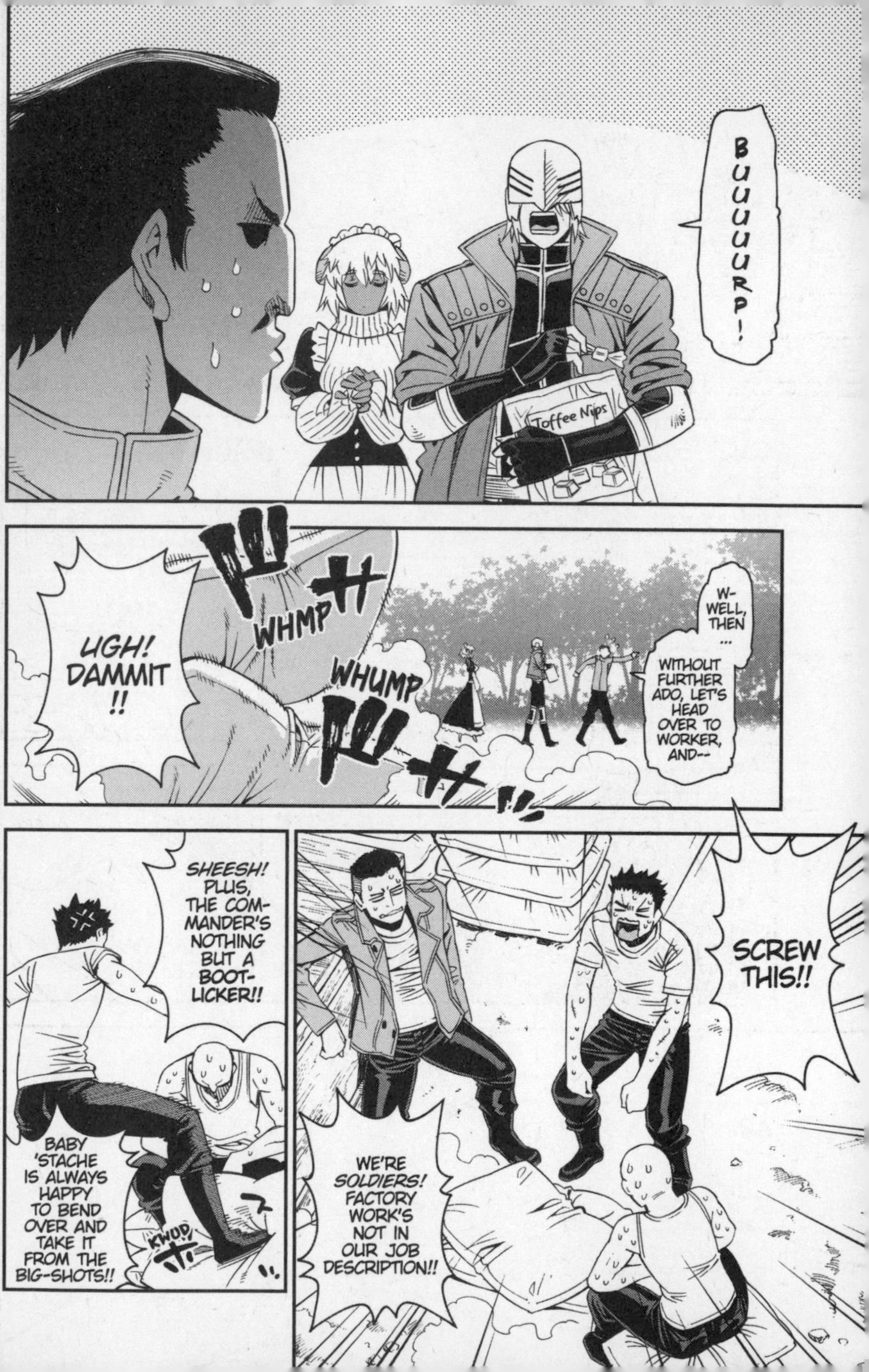
BUUUUURP!
Toffee Nips
W-WELL, THEN ... WITHOUT FURTHER ADO, LET'S HEAD OVER TO WORKER, AND--
WHMP
WHUMP
UGH! DAMMIT!!
SCREW THIS!!
WE'RE SOLDIERS! FACTORY WORK'S NOT IN OUR JOB DESCRIPTION!!
SHEESH! PLUS, THE COMMANDER'S NOTHING BUT A BOOT-LICKER!!
KWUD
BABY 'STACHE IS ALWAYS HAPPY TO BEND OVER AND TAKE IT FROM THE BIG-SHOTS!!

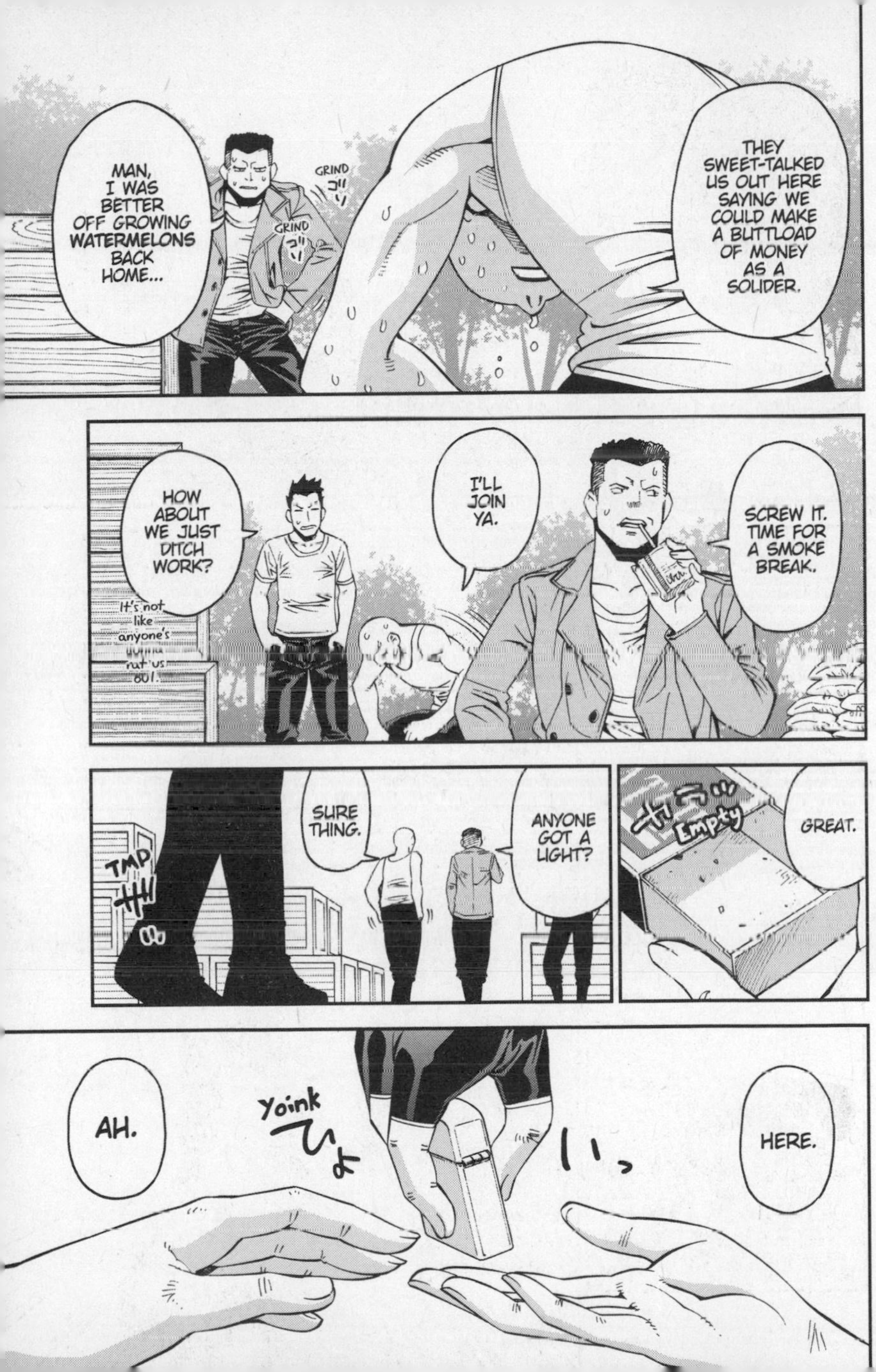
THEY SWEET-TALKED US OUT HERE SAYING WE COULD MAKE A BUTTLOAD OF MONEY AS A SOLIDER.
GRIND
GRIND
MAN, I WAS BETTER OFF GROWING WATERMELONS BACK HOME...
SCREW IT. TIME FOR A SMOKE BREAK.
I'LL JOIN YA.
HOW ABOUT WE JUST DITCH WORK?
It's not like anyone's gonna rat us out.
Empty
GREAT.
ANYONE GOT A LIGHT?
SURE THING.
TMP
HERE.
Yoink ひょ
AH.

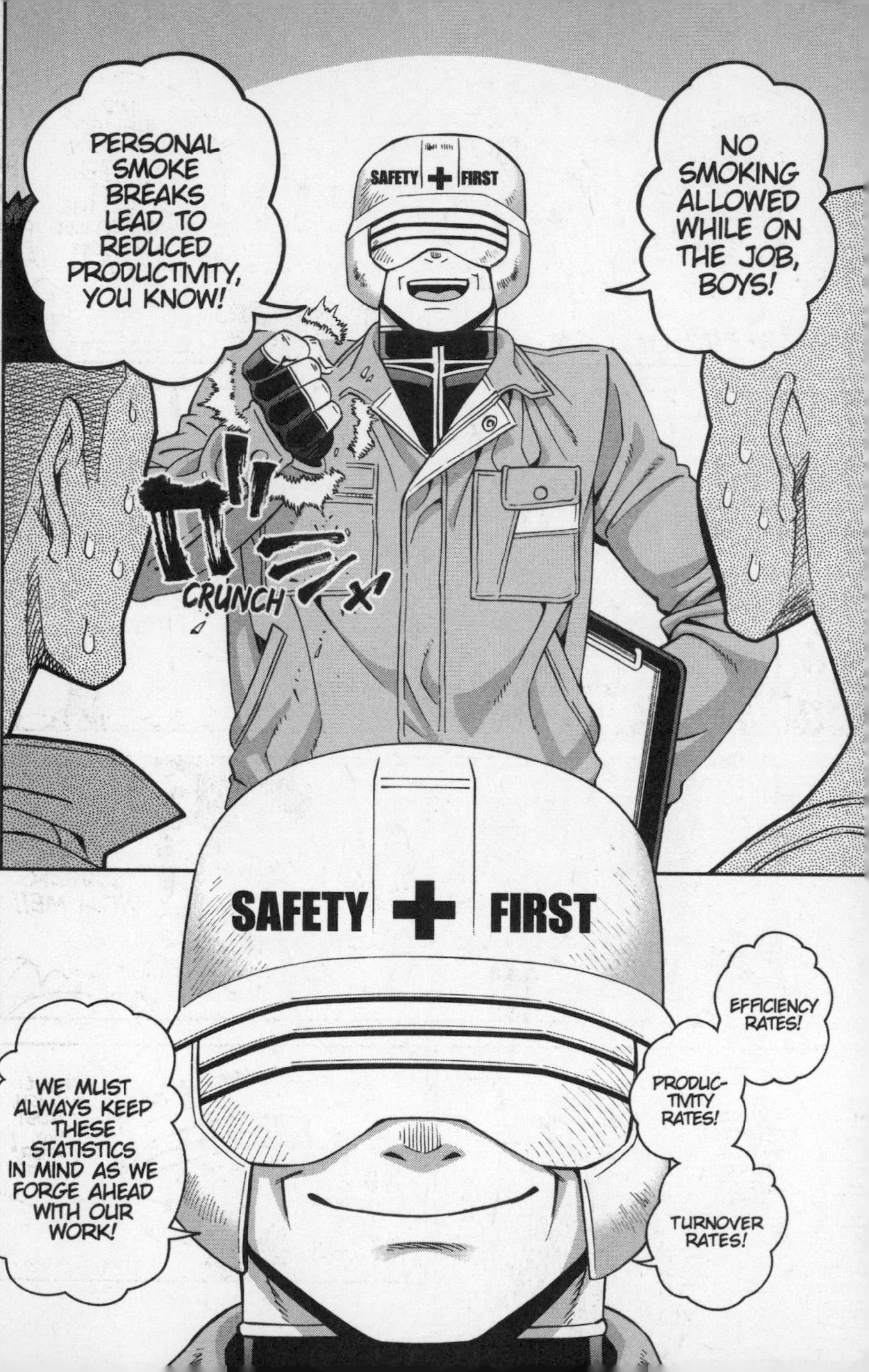
NO SMOKING ALLOWED WHILE ON THE JOB, BOYS!
SAFETY FIRST
PERSONAL SMOKE BREAKS LEAD TO REDUCED PRODUCTIVITY, YOU KNOW!
CRUNCH
SAFETY FIRST
EFFICIENCY RATES!
PRODUC-TIVITY RATES!
TURNOVER RATES!
WE MUST ALWAYS KEEP THESE STATISTICS IN MIND AS WE FORGE AHEAD WITH OUR WORK!

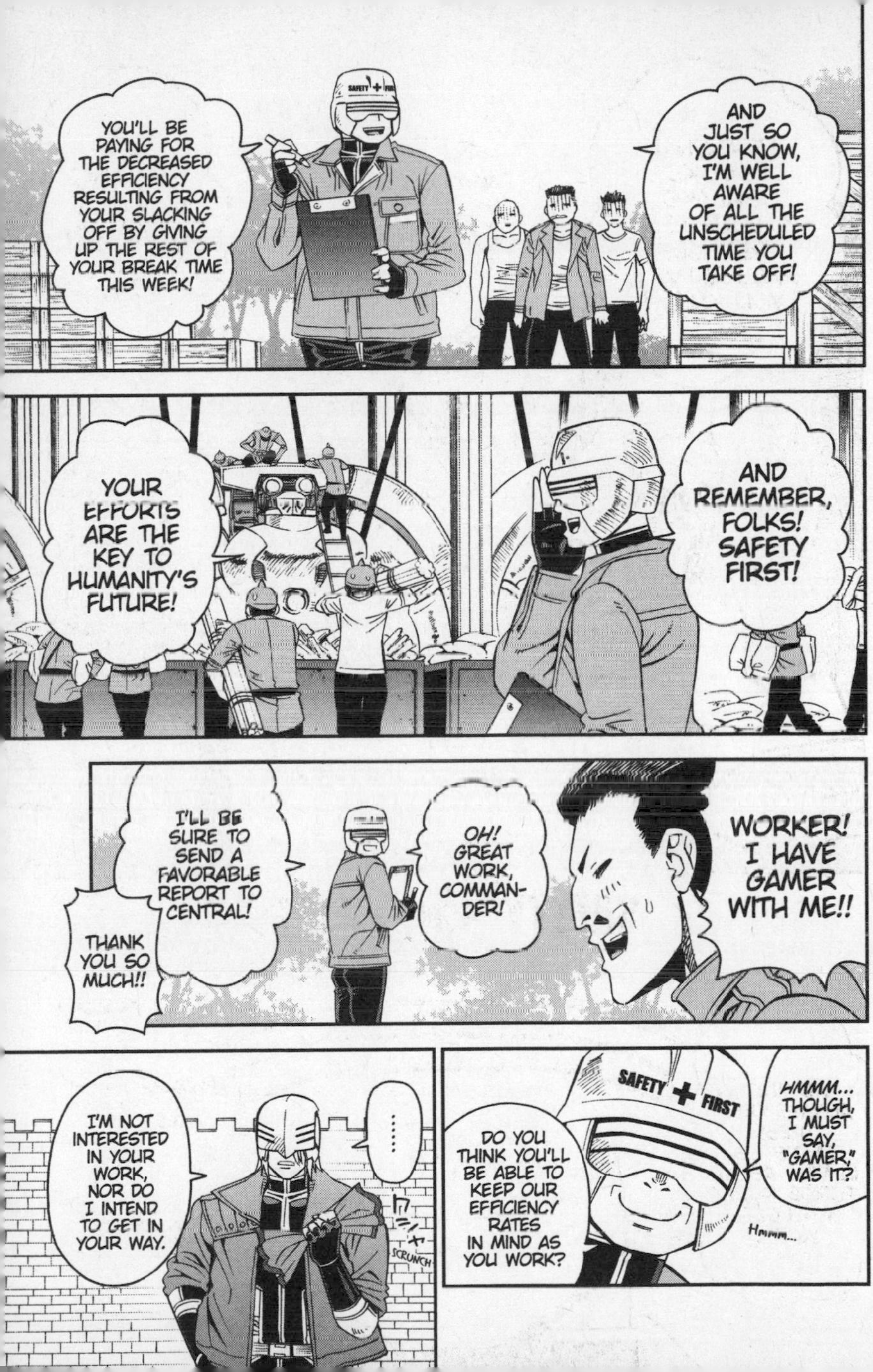
YOU'LL BE PAYING FOR THE DECREASED EFFICIENCY RESULTING FROM YOUR SLACKING OFF BY GIVING UP THE REST OF YOUR BREAK TIME THIS WEEK!
AND JUST SO YOU KNOW, I'M WELL AWARE OF ALL THE UNSCHEDULED TIME YOU TAKE OFF!
YOUR EFFORTS ARE THE KEY TO HUMANITY'S FUTURE!
AND REMEMBER, FOLKS! SAFETY FIRST!
WORKER! I HAVE GAMER WITH ME!!
OH! GREAT WORK, COMMANDER!
I'LL BE SURE TO SEND A FAVORABLE REPORT TO CENTRAL!
THANK YOU SO MUCH!!
SAFETY FIRST
HMMM... THOUGH, I MUST SAY, "GAMER," WAS IT?
DO YOU THINK YOU'LL BE ABLE TO KEEP OUR EFFICIENCY RATES IN MIND AS YOU WORK?
Hmmm...
......
I'M NOT INTERESTED IN YOUR WORK, NOR DO I INTEND TO GET IN YOUR WAY.
SCRUNCH

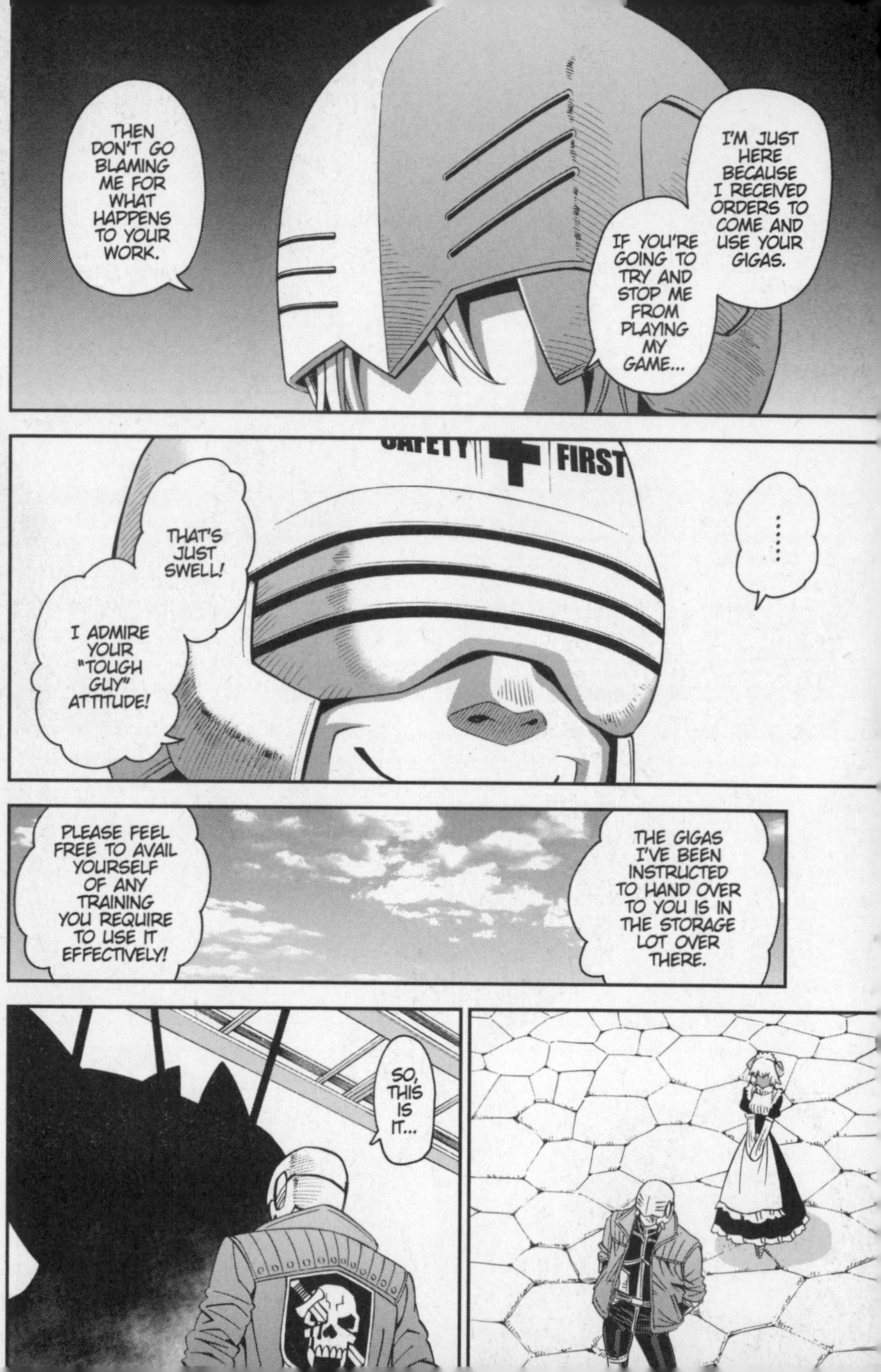
I'M JUST HERE BECAUSE I RECEIVED ORDERS TO COME AND USE YOUR GIGAS.
IF YOU'RE GOING TO TRY AND STOP ME FROM PLAYING MY GAME...
THEN DON'T GO BLAMING ME FOR WHAT HAPPENS TO YOUR WORK.
......
FIRST
THAT'S JUST SWELL!
I ADMIRE YOUR "TOUGH GUY" ATTITUDE!
THE GIGAS I'VE BEEN INSTRUCTED TO HAND OVER TO YOU IS IN THE STORAGE LOT OVER THERE.
PLEASE FEEL FREE TO AVAIL YOURSELF OF ANY TRAINING YOU REQUIRE TO USE IT EFFECTIVELY!
SO, THIS IS IT...

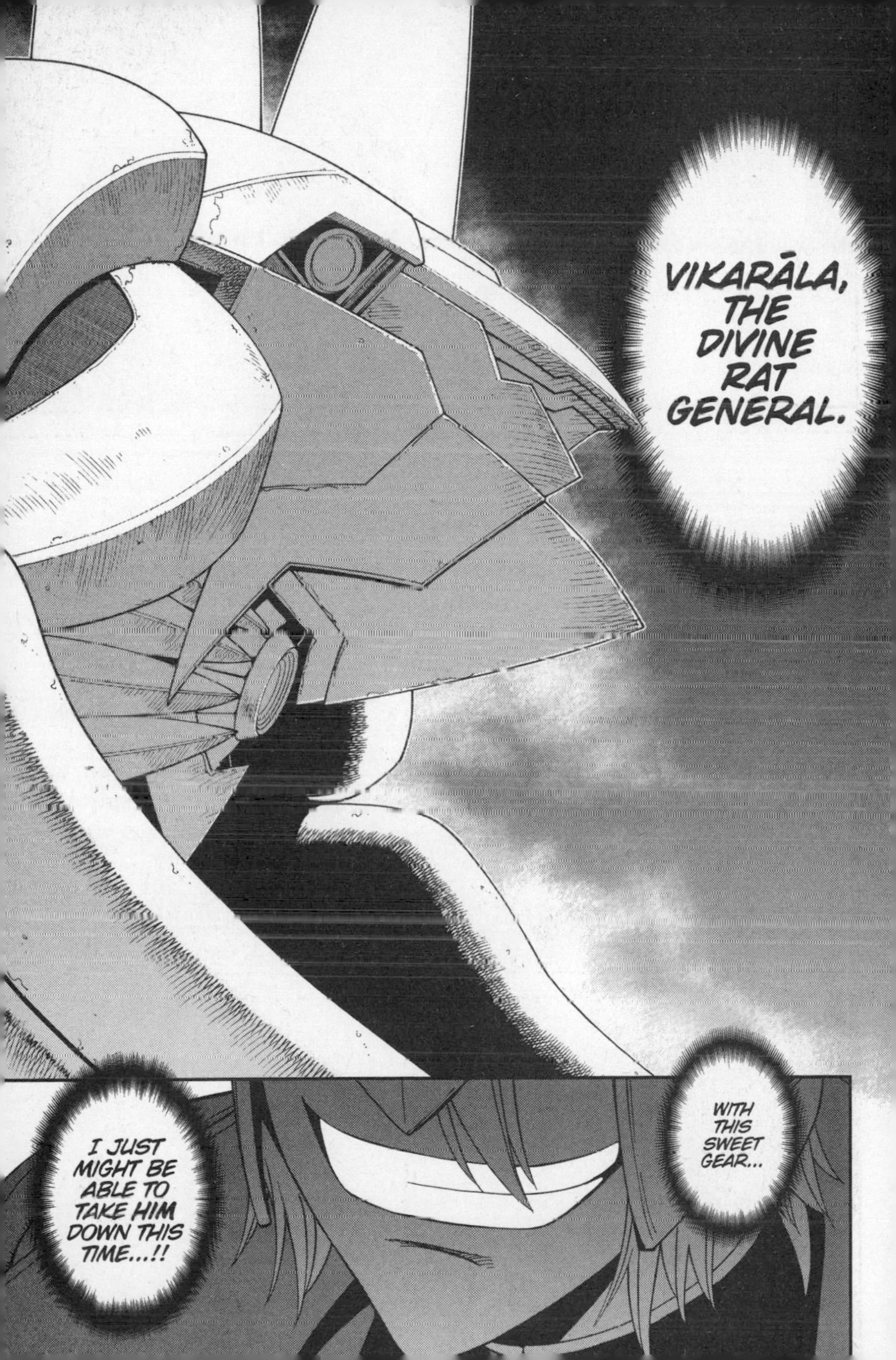
VIKARĀLA, THE DIVINE RAT GENERAL.
WITH THIS SWEET GEAR...
I JUST MIGHT BE ABLE TO TAKE HIM DOWN THIS TIME...!!

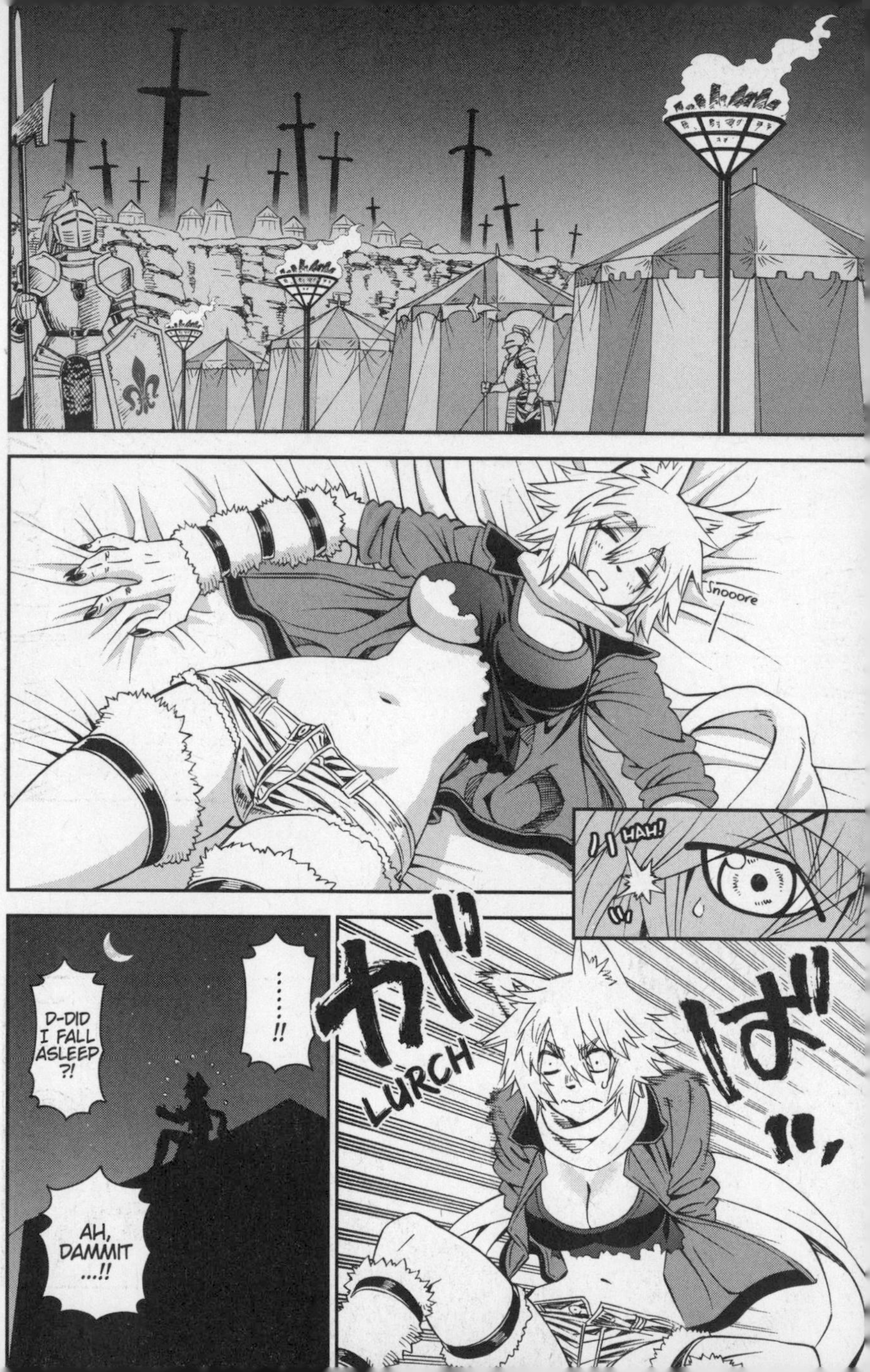

Snooore
HAH!
がば
LURCH
......!!
D-DID I FALL ASLEEP ?!
AH, DAMMIT ...!!

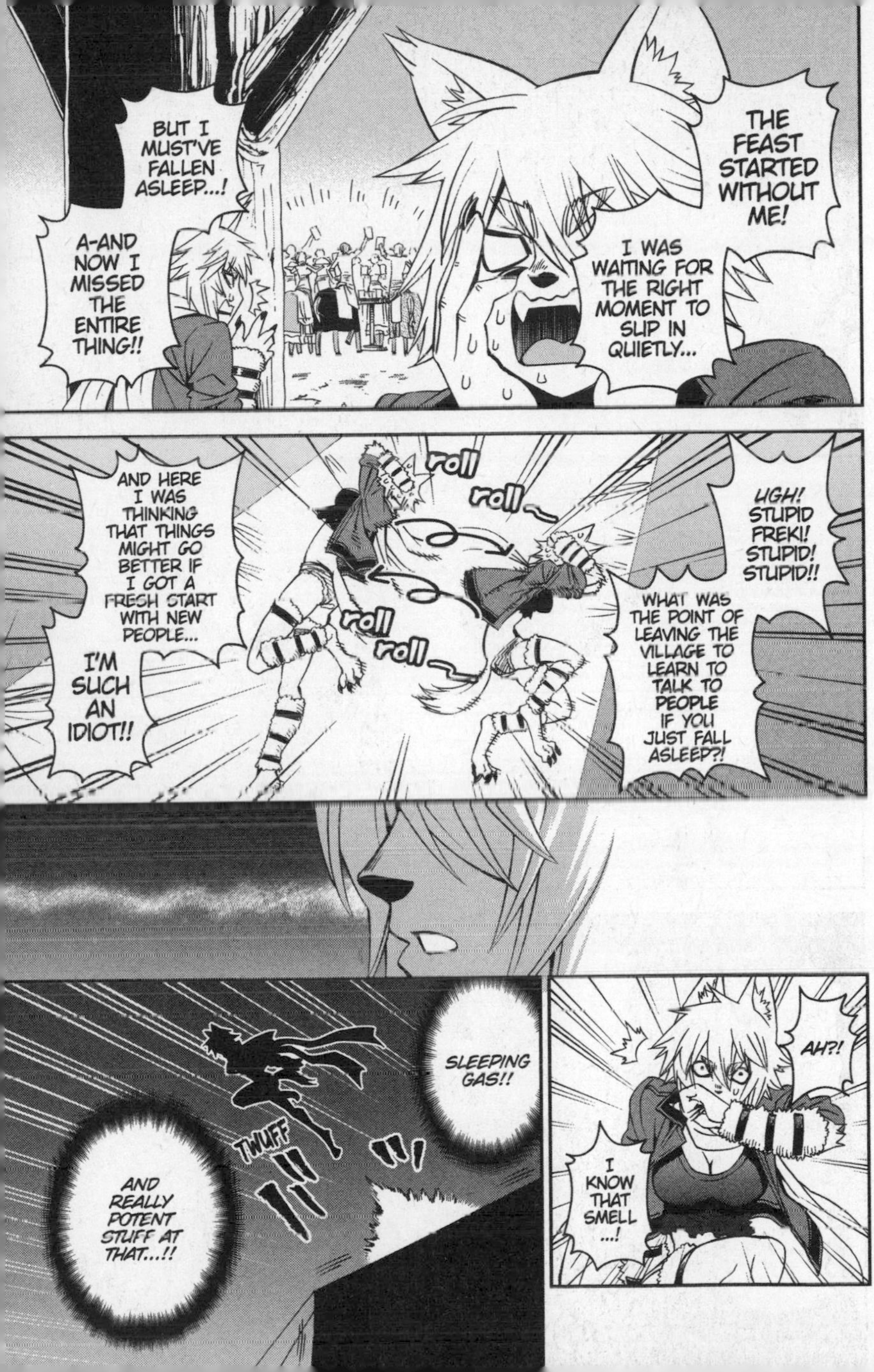
THE FEAST STARTED WITHOUT ME!
I WAS WAITING FOR THE RIGHT MOMENT TO SLIP IN QUIETLY...
BUT I MUST'VE FALLEN ASLEEP...!
A-AND NOW I MISSED THE ENTIRE THING!!
UGH! STUPID FREKI! STUPID! STUPID!!
WHAT WAS THE POINT OF LEAVING THE VILLAGE TO LEARN TO TALK TO PEOPLE IF YOU JUST FALL ASLEEP?!
roll
roll~
roll
roll~
AND HERE I WAS THINKING THAT THINGS MIGHT GO BETTER IF I GOT A FRESH START WITH NEW PEOPLE...
I'M SUCH AN IDIOT!!
AH?!
I KNOW THAT SMELL...!
SLEEPING GAS!!
TWUFF
AND REALLY POTENT STUFF AT THAT...!!

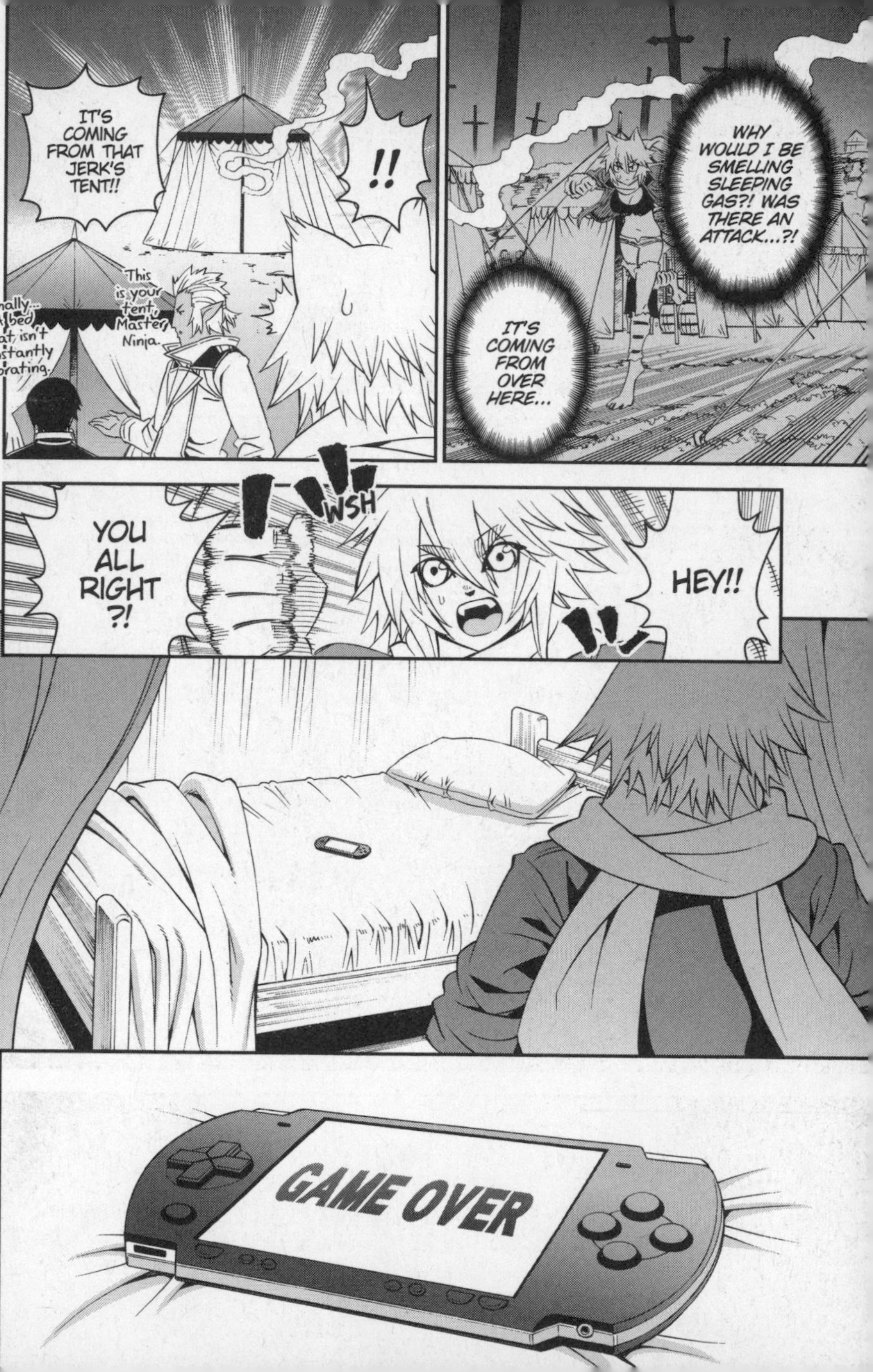
WHY WOULD I BE SMELLING SLEEPING GAS?! WAS THERE AN ATTACK...?!
IT'S COMING FROM OVER HERE...
!!
IT'S COMING FROM THAT JERK'S TENT!!
This is your tent, Master Ninja.
Finally... A bed that isn't constantly vibrating.
WSH
HEY!!
YOU ALL RIGHT?!
GAME OVER

Chapter 28:
The Lamias of Viper Forest

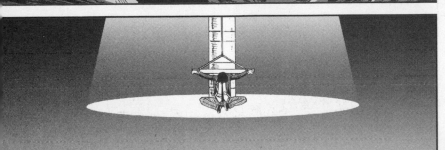

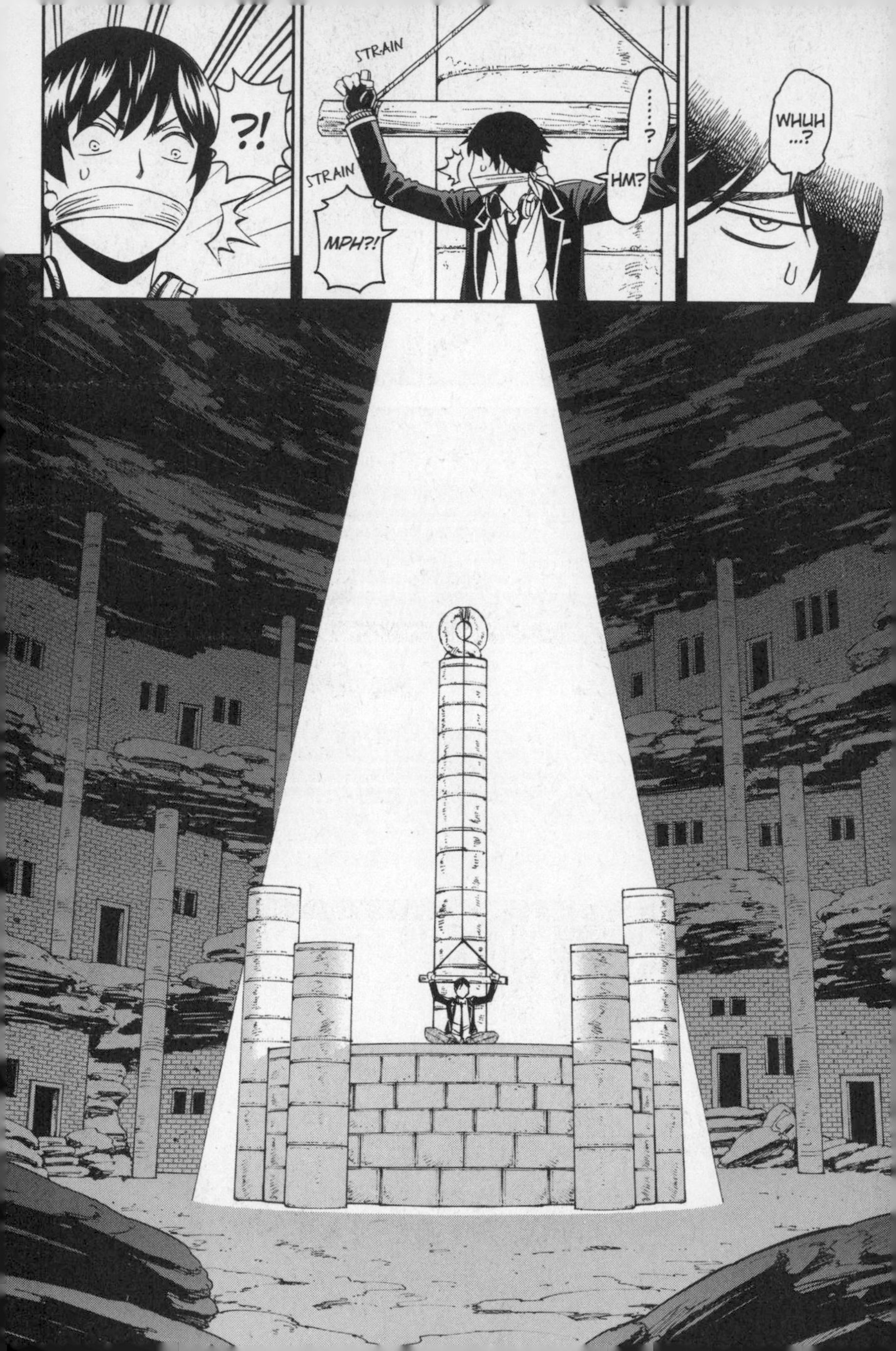
WHUH ...?
......?
HM?
STRAIN
STRAIN
MPH?!
?!

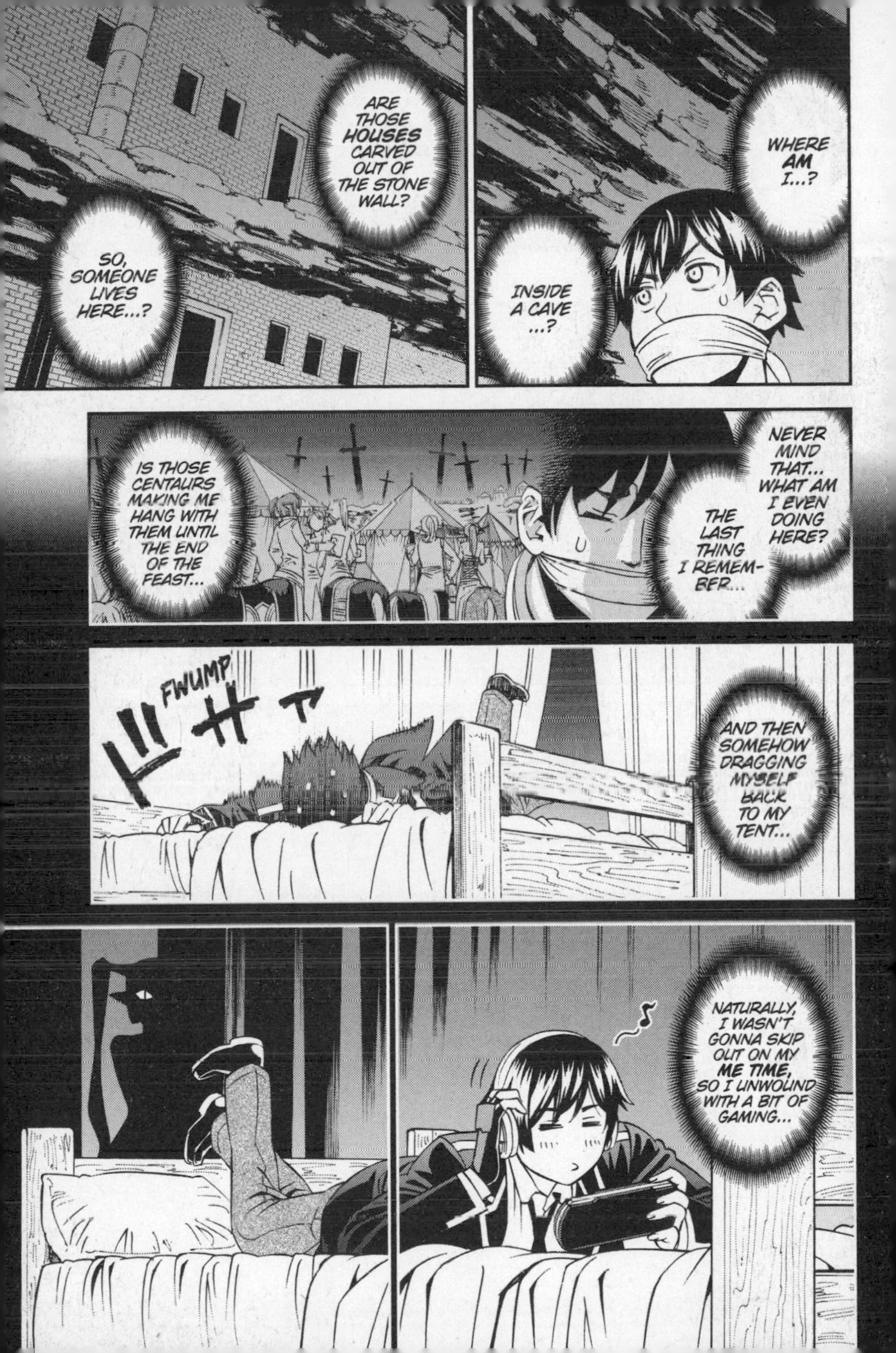
WHERE AM I...?
INSIDE A CAVE ...?
ARE THOSE HOUSES CARVED OUT OF THE STONE WALL?
SO, SOMEONE LIVES HERE...?
NEVER MIND THAT... WHAT AM I EVEN DOING HERE?
THE LAST THING I REMEMBER...
IS THOSE CENTAURS MAKING ME HANG WITH THEM UNTIL THE END OF THE FEAST...
AND THEN SOMEHOW DRAGGING MYSELF BACK TO MY TENT...
ドサッ
FWUMP
NATURALLY, I WASN'T GONNA SKIP OUT ON MY ME TIME, SO I UNWOUND WITH A BIT OF GAMING...

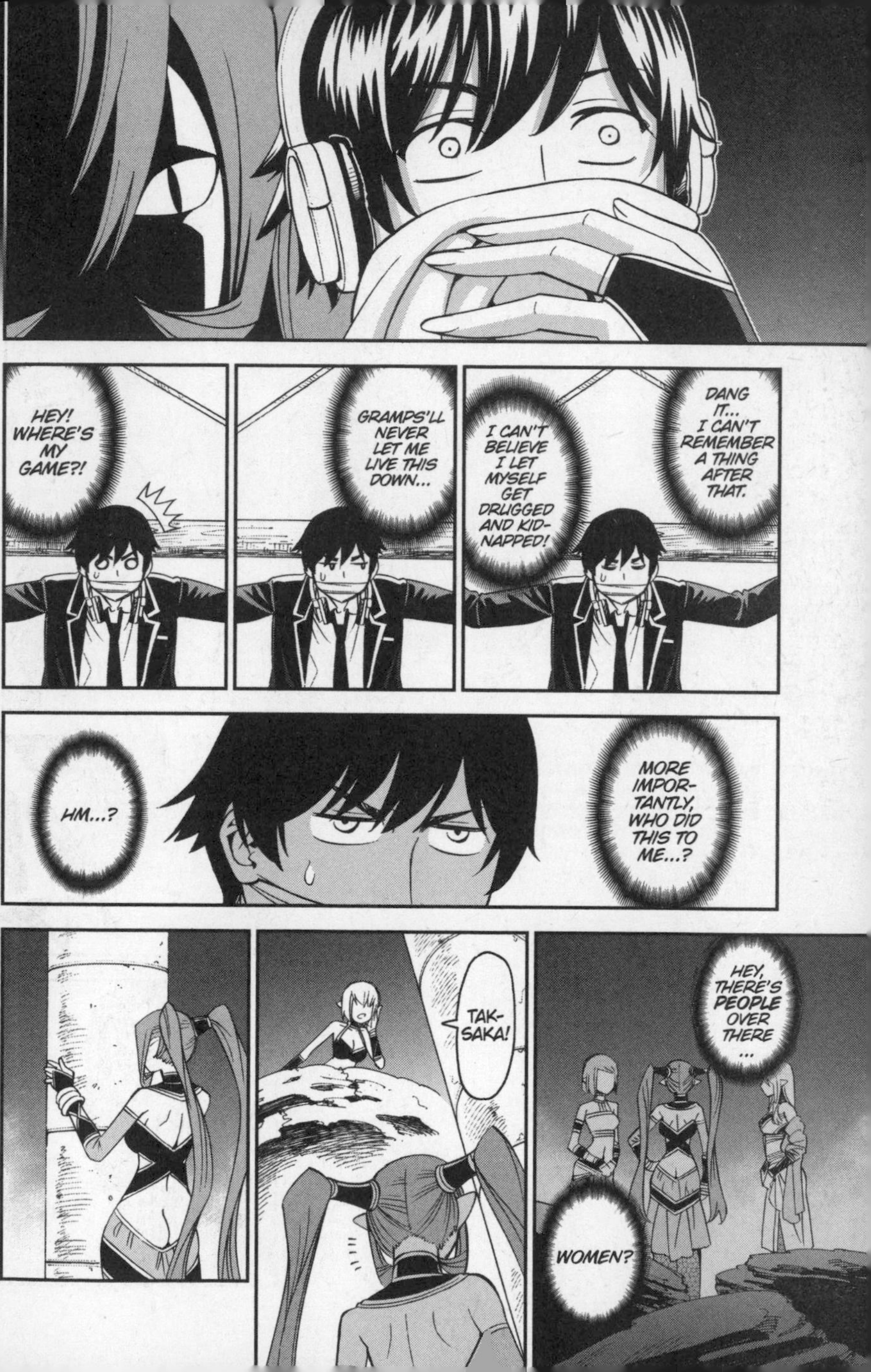
DANG IT... I CAN'T REMEMBER A THING AFTER THAT.
I CAN'T BELIEVE I LET MYSELF GET DRUGGED AND KID-NAPPED!
GRAMPS'LL NEVER LET ME LIVE THIS DOWN...
HEY! WHERE'S MY GAME?!
MORE IMPOR-TANTLY, WHO DID THIS TO ME...?
HM...?
HEY, THERE'S PEOPLE OVER THERE ...
WOMEN?
TAK-SAKA!

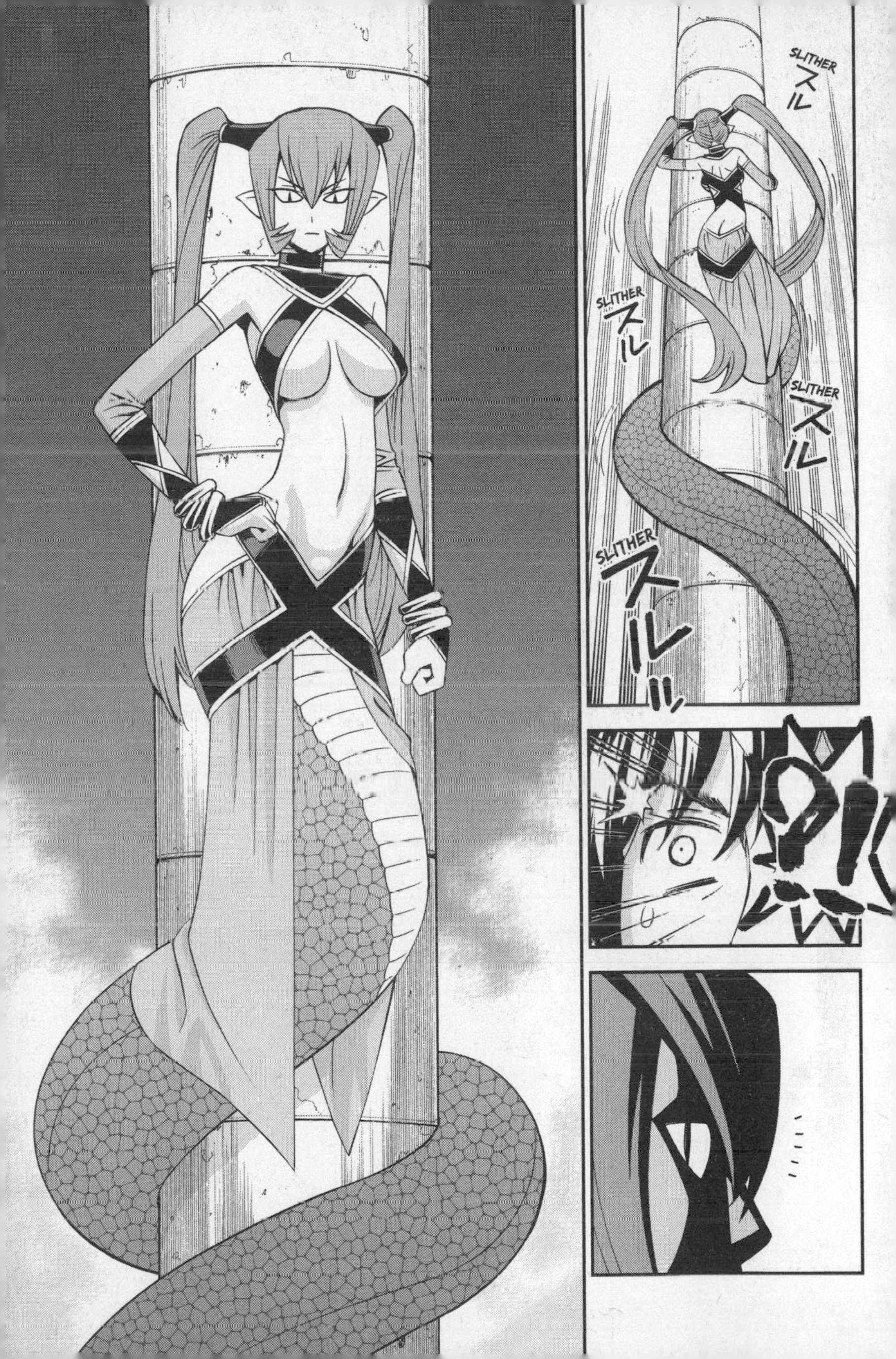
SLITHER
スル
SLITHER
スル
SLITHER
スル
SLITHER
スルルッ
?!
....

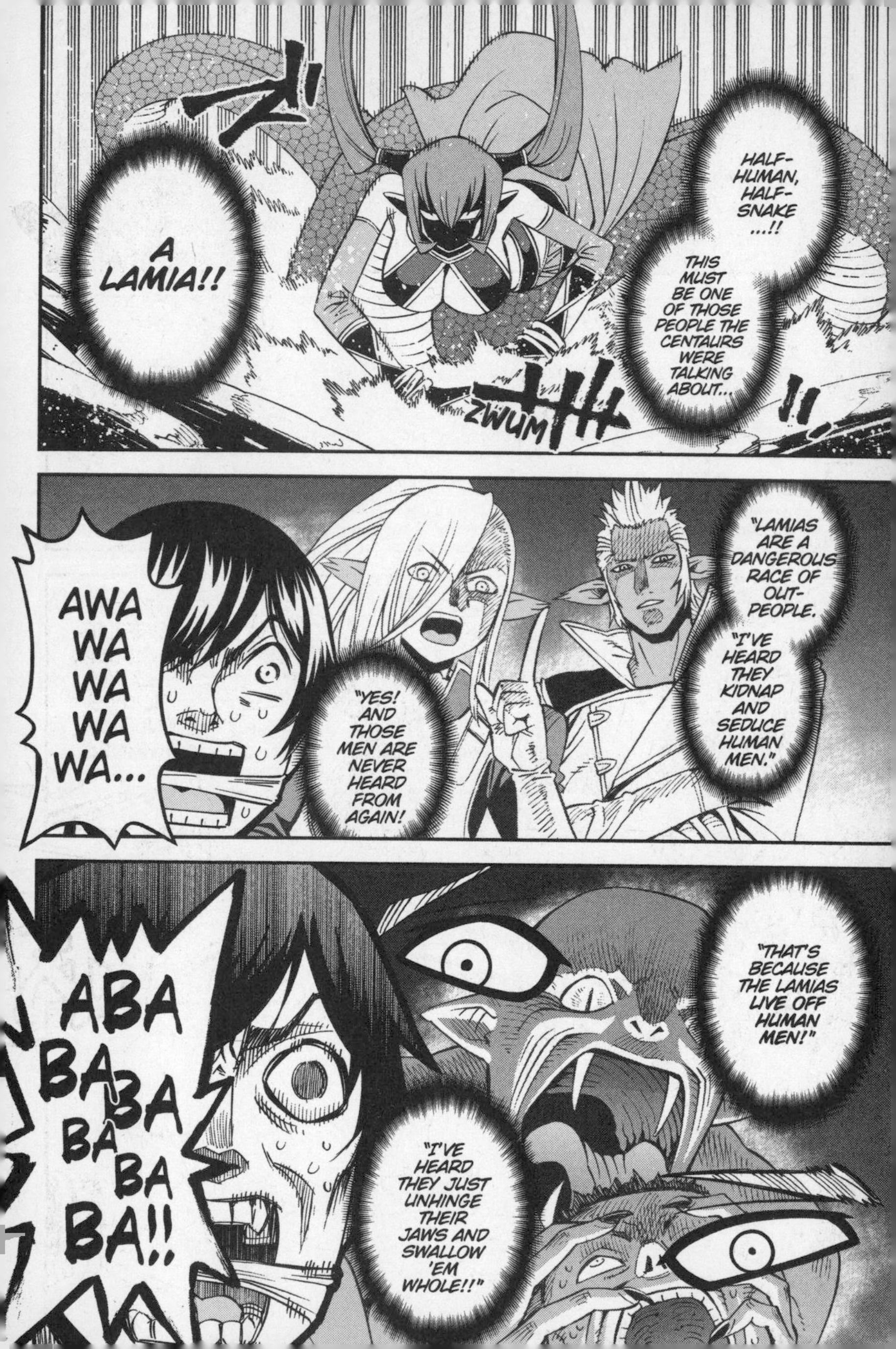

HALF-HUMAN, HALF-SNAKE ...!!
THIS MUST BE ONE OF THOSE PEOPLE THE CENTAURS WERE TALKING ABOUT...
ZWUM
A LAMIA!!
"LAMIAS ARE A DANGEROUS RACE OF OUT-PEOPLE.
"I'VE HEARD THEY KIDNAP AND SEDUCE HUMAN MEN."
"YES! AND THOSE MEN ARE NEVER HEARD FROM AGAIN!
AWA WA WA WA WA WA...
"THAT'S BECAUSE THE LAMIAS LIVE OFF HUMAN MEN!"
"I'VE HEARD THEY JUST UNHINGE THEIR JAWS AND SWALLOW 'EM WHOLE!!"
ABA BA BA BA BA BA BA!!

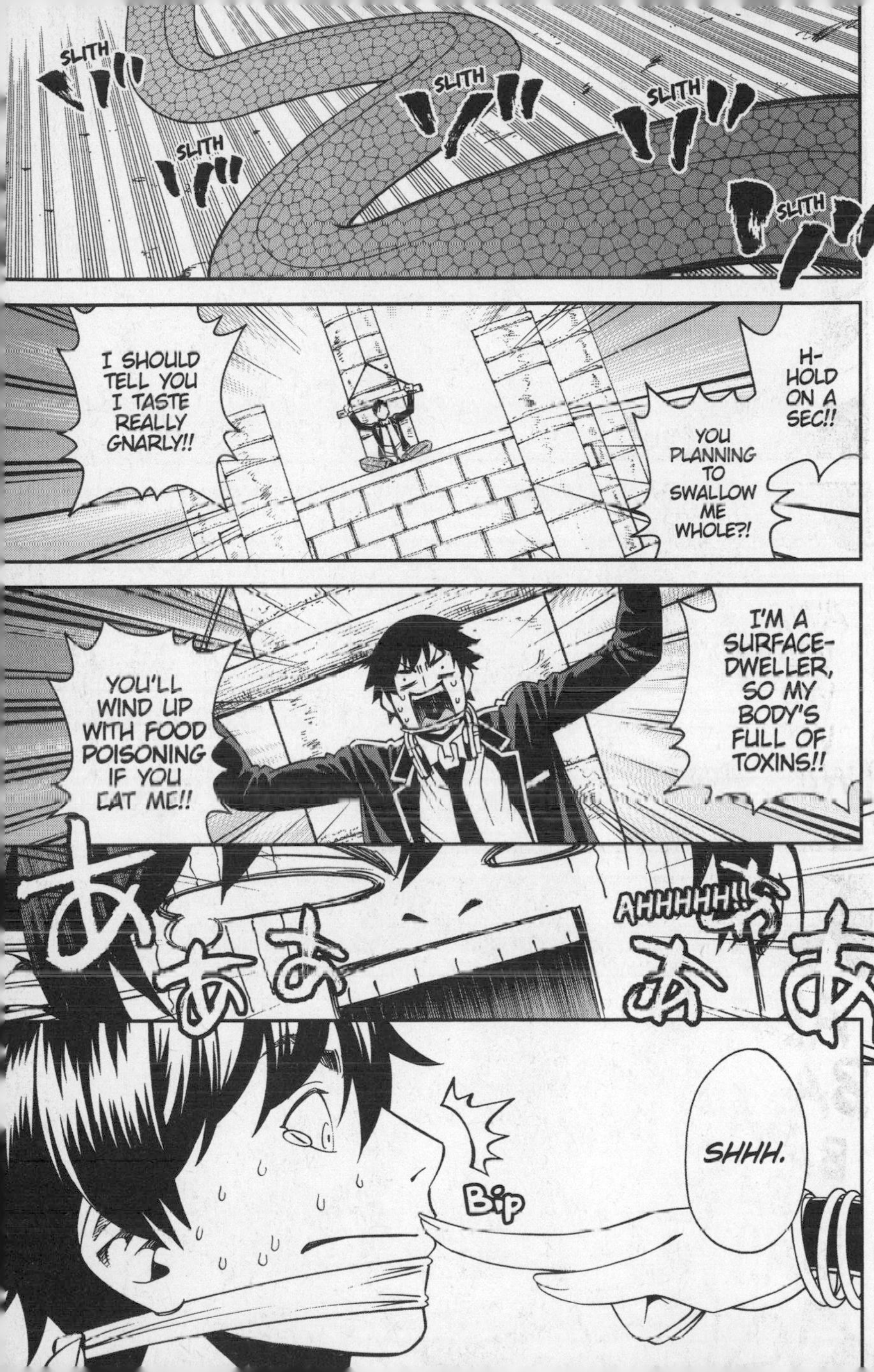
SLITH
SLITH
SLITH
SLITH
SLITH
H-HOLD ON A SEC!!
YOU PLANNING TO SWALLOW ME WHOLE?!
I SHOULD TELL YOU I TASTE REALLY GNARLY!!
I'M A SURFACE-DWELLER, SO MY BODY'S FULL OF TOXINS!!
YOU'LL WIND UP WITH FOOD POISONING IF YOU EAT ME!!
AHHHHH!!
ああああああ
SHHH.
Bip

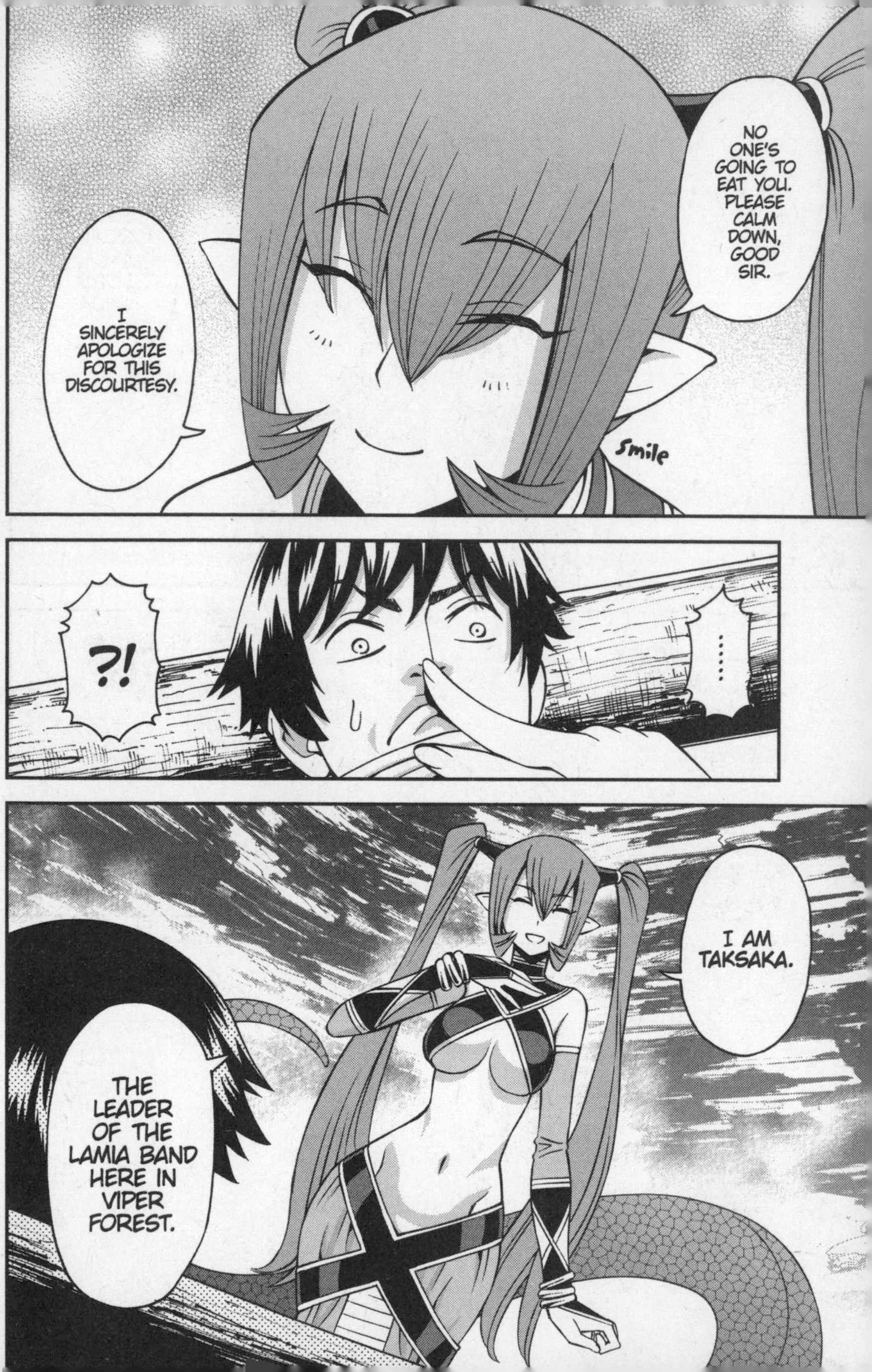
NO ONE'S GOING TO EAT YOU. PLEASE CALM DOWN, GOOD SIR.
I SINCERELY APOLOGIZE FOR THIS DISCOURTESY.
Smile
......
?!
I AM TAKSAKA.
THE LEADER OF THE LAMIA BAND HERE IN VIPER FOREST.

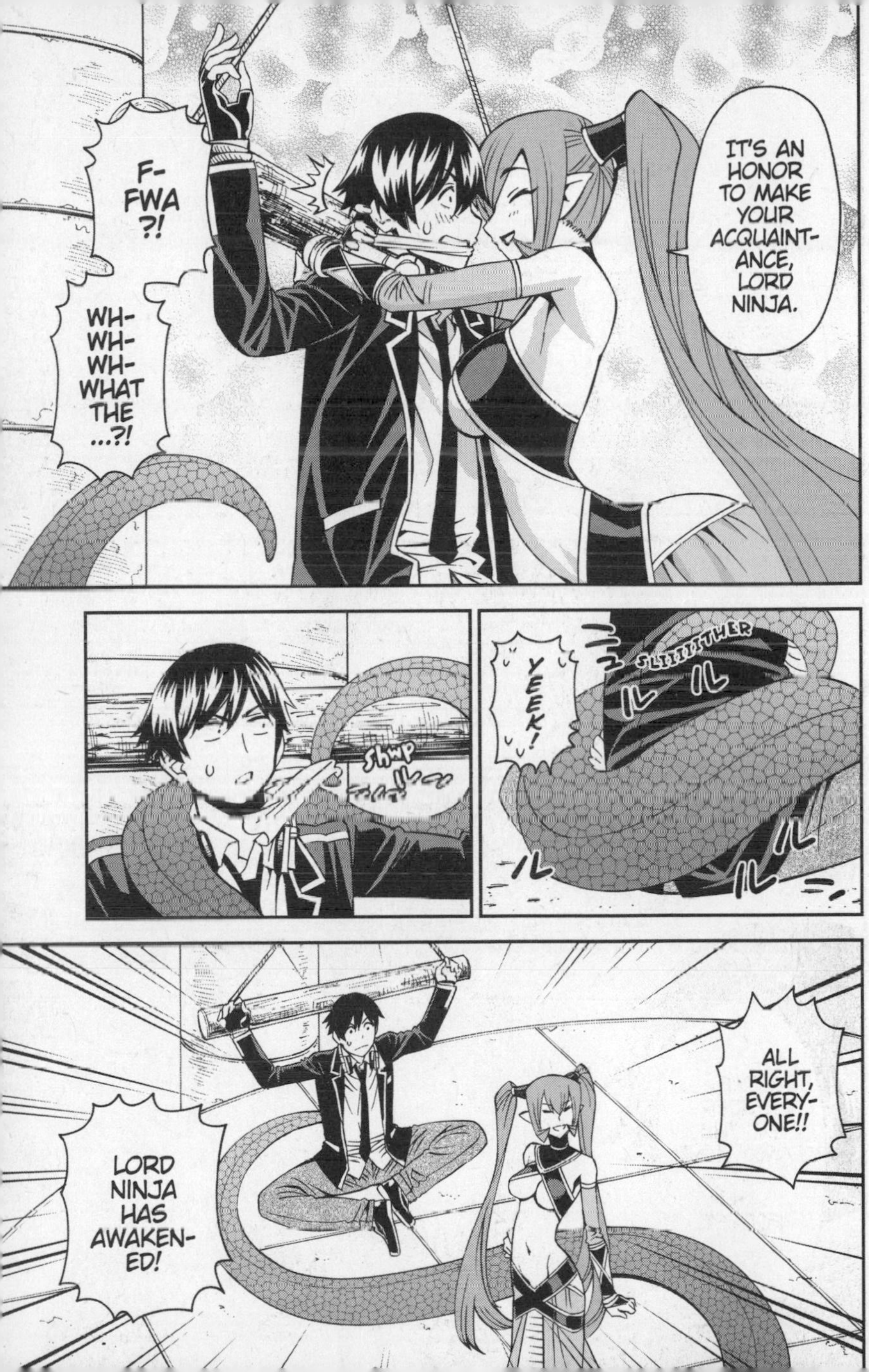
IT'S AN HONOR TO MAKE YOUR ACQUAINTANCE, LORD NINJA.
F-FWA?!
WH-WH-WH-WHAT THE ...?!
YEEEK!
SLIIIIITHER
shwp
ALL RIGHT, EVERYONE!!
LORD NINJA HAS AWAKENED!

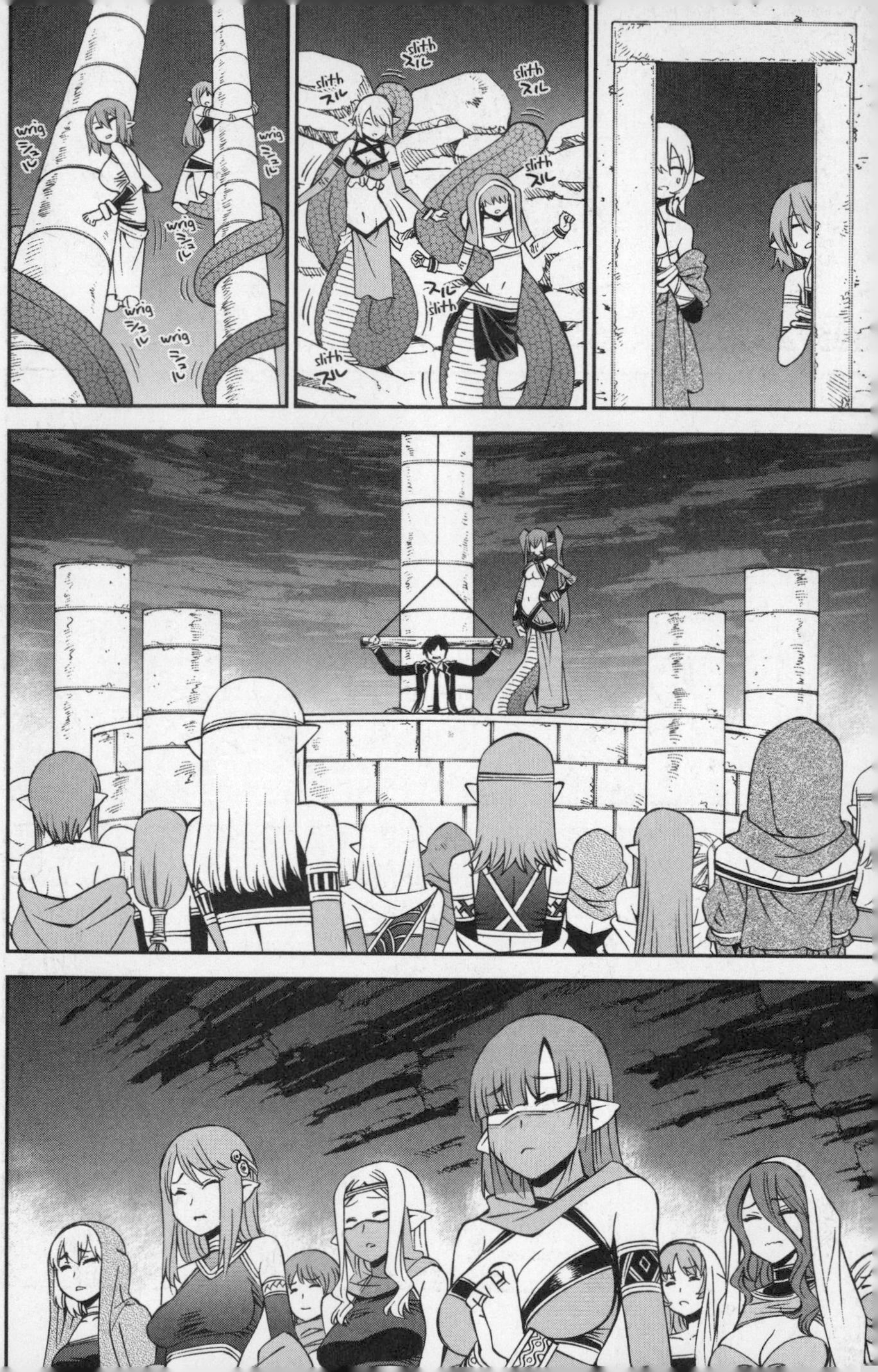
slith スル
slith スル
slith スル
slith スル
スル slith
slith スル
wrig
wrig
wrig
wrig
wrig

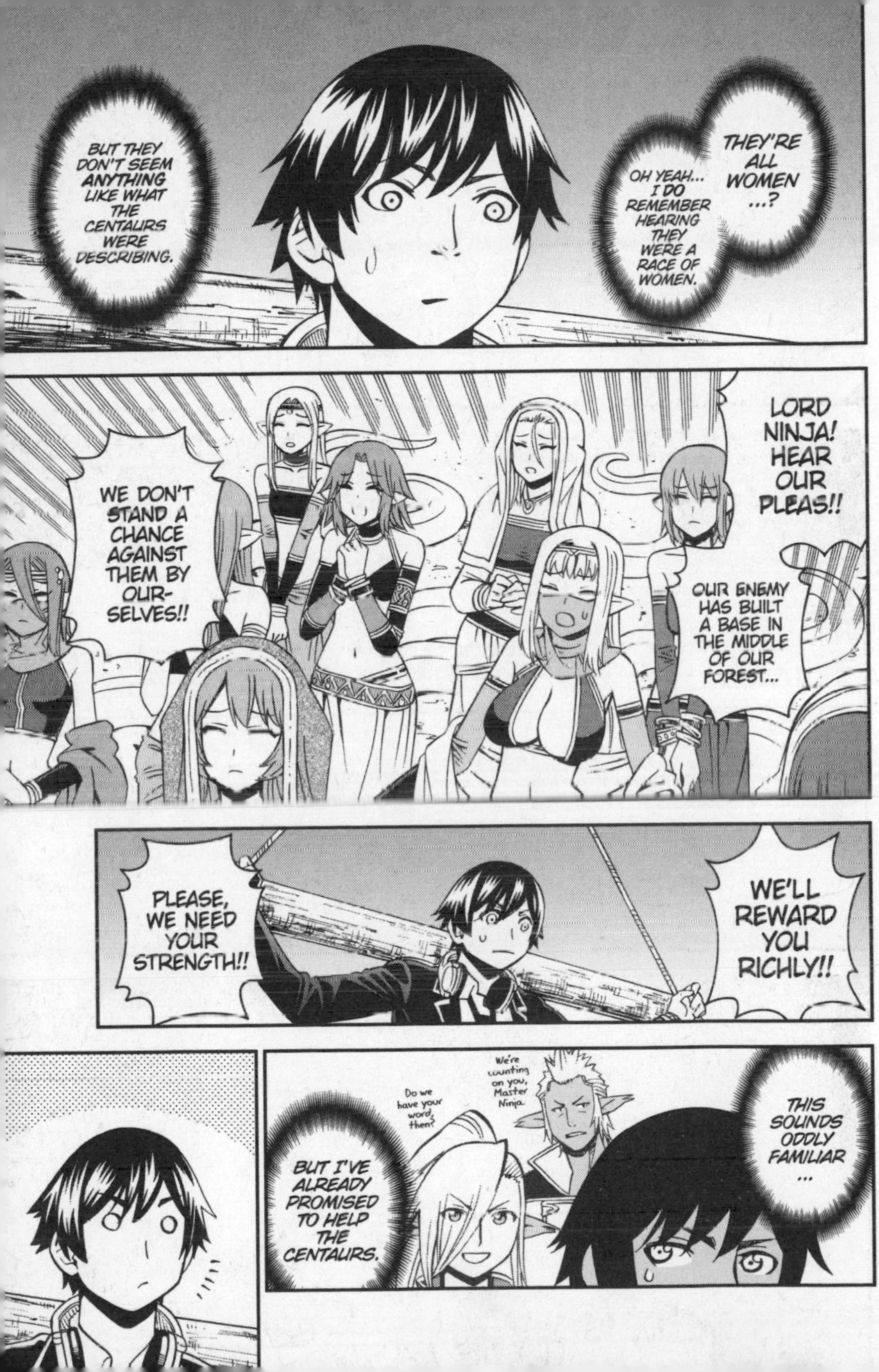
THEY'RE ALL WOMEN ...?
OH YEAH... I DO REMEMBER HEARING THEY WERE A RACE OF WOMEN.
BUT THEY DON'T SEEM ANYTHING LIKE WHAT THE CENTAURS WERE DESCRIBING.
LORD NINJA! HEAR OUR PLEAS!!
OUR ENEMY HAS BUILT A BASE IN THE MIDDLE OF OUR FOREST...
WE DON'T STAND A CHANCE AGAINST THEM BY OUR-SELVES!!
WE'LL REWARD YOU RICHLY!!
PLEASE, WE NEED YOUR STRENGTH!!
THIS SOUNDS ODDLY FAMILIAR ...
We're counting on you, Master Ninja.
Do we have your word, then?
BUT I'VE ALREADY PROMISED TO HELP THE CENTAURS.

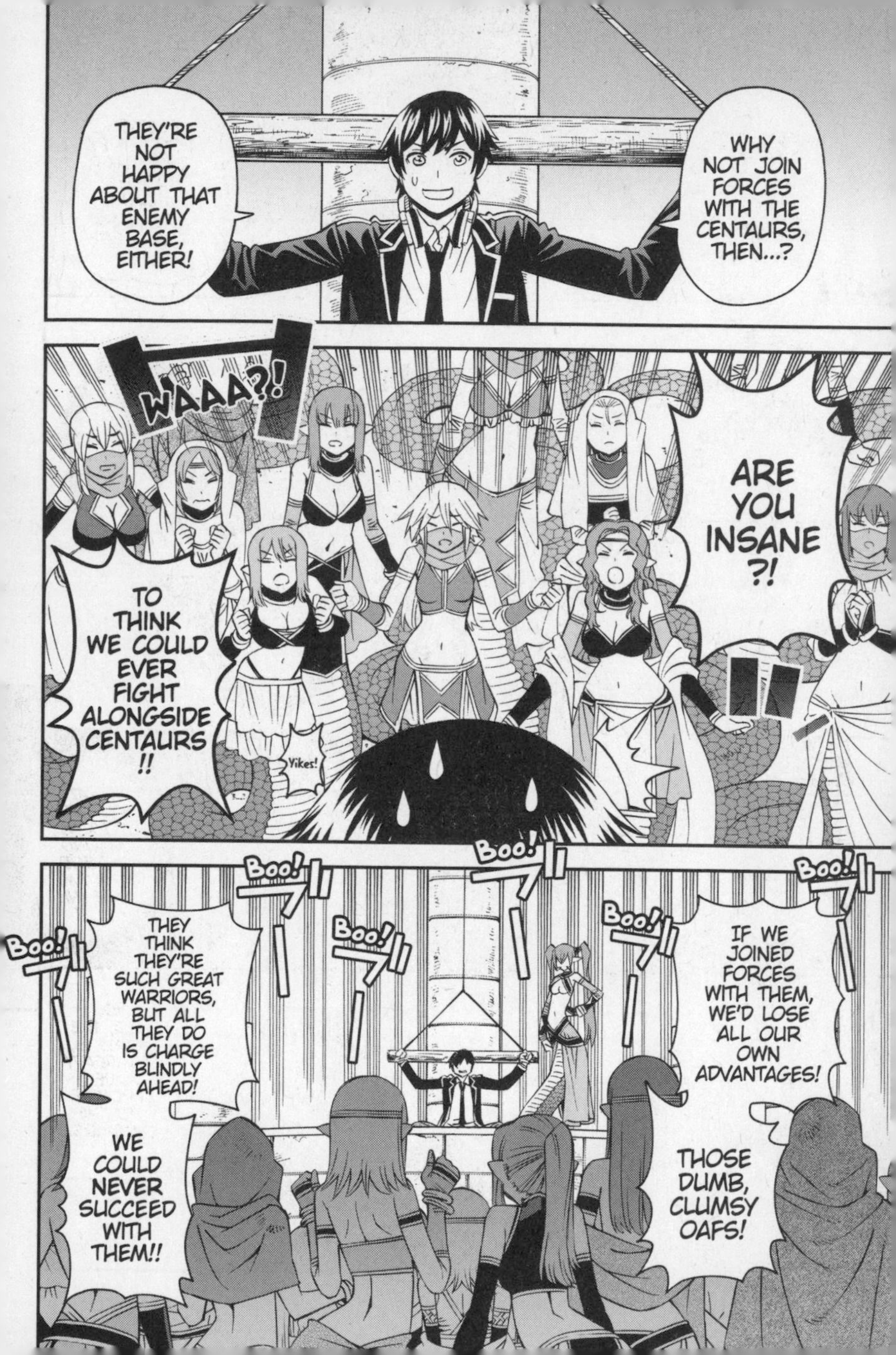
THEY'RE NOT HAPPY ABOUT THAT ENEMY BASE, EITHER!
WHY NOT JOIN FORCES WITH THE CENTAURS, THEN...?
ARE YOU INSANE?!
WAAA?!
TO THINK WE COULD EVER FIGHT ALONGSIDE CENTAURS!!
Yikes!
Boo!
Boo!
Boo!
IF WE JOINED FORCES WITH THEM, WE'D LOSE ALL OUR OWN ADVANTAGES!
Boo!
Boo!
THEY THINK THEY'RE SUCH GREAT WARRIORS, BUT ALL THEY DO IS CHARGE BLINDLY AHEAD!
Boo!
THOSE DUMB, CLUMSY OAFS!
WE COULD NEVER SUCCEED WITH THEM!!

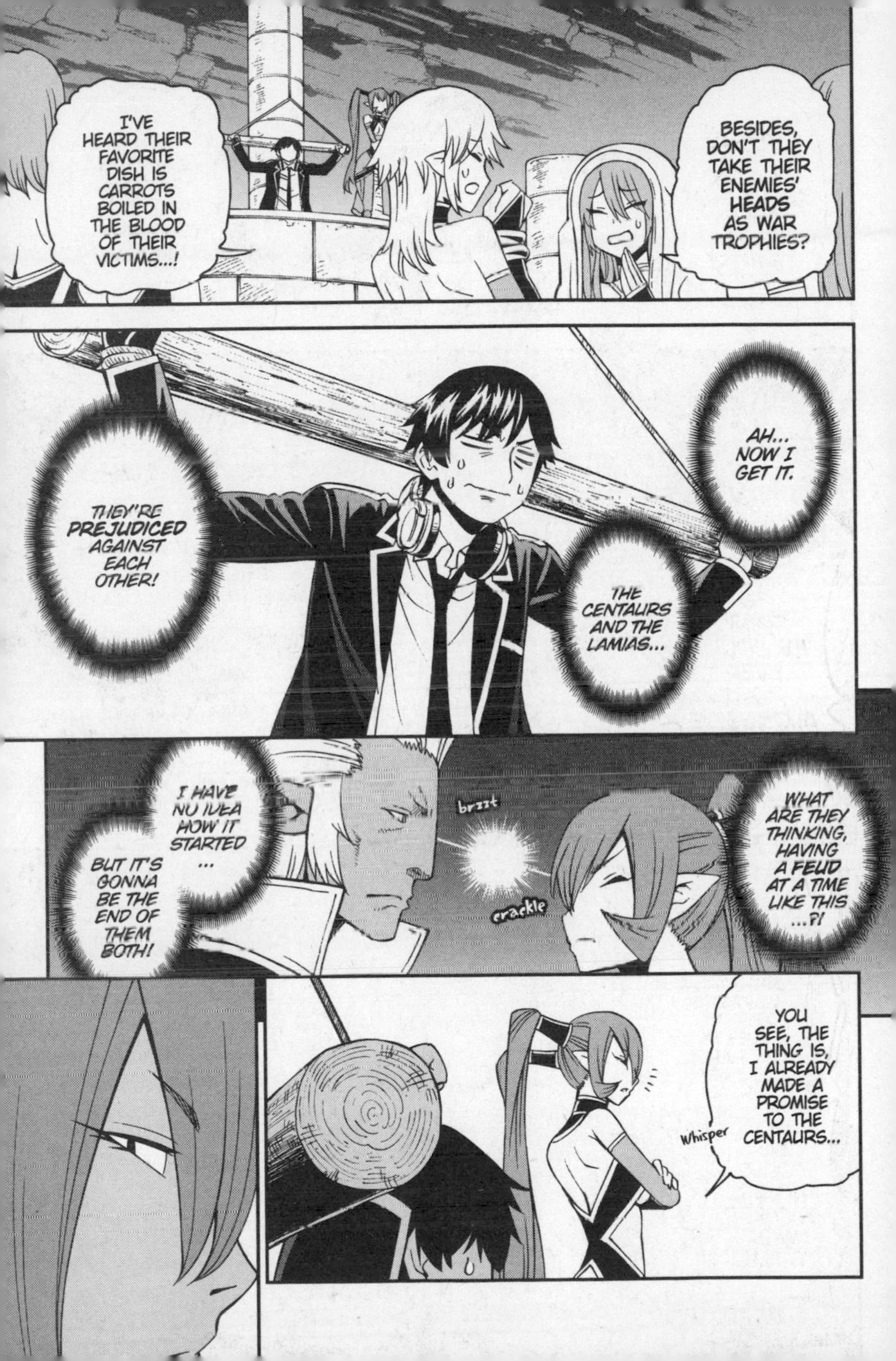
BESIDES, DON'T THEY TAKE THEIR ENEMIES' HEADS AS WAR TROPHIES?
I'VE HEARD THEIR FAVORITE DISH IS CARROTS BOILED IN THE BLOOD OF THEIR VICTIMS...!
AH... NOW I GET IT.
THE CENTAURS AND THE LAMIAS...
THEY'RE PREJUDICED AGAINST EACH OTHER!
WHAT ARE THEY THINKING, HAVING A FEUD AT A TIME LIKE THIS...?!
brzzt
crackle
I HAVE NO IDEA HOW IT STARTED...
BUT IT'S GONNA BE THE END OF THEM BOTH!
YOU SEE, THE THING IS, I ALREADY MADE A PROMISE TO THE CENTAURS...
Whisper

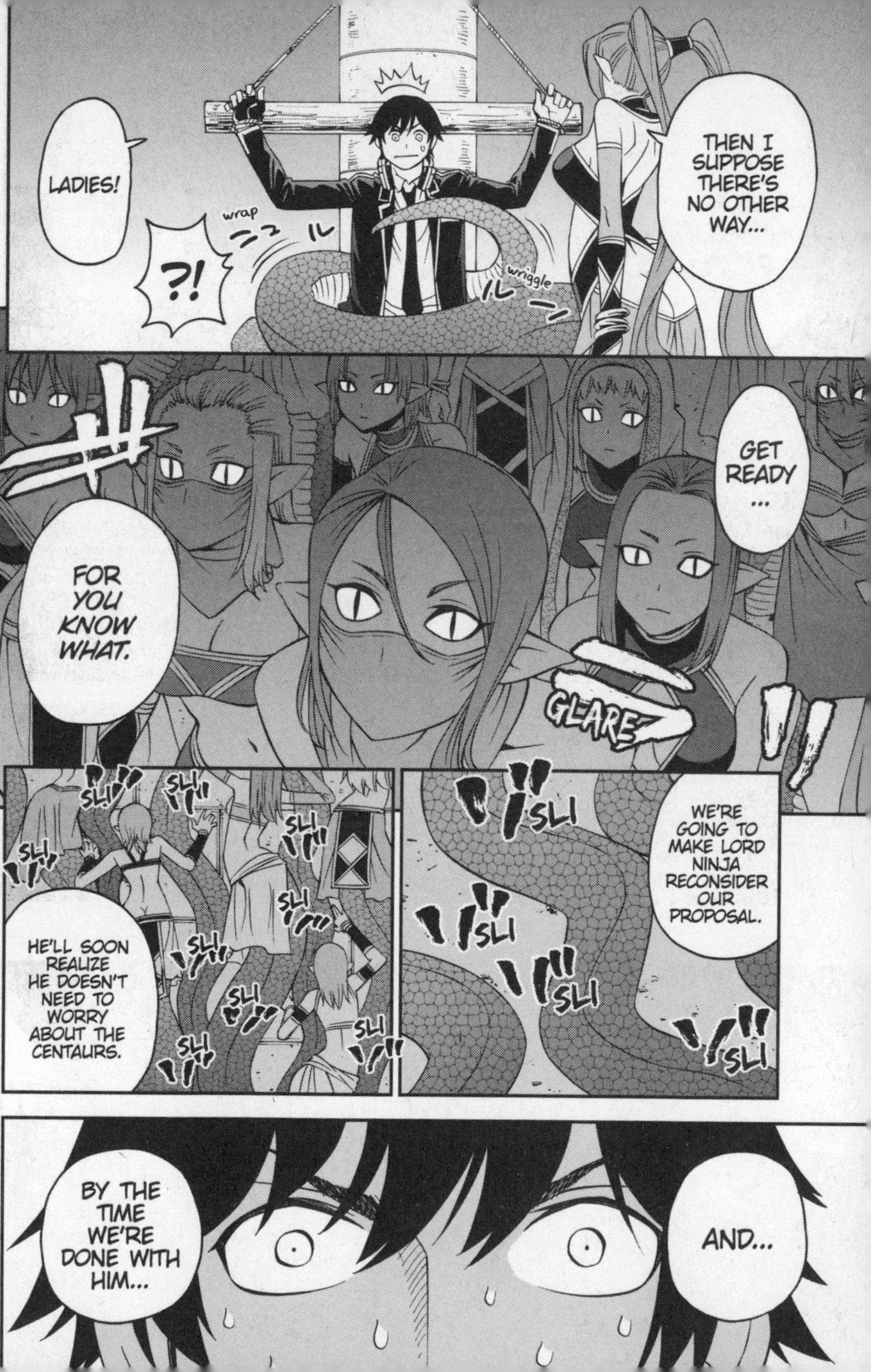
THEN I SUPPOSE THERE'S NO OTHER WAY...
LADIES!
wrap
?!
wriggle
GET READY ...
GLARE
FOR YOU KNOW WHAT.
WE'RE GOING TO MAKE LORD NINJA RECONSIDER OUR PROPOSAL.
SLI
SLI
SLI
SLI
SLI!
SLI
SLI
SLI
SLI
SLI
SLI
SLI
SLI
HE'LL SOON REALIZE HE DOESN'T NEED TO WORRY ABOUT THE CENTAURS.
AND...
BY THE TIME WE'RE DONE WITH HIM...

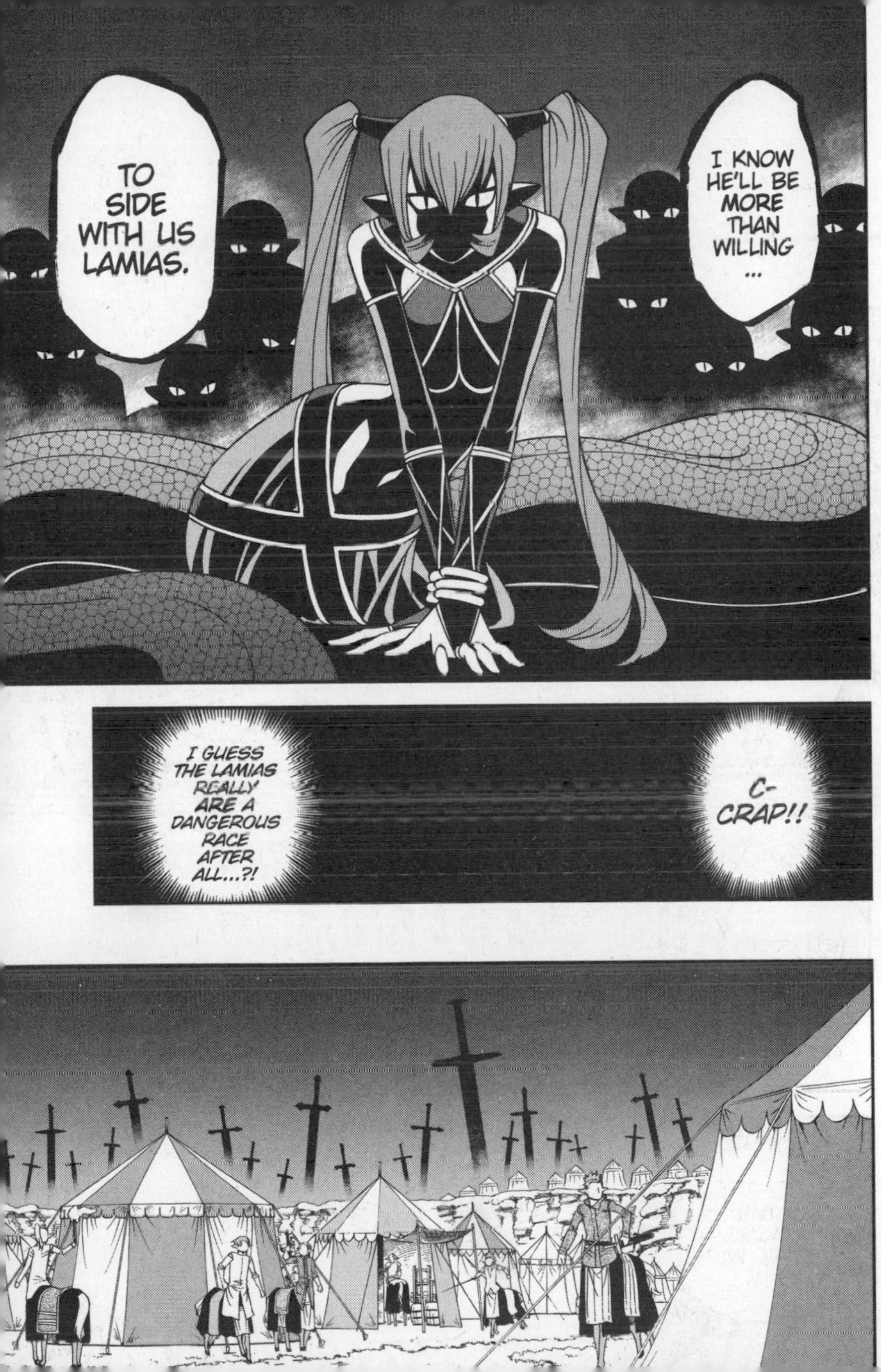
I KNOW HE'LL BE MORE THAN WILLING ...
TO SIDE WITH US LAMIAS.
C- CRAP!!
I GUESS THE LAMIAS REALLY ARE A DANGEROUS RACE AFTER ALL...?!

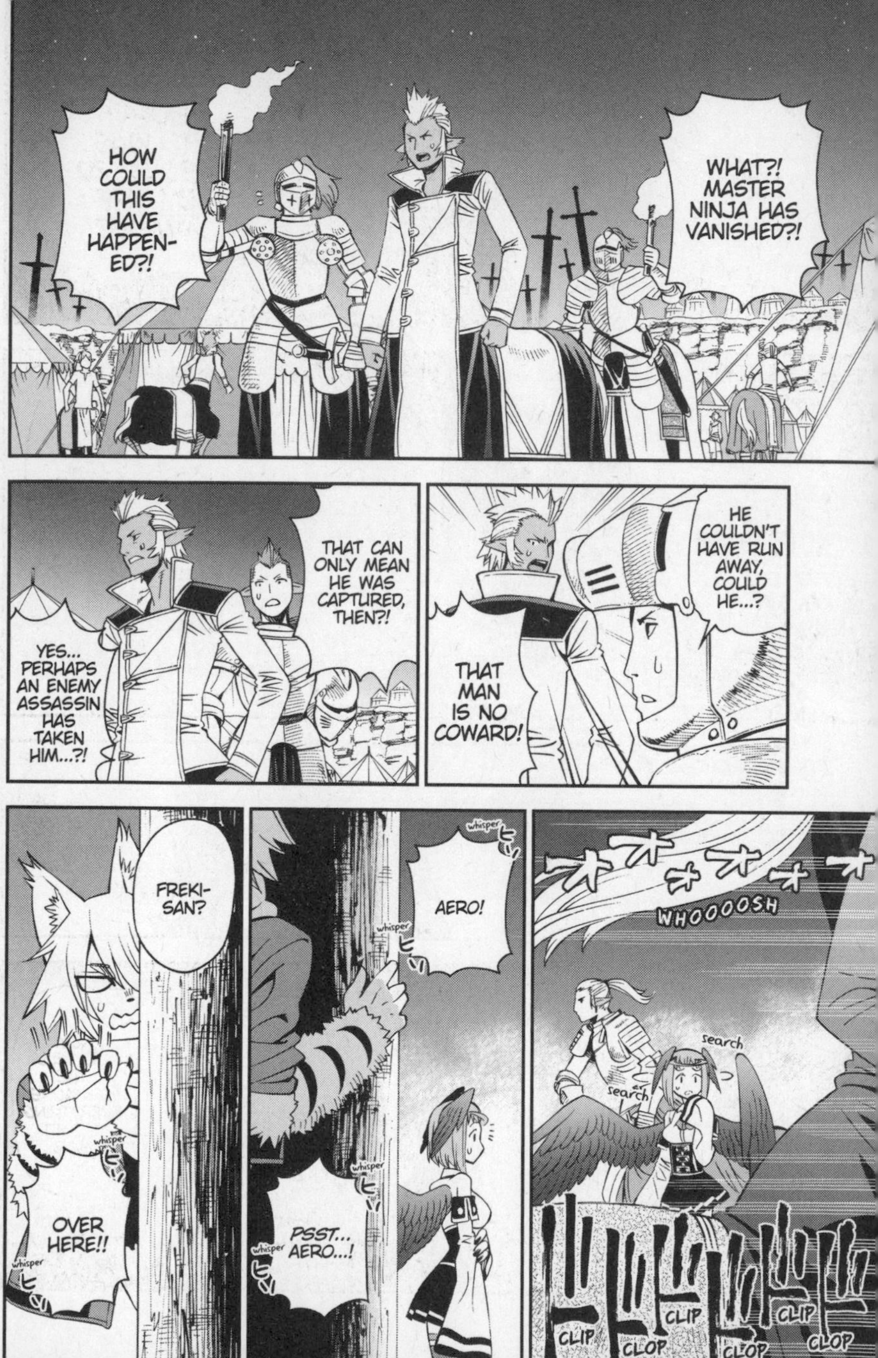
WHAT?! MASTER NINJA HAS VANISHED?!
HOW COULD THIS HAVE HAPPEN-ED?!
HE COULDN'T HAVE RUN AWAY, COULD HE...?
THAT MAN IS NO COWARD!
THAT CAN ONLY MEAN HE WAS CAPTURED, THEN?!
YES... PERHAPS AN ENEMY ASSASSIN HAS TAKEN HIM...?!
WHOOOOSH
search
search
CLIP CLOP CLIP CLOP CLIP CLOP
whisper
AERO!
whisper
whisper
PSST... AERO...!
whisper
FREKI-SAN?
whisper
OVER HERE!!
whisper

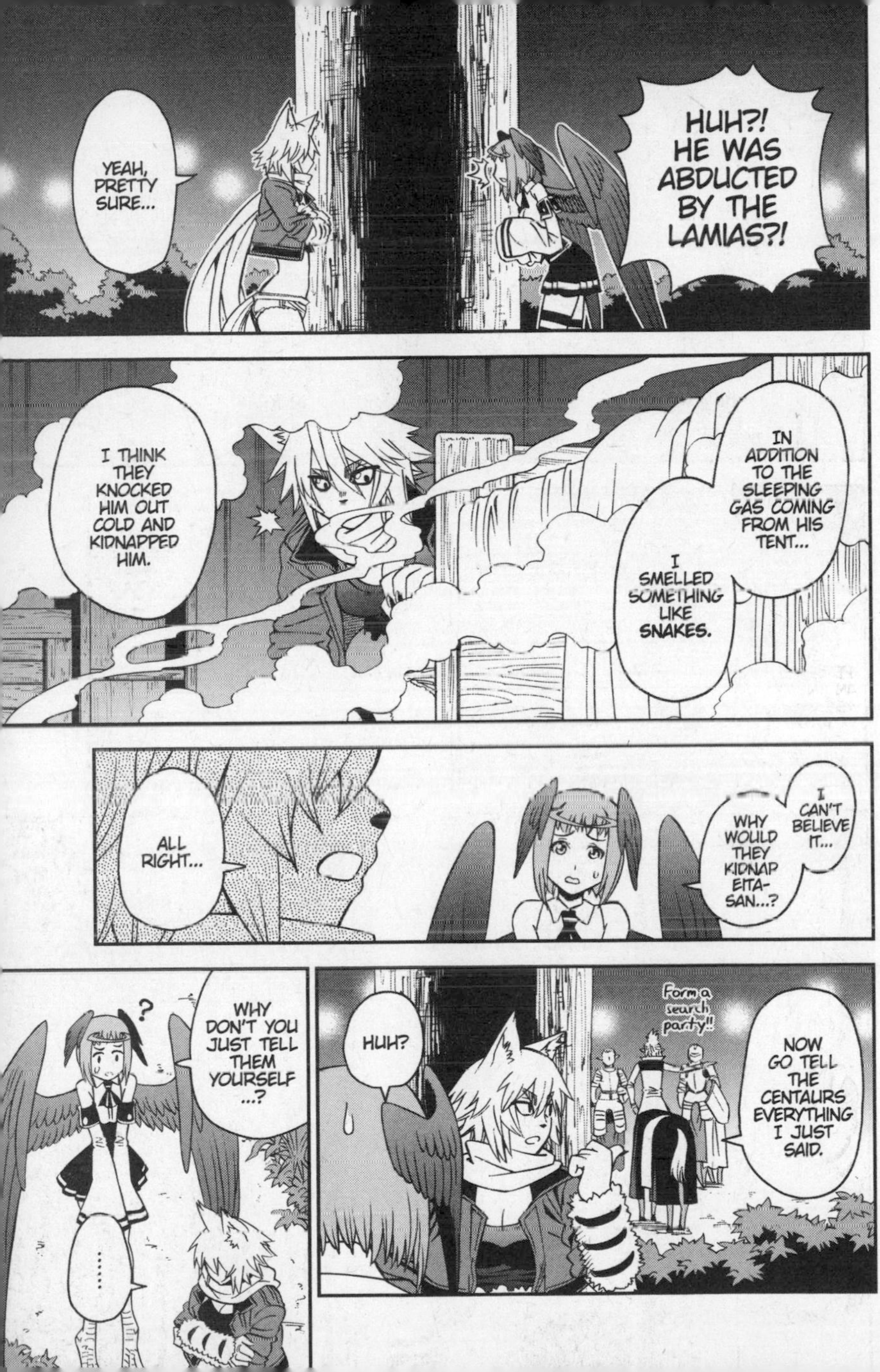
HUH?! HE WAS ABDUCTED BY THE LAMIAS?!
YEAH, PRETTY SURE...
IN ADDITION TO THE SLEEPING GAS COMING FROM HIS TENT...
I SMELLED SOMETHING LIKE SNAKES.
I THINK THEY KNOCKED HIM OUT COLD AND KIDNAPPED HIM.
I CAN'T BELIEVE IT...
WHY WOULD THEY KIDNAP EITA-SAN...?
ALL RIGHT...
NOW GO TELL THE CENTAURS EVERYTHING I JUST SAID.
Form a search party!!
HUH?
WHY DON'T YOU JUST TELL THEM YOURSELF...?
?
......

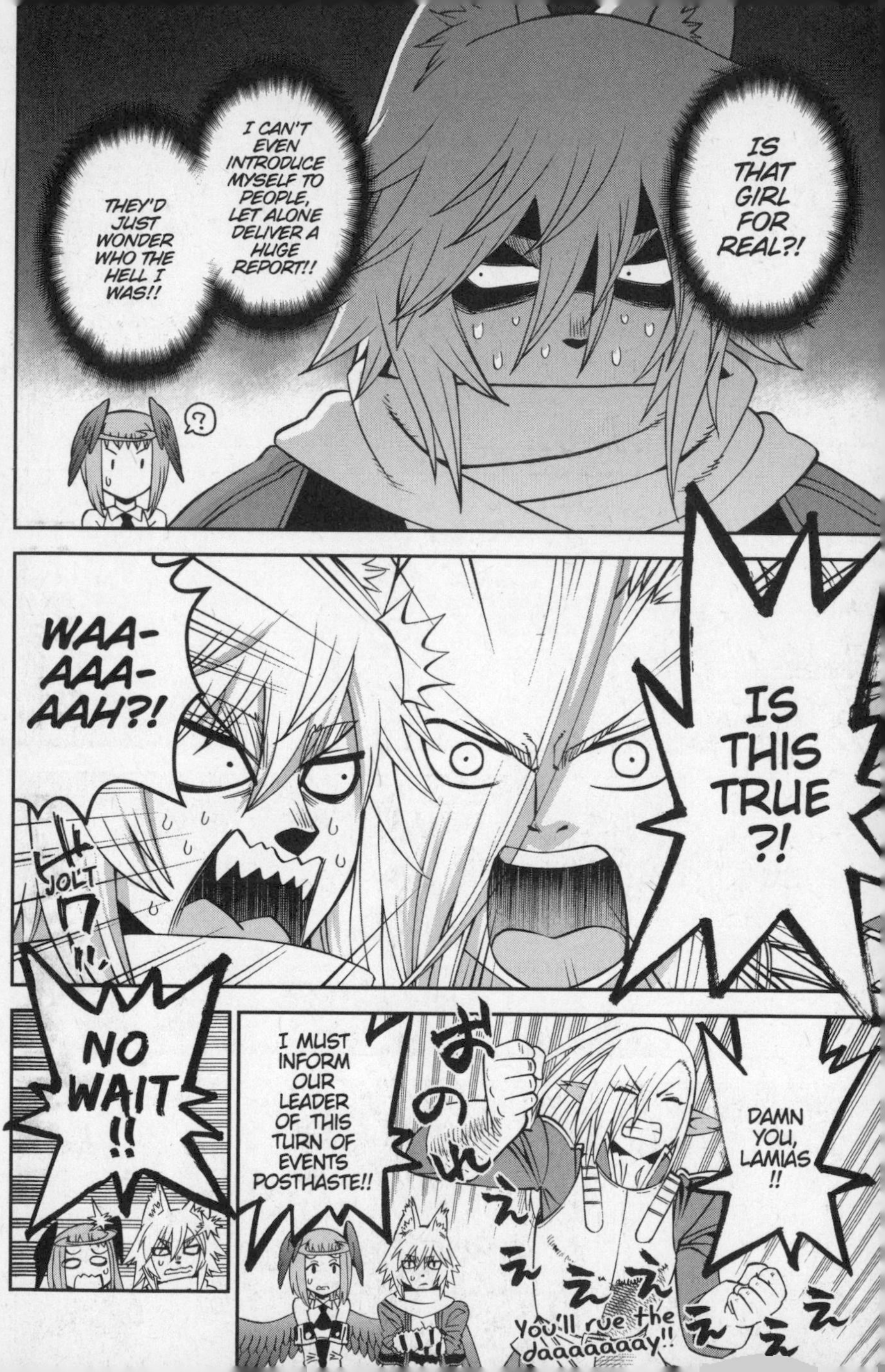
IS THAT GIRL FOR REAL?!
I CAN'T EVEN INTRODUCE MYSELF TO PEOPLE, LET ALONE DELIVER A HUGE REPORT!!
THEY'D JUST WONDER WHO THE HELL I WAS!!
?
IS THIS TRUE?!
WAA-AAA-AAH?!
JOLT
DAMN YOU, LAMIAS!!
I MUST INFORM OUR LEADER OF THIS TURN OF EVENTS POSTHASTE!!
You'll rue the daaaaaaaay!!
NO WAIT!!

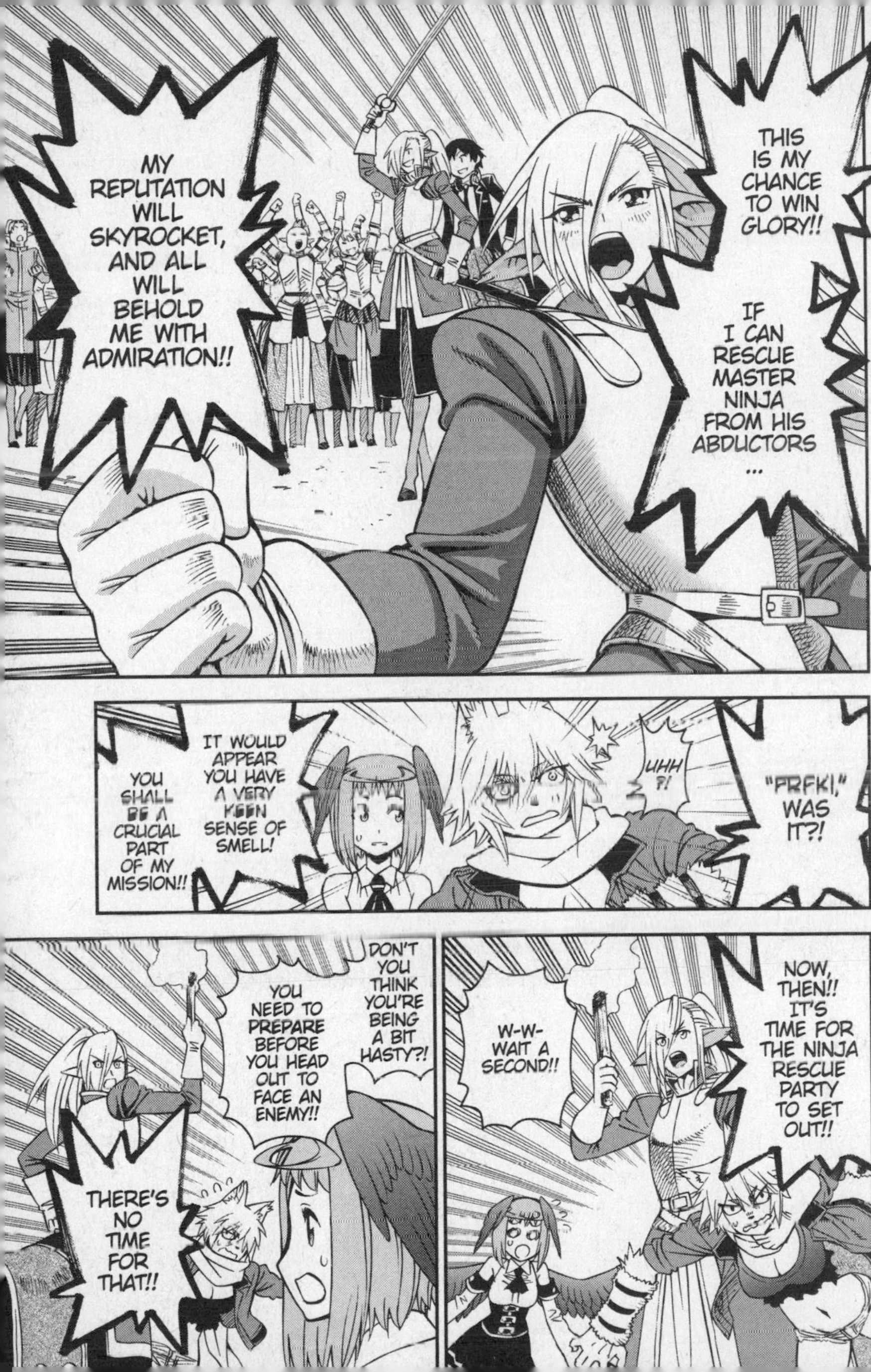
THIS IS MY CHANCE TO WIN GLORY!!
IF I CAN RESCUE MASTER NINJA FROM HIS ABDUCTORS ...
MY REPUTATION WILL SKYROCKET, AND ALL WILL BEHOLD ME WITH ADMIRATION!!
"FRFKI," WAS IT?!
UHH ?!
IT WOULD APPEAR YOU HAVE A VERY KEEN SENSE OF SMELL!
YOU SHALL BE A CRUCIAL PART OF MY MISSION!!
NOW, THEN!! IT'S TIME FOR THE NINJA RESCUE PARTY TO SET OUT!!
W-W-WAIT A SECOND!!
DON'T YOU THINK YOU'RE BEING A BIT HASTY?!
YOU NEED TO PREPARE BEFORE YOU HEAD OUT TO FACE AN ENEMY!!
THERE'S NO TIME FOR THAT!!

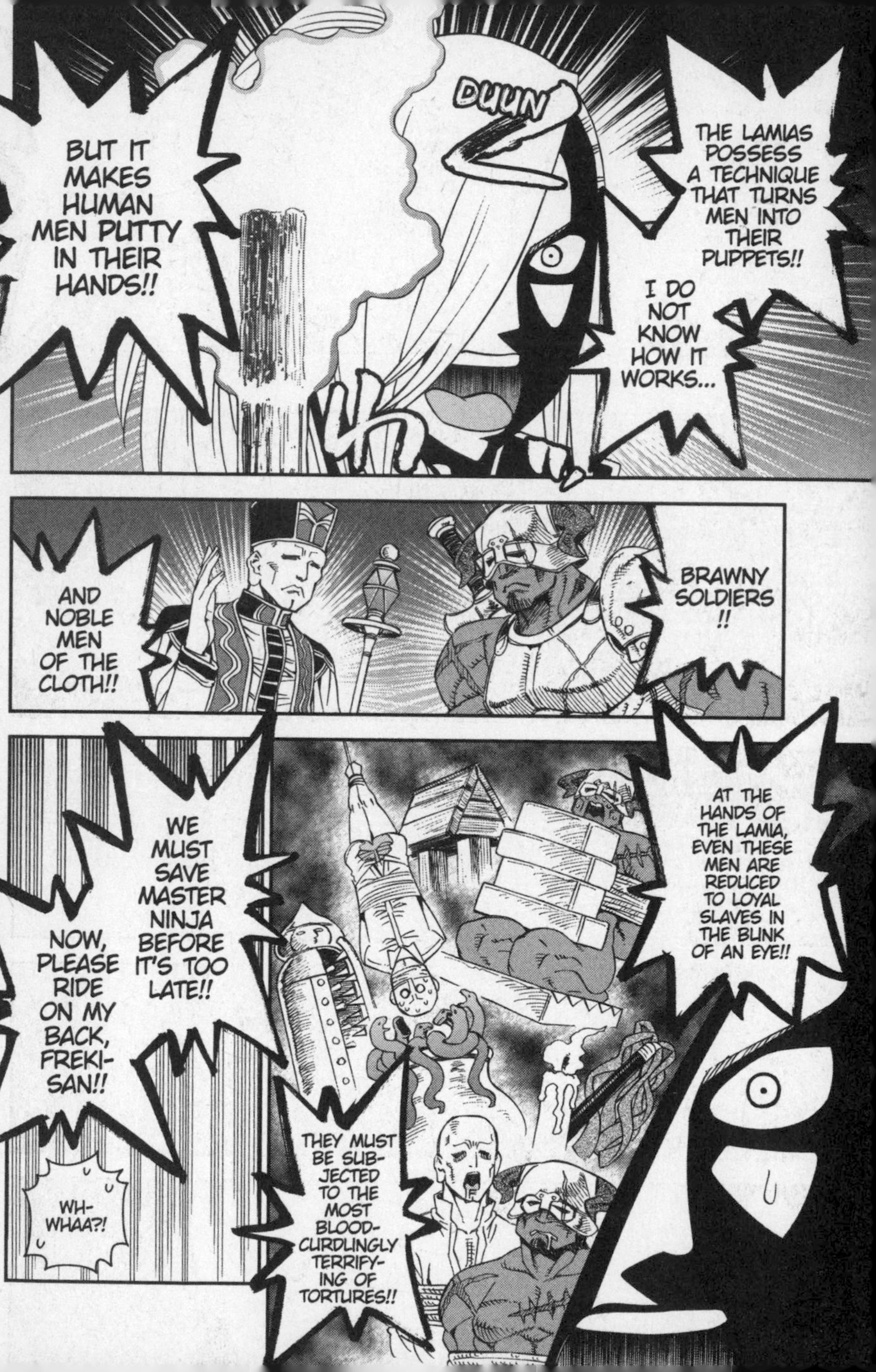
DUUN
THE LAMIAS POSSESS A TECHNIQUE THAT TURNS MEN INTO THEIR PUPPETS!!
I DO NOT KNOW HOW IT WORKS...
BUT IT MAKES HUMAN MEN PUTTY IN THEIR HANDS!!
BRAWNY SOLDIERS !!
AND NOBLE MEN OF THE CLOTH!!
AT THE HANDS OF THE LAMIA, EVEN THESE MEN ARE REDUCED TO LOYAL SLAVES IN THE BLINK OF AN EYE!!
THEY MUST BE SUB-JECTED TO THE MOST BLOOD-CURDLINGLY TERRIFY-ING OF TORTURES!!
WE MUST SAVE MASTER NINJA BEFORE IT'S TOO LATE!!
NOW, PLEASE RIDE ON MY BACK, FREKI-SAN!!
WH-WHAA?!

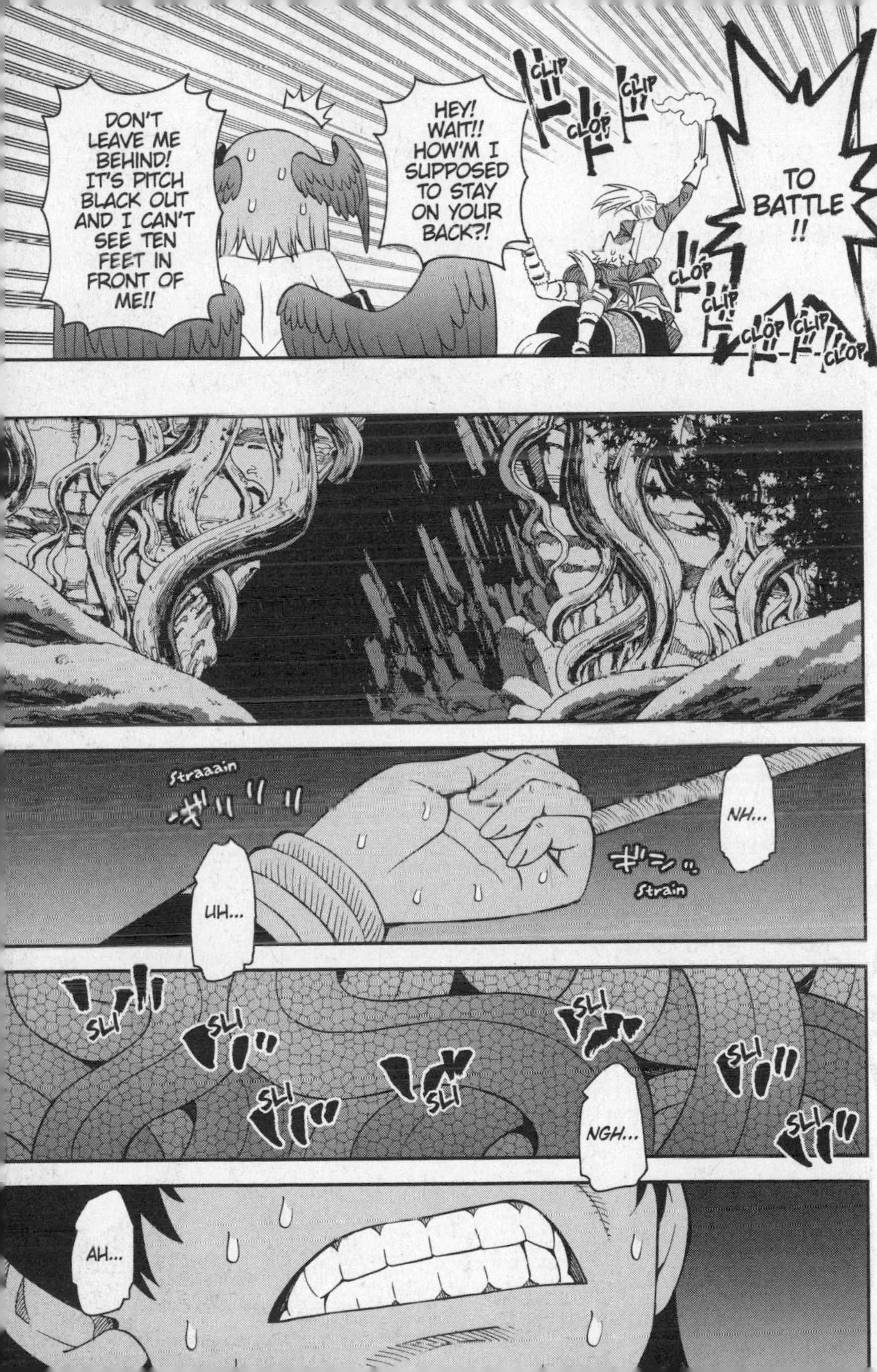
TO BATTLE!!
CLIP
CLOP
CLIP
CLOP
CLIP
CLOP
CLIP
CLOP
HEY! WAIT!! HOW'M I SUPPOSED TO STAY ON YOUR BACK?!
DON'T LEAVE ME BEHIND! IT'S PITCH BLACK OUT AND I CAN'T SEE TEN FEET IN FRONT OF ME!!
NH...
Strain
Straaain
UH...
SLI
SLI
NGH...
SLI
SLI
SLI
SLI
SLI
AH...

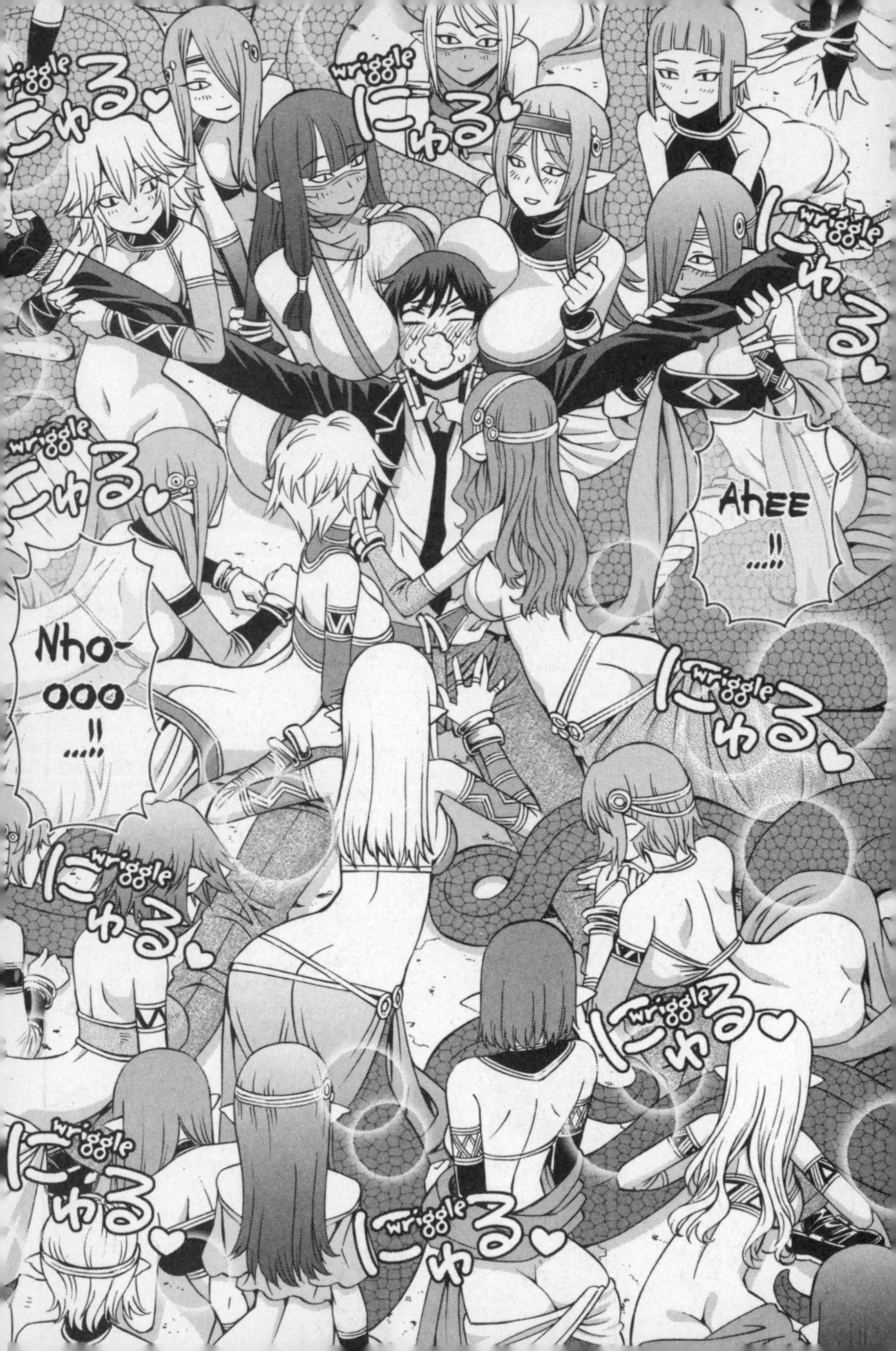
wriggle にゅる
wriggle にゅる
wriggle にゅる
Ahee ...!!
wriggle にゅる
wriggle にゅる
Nho-ooo ...!!
wriggle にゅる
wriggle にゅる
wriggle にゅる
wriggle にゅる

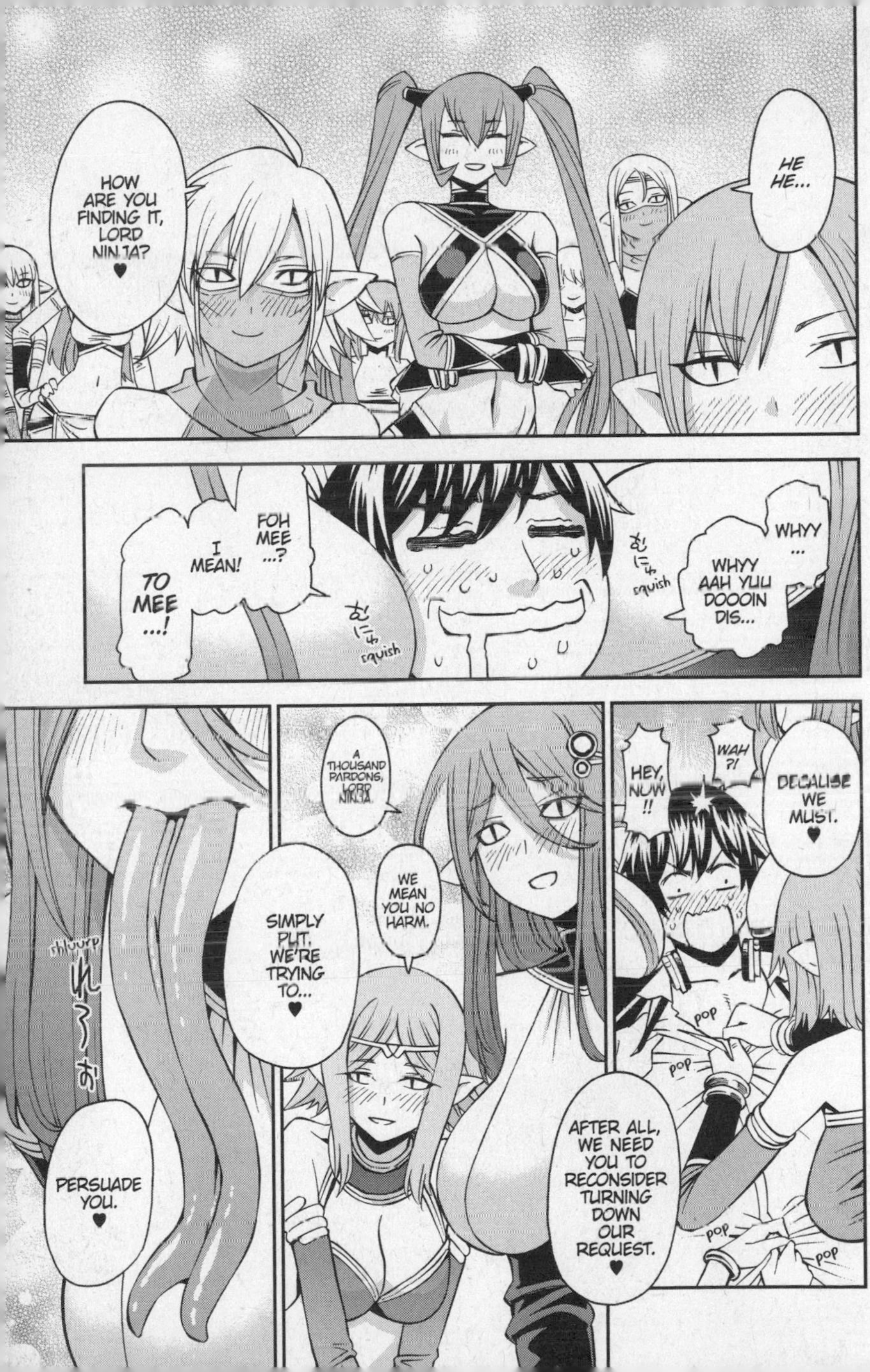
HE HE...
HOW ARE YOU FINDING IT, LORD NINJA? ♥
WHYY...
WHYY AAH YUU DOOOIN DIS...
むにゅ squish
むにゅ squish
FOH MEE...?
I MEAN!
TO MEE...!
WAH?!
BECAUSE WE MUST. ♥
HEY, NOW!!
pop
pop
pop
pop
A THOUSAND PARDONS, LORD NINJA.
WE MEAN YOU NO HARM.
SIMPLY PUT, WE'RE TRYING TO... ♥
AFTER ALL, WE NEED YOU TO RECONSIDER TURNING DOWN OUR REQUEST. ♥
れろお shluurp
PERSUADE YOU. ♥

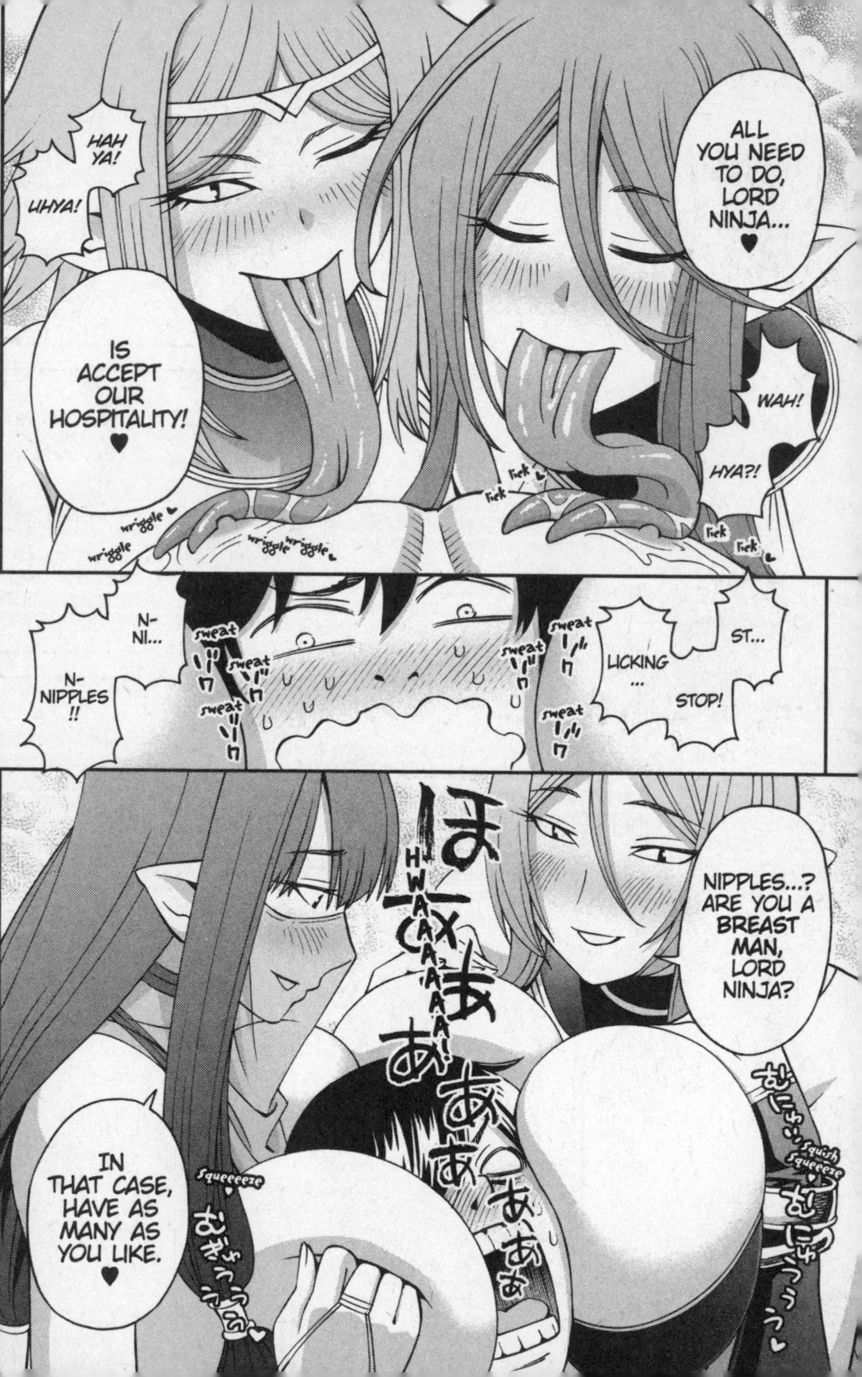
ALL YOU NEED TO DO, LORD NINJA... ♥
WAH!
HYA?!
lick lick ♥
lick lick ♥
HAH YA!
UHYA!
IS ACCEPT OUR HOSPITALITY! ♥
wriggle wriggle ♥
wriggle wriggle ♥
ST...
LICKING ...
STOP!
sweat sweat sweat sweat sweat
N- NI...
N- NIPPLES !!
NIPPLES...? ARE YOU A BREAST MAN, LORD NINJA?
HWAAAAAAA!
Squish Squeeeeze ♥
IN THAT CASE, HAVE AS MANY AS YOU LIKE. ♥
Squeeeeze ♥

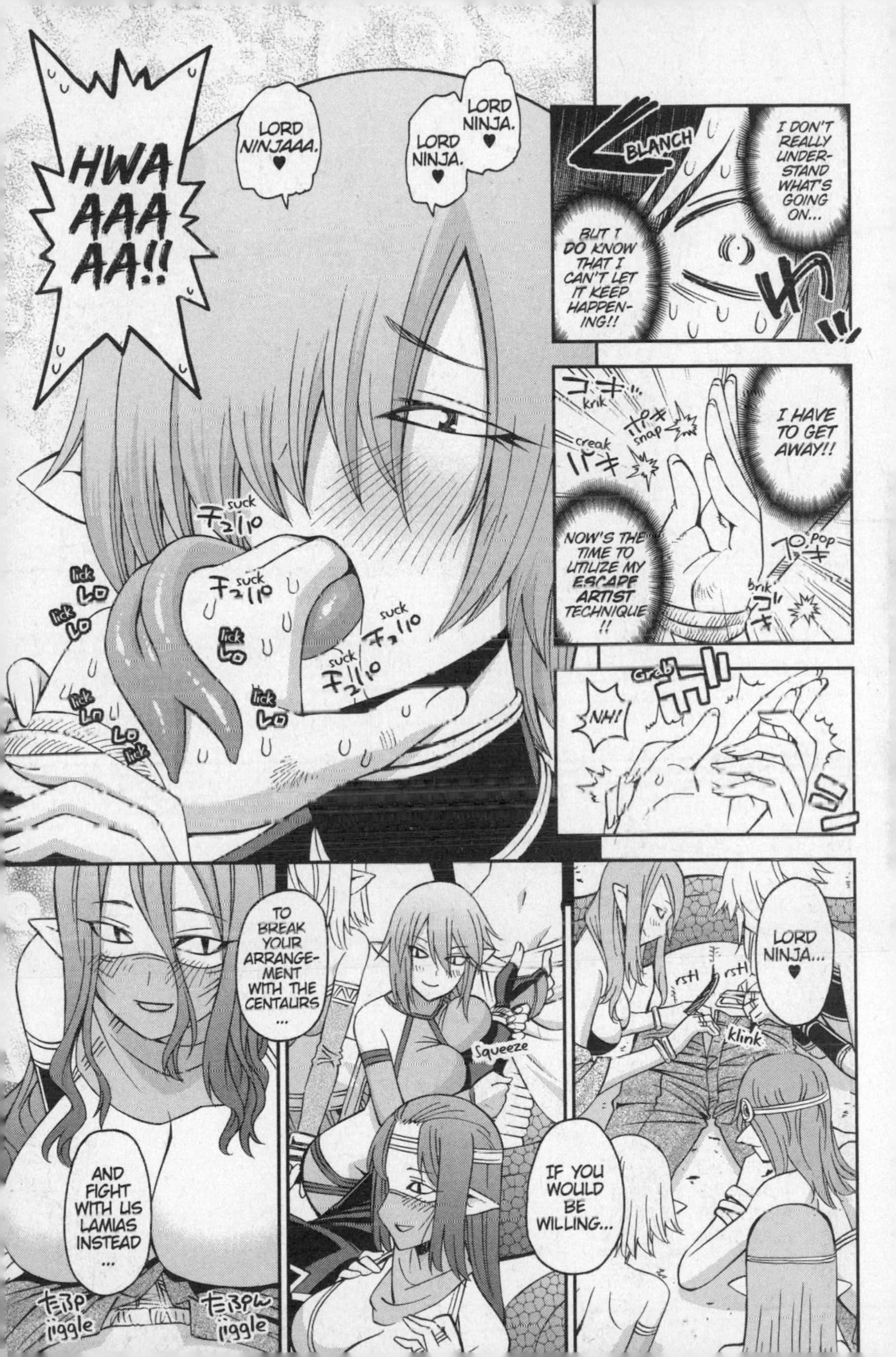
LORD NINJA. ♥
LORD NINJA. ♥
LORD NINJAAA. ♥
HWAAAAAAA!!
suck
suck
suck
suck
lick
lick
lick
lick
lick
lick
BLANCH
I DON'T REALLY UNDERSTAND WHAT'S GOING ON...
BUT I DO KNOW THAT I CAN'T LET IT KEEP HAPPENING!!
krik
snap
creak
I HAVE TO GET AWAY!!
pop
brik
NOW'S THE TIME TO UTILIZE MY ESCAPE ARTIST TECHNIQUE!!
Grab
NH!
LORD NINJA... ♥
rstl
rstl
klink
TO BREAK YOUR ARRANGEMENT WITH THE CENTAURS...
Squeeze
IF YOU WOULD BE WILLING...
AND FIGHT WITH US LAMIAS INSTEAD...
jiggle
jiggle

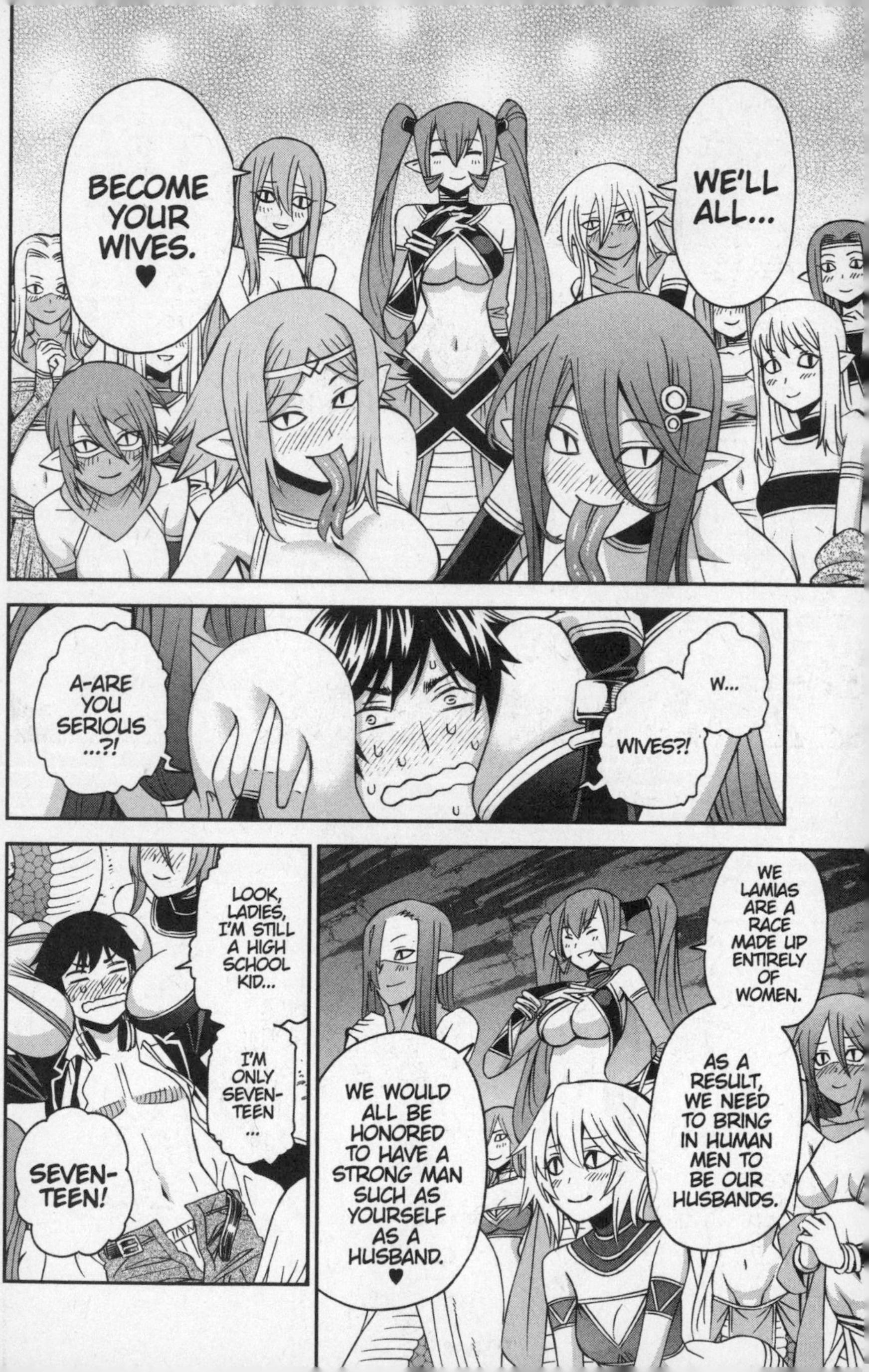
WE'LL ALL...
BECOME YOUR WIVES. ♥
W... WIVES?!
A-ARE YOU SERIOUS...?!
WE LAMIAS ARE A RACE MADE UP ENTIRELY OF WOMEN.
AS A RESULT, WE NEED TO BRING IN HUMAN MEN TO BE OUR HUSBANDS.
WE WOULD ALL BE HONORED TO HAVE A STRONG MAN SUCH AS YOURSELF AS A HUSBAND. ♥
LOOK, LADIES, I'M STILL A HIGH SCHOOL KID...
I'M ONLY SEVEN-TEEN...
SEVEN-TEEN!

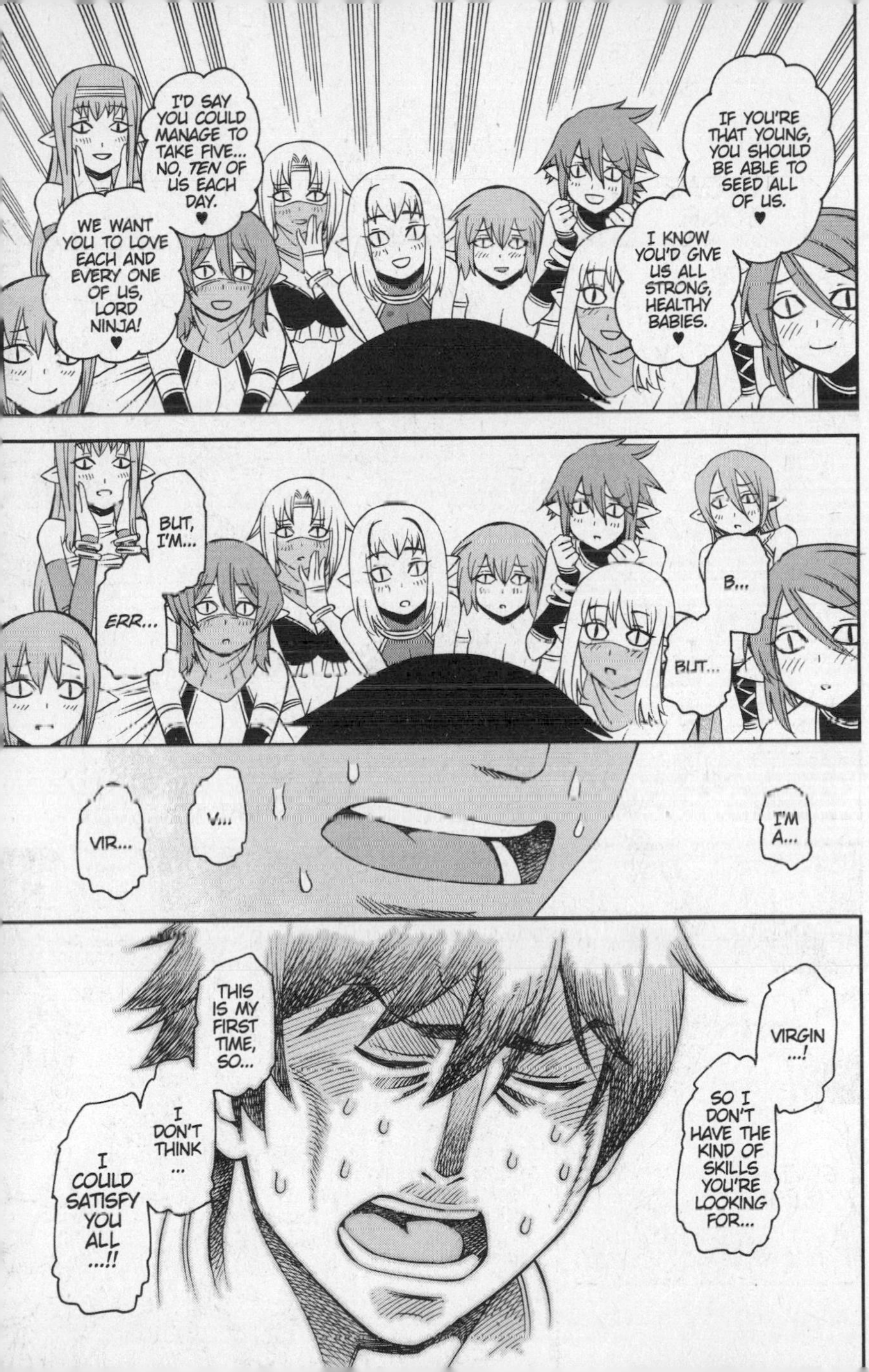
IF YOU'RE THAT YOUNG, YOU SHOULD BE ABLE TO SEED ALL OF US. ♥
I KNOW YOU'D GIVE US ALL STRONG, HEALTHY BABIES. ♥
I'D SAY YOU COULD MANAGE TO TAKE FIVE... NO, *TEN* OF US EACH DAY. ♥
WE WANT YOU TO LOVE EACH AND EVERY ONE OF US, LORD NINJA! ♥
B...
BUT...
BUT, I'M...
ERR...
I'M A...
V...
VIR...
VIRGIN ...!
SO I DON'T HAVE THE KIND OF SKILLS YOU'RE LOOKING FOR...
THIS IS MY FIRST TIME, SO...
I DON'T THINK ...
I COULD SATISFY YOU ALL ...!!

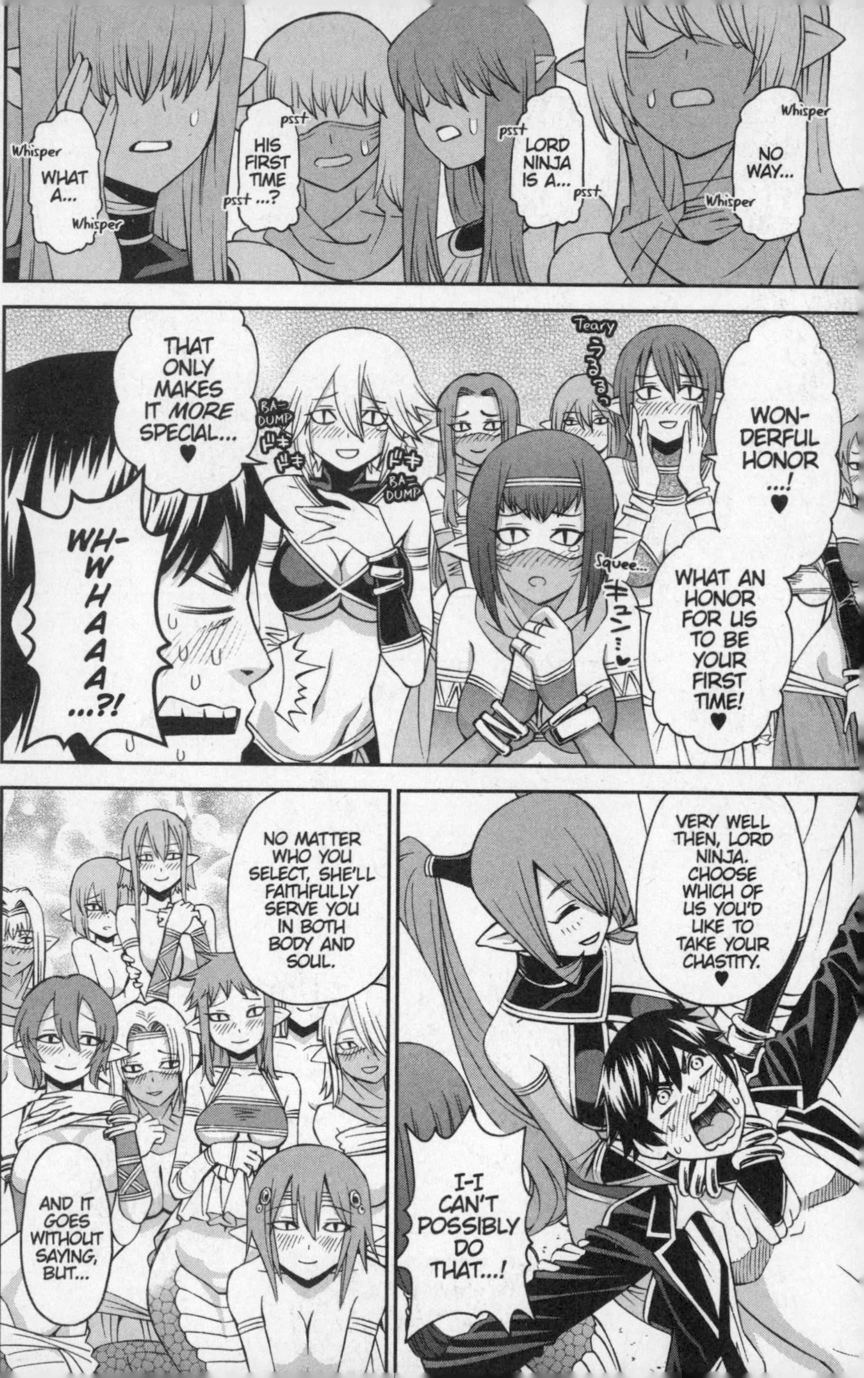
Whisper
NO WAY...
Whisper
psst
LORD NINJA IS A...
psst
psst
HIS FIRST TIME ...?
psst
Whisper
WHAT A...
Whisper
Teary
うるる
WON-DERFUL HONOR ...!
WHAT AN HONOR FOR US TO BE YOUR FIRST TIME!
Squee...
キュン...
BA-DUMP
ドキ
BA-DUMP
ドキ
THAT ONLY MAKES IT MORE SPECIAL...
WH-WHAAAA...?!
VERY WELL THEN, LORD NINJA. CHOOSE WHICH OF US YOU'D LIKE TO TAKE YOUR CHASTITY.
I-I CAN'T POSSIBLY DO THAT...!
NO MATTER WHO YOU SELECT, SHE'LL FAITHFULLY SERVE YOU IN BOTH BODY AND SOUL.
AND IT GOES WITHOUT SAYING, BUT...

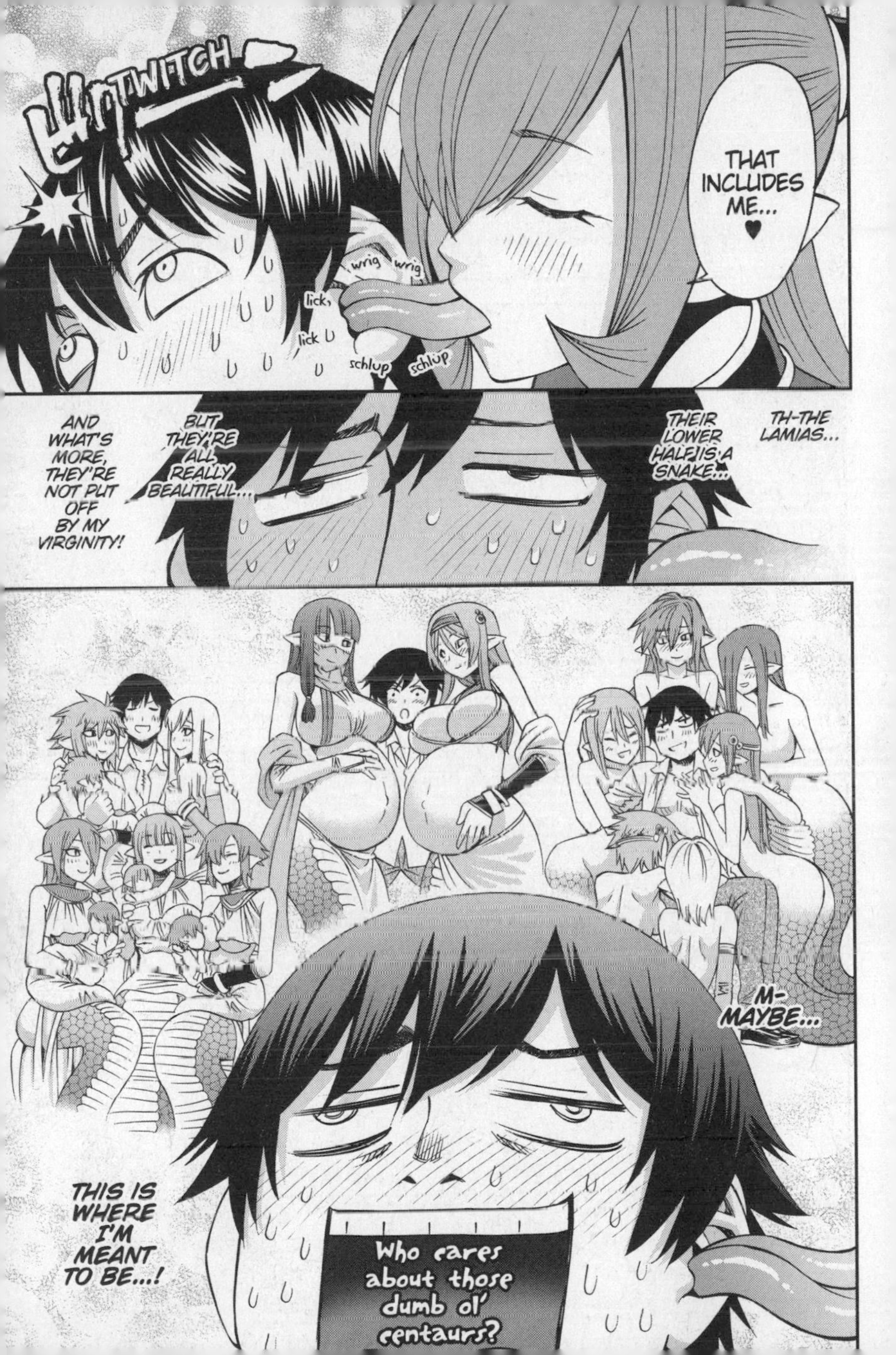
THAT INCLUDES ME... ♥
TWITCH
wrig wrig
lick, lick
schlup schlup
TH-THE LAMIAS...
THEIR LOWER HALF IS A SNAKE...
BUT THEY'RE ALL REALLY BEAUTIFUL...
AND WHAT'S MORE, THEY'RE NOT PUT OFF BY MY VIRGINITY!
M-MAYBE...
Who cares about those dumb ol' centaurs?
THIS IS WHERE I'M MEANT TO BE...!

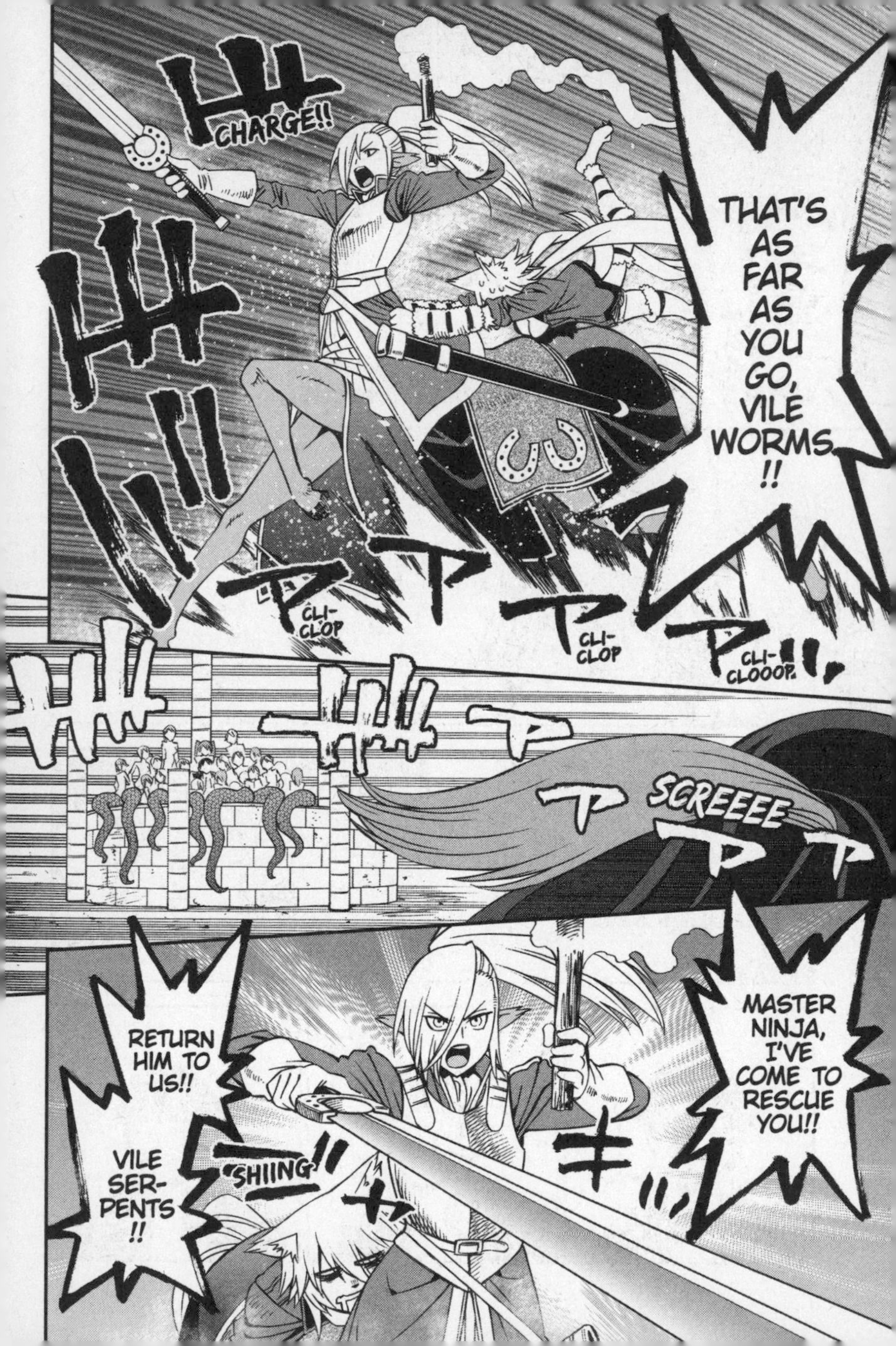
THAT'S AS FAR AS YOU GO, VILE WORMS!!
CHARGE!!
CLI-CLOOP!!
CLI-CLOP
CLI-CLOP
SCREEEE
MASTER NINJA, I'VE COME TO RESCUE YOU!!
RETURN HIM TO US!!
SHIING!!
VILE SERPENTS!!

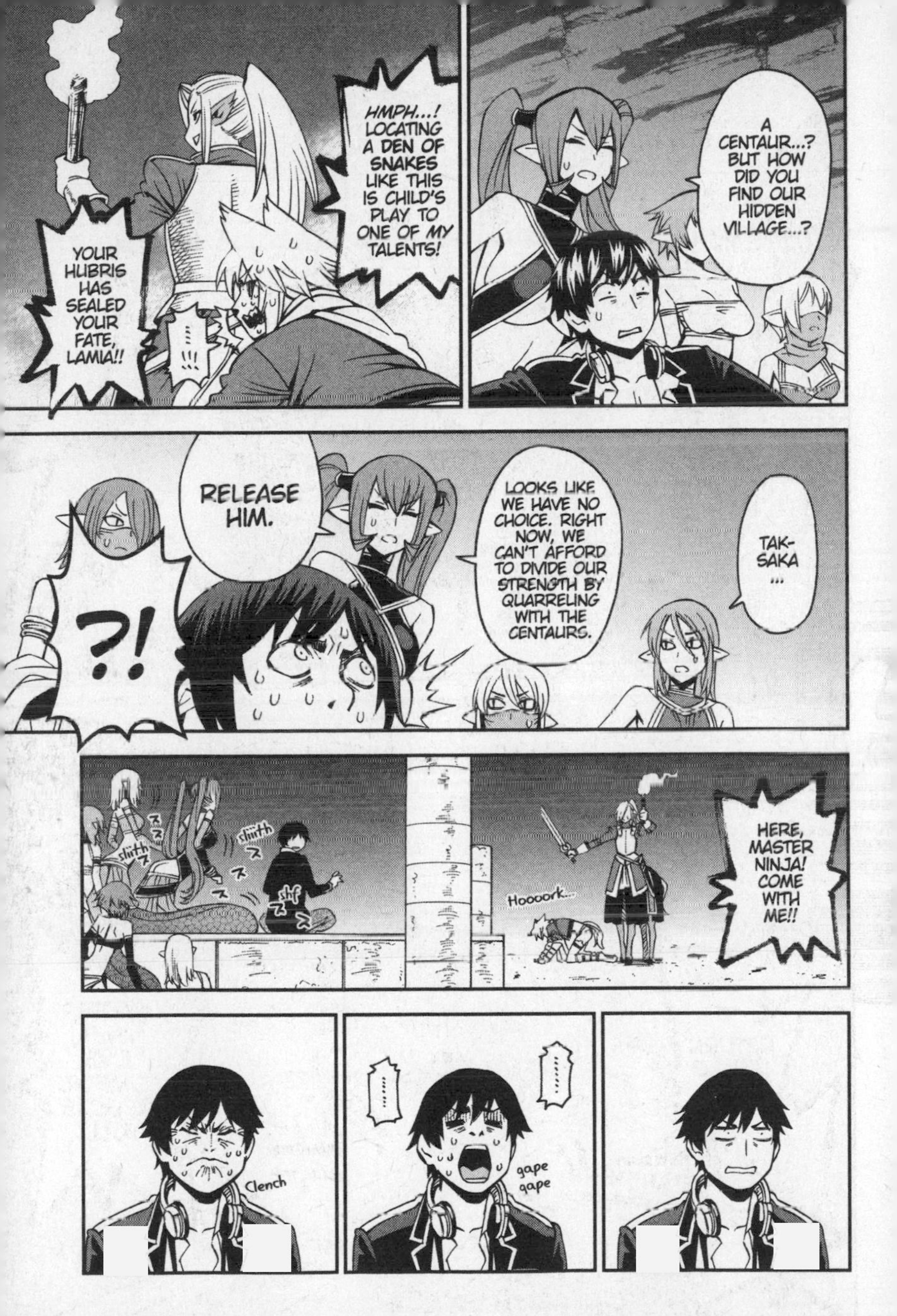
A CENTAUR...? BUT HOW DID YOU FIND OUR HIDDEN VILLAGE...?
HMPH...! LOCATING A DEN OF SNAKES LIKE THIS IS CHILD'S PLAY TO ONE OF MY TALENTS!
...!!!
YOUR HUBRIS HAS SEALED YOUR FATE, LAMIA!!
TAK-SAKA ...
LOOKS LIKE WE HAVE NO CHOICE. RIGHT NOW, WE CAN'T AFFORD TO DIVIDE OUR STRENGTH BY QUARRELING WITH THE CENTAURS.
RELEASE HIM.
?!
HERE, MASTER NINJA! COME WITH ME!!
Hoooork...
shf
sliith
sliith
......
......
gape gape
Clench

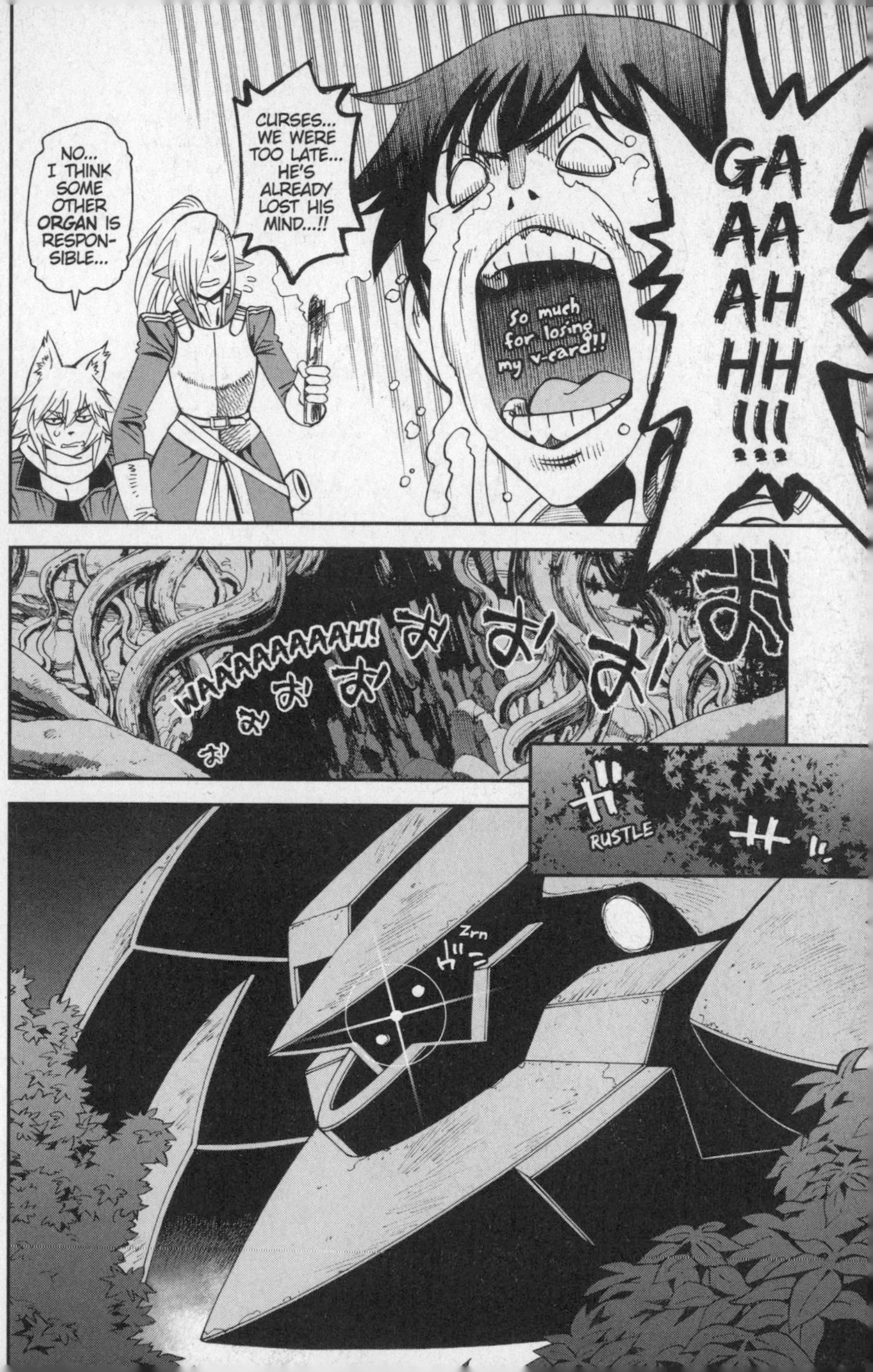
GAAAAHHH!!!
So much for losing my v-card!!
CURSES... WE WERE TOO LATE... HE'S ALREADY LOST HIS MIND...!!
NO... I THINK SOME OTHER ORGAN IS RESPONSIBLE...
WAAAAAAAAAH!
RUSTLE
Zrn

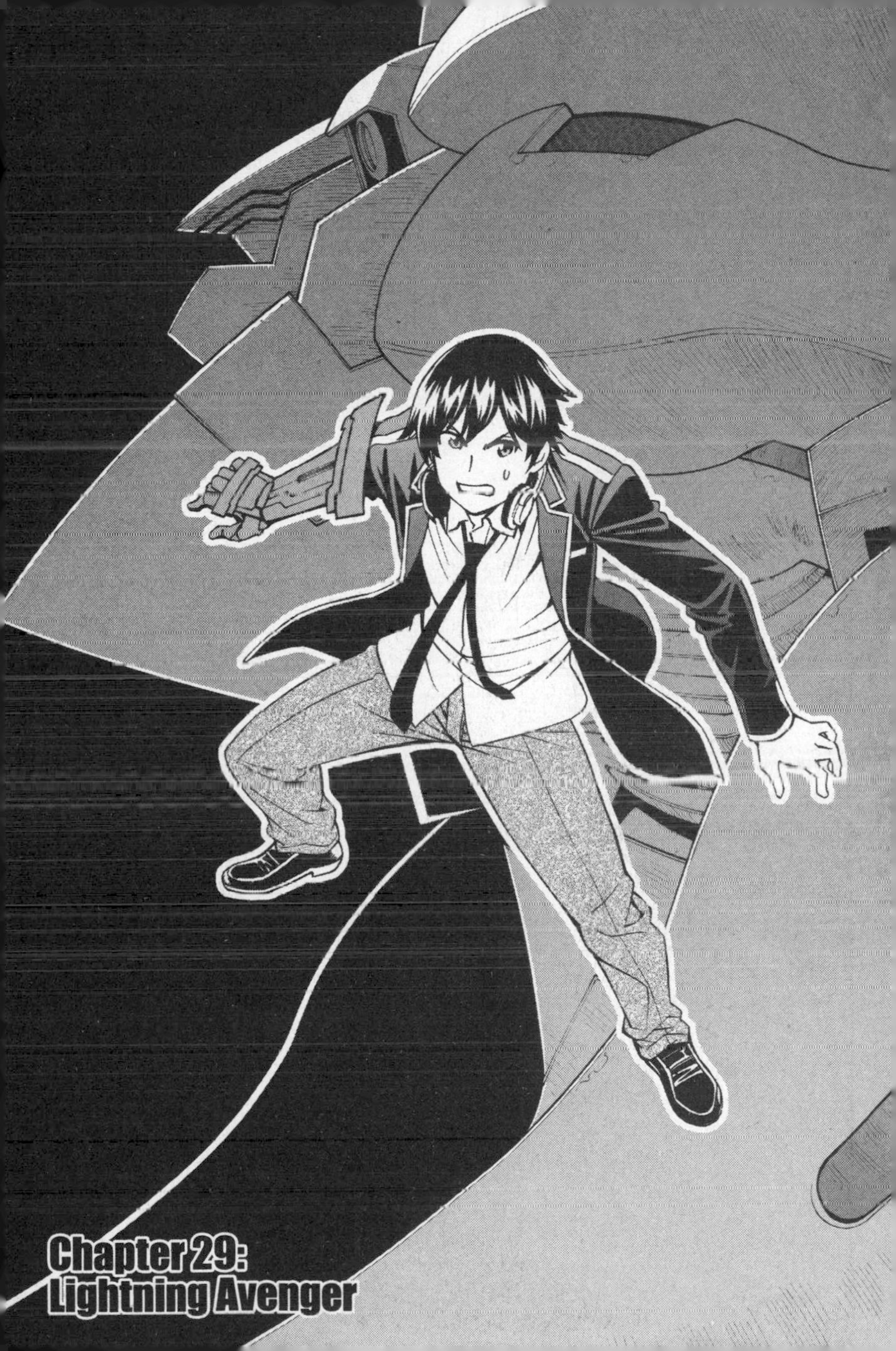
Chapter 29:
Lightning Avenger

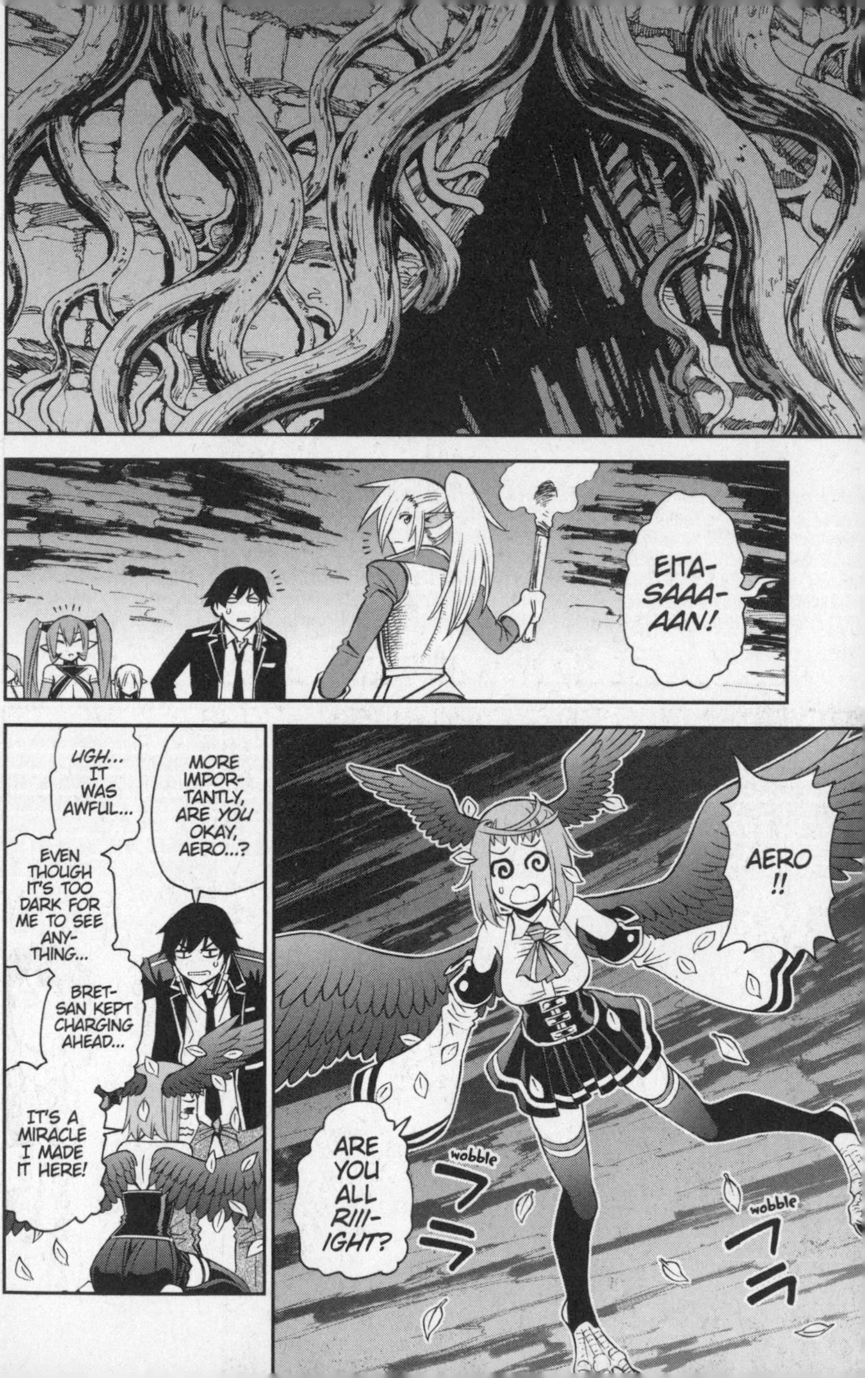
EITA-SAAAA-AAN!
AERO !!
ARE YOU ALL RIIII-IGHT?
wobble
wobble
MORE IMPORTANTLY, ARE YOU OKAY, AERO...?
UGH... IT WAS AWFUL...
EVEN THOUGH IT'S TOO DARK FOR ME TO SEE ANYTHING...
BRET-SAN KEPT CHARGING AHEAD...
IT'S A MIRACLE I MADE IT HERE!

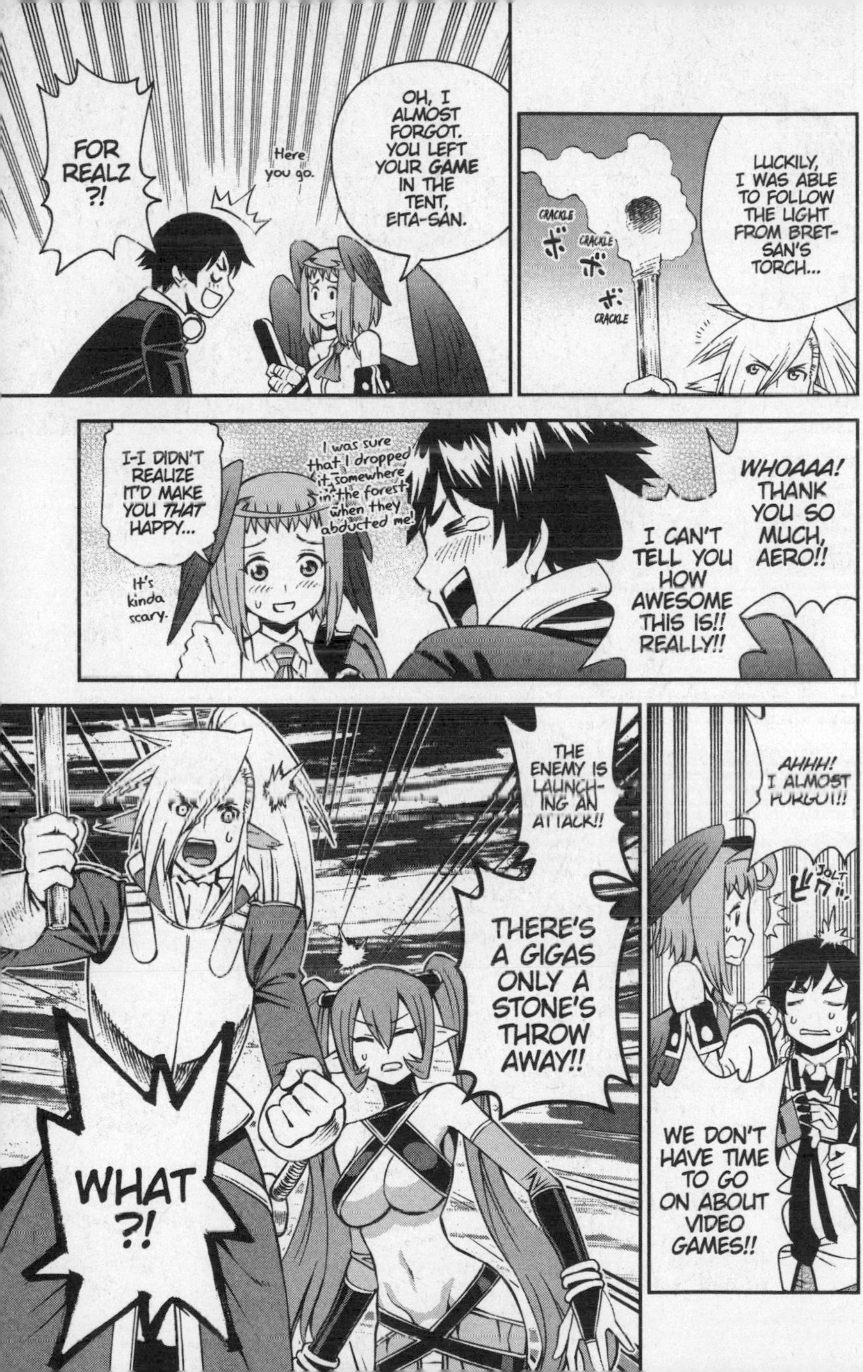
LUCKILY, I WAS ABLE TO FOLLOW THE LIGHT FROM BRET-SAN'S TORCH...
CRACKLE
CRACKLE
CRACKLE
OH, I ALMOST FORGOT. YOU LEFT YOUR GAME IN THE TENT, EITA-SAN.
Here you go.
FOR REALZ ?!
WHOAAA! THANK YOU SO MUCH, AERO!!
I CAN'T TELL YOU HOW AWESOME THIS IS!! REALLY!!
I was sure that I dropped it somewhere in the forest when they abducted me!
I-I DIDN'T REALIZE IT'D MAKE YOU THAT HAPPY...
It's kinda scary.
AHHH! I ALMOST FORGOT!!
JOLT
WE DON'T HAVE TIME TO GO ON ABOUT VIDEO GAMES!!
THE ENEMY IS LAUNCHING AN ATTACK!!
THERE'S A GIGAS ONLY A STONE'S THROW AWAY!!
WHAT ?!

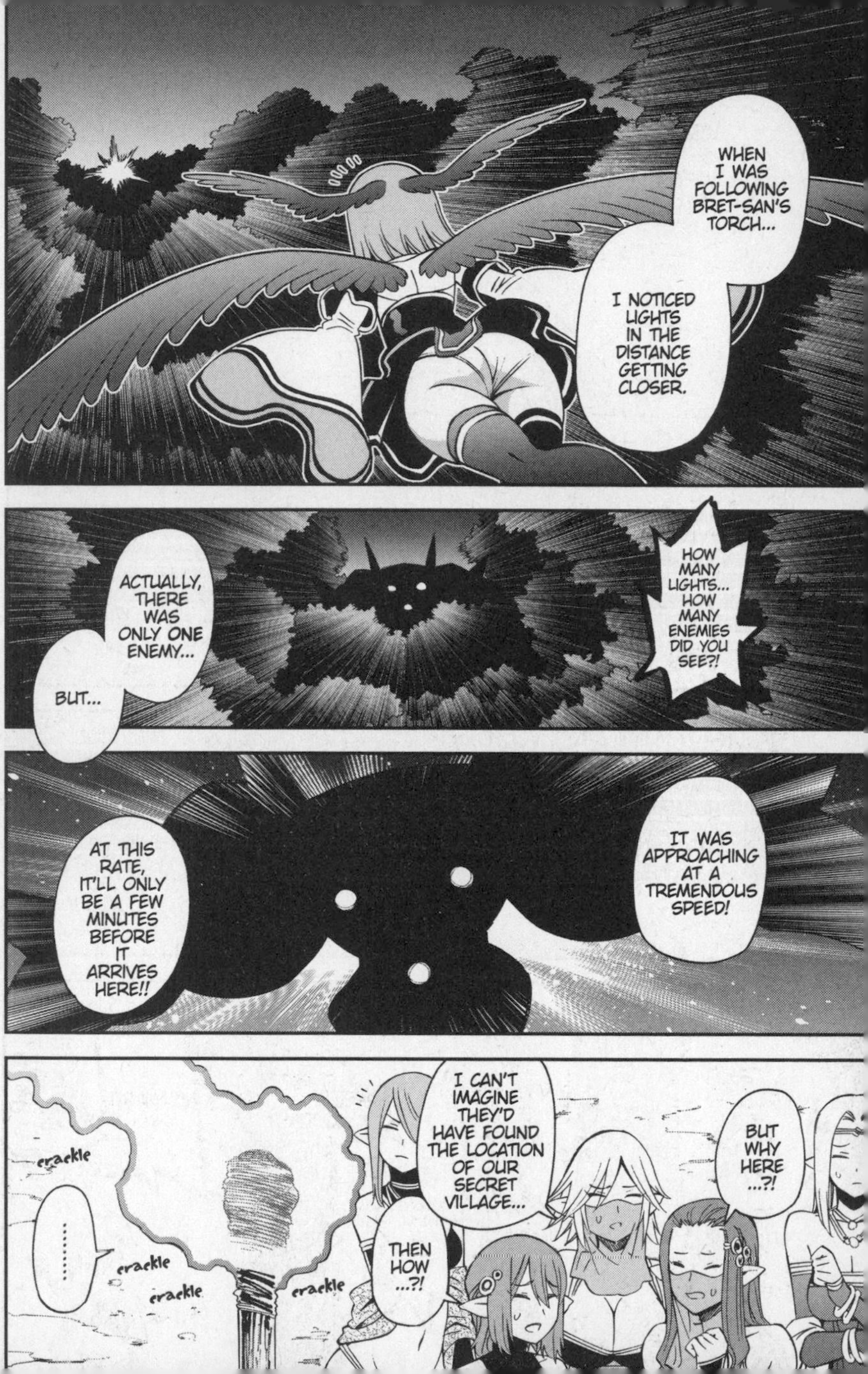
WHEN I WAS FOLLOWING BRET-SAN'S TORCH...
I NOTICED LIGHTS IN THE DISTANCE GETTING CLOSER.
HOW MANY LIGHTS... HOW MANY ENEMIES DID YOU SEE?!
ACTUALLY, THERE WAS ONLY ONE ENEMY...
BUT...
IT WAS APPROACHING AT A TREMENDOUS SPEED!
AT THIS RATE, IT'LL ONLY BE A FEW MINUTES BEFORE IT ARRIVES HERE!!
BUT WHY HERE ...?!
I CAN'T IMAGINE THEY'D HAVE FOUND THE LOCATION OF OUR SECRET VILLAGE...
THEN HOW ...?!
crackle
crackle
crackle
crackle
......

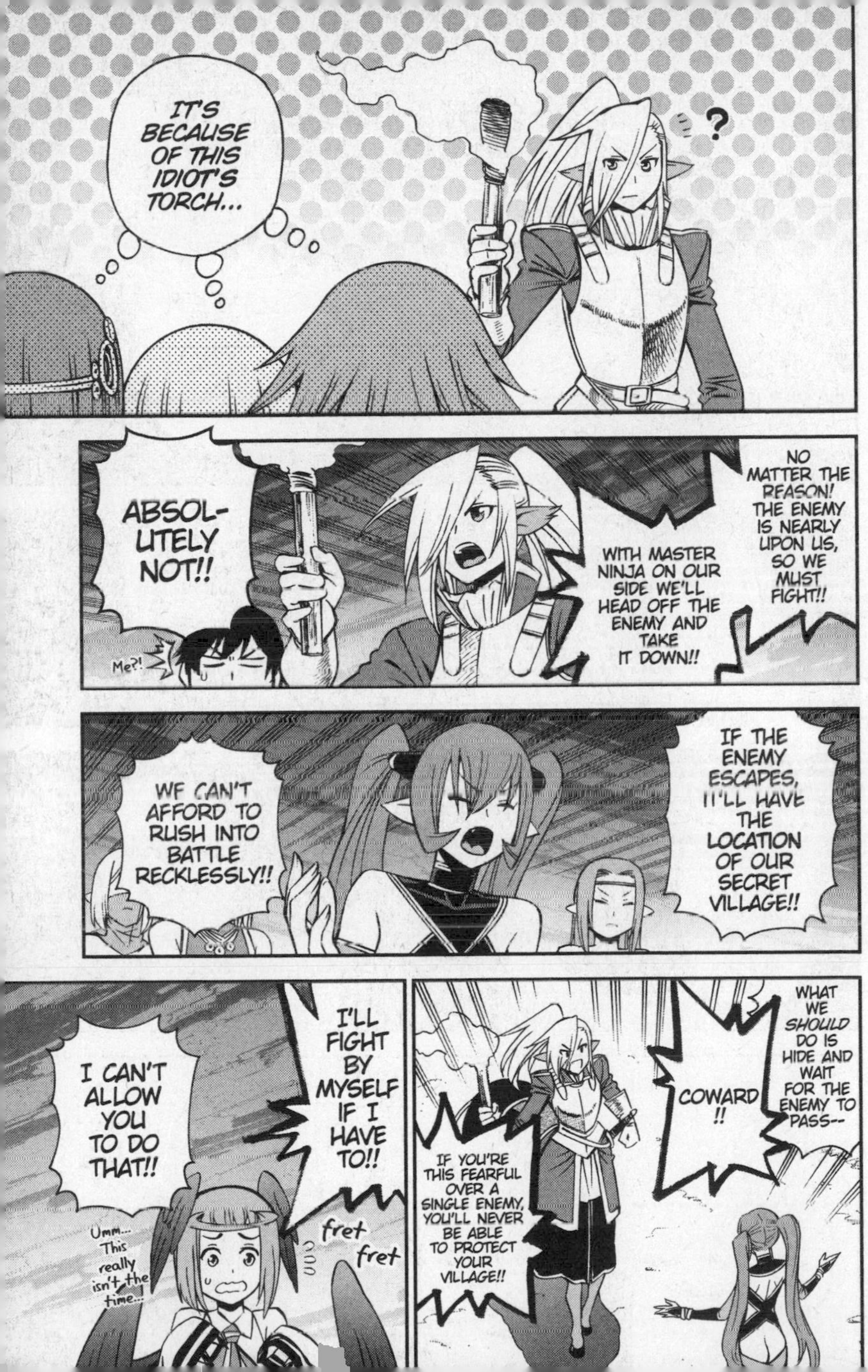

IT'S BECAUSE OF THIS IDIOT'S TORCH...
?
NO MATTER THE REASON! THE ENEMY IS NEARLY UPON US, SO WE MUST FIGHT!!
WITH MASTER NINJA ON OUR SIDE WE'LL HEAD OFF THE ENEMY AND TAKE IT DOWN!!
ABSOL-UTELY NOT!!
Me?!
IF THE ENEMY ESCAPES, IT'LL HAVE THE LOCATION OF OUR SECRET VILLAGE!!
WE CAN'T AFFORD TO RUSH INTO BATTLE RECKLESSLY!!
WHAT WE SHOULD DO IS HIDE AND WAIT FOR THE ENEMY TO PASS--
COWARD!!
IF YOU'RE THIS FEARFUL OVER A SINGLE ENEMY, YOU'LL NEVER BE ABLE TO PROTECT YOUR VILLAGE!!
I'LL FIGHT BY MYSELF IF I HAVE TO!!
I CAN'T ALLOW YOU TO DO THAT!!
fret fret
Umm... This really isn't the time...

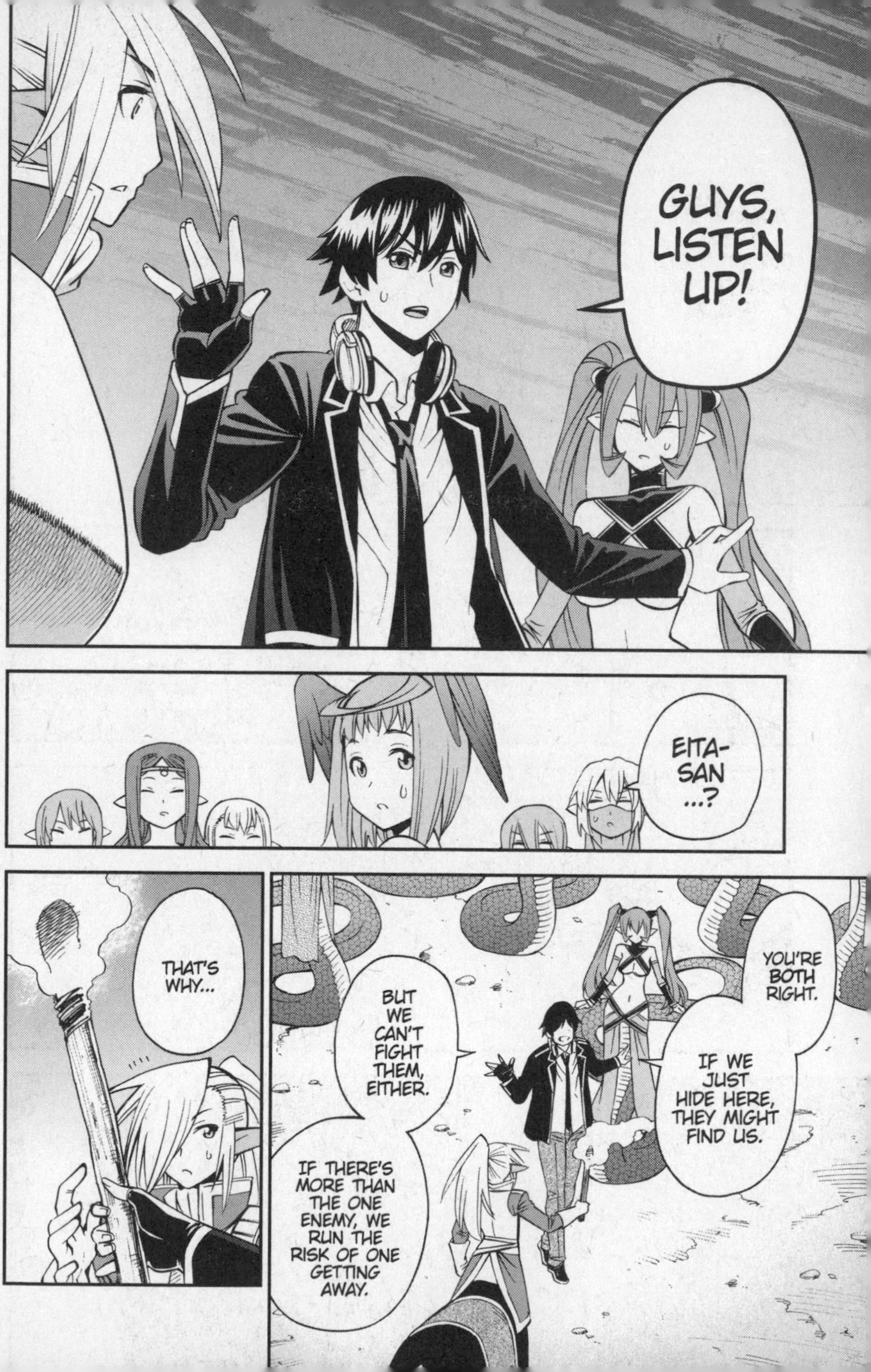
GUYS, LISTEN UP!
EITA-SAN ...?
YOU'RE BOTH RIGHT.
IF WE JUST HIDE HERE, THEY MIGHT FIND US.
BUT WE CAN'T FIGHT THEM, EITHER.
IF THERE'S MORE THAN THE ONE ENEMY, WE RUN THE RISK OF ONE GETTING AWAY.
THAT'S WHY...

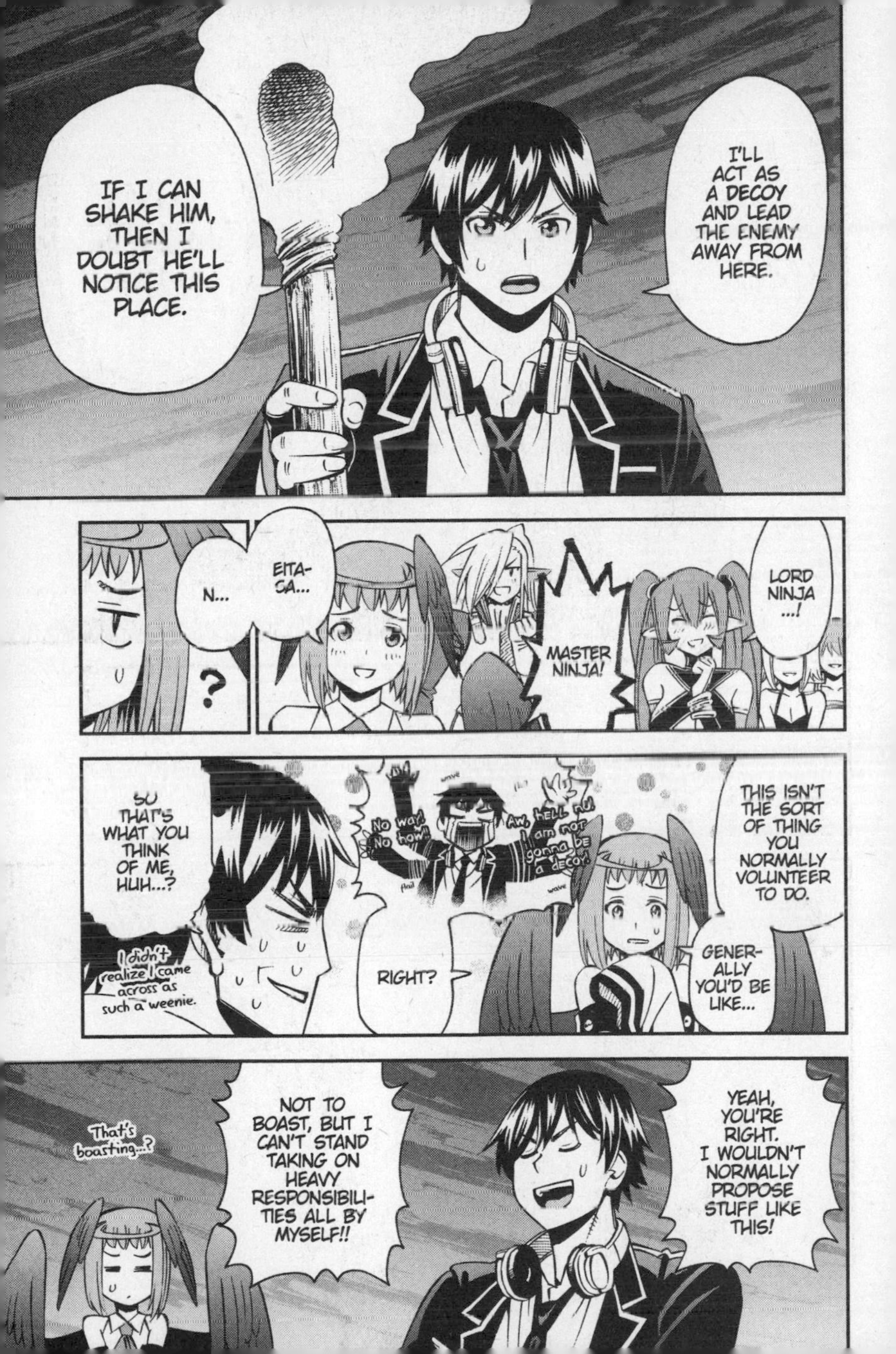
I'LL ACT AS A DECOY AND LEAD THE ENEMY AWAY FROM HERE.
IF I CAN SHAKE HIM, THEN I DOUBT HE'LL NOTICE THIS PLACE.
LORD NINJA ...!
MASTER NINJA!
EITA-SA...
N...
?
THIS ISN'T THE SORT OF THING YOU NORMALLY VOLUNTEER TO DO.
GENER-ALLY YOU'D BE LIKE...
wave
Aw, hell no! I am not gonna be a decoy!
wave
No way! No how!
flail
RIGHT?
SO THAT'S WHAT YOU THINK OF ME, HUH...?
I didn't realize I came across as such a weenie.
YEAH, YOU'RE RIGHT. I WOULDN'T NORMALLY PROPOSE STUFF LIKE THIS!
NOT TO BOAST, BUT I CAN'T STAND TAKING ON HEAVY RESPONSIBILI-TIES ALL BY MYSELF!!
That's boasting...?

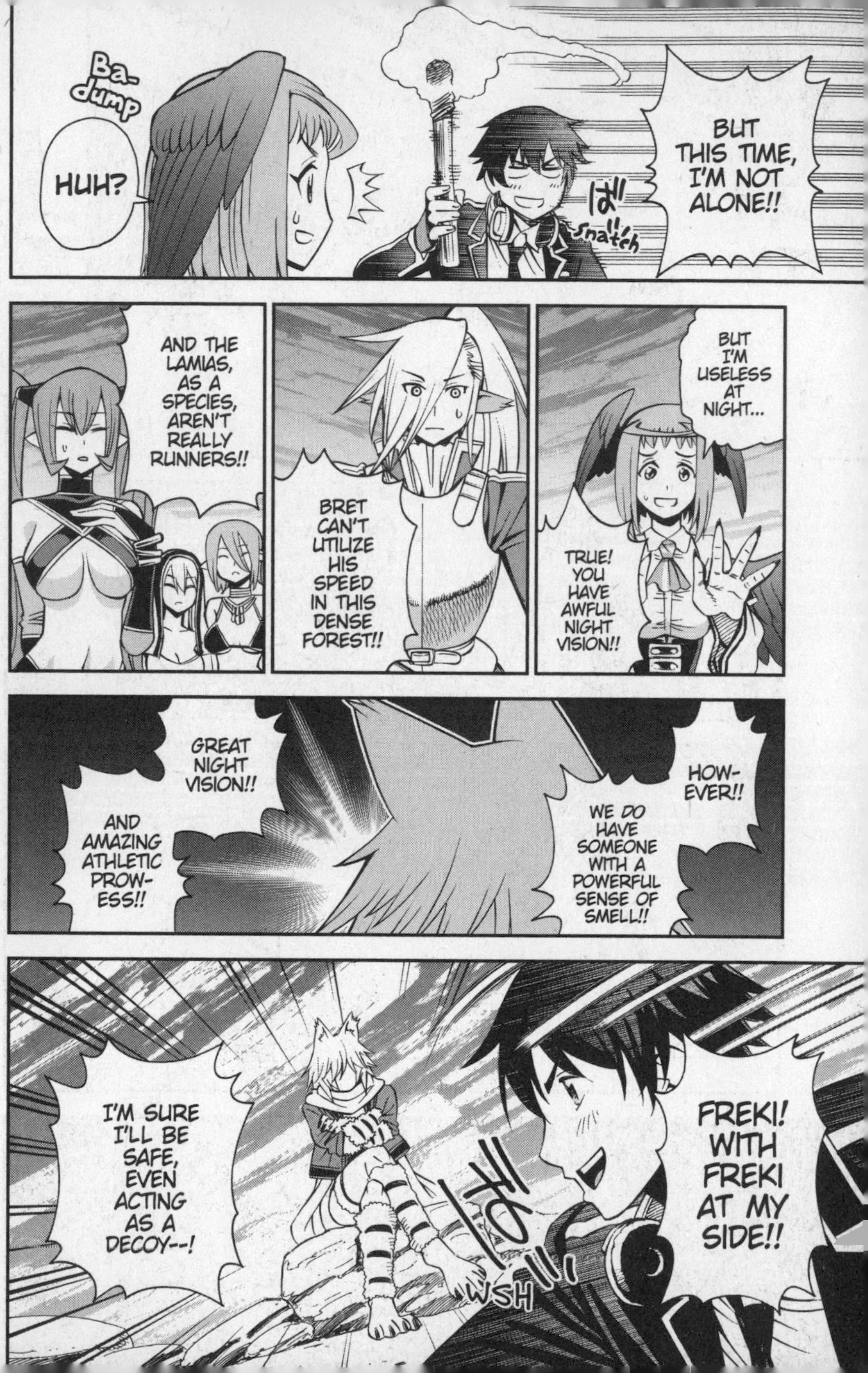
BUT THIS TIME, I'M NOT ALONE!!
ぱ
Snatch!!
Ba-dump
HUH?
BUT I'M USELESS AT NIGHT...
TRUE! YOU HAVE AWFUL NIGHT VISION!!
BRET CAN'T UTILIZE HIS SPEED IN THIS DENSE FOREST!!
AND THE LAMIAS, AS A SPECIES, AREN'T REALLY RUNNERS!!
HOW-EVER!!
WE DO HAVE SOMEONE WITH A POWERFUL SENSE OF SMELL!!
GREAT NIGHT VISION!!
AND AMAZING ATHLETIC PROW-ESS!!
FREKI! WITH FREKI AT MY SIDE!!
WSH!!!
I'M SURE I'LL BE SAFE, EVEN ACTING AS A DECOY--!

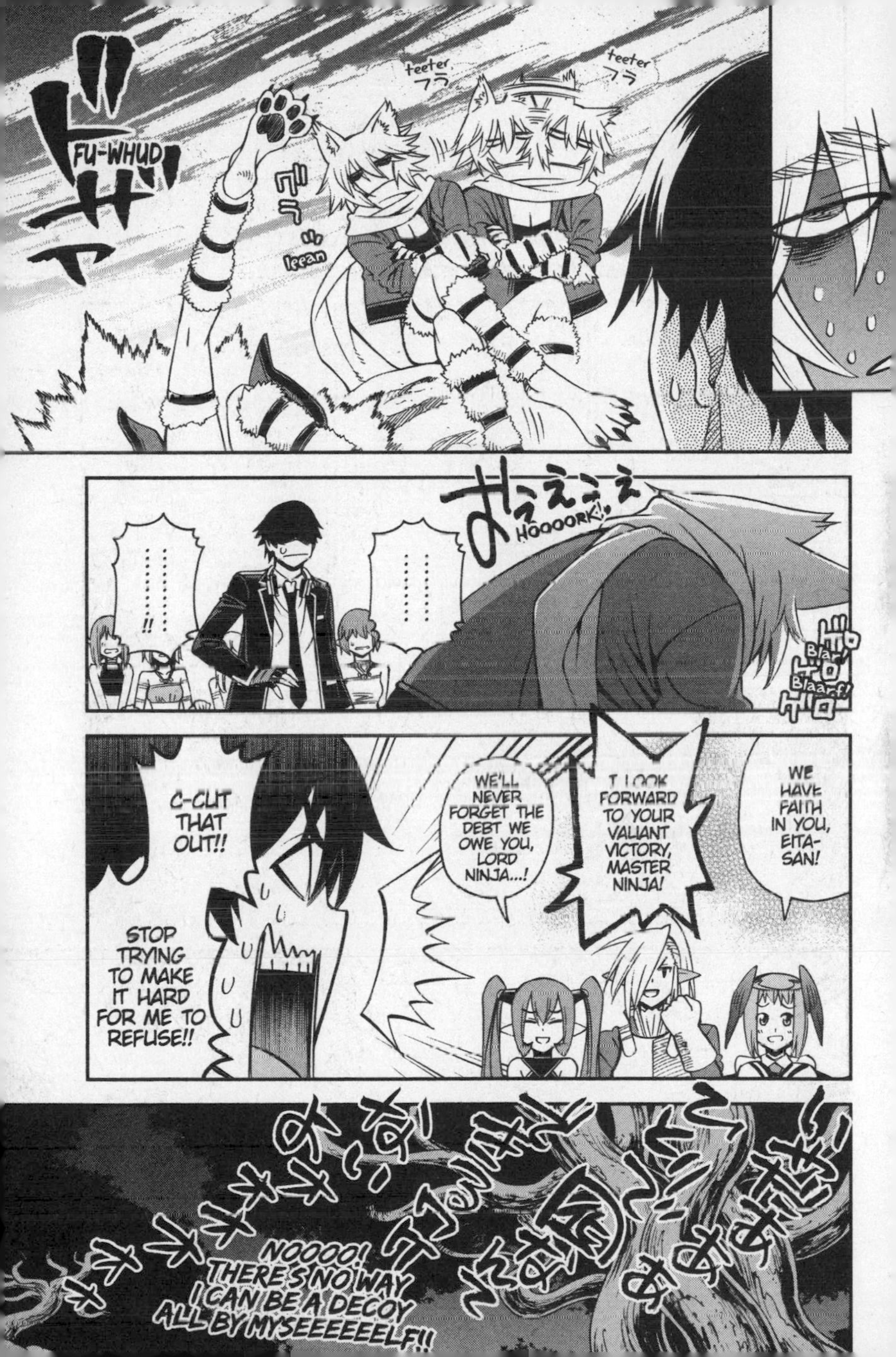
teeter
teeter
lean
FU-WHUD
Blarf! Blaarf!
HOOOORK!
……
……!!
WE HAVE FAITH IN YOU, EITA-SAN!
I LOOK FORWARD TO YOUR VALIANT VICTORY, MASTER NINJA!
WE'LL NEVER FORGET THE DEBT WE OWE YOU, LORD NINJA...!
C-CUT THAT OUT!!
STOP TRYING TO MAKE IT HARD FOR ME TO REFUSE!!
NOOOO! THERE'S NO WAY I CAN BE A DECOY ALL BY MYSEEEEEELF!!

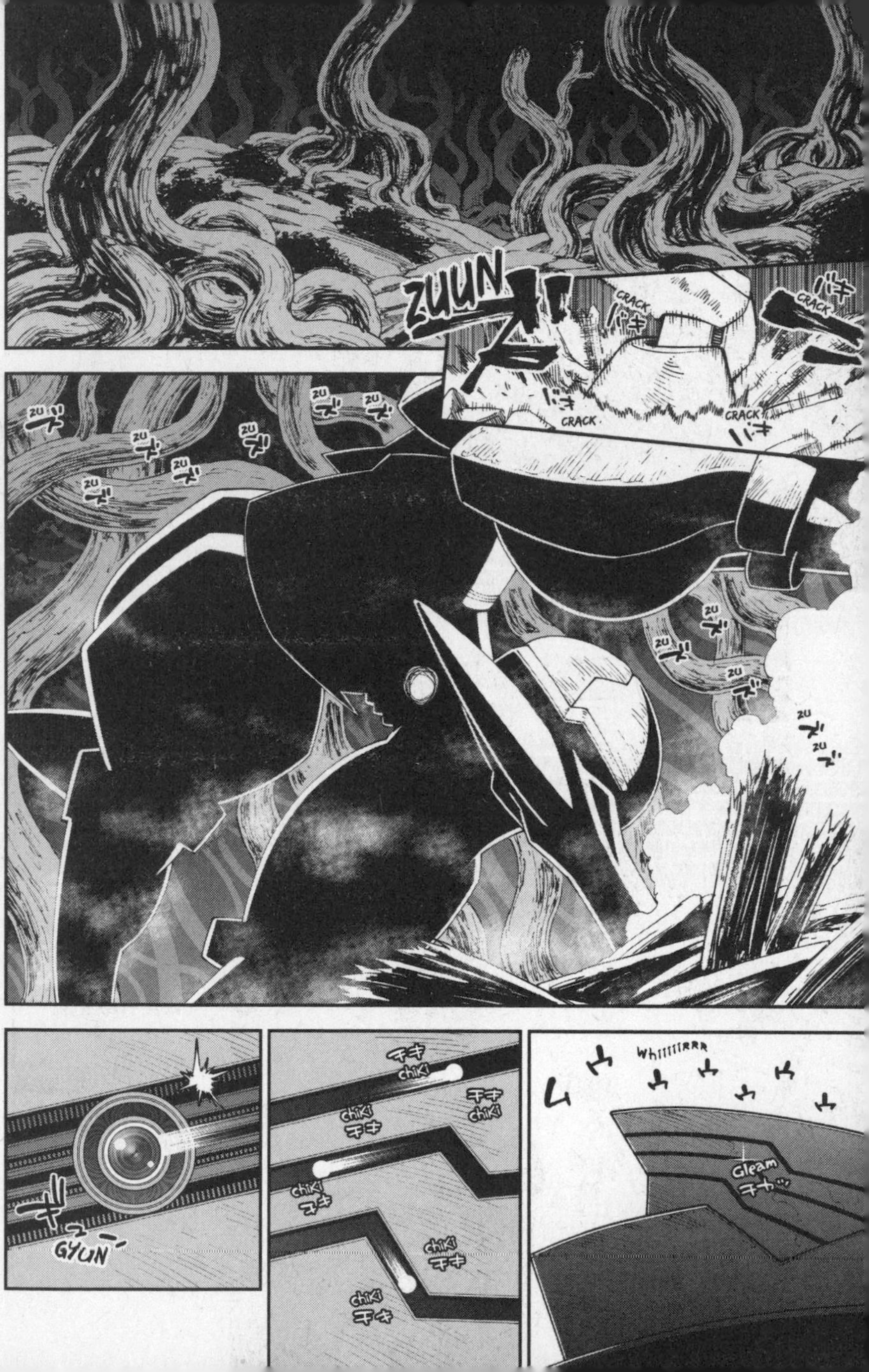

バキ CRACK
CRACK バキ
ZUUN
バキ CRACK
CRACK バキ
ZU ズ
ZU ズ
ZU ズ
ZU ズ
ZU ズ
ZU ズ
ZU ズ
ZU ズ
ZU ズ
ZU ズ
ZU ズ
ZU ズ
Whiiiiirrr
Gleam
チキ chiki
チキ chiki
chiki チキ
chiki チキ
chiki チキ
chiki チキ
GYUN

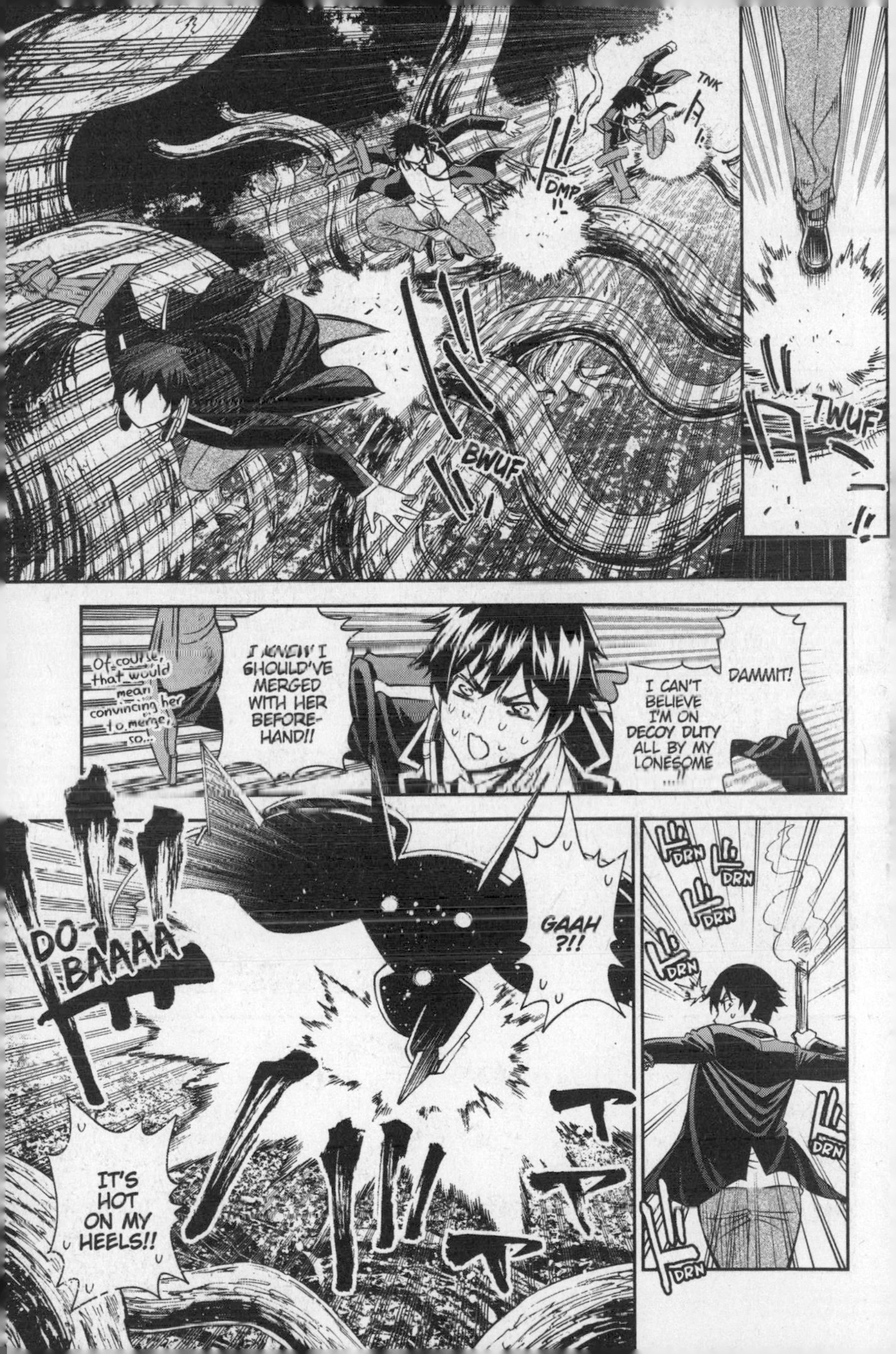
TWUF
TNK
DMP
BWUF
DAMMIT!
I CAN'T BELIEVE I'M ON DECOY DUTY ALL BY MY LONESOME ...
I KNEW I SHOULD'VE MERGED WITH HER BEFORE-HAND!!
Of course, that would mean convincing her to merge, so...
DRN
DRN
DRN
DRN
DRN
DRN
DRN
GAAH ?!!
DO-BAAAA
IT'S HOT ON MY HEELS!!

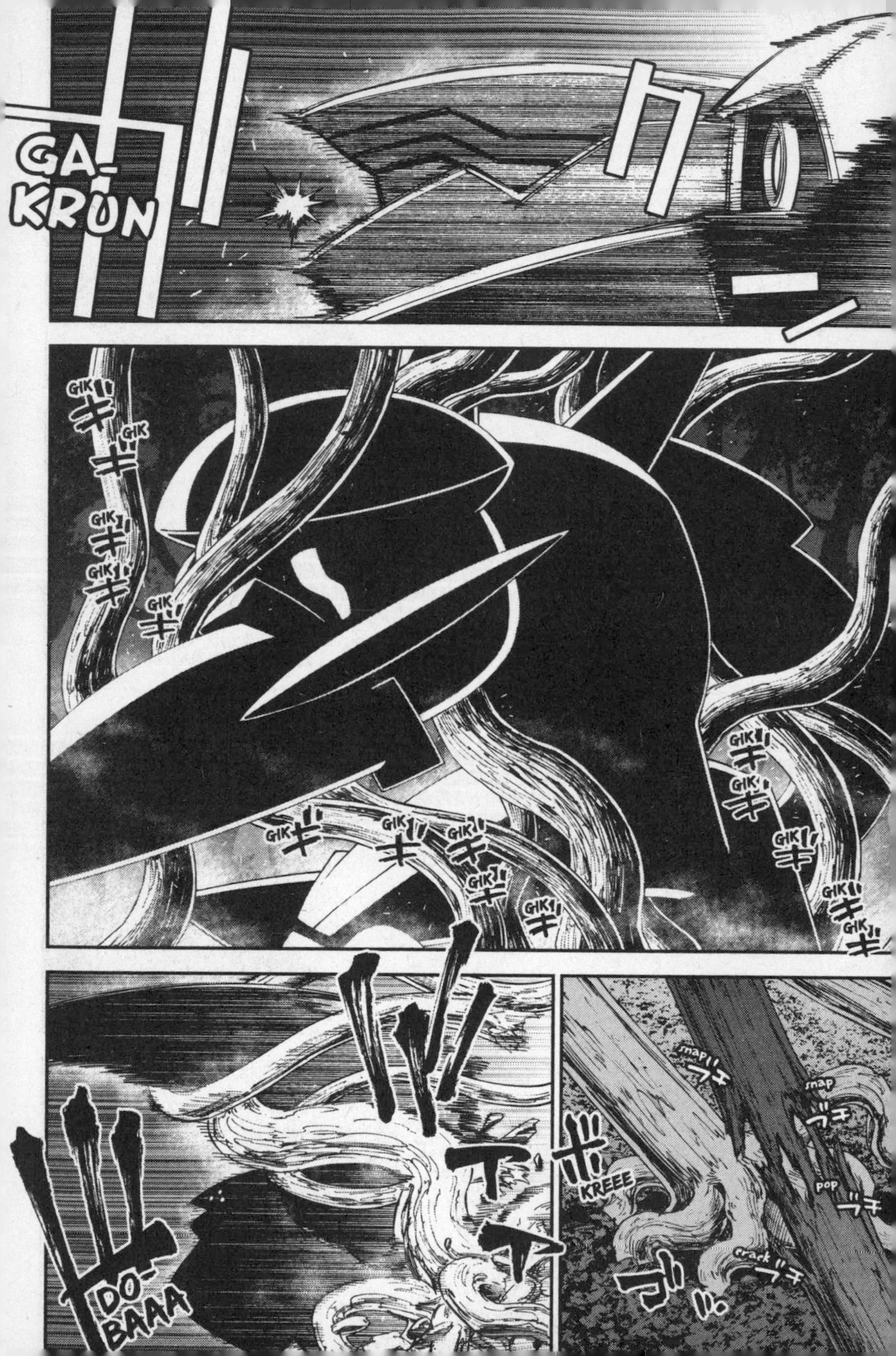
GA-KRUN
GIK
GIK
GIK
GIK
GIK
GIK
GIK
GIK
GIK
GIK
GIK
GIK
GIK
GIK
GIK
snap
snap
KREEE
pop
crack
DO-BAAA

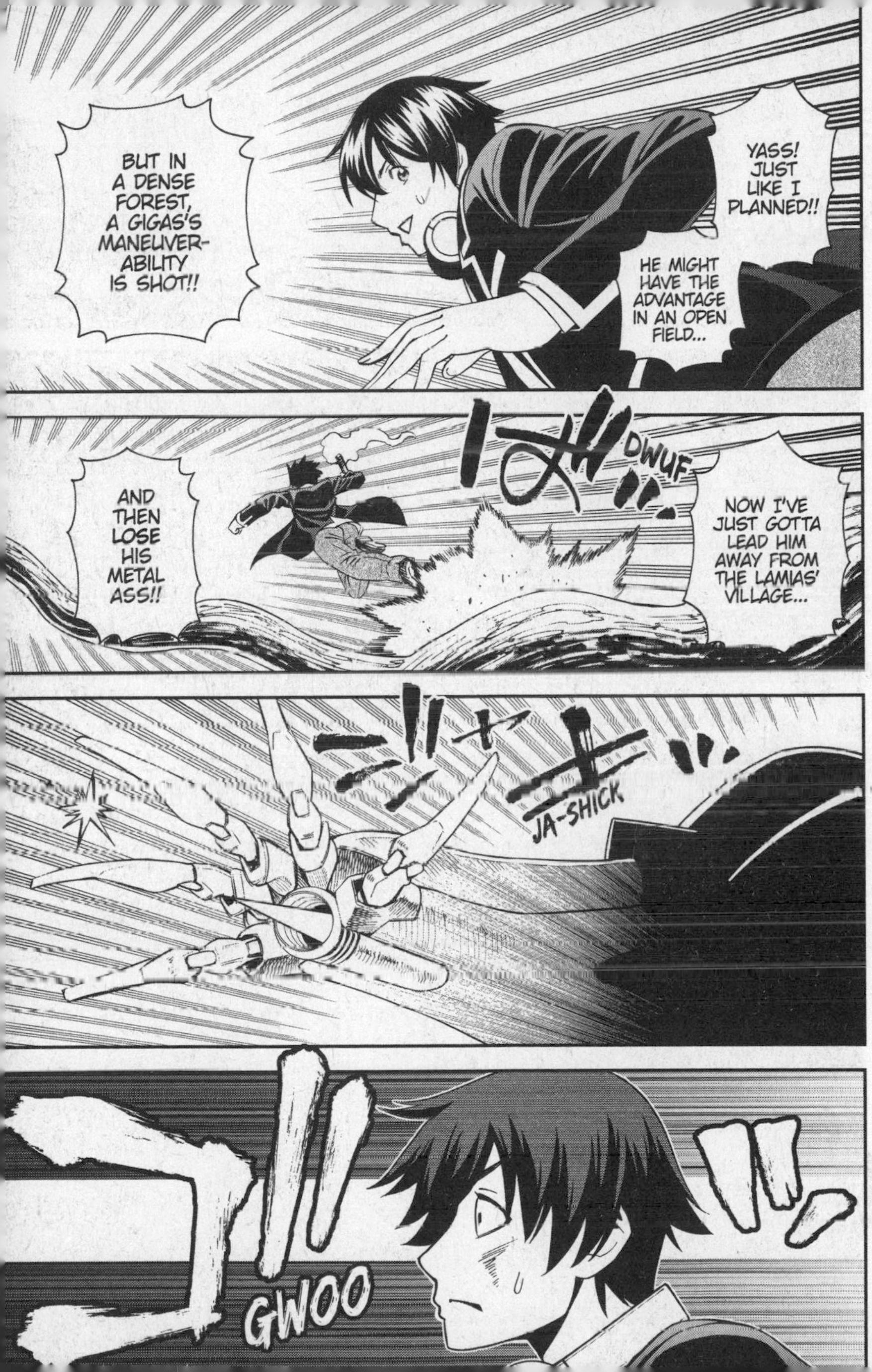
YASS! JUST LIKE I PLANNED!!
HE MIGHT HAVE THE ADVANTAGE IN AN OPEN FIELD...
BUT IN A DENSE FOREST, A GIGAS'S MANEUVER-ABILITY IS SHOT!!
DWUF
NOW I'VE JUST GOTTA LEAD HIM AWAY FROM THE LAMIAS' VILLAGE...
AND THEN LOSE HIS METAL ASS!!
JA-SHICK
GWOO

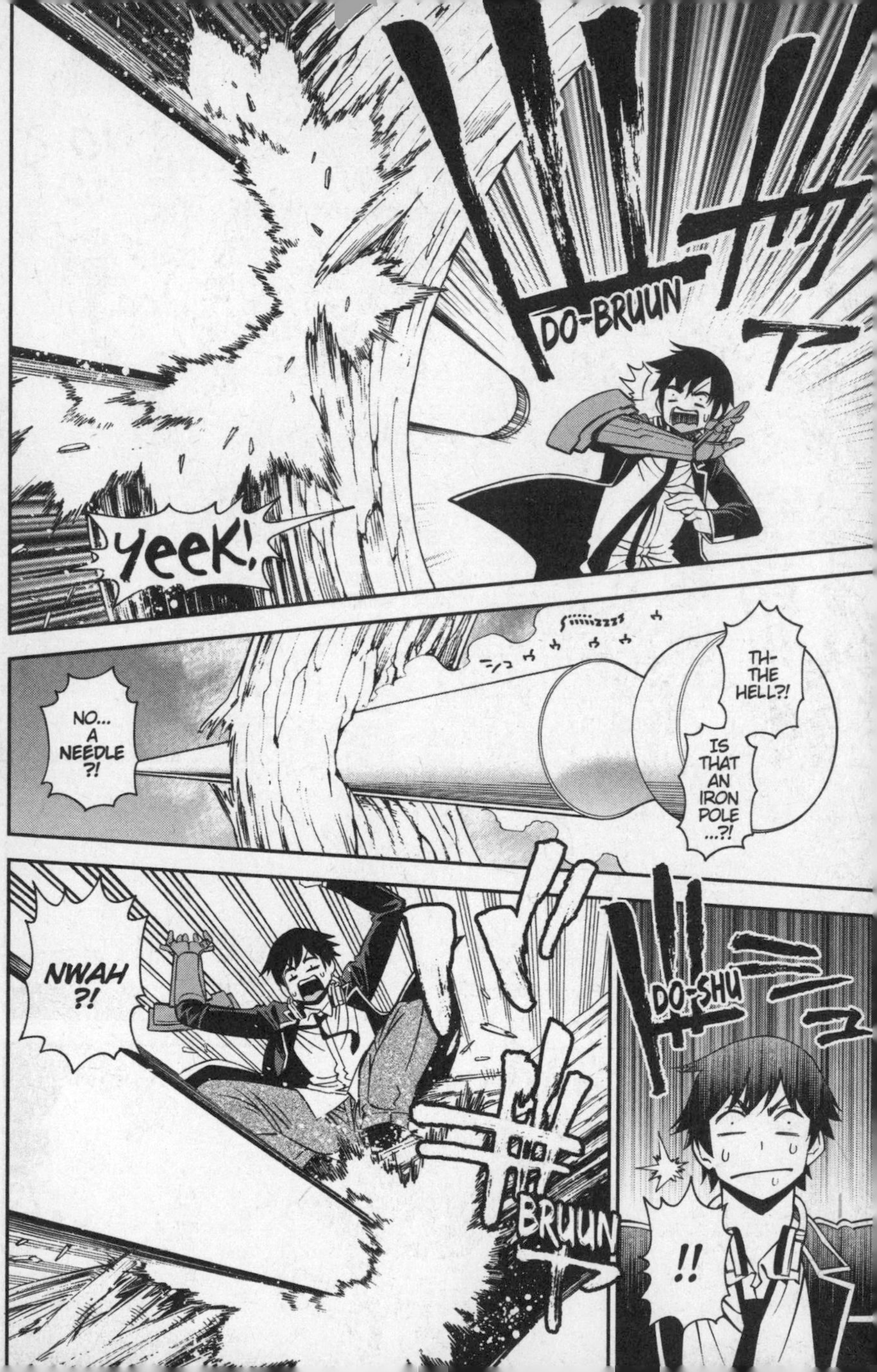
DO-BRUUN
yeek!
TH- THE HELL?!
IS THAT AN IRON POLE ...?!
NO... A NEEDLE ?!
DO-SHU
NWAH ?!
!!
BRUUN

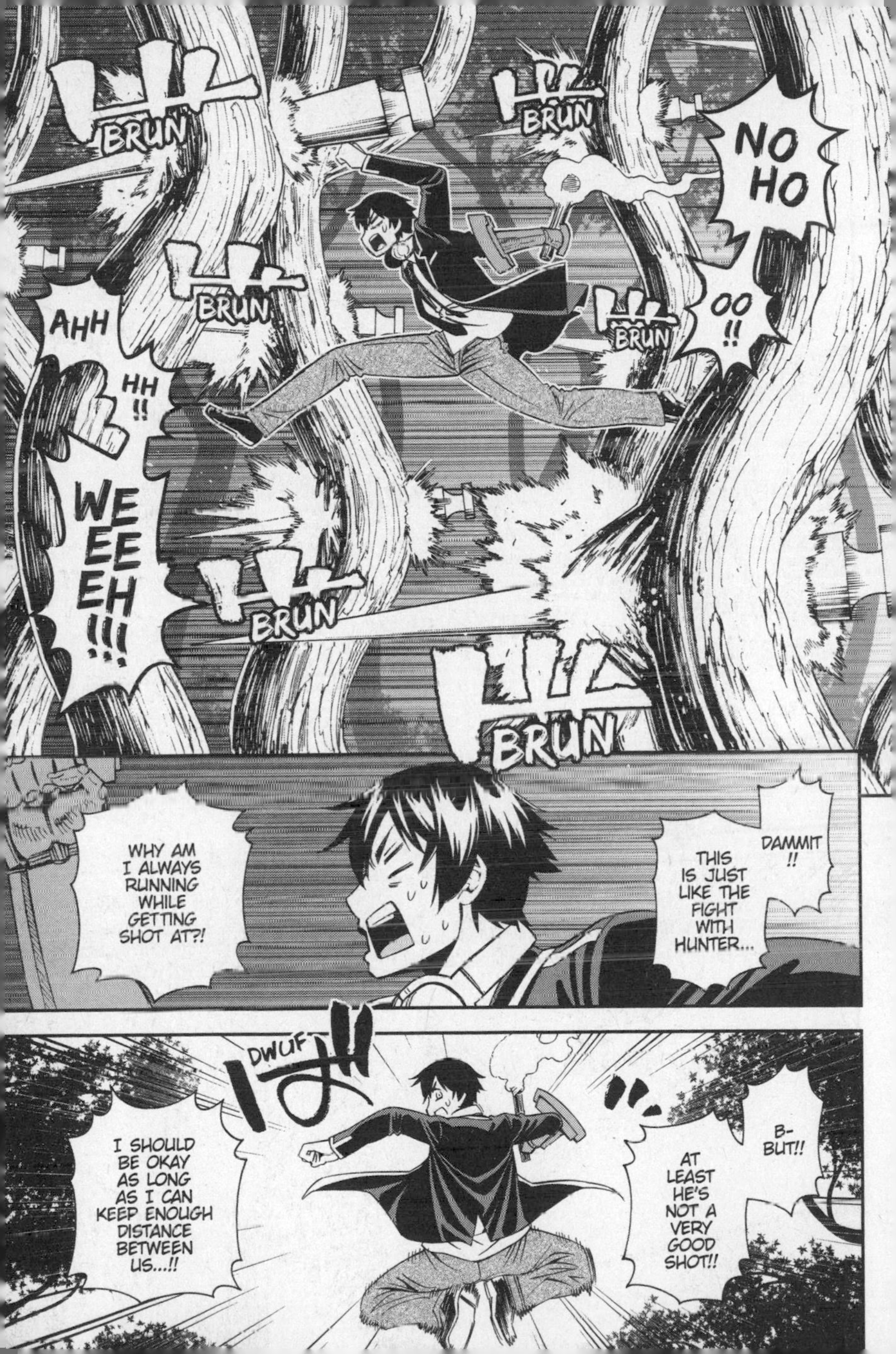
BRUN
NO HO
OO!!
BRUN
BRUN
BRUN
AHH HH!!
WE EE EH!!!
BRUN
BRUN
DAMMIT!!
THIS IS JUST LIKE THE FIGHT WITH HUNTER...
WHY AM I ALWAYS RUNNING WHILE GETTING SHOT AT?!
B-BUT!!
AT LEAST HE'S NOT A VERY GOOD SHOT!!
DWUF
I SHOULD BE OKAY AS LONG AS I CAN KEEP ENOUGH DISTANCE BETWEEN US...!!

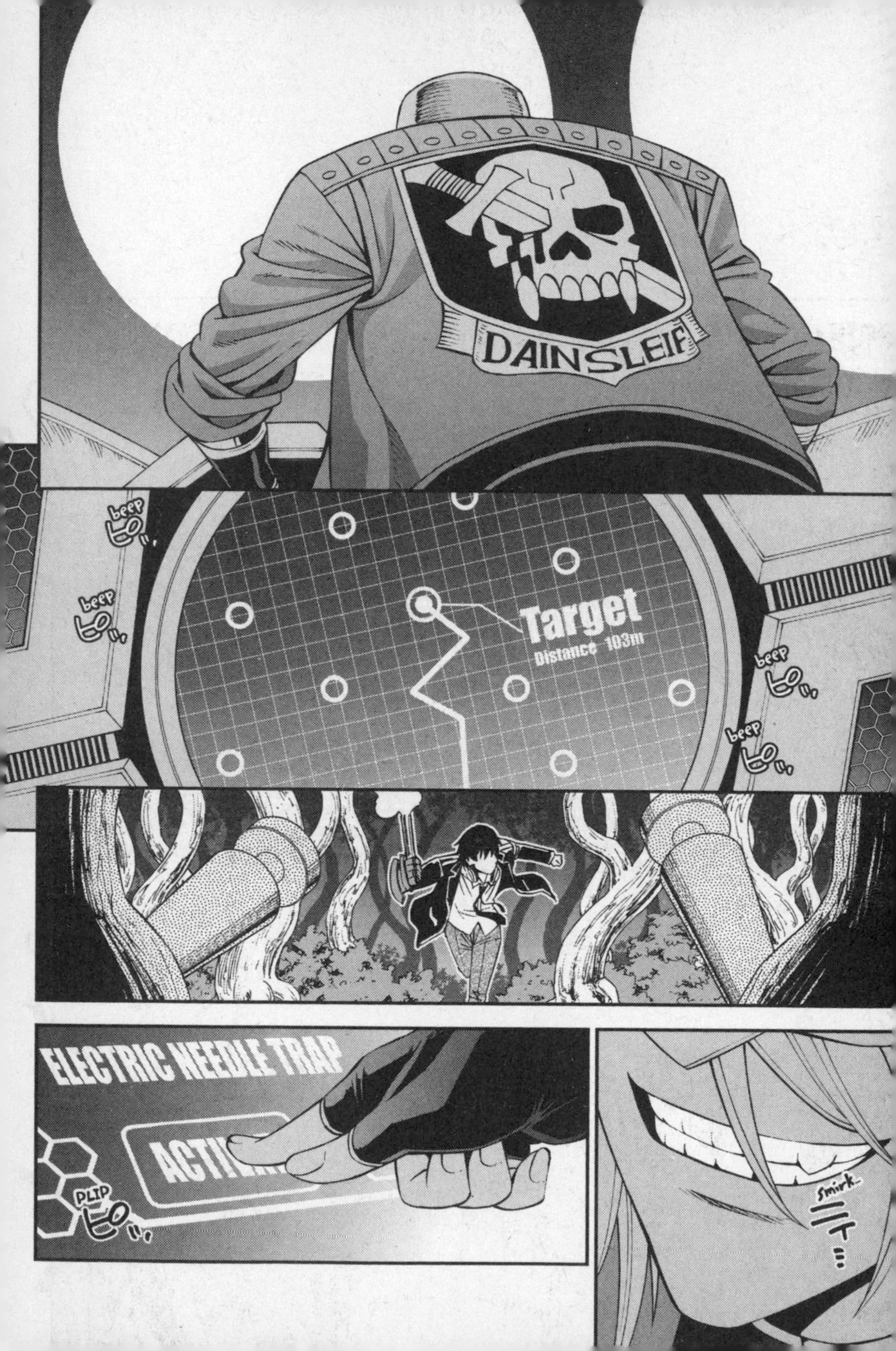
DAINSLEIF
beep ピッ
beep ピッ
Target
Distance 103m
beep ピッ
beep ピッ
Smirk... ニヤ…
ELECTRIC NEEDLE TRAP
PLIP ピッ

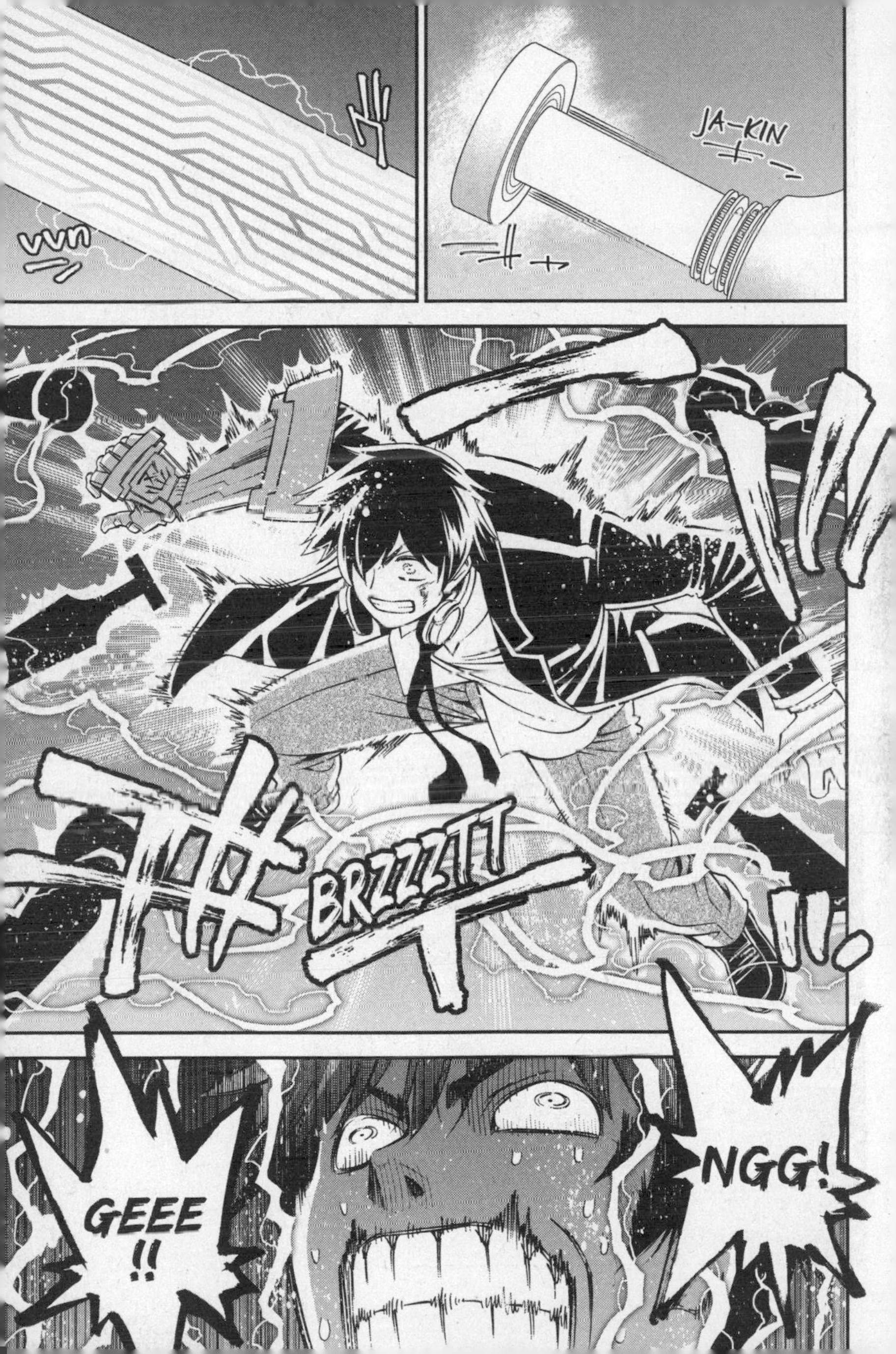
JA-KIN
VVN
BRZZZZTT
NGG!
GEEE !!

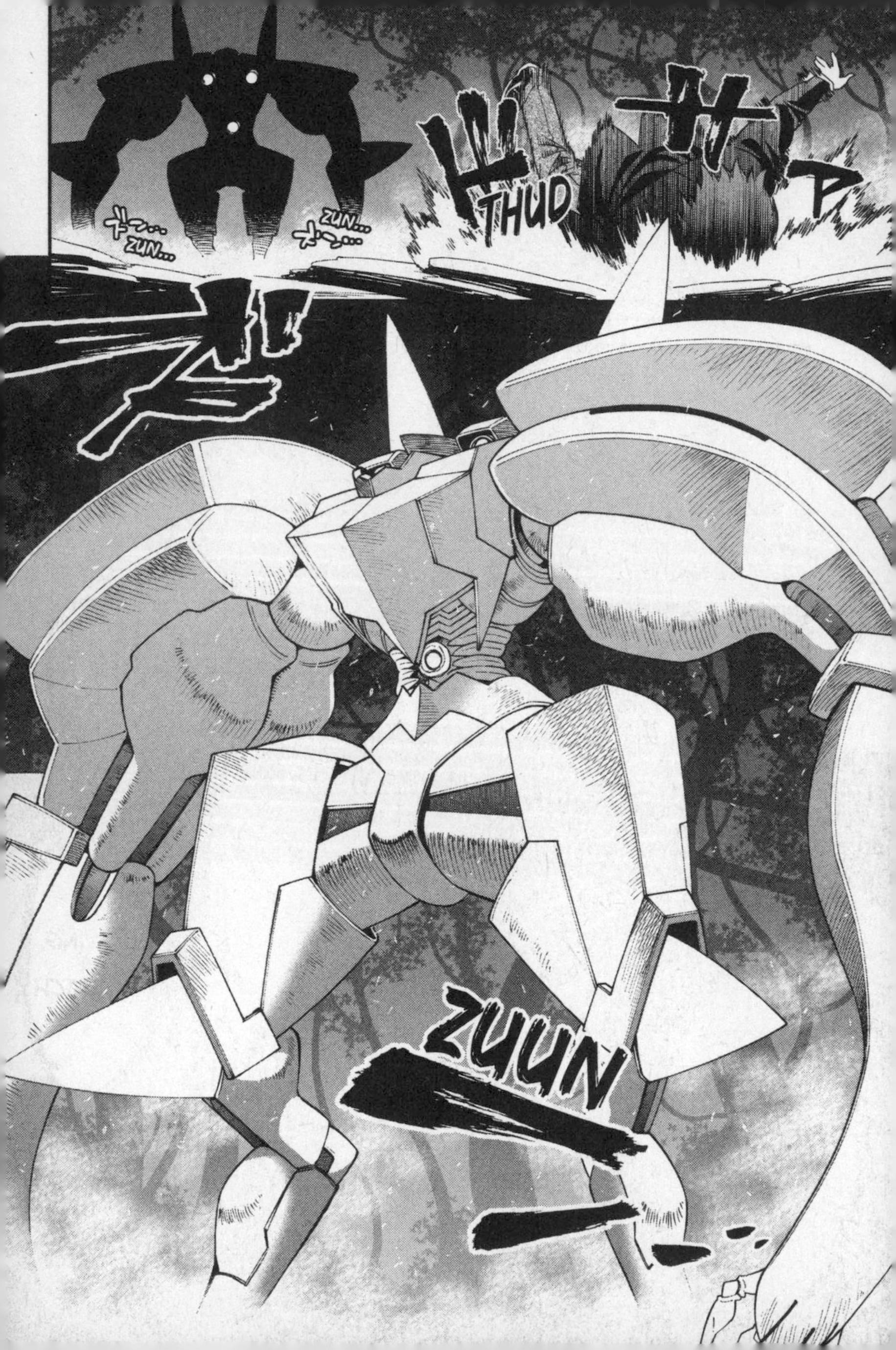
THUD
ZUN...
ZUN...
ZUUN

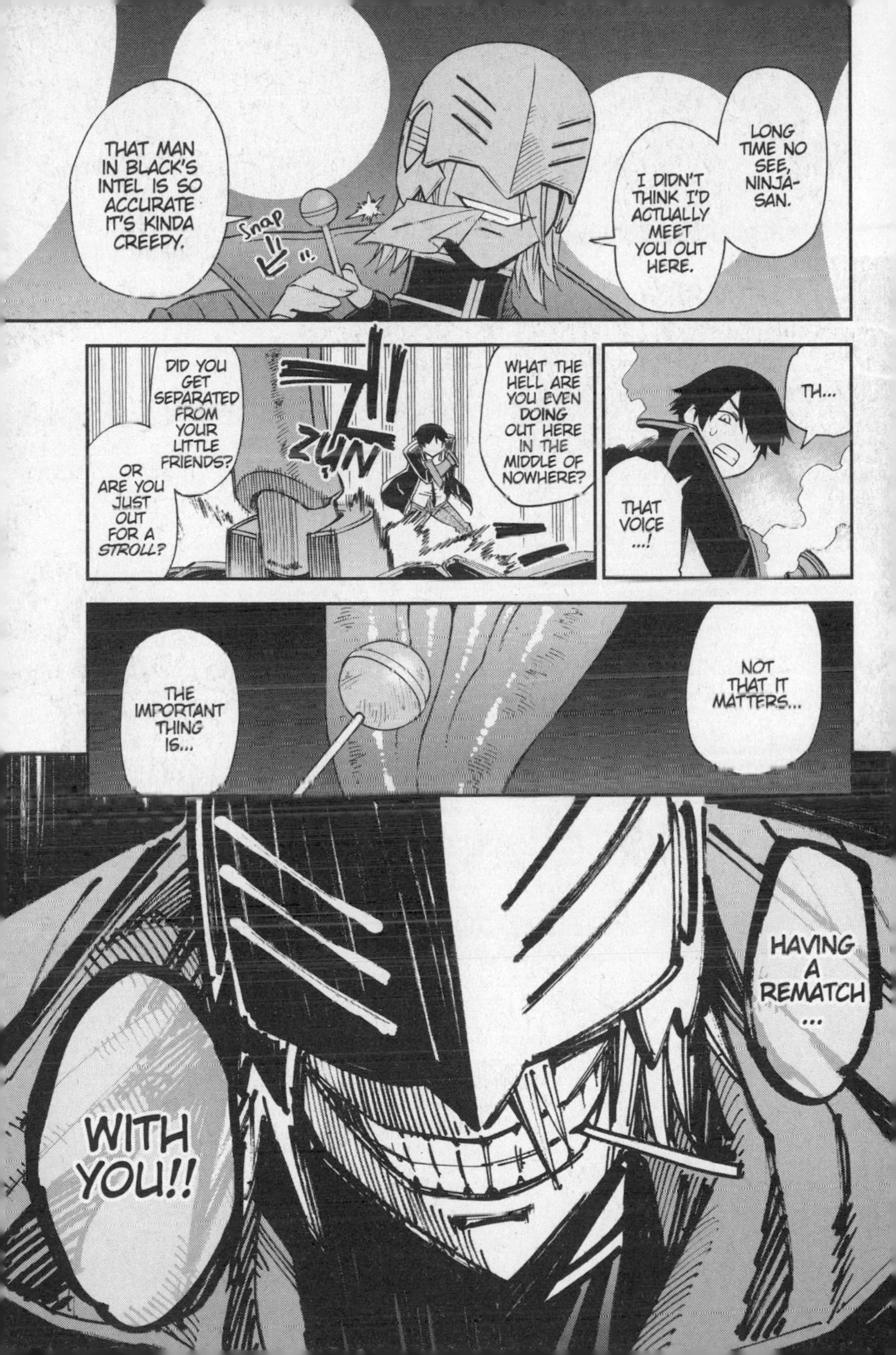
LONG TIME NO SEE, NINJA-SAN.
I DIDN'T THINK I'D ACTUALLY MEET YOU OUT HERE.
Snap
THAT MAN IN BLACK'S INTEL IS SO ACCURATE IT'S KINDA CREEPY.
TH...
THAT VOICE ...!
WHAT THE HELL ARE YOU EVEN DOING OUT HERE IN THE MIDDLE OF NOWHERE?
ZUN
DID YOU GET SEPARATED FROM YOUR LITTLE FRIENDS?
OR ARE YOU JUST OUT FOR A STROLL?
NOT THAT IT MATTERS...
THE IMPORTANT THING IS...
HAVING A REMATCH ...
WITH YOU!!

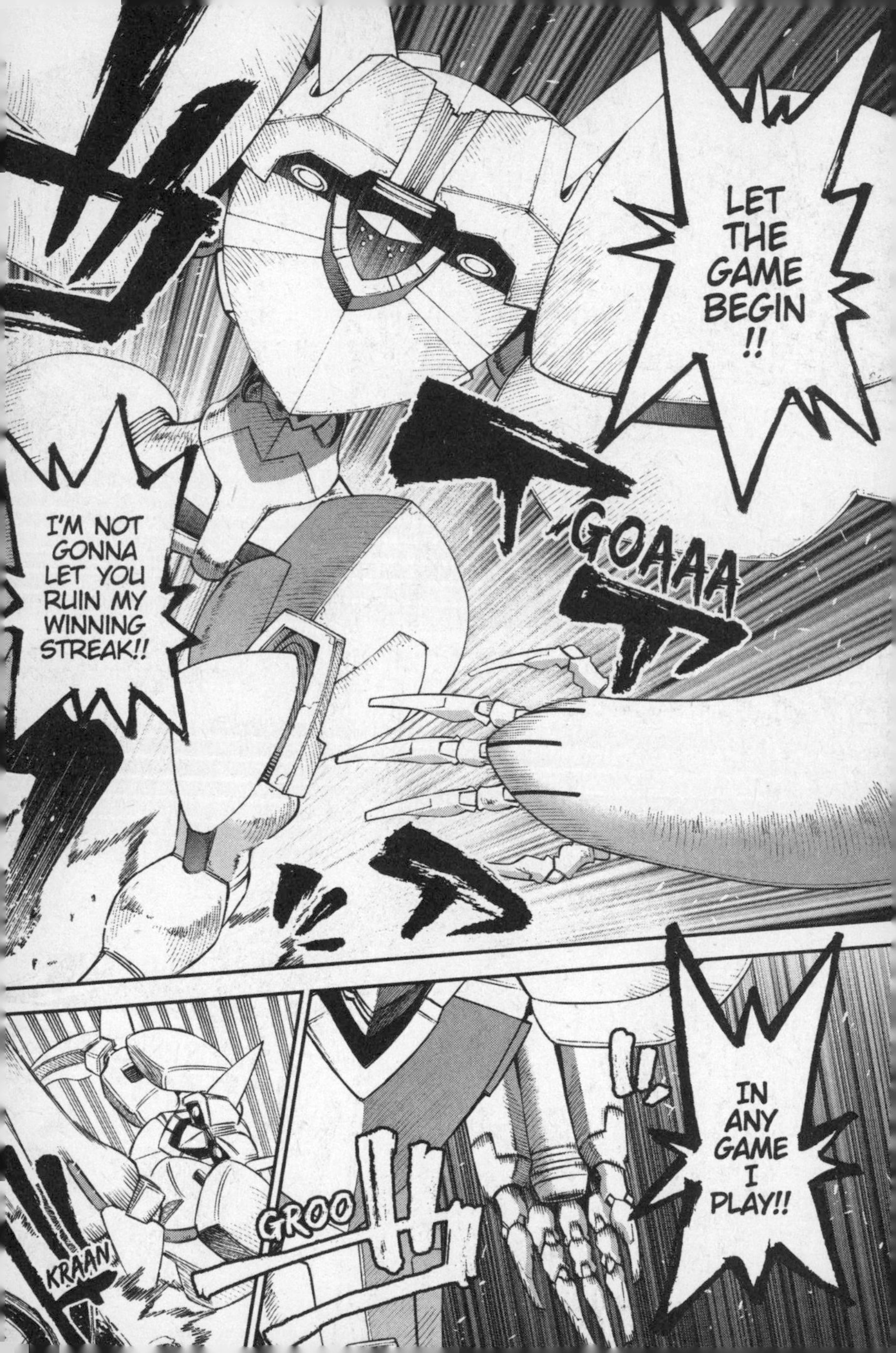
LET THE GAME BEGIN!!
GOAAA
I'M NOT GONNA LET YOU RUIN MY WINNING STREAK!!
IN ANY GAME I PLAY!!
GROO
KRAAN

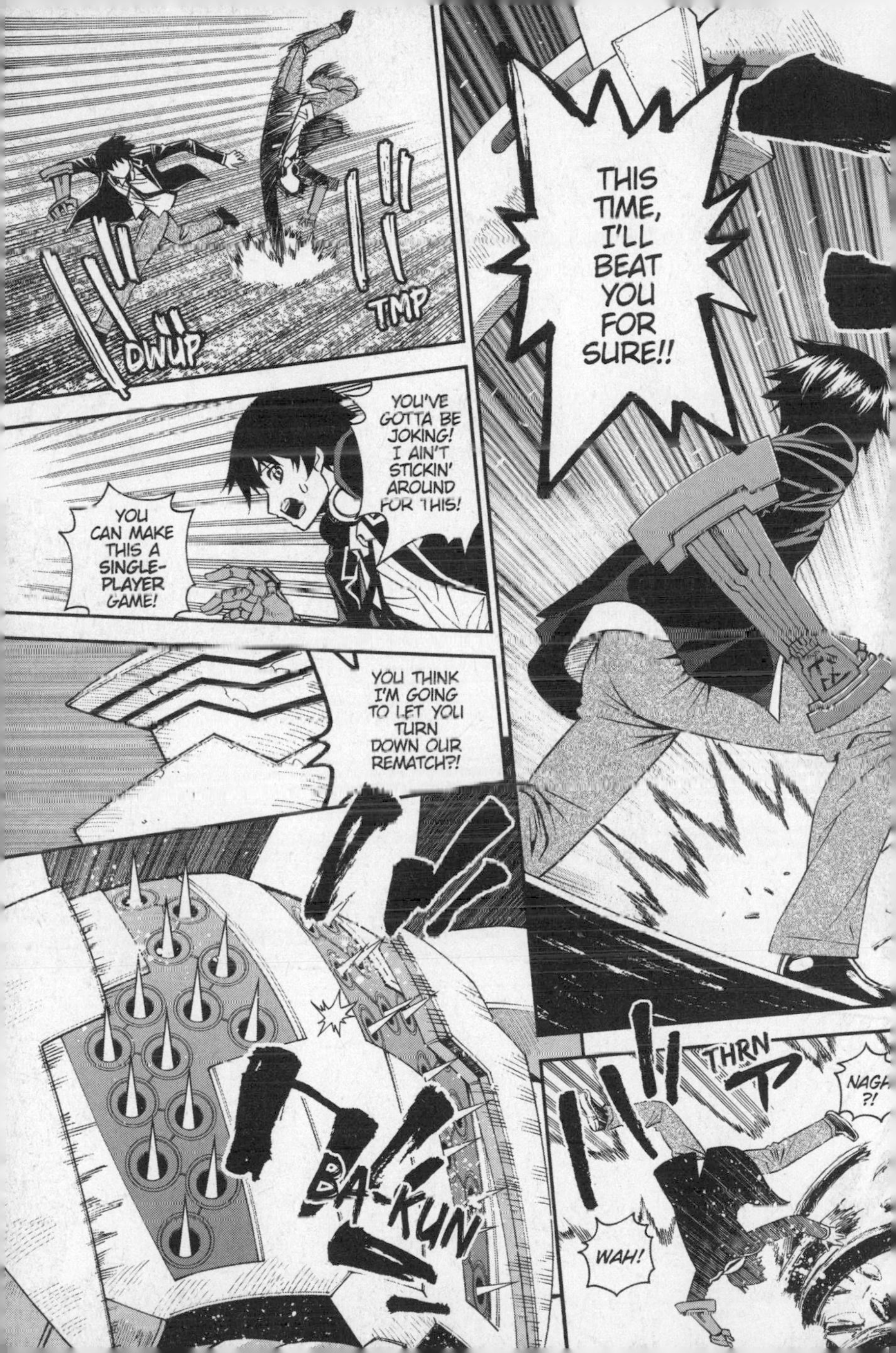

THIS TIME, I'LL BEAT YOU FOR SURE!!
TMP
DWUP
YOU'VE GOTTA BE JOKING! I AIN'T STICKIN' AROUND FOR THIS!
YOU CAN MAKE THIS A SINGLE-PLAYER GAME!
YOU THINK I'M GOING TO LET YOU TURN DOWN OUR REMATCH?!
BA-KUN
NAGH?!
THRN
WAH!

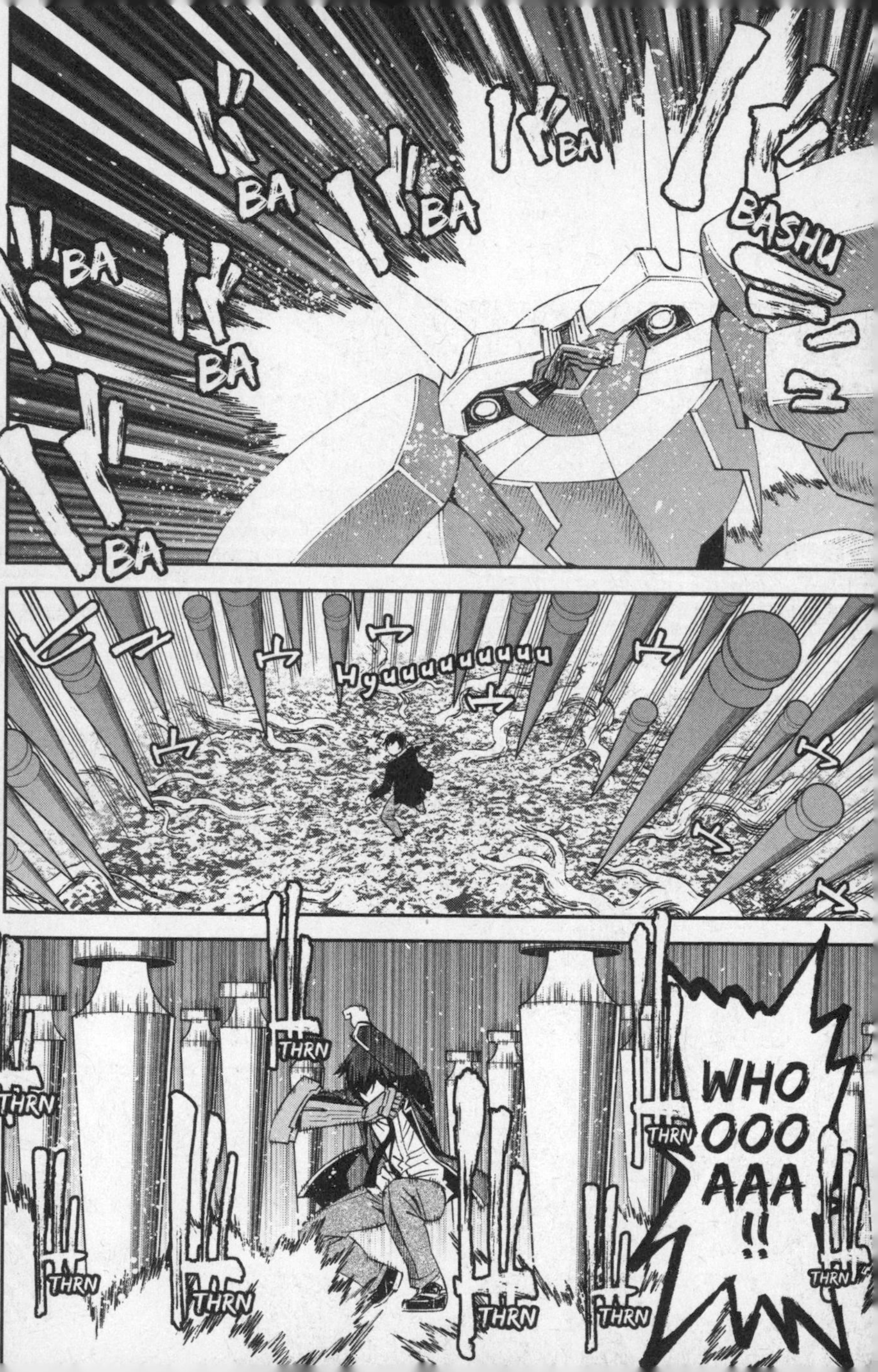
BASHU
BA
BA
BA
BA
BA
BA
Hyuuuuuuuuuu
WHOOOOAAA!!
THRN
THRN
THRN
THRN
THRN
THRN
THRN
THRN

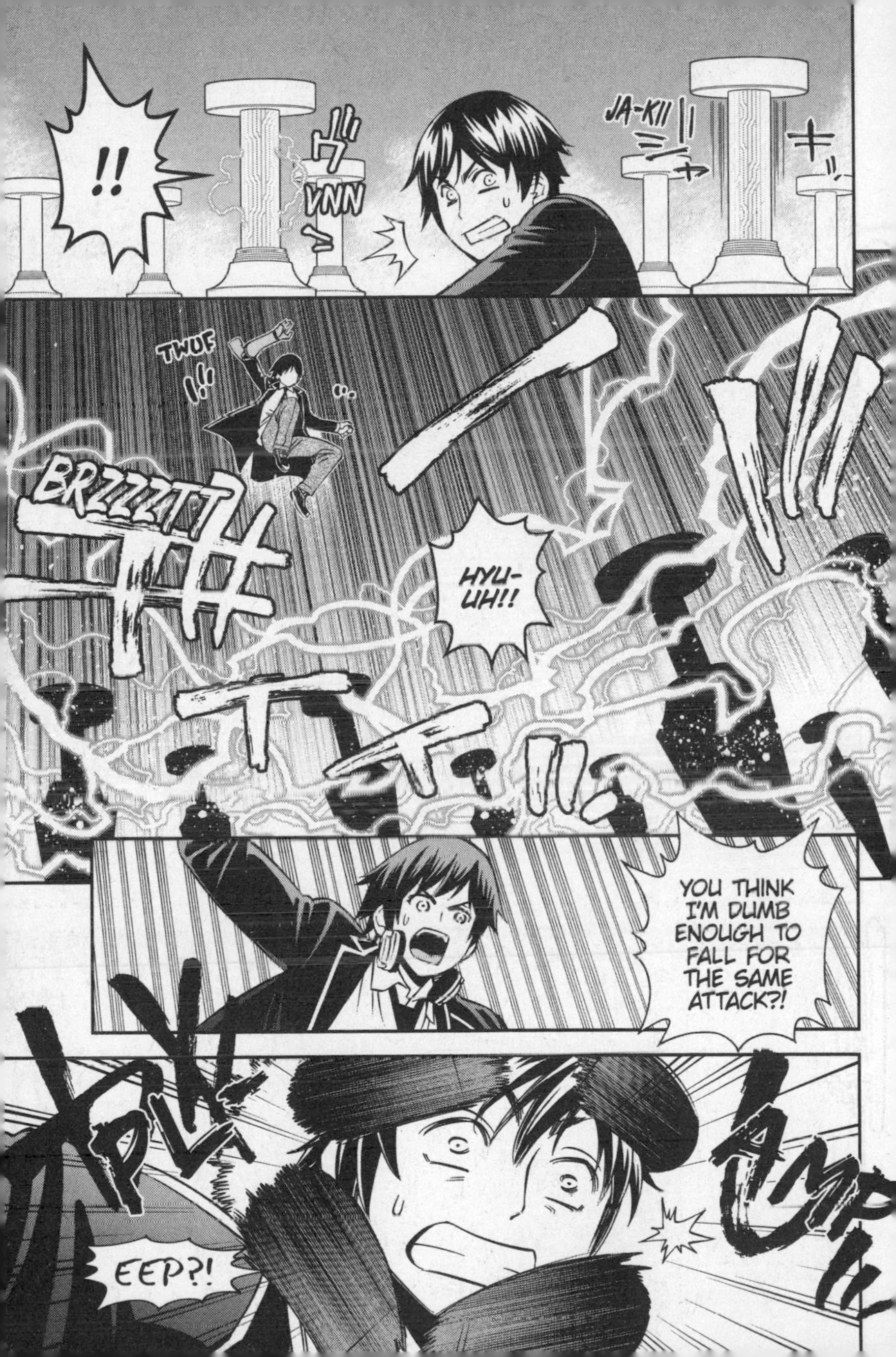
JA-KII
VNN
!!
HYU-UH!!
TWUF
BRZZZTT
YOU THINK I'M DUMB ENOUGH TO FALL FOR THE SAME ATTACK?!
EEP?!

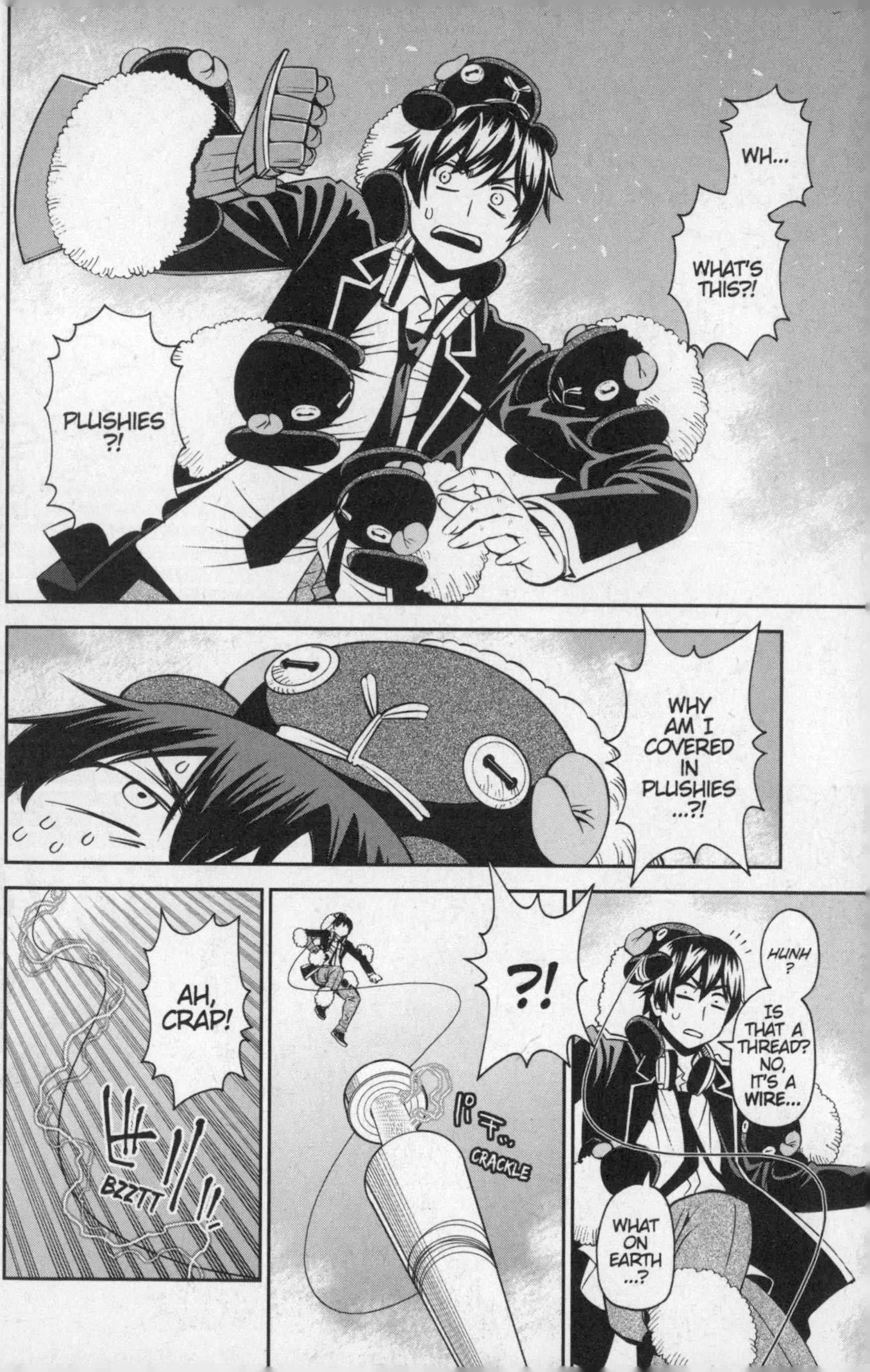
WH...
WHAT'S THIS?!
PLUSHIES ?!
WHY AM I COVERED IN PLUSHIES ...?!
HUNH ?
IS THAT A THREAD? NO, IT'S A WIRE...
WHAT ON EARTH ...?
?!
パチ..
CRACKLE
AH, CRAP!
BZZTT!!

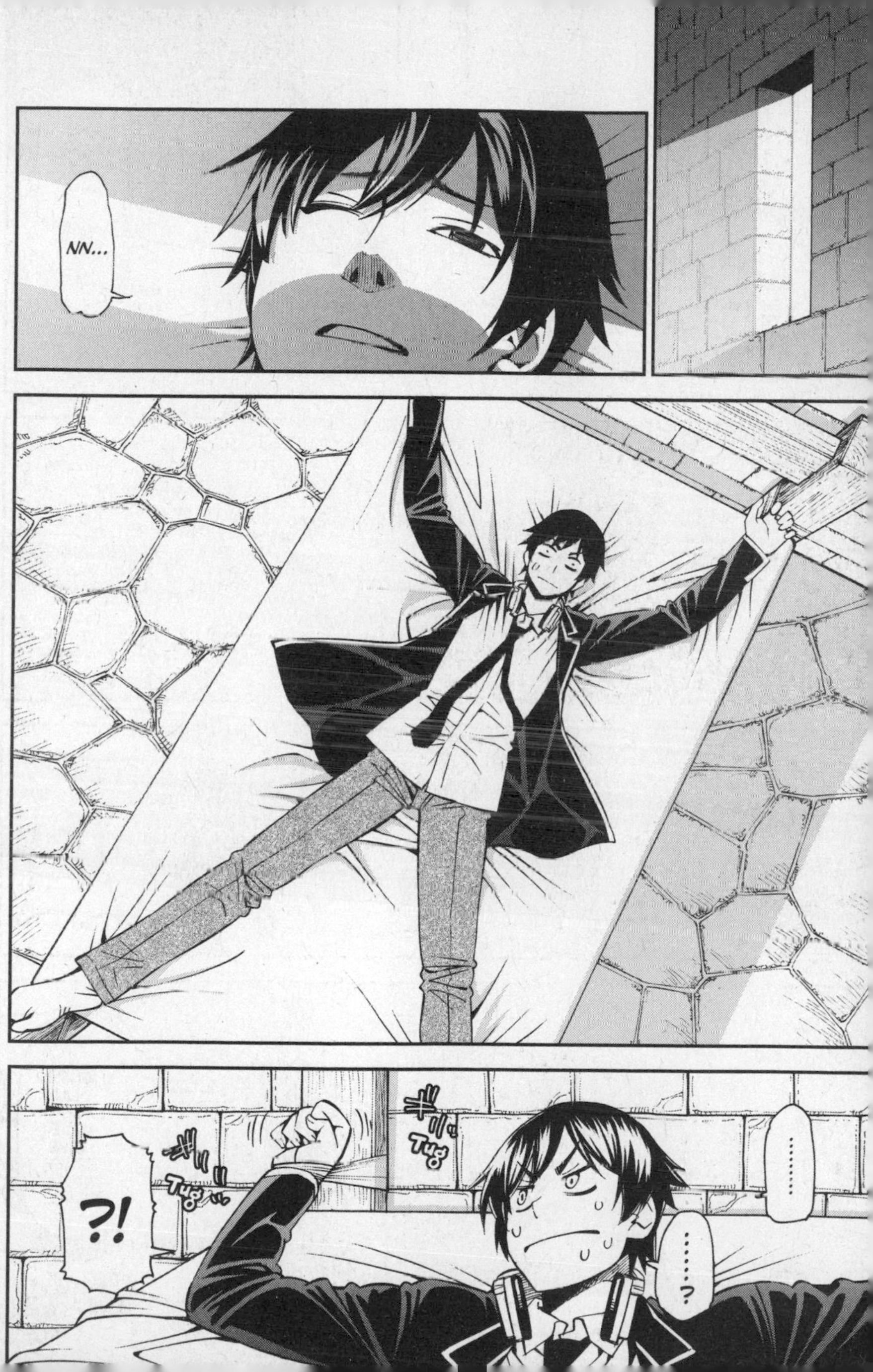
NN...
......
Tug
Tug
......?
?!

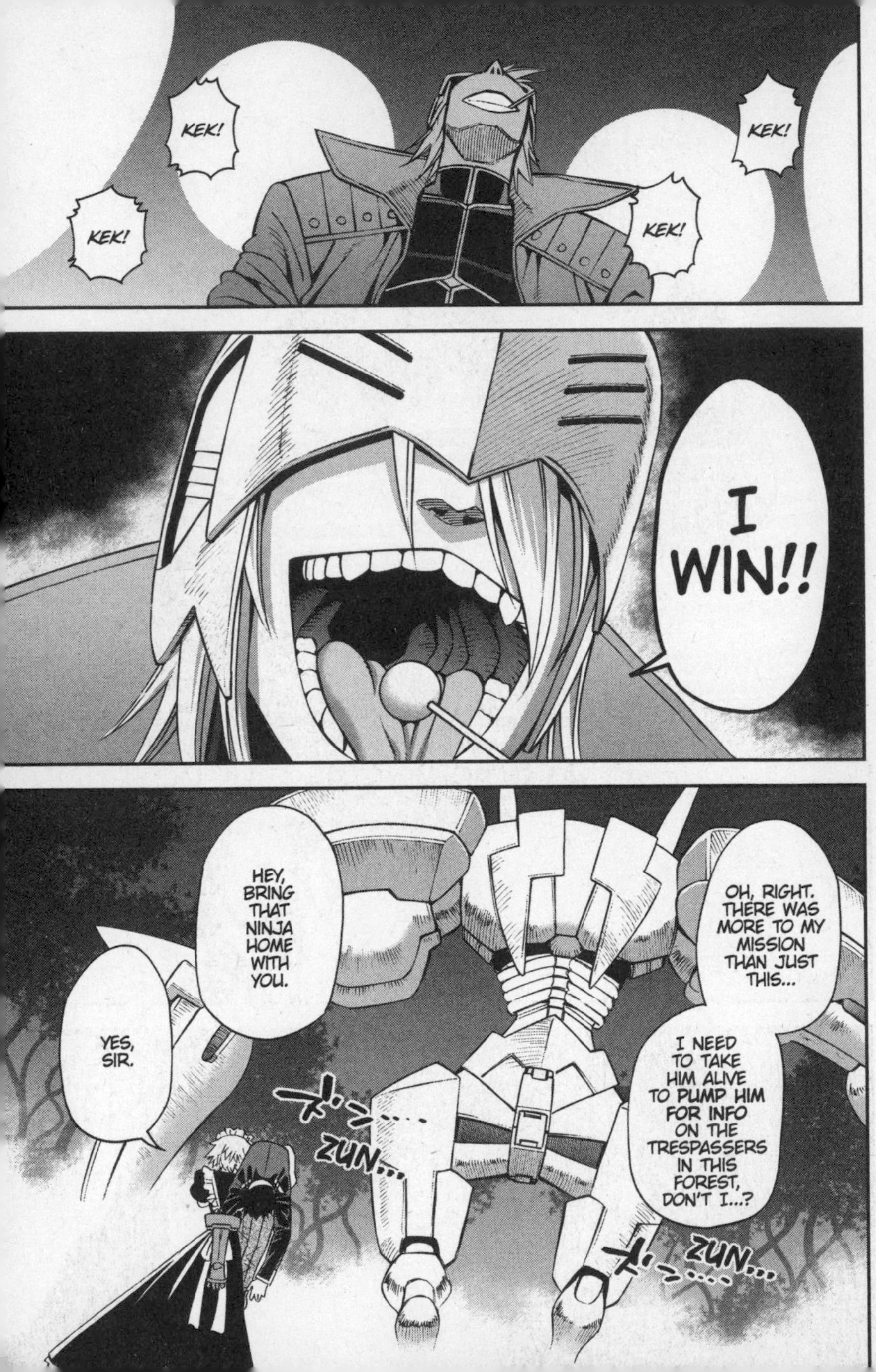
KEK!
KEK!
KEK!
KEK!
I WIN!!
OH, RIGHT. THERE WAS MORE TO MY MISSION THAN JUST THIS...
I NEED TO TAKE HIM ALIVE TO PUMP HIM FOR INFO ON THE TRESPASSERS IN THIS FOREST, DON'T I...?
HEY, BRING THAT NINJA HOME WITH YOU.
YES, SIR.
ZUN...
ZUN...

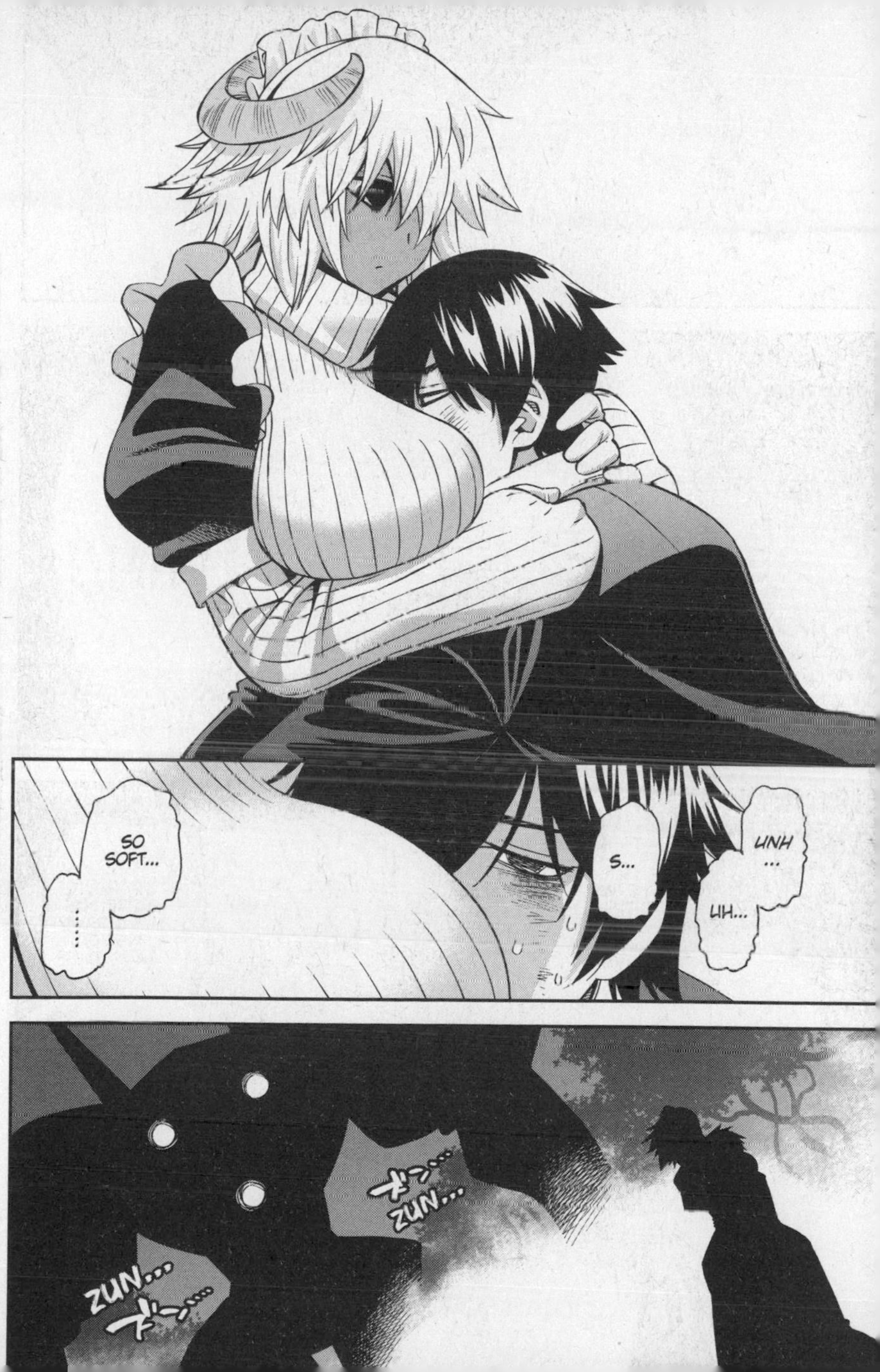
UNH ...
S...
UH...
SO SOFT...
......
ズー…
ZUN...
ZUN...
ズー…

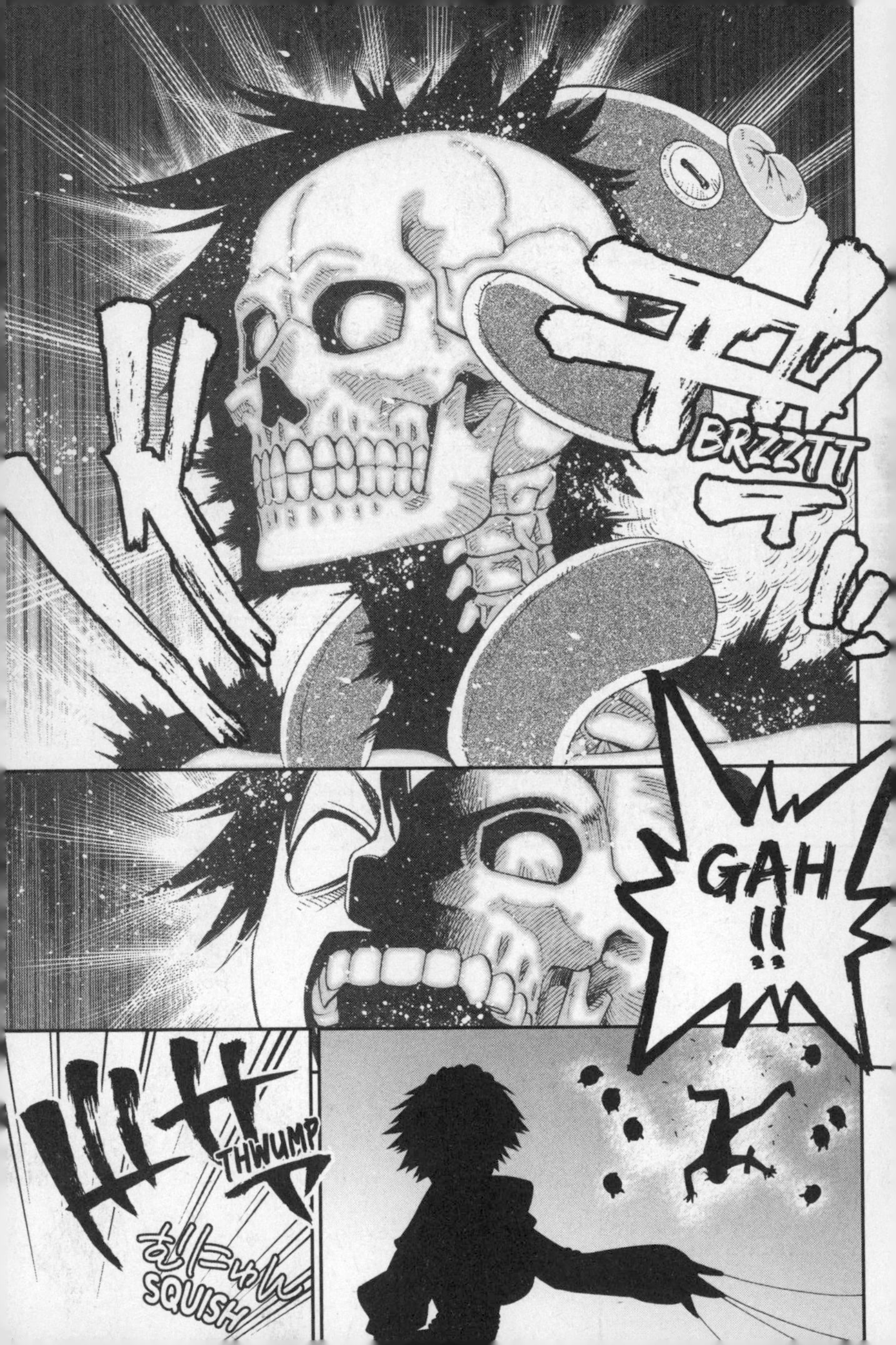
BRZZTT
GAH!!
THWUMP
むにゅん
SQUISH

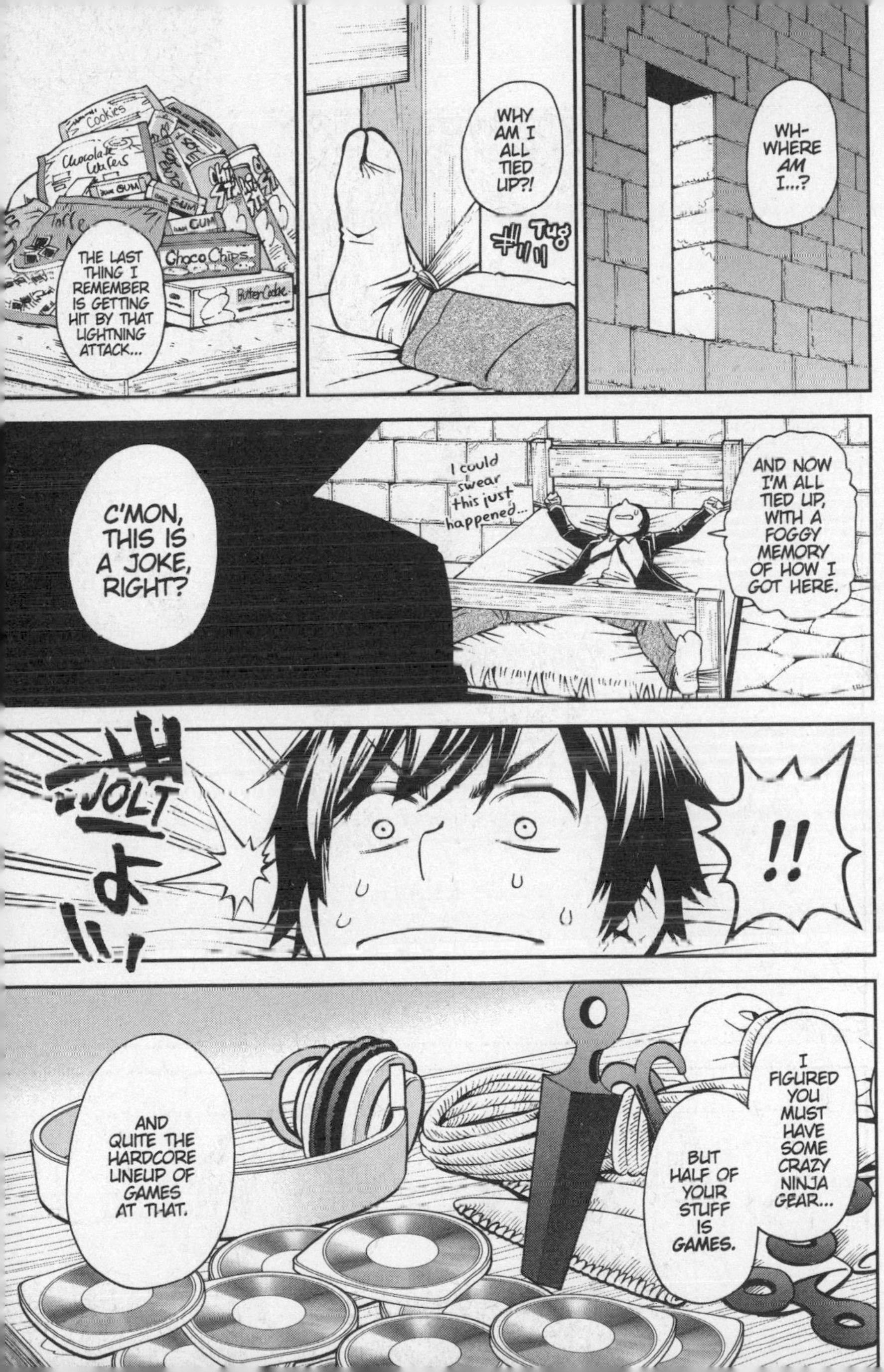

WH-WHERE AM I...?
WHY AM I ALL TIED UP?!
Tug
Cookies
Chocolate Wafers
GUM
Choco Chips
Butter Cookie
THE LAST THING I REMEMBER IS GETTING HIT BY THAT LIGHTNING ATTACK...
AND NOW I'M ALL TIED UP, WITH A FOGGY MEMORY OF HOW I GOT HERE.
I could swear this just happened...
C'MON, THIS IS A JOKE, RIGHT?
!!
JOLT
I FIGURED YOU MUST HAVE SOME CRAZY NINJA GEAR...
BUT HALF OF YOUR STUFF IS GAMES.
AND QUITE THE HARDCORE LINEUP OF GAMES AT THAT.

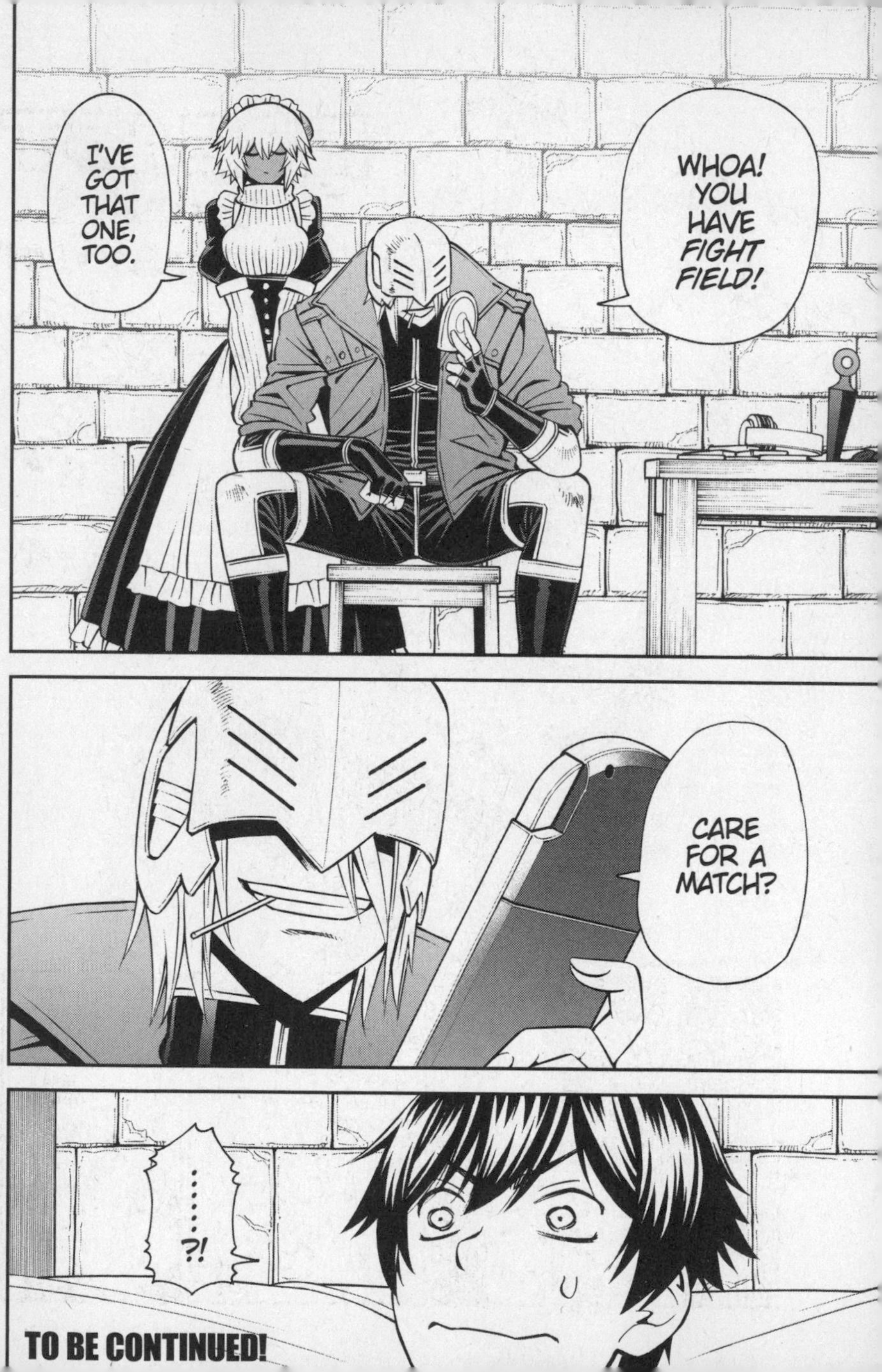
WHOA! YOU HAVE FIGHT FIELD!
I'VE GOT THAT ONE, TOO.
CARE FOR A MATCH?
......?!
TO BE CONTINUED!

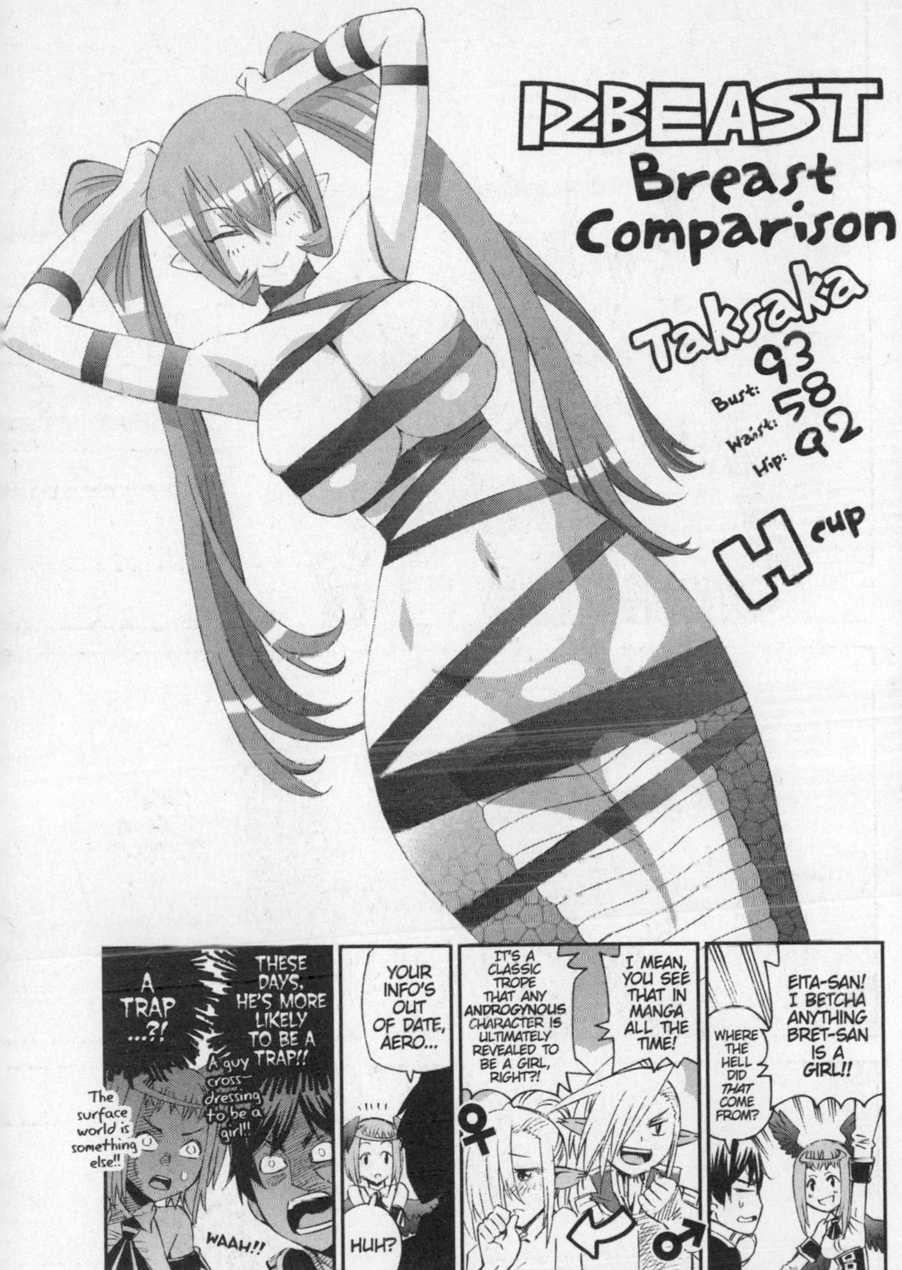
12BEAST
Breast Comparison
Taksaka
Bust: 93
Waist: 58
Hip: 92
H cup
EITA-SAN! I BETCHA ANYTHING BRET-SAN IS A GIRL!!
WHERE THE HELL DID THAT COME FROM?
I MEAN, YOU SEE THAT IN MANGA ALL THE TIME!
IT'S A CLASSIC TROPE THAT ANY ANDROGYNOUS CHARACTER IS ULTIMATELY REVEALED TO BE A GIRL, RIGHT?!
YOUR INFO'S OUT OF DATE, AERO...
HUH?
THESE DAYS, HE'S MORE LIKELY TO BE A TRAP!!
A TRAP ...?!
A guy cross-dressing to be a girl!!
The surface world is something else!!
WAAH!!

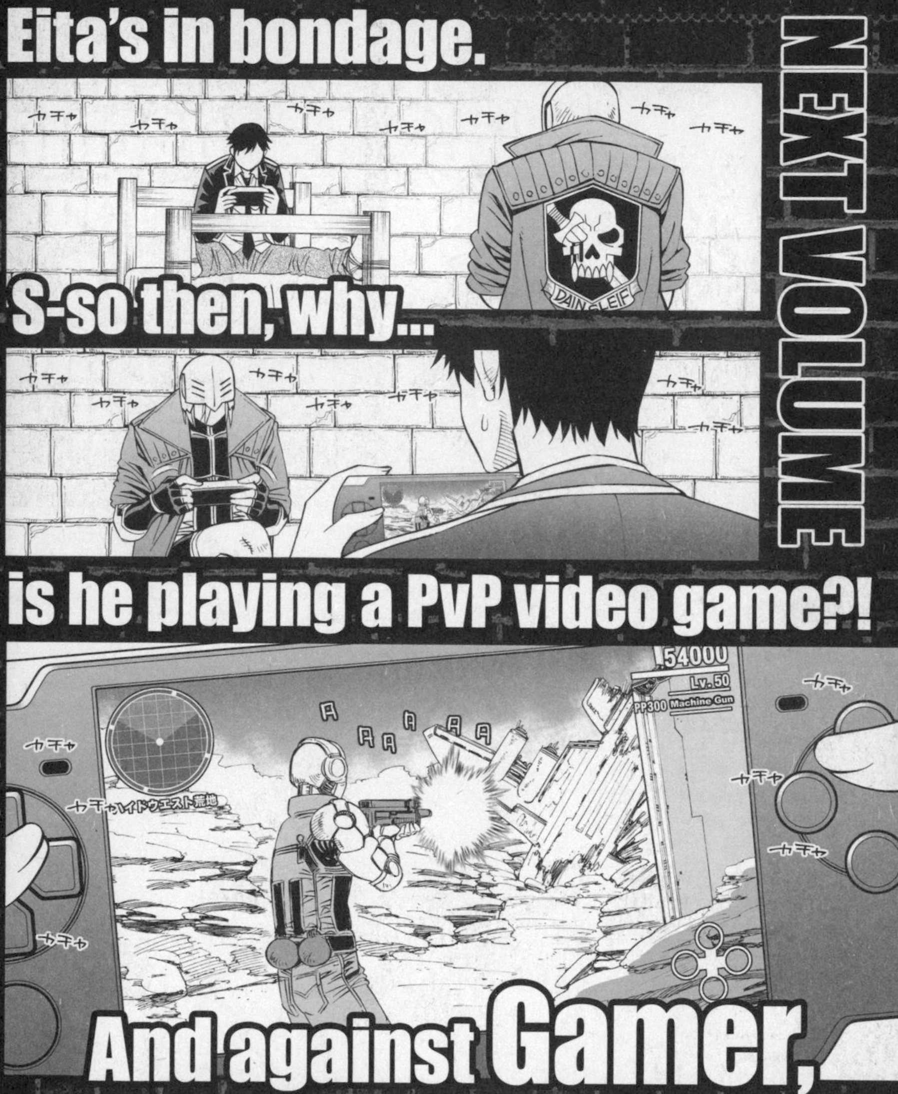
NEXT VOLUME
Eita's in bondage.
カチャ
S-so then, why...
カチャ
is he playing a PvP video game?!
54000
Lv. 50
PP300 Machine Gun
ハイドウエスト荒地
カチャ
And against Gamer,
of all people?!

COMING SOON!